Politics in Scotland brings together experts in their subject areas and delivers engaging and informed discussion. Important themes are investigated, from the 'quality' of democracy in Scotland and the policy performance of devolved institutions to Scotland's role in the international sphere. This collection captures the rapidly evolving nature of constitutional politics in Scotland and the UK and deserves to be widely read.

Lynn Bennie, *University of Aberdeen, UK*

An independent Scotland would seek to 'punch above its weight' and so does this book and it succeeds because of the quality of its contributions. The book delivers a reasoned understanding of the motivations and dynamics for modern Scottish politics within its UK, domestic and international context. Qvortrup's scathing observation in his chapter, that the attempts of the political pygmies of contemporary British politics to enact political reform can be summarised by Britney Spears' refrain, "Whoops! I've done it again" lingers long after the book is finished.

Andrew Massey, *University of Exeter, UK*

Scotland has a lot to teach us about how identities are negotiated in multi-national states. This book is an essential read for anyone wishing to gain a nuanced and updated understanding of the Scottish and British political landscapes.

S. Karly Kehoe, *Saint Mary's University, Canada*

This is a major contribution to the understanding of *Politics in Scotland* in its many facets. It covers the key themes and addresses the main issues through a range of chapters highly insightful and written by leading authors in the field. An essential reading both for experts in Scottish politics and the profound reader wishing to acquire knowledge about a fascinating country and its recent developments and transformations.

Edoardo Ongaro, *Professor of International Public Services Management, Northumbria University, Newcastle, UK, and President, European Group for Public Administration (EGPA)*

Scottish politics has never been more alive nor hotly contested. This highly timely and comprehensive collection shines a light into the brightest and darkest corners of Scottish Politics. It is unrivalled in illuminating key issues and debates, blending together our understandings of the past, present and contested futures of Scotland.

Allan McConnell, *University of Sydney, Australia*

How different are Scottish policy and politics from the rest of the UK? *Politics in Scotland* brings together a strong group of expert authors to examine the cutting-edge issues. They provide a comprehensive and informative guide to this question of where Scottish policy and politics is now and where it is heading in the future.

Martin Laffin, *Queen Mary University of London, UK*

Politics in Scotland

Politics in Scotland is an authoritative introduction to the contemporary political landscape in Scotland and an essential text for undergraduate and postgraduate students of Scottish Politics. Written by leading experts in the field, it is coherently organised to provide a clear and comprehensive overview of a range of themes in contemporary Scottish Politics.

Key topics include:

- Government and electoral behaviour.
- Representation and political parties in Scotland.
- Public policy and Scotland's relationship with the rest of the world.
- Scottish politics both in the run up to and after the 2014 referendum.
- The future of Scottish government and politics.

This textbook will be essential reading for students of Scottish Politics, British Politics, devolution, government and policy.

Duncan McTavish is Professor of Public Policy and Management at Glasgow Caledonian University, UK. He has published extensively in public policy and management, multi-level government and politics of the nation State, and edited leading academic journals.

Politics in Scotland

Edited by
Duncan McTavish

LONDON AND NEW YORK

First published 2016
by Routledge
2 Park Square, Milton Park, Abingdon, Oxon OX14 4RN

and by Routledge
711 Third Avenue, New York, NY 10017

Routledge is an imprint of the Taylor & Francis Group, an informa business

© 2016 Selection and editorial matter: Duncan McTavish; individual chapters: the contributors

The right of the editor to be identified as the author of the editorial material, and of the authors for their individual chapters, has been asserted in accordance with sections 77 and 78 of the Copyright, Designs and Patents Act 1988.

All rights reserved. No part of this book may be reprinted or reproduced or utilised in any form or by any electronic, mechanical, or other means, now known or hereafter invented, including photocopying and recording, or in any information storage or retrieval system, without permission in writing from the publishers.

Trademark notice: Product or corporate names may be trademarks or registered trademarks, and are used only for identification and explanation without intent to infringe.

British Library Cataloguing in Publication Data
A catalogue record for this book is available from the British Library

Library of Congress Cataloging in Publication Data
Names: McTavish, Duncan, editor.
Title: Politics in Scotland / edited by Duncan McTavish.
Description: Abingdon, Oxon ; New York, NY : Routledge, 2016. | Includes bibliographical references and index.
Identifiers: LCCN 2016003608| ISBN 9781138933200 (hardback) | ISBN 9781138933217 (pbk.) | ISBN 9781315678672 (ebook)
Subjects: LCSH: Scotland–Politics and government–21st century. | Scotland–Foreign relations–21st century. | Public administration–Scotland. | Local government–Scotland. | Home rule–Scotland. | Voting–Scotland.
Classification: LCC JN1228 .P65 2016 | DDC 320.9411–dc23
LC record available at http://lccn.loc.gov/2016003608

ISBN: 978-1-138-93320-0 (hbk)
ISBN: 978-1-138-93321-7 (pbk)
ISBN: 978-1-315-67867-2 (ebk)

Typeset in Times New Roman
by Taylor & Francis Books

Contents

List of illustrations		ix
List of contributors		xi
	Politics in Scotland: Introduction DUNCAN MCTAVISH	1
1	Unionism and nationalism: The historical context of Scottish politics EWEN A. CAMERON	6
2	How Scotland votes: Elections and electoral behaviour in Scotland CRAIG MCANGUS	24
3	Quality of Scottish democracy THOMAS LUNDBERG	42
4	Political parties in Scotland DUNCAN MCTAVISH	59
5	Corks on a beach? Finding a hard budget constraint for the Scottish Government PAUL HALLWOOD AND RONALD MACDONALD	91
6	Scottish local government: Past, present and futures COLIN MAIR	108
7	Civil service and machinery of government RICHARD PARRY	123
8	Social policy in a devolved Scotland: Different, fairer? KIRSTEIN RUMMERY	140
9	Gender and equality in Scotland: Mind the gap GILLIAN FYFE AND KAREN JOHNSTON	160
10	Scotland and the world MICHAEL KEATING	180

11	A small country in a bigger country or a small country in a big world? RICHARD KERLEY	195
12	The future of Scottish government and public policy: A distinctive Scottish style? PAUL CAIRNEY	213
13	Scotland and British constitutional reform: 'Oops, I did it again!' Blair, Cameron and the Britney Spears model of constitutional reform MATT QVORTRUP	229
14	The media and politics in Scotland DAVID HUTCHISON	243
	Politics in Scotland: Conclusion DUNCAN MCTAVISH	259
	Index	263

List of illustrations

Figures

2.1	Share of the vote won at UK general elections in Scotland, 1945–2015	29
2.2	Percentage of seats won at Scottish general elections, 1945–2015	30
2.3	Share of the constituency vote in Scottish Parliament elections, 1999–2015	33
2.4	Share of the regional vote in Scottish Parliament elections, 1999–2015	34
2.5	National identity in Scotland, 1999–2014	37
8.1	Relative poverty after housing costs, Scotland and the UK	146
8.2	Equality of household income, as measured by the Gini coefficient, Scotland and the UK	146
8.3	Employment rates (16–64) in the four countries of the UK, Q1 2002–Q1 2014	148
8.4	Throughout the last decade the rate of premature deaths in Scotland has been much higher than in England and Wales	150
8.5	The standardised mortality rate for stomach cancer, lung cancer and heart disease in Glasgow is almost twice as high as that in the best areas	150
8.6	Funding sources (£ billion)	155

Tables

2.1	First three rounds of the North East Scotland regional list result, 2011 Scottish Parliament election	26
2.2	Seats won at Scottish general elections, 1945–1970	27
2.3	Seats won at Scottish general elections, February 1974–2015	27
2.4	Constituency (and regional) seats won at Scottish Parliament elections, 1999–2011	32
3.1	Conceptualisations of democratic quality	46
3.2	Democratic quality rankings	47
3.3	Female membership of the Scottish Parliament (percentages) at each election, 1999–2011	52
3.4	Voter turnout (percentages) at Scottish Parliament elections, 1999–2011	55
4.1	UK general elections 1979–1997: party representation from Scotland	62
4.2	Scottish parliamentary election 1999: main parties' constituency and regional representation	66

x *List of illustrations*

4.3	Scotland 2015: background of MEPs, MSPs, candidates for Scottish seats in the UK election, and MPs elected	74
4.4	Scotland 2015: background of MEPs, MSPs, candidates for Scottish seats at UK election by party affiliation	75
7.1	Public employment in Scotland, 1999 and 2015	125
10.1	Attitudes to EU, 2014	189
10.2	Voting intention in EU referendum, 2014	189
11.1	Constitutional and statutory position of local government: some international comparators	205
14.1	Daily newspaper ciculations in Scotland	246

List of contributors

Paul Cairney is Professor of Politics and Public Policy, University of Stirling. He is a well recognised specialist in Scottish politics and public policy and publishes extensively in this area, in academic books and journals, also including social and digital media. His research interests also encompass comparative public policy, including comparisons of policy theories, policy outcomes in different countries, the UK and devolved government policy making, and complexity theory and policy making.

Ewen A. Cameron is the Sir William Fraser Professor of Scottish History at the University of Edinburgh. His research has focused on the history of the land question in Scotland and Ireland, the development of modern Scottish politics since the nineteenth century and the modern history of the relationship between the UK state and the Scottish universities. He has numerous publications and his most recent book is *Impaled on the Thistle: Scotland Since 1880* (Edinburgh University Press, 2010).

Gillian Fyfe is Research Policy Manager with the Confederation of Scottish Local Authorities (COSLA) and was awarded her Ph.D. from Glasgow Caledonian University in 2014. She has a legal background, having graduated with an L.L.B. (Hons) from the University of Glasgow. Her research interests include public policy, governance, and equality policy. She has published in academic journals in the area of equality policy and written numerous research-based reports used to inform public policy at senior levels.

Paul Hallwood is Professor of Economics at the University of Connecticut, USA, previously Senior Lecturer at Aberdeen University. He has authored ten books including two jointly authored on financing the Scottish Government, as well as several papers on the same subject including 'Reforming Taxation and the Scotland Act 1988: Hard Budget Constraints and the Inadequacy of Calman Commission Proposals' (University of Connecticut, 2010).

David Hutchison is Professor of Media Policy at Glasgow Caledonian University. He has researched, written and published extensively on various aspects of media and media policy, including news media ownership, metropolitan and non-metropolitan journalism, British and European media policy, media in Scotland, and media in Canada. His most recent publication is *Scotland's Referendum and the Media* (Edinburgh University Press, 2016). He is also chair of Regional Screen Scotland.

Karen Johnston is Professor of Organisation Studies, University of Portsmouth. She has extensive academic and research experience, having worked at leading universities in

xii *List of contributors*

South Africa, the USA and the UK. Her research expertise includes public policy, political-administrative leadership, public governance, public management and gender equality, and she has published numerous peer-reviewed journal articles and books on representative bureaucracy and public policy. She has edited leading academic journals.

Michael Keating is Professor of Scottish Politics at the University of Aberdeen, and also holds a professorial appointment at the University of Edinburgh. He is Director of the Scottish Centre for Constitutional Change. He has considerable international research standing and is widely recognised as one of the world's leading experts on nations and nationalism in autonomous, home rule, federal and devolved contexts. He has numerous publications, has advised the Scottish Government and provided evidence to the Scottish Parliament. He has edited leading national and international academic journals.

Richard Kerley is Professor of Management at Queen Margaret University, Edinburgh. He has a special interest in public service management. He previously held posts with the Scottish Local Authorities Management Centre at Strathclyde University and at the University of Edinburgh. He has published in the area of public service performance management in leading journals. He chaired the Scottish Executive Working Party on Renewing Local Democracy which resulted in the 2004 Local Governance Act.

Thomas Lundberg is Lecturer in Politics at the University of Glasgow. His research interests are in comparative politics and the quality of democracy, focusing on political parties, constituencies and electoral systems and the relationship between citizens and their representatives. He has published a major work on *Proportional Representation and the Constituency Role in Britain* (Palgrave Macmillan, 2000) and articles on minority government, referendums, anti-political establishment parties and politics in Scotland since devolution.

Ronald MacDonald is Adam Smith Professor of Political Economy at the University of Glasgow. His research interests are in macroeconomics, international finance and finance and he has published widely in these areas. He contributed to the 2014 referendum debate in Scotland. He has been a consultant to the IMF, central banks, governments and public agencies. He is also a Research Fellow at the CESifi research network Munich and an International Fellow of the Keil Institute of the World Economy.

Colin Mair is Chief Executive of the Improvement Service, a partnership set up by the Confederation of Scottish Local Authorities (COSLA) and the Society of Local Authority Chief Executives (SOLACE) to support local government across Scotland. He was Director of the Scottish Local Authority Management Centre at Strathclyde University and Director of International Programmes at that university, where he worked on local government and public sector development in India, sub-Saharan Africa and Eastern Europe.

Craig McAngus is Lecturer in Politics and International Relations at the University of Aberdeen, previously Research Fellow at the University of Stirling working on the Economic and Social Research Council (ESRC) Future of the UK and Scotland project. He has undertaken detailed research (with publications) analysing how

Plaid Cymru and the Scottish National Party have adapted to changed opportunity structures created by devolution in the UK, in particular how they have reconciled their identities as autonomist parties with governmental status.

Duncan McTavish is Professor of Public Policy and Management at Glasgow Caledonian University. He has published extensively in public policy and management, multi-level government and politics of the nation state. He also has considerable experience in public engagement and operating at the academic–practitioner interface, is a board member of the Institute for Public Policy and Professional Practice (I4P) based in the north of England and a non-executive director of Glasgow Council for the Voluntary Sector (GCVS). He has edited leading academic journals and provided advice to public and private sector organisations.

Richard Parry is Honorary Fellow, previously Reader, in the School of Social and Political Science at the University of Edinburgh. He has researched extensively in the area of the UK and Scottish public policy and administration, and he was a member of the ESRC Whitehall and Devolution and Constitutional Change Programmes. He has numerous publications and conference papers on the role of the civil service in Scotland before and after devolution.

Matt Qvortrup is Professor and Chair of Political Science at Coventry University. He has previously worked at Cranfield University. He is internationally recognised as a comparative political scientist and constitutional lawyer with a particularly notable expertise in referenda. He has won the Oxford University Press Law Prize (2012) and is winner of the British Journal of Politics and International Relations Prize (2013). He has numerous publications (books, articles), including works on referenda, political divorce settlements, and electoral systems.

Kirstein Rummery is Professor of Social Policy at the University of Stirling and Co-Director of the Centre for Gender and Feminist Studies. She carries out research on health and social care policy, gender equality, disability rights and dementia, and has published extensively in these areas. She is currently working on an ESRC-funded project, 'Fairer, Caring Nations', looking comparatively at the links between care policy and gender equality in developed welfare states as part of the Scottish Centre on Constitutional Change.

Politics in Scotland

Introduction

Duncan McTavish

There is a lively interest in Scottish politics at the present time. Although the country has long had administrative devolution and distinctiveness in certain aspects of political, public and professional life, the visibility of Scottish politics became much more pronounced from the late 1990s among scholars, students and the general public. The establishment of a devolved Scottish Parliament with a (partially) proportional voting system gave prominence to the Scottish National Party (SNP), and despite the difficulties of gaining single party majority in such an electoral system the party gained an overall majority government in Holyrood in 2011, having run the government as the biggest party but without an overall majority from 2007. A referendum on Scottish independence was held in 2014 engaging a very large proportion of the population resulting in a turnout of 85 per cent, considerably higher than general elections to Scottish and UK parliaments; fearing a 'yes' vote in the closing stages of the referendum, the main UK parties 'vowed' to give the Scottish Parliament significantly greater powers if voters returned a no vote, which they did by a margin of 55–45 per cent. In May 2015, the UK general election saw the SNP win 56 of Scotland's 59 parliamentary seats. Such a result from a party whose main objective is constitutional change has not been seen at Westminster since Redmond's Irish nationalists' success in 1910 (when the nationalists held the balance of power at Westminster and 'almost' achieved Irish home rule).

The chapters in this volume, contributed by leading scholars and practitioners in the field, are organized around broad themes which collectively give a coherent picture of some key areas of concern for the study of Scottish politics. The conclusion contextualizes all this (with some international comparison) against (a) the reality that Scotland is not part of a federal UK structure; (b) by questioning conventional approaches to structures and institutions with regard to conceptualizations of unionism, nationalism, nation building and political and policy distinctiveness; and (c) through addressing the issue of new politics and Scotland.

The first theme is historical foregrounding. The chapter by Ewen A. Cameron ('Unionism and Nationalism: the Historical Context of Scottish Politics') explores different political traditions pre-and post-1945, showing interactions between unionism and nationalism. It also identifies the accommodating nature of unionism in the 1950s and the demise of the form of unionism displayed then. It addresses the rise of nationalism – Labour and Liberal nationalism and the rise of the SNP – and examines the trajectory from administrative devolution to political devolution within the Westminster system. Finally it addresses the post-referendum period: accommodation within UK government understandings of parliamentary sovereignty, or the undermining of that idea. The importance of this historical understanding is vital to an appreciation of the present in Scottish political life.

The operation of government provides a theme. The government machine (i.e. the civil service or core executive), funding and taxation arrangements and the operation of government at local government level are the main elements addressed. Richard Parry ('Civil Service and the Machinery of Government') analyses the civil service in terms of Scottish practices and wider UK institutional norms, similarities in Scotland to UK practices and structures, and the embedding of such within devolution legislation – and the SNP government's compatibility of policy initiatives within these arrangements. The relevance of such an analysis is obvious: the civil service in Scotland is part of the UK civil service, and the party forming the government in Scotland since 2007 has the aim of independence from the existing UK state. Parry's evaluation is interesting. Amongst other findings he observes that while there is a recognized 'Scottish model', traditional UK norms of neutral advice and support to the democratically elected government have been sustained. Paul Hallwood and Ronald MacDonald ('Corks on a Beach? Finding a Hard Budget Constraint for the Scottish Government') examine the Scotland Act 2016 approach to funding of the Scottish Government and conclude that while this represents a harder budget constraint than previous arrangements, there is still an element of continuing soft budget constraint – that is, according to the authors, the continuation of Scottish Parliament and Government spending without having to consider all of the tax and the political consequences of that spending (and therefore presumably leading to an accountability deficit). The authors also show that much of the actual funding arrangements set out in the 2016 Act were discussed at senior political and policy level (facilitated by the largest party of government at the time) over a decade previously – perhaps an indication that much of the thinking behind fiscal aspects of the 2015 Act is hardly novel. It is of course true that while a hard budget constraint may have been limited in the years preceding 2015, political choices were made with 'hard expenditure constraints' within the fixed overall devolved budget: for example, the Scottish Government elected in 2011 has in effect reduced and constrained expenditure on further (college) education to protect higher education and has not increased health spending quite as much as in England, both evidence of hard budget constraints and consequent political choices. In the chapter addressing local government, Colin Mair ('Scottish Local Government: Past, Present and Futures') underlines the rationalistic, technocratic approach to local government from the mid-1970s, implying the centralization of provision and the removal of much provision from local governance, the national prescription of policy and finance for local government. Mair points out that this is not necessarily the norm throughout Europe and he addresses the balancing of, on the one hand centralization and national prescription, and on the other subsidiarity and localization initiatives.

The third theme is elections, representation and politics, significant in three key respects. First, electoral behaviour is a vital aspect of politics in any democracy; and second, political parties as the vehicles of political ideas and actions are clearly of interest to any study of Scottish politics. A third component is (increasingly) important, and that is the quality of Scottish democracy. Craig McAngus ('How Scotland Votes: Elections and Electoral Behaviour in Scotland') includes an outline of how Scotland votes, overviewing electoral behaviour from 1945 up to the most recent UK general election in 2015. His chapter includes devolved elections and comment on the 2014 independence referendum. He also looks at the extent to which elections to the devolved Parliament are treated by the electorate as 'second order elections'. A detailed account of Scotland's political parties, their positioning in Scottish politics up to the present, and engagement with the national dimension of Scottish politics, as well as an analysis of membership and party representation, is provided in Duncan McTavish's chapter ('Political Parties in Scotland'). This treatment includes a perspective on the varying fortunes of the main parties in Scotland and evaluates them in terms of current literature and thinking on party type, membership levels, member–leader relationships, and representativeness of elected members. Thomas Lundberg ('Quality of Scottish Democracy') explores the extent to which devolution has led to a 'new politics' distinct from Westminster-styled politics alongside the persistence of adversarial models. Lundberg also looks at the Scottish referendum campaign and democratic engagement, and uses some comparative information, posing the question of whether small nations are more likely to display better democratic quality.

An important theme is representation and equality; important for a number of reasons, not least of which is the stated commitment of the Scottish Parliament (from its establishment) to equal opportunities, restated at the commencement of the current Parliament. Gillian Fyfe and Karen Johnston ('Gender and Equality in Scotland: Mind the Gap') assess the position of gender equality and representation in Scottish politics and public policy, specifically examining gender inclusion and exclusion in devolved institutions and addressing participation and mainstreaming of equality in the policy process. The authors identify significant gaps in policy formulation and implementation caused by a split between devolved and reserved powers, and raise some questions over the political will and commitment to equality, noting that while under the terms of the 2016 Scotland Act equality remains reserved, considerable powers to advance equality will exist and it remains to be seen if there will be a renewed drive for equality in light of the current First Minister's early statements and actions. Kirstein Rummery ('Social Policy in a Devolved Scotland: Different, Fairer?') examines the evidence for the claim that Scotland is different and fairer in social policy terms from the rest of the UK. She outlines developments in Scottish social policy since devolution in the context of long standing differences in legislative and administrative frameworks in Scotland vis-à-vis other parts of the UK and appraises differences in actual policy outputs and trajectories in terms of core social policy concerns – Beveridge's 'five evils' of disease, ignorance, poverty, homelessness, idleness. The analysis concludes that while there has been some policy divergence from other parts of the UK, Scottish social policy has not been especially radical with regard to creating a much fairer society; and that currently – and also with enhanced powers devolved with the 2016 Scotland Act – the resource envelope available to Scotland could be used to re-prioritize policies and create greater fairness. But the author also notes that some adopted policies, while not optimal in terms of creating a fairer society, do have positive outcomes through universality and social solidarity. It is likely that responsive government will wish to take cognizance of such outcomes when drawing up policy priorities. Scottish administrations will also consider the fiscal and welfare configuration between Scottish and UK governments under current arrangements and after the 2016 Act: fiscal and welfare federalism it is not, but rather a mélange of Scottish raised taxes (mainly income tax), UK raised taxes, continuing Barnett or Barnett style expenditure allocation from Westminster to Holyrood, a UK based universal credit welfare system with calculations of benefits based at Westminster, some competences devolved to Holyrood to top up a range of benefits, and so on. In this complex picture of UK–Scottish Governments' interrelationships, a total reconfiguration of welfare policy may not be risk free in terms of possible resource impact. For example when an earlier (Labour–Liberal Democrat) coalition government in Holyrood introduced free personal care this led to a loss of Attendance Allowance from the UK Department of Work and Pensions, a loss which had to be made good from the Scottish Executive's block grant. The point being that any Scottish government is likely to move with caution rather than speed, and only after a form of risk assessment and political calculation is undertaken.

There are themed chapters looking at aspects of Scotland in a UK and international context. Richard Kerley ('A Small Country in a Bigger Country or a Small Country in a Big World?') discusses some of the characteristics and complexities of Scotland's status, using categorizations like country, nation and state, and how these characterize relationships between the four jurisdictions of the UK. A range of international comparisons is drawn and he concludes with an outline of some current issues, for example the prospect of further institutional and constitutional change of an emergent and confused nature emanating from Westminster; the challenges of scrutinizing government in a unicameral legislature; and the importance of historical legacy or path dependency in any redesigned institutional or political architecture. Michael Keating analyses 'Scotland and the World' through developments in para-diplomacy and proto-diplomacy. The relevance of these concepts is seen in the reality that devolved governments are increasingly involved in international affairs. The conceptual distinction between the 'high politics' of international affairs and matters of state on the one hand and domestic matters on the other, at best requires nuancing and at worst is not particularly useful in the study of many policy areas, though the reserved/devolved distinction is clearly embedded in the Scottish devolution legislation. As Keating points out, transnational integration has led to governmental and policy rescaling, and while para-diplomacy (essentially the extension of domestic policy competences into the international arena) is relatively uncontentious, proto-diplomacy (which is about region- or nation building, accentuating national identity or greater autonomy in the international sphere) can be highly contested. As the author concludes, such external engagement (para- and proto-diplomacy) is becoming ingrained in multi-level governance, and this is highly visible in the case of Scotland.

The final theme addresses some aspects of contemporary Scottish politics and the significance of these for future directions. Paul Cairney examines the notion of a distinct Scottish policy style ('The Future of Scottish Government and Public Policy: a Distinctive Scottish Style?'). While there is much evidence of the distinctiveness thesis (e.g. greater participation and consultative roles for local government and others in policy formation and implementation), a powerful explanatory fact is found in the size and capacity of central government and key interest groups in Scotland; and there appears to be something of a deficit regarding parliamentary scrutiny – the author suggests future possibilities to reform this. A relatively neglected area of study in Scottish politics is the media. Yet the importance of this is obvious. The media provide the channel for political communication and discourse essential in a modern democracy, providing information on political and policy initiatives as well as opportunities for civic debate, and enabling citizens formulate judgments on matters of the day. David Hutchison ('The Media and Politics in Scotland') outlines the 'health' of print and broadcast media in Scotland, noting the relative position of Scottish editions of predominantly English titles. The situation of Scottish-produced output in the broadcast media is examined and the media bias (including online media) during the Scottish referendum is addressed. The chapter also addresses relationships between the media and government in Scotland. Matt Qvortrup's account of British constitutional reform and the relevance for Scotland has a humorous subtitle but a serious intent ('Scotland and British Constitutional Reform: "Oops, I Did It Again!" Blair, Cameron and the Britney Spears Model of Constitutional Reform'). Constitutional reform in Britain, somewhat exceptional by international comparison, has not been characterized by 'constitutional moments', but driven by party political short-term interest. While this has displayed a degree of flexibility resulting in positive and pragmatic outcomes, it can be stretched beyond practical application with negative results. There are a number of aspects of the current political environment which make this a possible scenario, including the somewhat haphazard and asymmetric devolution across the UK, the workability and symbolism of 'English votes for English laws', the strong presence of the SNP both in Holyrood and Westminster, and the possibility of another referendum on Scottish independence.

There is a concluding chapter which synthesizes the above in the context of key dimensions facing Scottish politics as it looks to the future. These dimensions are the key governance relationship between Holyrood and Westminster, which is contextualised by devolution not federalism; the role of structures and institutions and how these play against definitions of unionism and nationalism; dimensions of new politics in Scotland.

1 Unionism and nationalism
The historical context of Scottish politics

Ewen A. Cameron

Although the referendum campaign of 2014 took place without very much reference to political history, it will be the contention of this chapter that its historical contextualisation is vitally important. What reference to history that there was tended to focus on appeals to the shared history of Britishness during the Great War and the Second World War, anniversaries of both of which occurred during the referendum campaign. The SNP and the Yes campaign seemed deliberately to eschew appeals to the Scottish historical past, perhaps on the grounds that this would be seen as exclusive. A range of books was published during the campaign that sought to explain and contextualise the referendum for a broader audience but, once again, very little of this material was explicitly historical (Cameron 2013). There was an exchange of views between two of Scotland's leading historians, but their interesting debate concentrated on broad historical issues rather than the specifics of Scottish political history (Devine 2014; Whatley 2014).

The objective of this chapter will be to provide an overview of the modern political history of Scotland, with the focus on points of political change since the late nineteenth century. It is important to delve into a slightly longer period than the recent past in order to understand some of the key themes, such as the history of unionism or the way in which Scotland has been governed within the United Kingdom in the period before the creation of the Scottish Parliament in 1999. It is argued here that there was a series of developments in the late nineteenth century – the establishment of the Scottish Office, electoral reform and redistribution of constituencies in 1885 and the debate over Irish Home Rule in 1886 – which had a defining role in the creation of modern Scottish politics.

It would be misleading to see the political history of modern Scotland as forming a single narrative leading to this point, important though the current moment is. It would be easy to construct a Whiggish narrative, glorifying the present moment, to show that Scottish politics has always been distinct and divergent from a British norm and that this can explain readily the route by which we came to the referendum in September 2014. This chapter, however, will look at the different political traditions in Scottish political history and will emphasise that the polarisation evident in the referendum campaign masks significant ways in which unionism and nationalism represent broad and overlapping understandings. In periods, such as the 1950s, when the Scottish Unionist Party was popular, its strength was based on a subtle understanding of the accommodating nature of the Union and a series of policy demonstrations – housing or administrative reform – of the way in which the idea of Scotland could thrive within its structures. It is a significant feature of later periods that this conception of the Union was lost, even by unionists. The demise of this inclusive form of unionism will be charted. The chapter will also look at the rise of nationalism as a force within Scottish politics that goes beyond the history of the SNP. The ways in which Labour and Liberalism attempted to bolster their nationalist credentials, partly as a response to the rise of the SNP from the late 1960s, will be stressed. The chapter will thereby contextualise the politics of the home rule question. An important theme running through the chapter will be examination of a series of points at which fundamental changes in the political landscape became evident and the ways in which those whose position was under threat sought to respond to these changes. The Scottish historical context of ideas for post-referendum development will also be discussed. The conclusion will look at the extent to which these formulations can be accommodated within UK-government understandings of parliamentary sovereignty and the extent to which the current moment has the potential to undermine the long continuity and centrality of that idea.

A monolithic Liberalism?

Three phases can be identified in the modern political history of Scotland that commenced with the 1832 Reform Acts. Prior to 1832 the Scottish electorate was tiny, with only around 4,500 voters in 1832 (Pentland 2008). They elected forty-five members of the United Kingdom Parliament at Westminster, an arrangement arising from the Union of 1707. Indeed, in the influence of feudalism in the Scottish franchise there were continuities with the period before the Union (Ferguson 1959; 1998). With the 1832 Act the Scottish electorate was extended to about 64,000 and the number of Scottish MPs grew to fifty-three. From 1832 to 1918 Scottish politics was dominated by the Whigs, and from the middle of the nineteenth century a clearly defined Liberal political identity had emerged and this continued to virtually monopolise Scottish representation at Westminster down to the Great War. During this period there was only one general election – that of 1900, fought at the height of the Boer War – at which the Liberals did not win a majority of Scottish seats (Brown 1992). On some occasions, such as 1868 or 1885, their dominance was almost complete; on other occasions, such as 1846 or 1874, it was a little less so. The Conservatives were extraordinarily weak in Scotland, especially in the burgh seats, where they had hardly any success (Hutchison 1986: 1–217). The electorate was expanded with the enfranchisement of householders in the burghs in 1868 and the extension of this franchise to the counties in 1885. The year 1885 also saw a redistribution of seats, confirming a trend towards the increased representation of populous urban areas and a recognisably modern constituency map. We can trace the modern electoral map of Scotland to these reforms, although the rural areas were still over-represented. This new system remained manifestly undemocratic, although that test is anachronistic. Across the country only around 60 per cent of adult males were able to vote and women remained outside the franchise, although some could vote in school board elections after 1872 and county council elections after 1889 (Hoppen 1985).

The Liberalism that dominated this period was characterised by free trade, low taxation, an aspiration to minimise government expenditure and a foreign policy that sought to avoid wars, which were expensive undertakings (as the Boer War was to prove in a way that disrupted both the fiscal and the political consensus around free trade) (Biagini 1992). These ideas were expounded by Gladstone in his Midlothian campaigns in 1879 and 1880, as he sought election for that seat. He appealed to his own electors in a direct manner at meetings across the county and, through the power of the press, to the wider electorate in an innovative campaign that exploited technological advances in the form of railway travel and telegraphic communication (Brooks 1985). The strength of Liberalism in this period was all the more remarkable when one considers that they were able to see off challenges from a variety of different directions. In Highland seats at the elections of 1885 and 1886 the Liberals were challenged by new voters who, uniquely across Britain, used their votes to support 'Crofter' candidates from outside the traditional party system but by 1895 these had been largely reabsorbed by the Liberal party (Cameron 1996).

The threat to Liberalism from independent Labour candidates was muted in Scotland. Such was the power of the Liberal party and the range of issues that it campaigned on that it was difficult for Labour candidates to carve out a distinctive political identity. Although Labour organisation was precocious in Scotland, with a Scottish Labour party founded in 1888, its electoral performance before the Great War was weaker in Scotland than in other industrial areas of the country. The Liberals in Scotland eschewed the pact with Labour that operated in other parts of the country, although they did have some concerns about the extent to which Labour could grow to become a threat in the longer term (Hutchison 1986: 218–65).[1] Conditions were difficult for Labour in Scotland, as one activist pointed out in 1906: 'we have not a clear fight anywhere, in every constituency we have to fight both Liberal and Tory'.[2] Nevertheless, the fact is that there were only three Labour MPs in Scotland elected in December 1910, the last election before the Great War, and the Labour share of the vote in that election was only 3.6 per cent, compared to 6.4 per cent across the United Kingdom as a whole (Cameron 2010: 80).

A more serious challenge was from those who left the Liberal party after 1886 in opposition to Irish Home Rule. They styled themselves Liberal Unionists, sought to defend the 1800/01 Union with Ireland and pursued an electoral pact with the Conservatives at the 1886 and subsequent elections down to December 1910, prior to a full merger in 1912 (Burness 2003). That merger created in Scotland the Scottish Unionist Party, nomenclature that survived until the reintroduction of the word 'Conservative' in 1965. The emergence of Unionism gave the Conservatives partners who allowed them to build a new identity and develop a much greater possibility of connecting with the Scottish electorate. There was some evidence of success in the elections of 1886, 1895 and 1900, but by 1906 the Liberals appeared to have seen off this challenge too and they won 56, 58 and 59 of the new 70 Scottish seats in the 1906, January 1910 and December 1910 elections (Cameron 2010: 79–101). The ramifications of Gladstone's first Irish Home Rule bill were very important in the longer term. This bill established many of the themes in the argument about devolution that would rumble on across the twentieth century and beyond. Equally important was its role as the midwife of unionism as a political theme in modern Scottish politics.[3] Although unionism was initiated by a threat to the union with Ireland, it developed a Scottish context as the twentieth century went on. At first this was implicit, 'the Union' encompassed the unions of 1800/01 and 1707, but became explicit after the partition of Ireland in 1922 and as the future of the Union of 1707 became a matter of more direct debate in the later twentieth century (Mitchell 1998a). The debate about the Irish question in the period from 1886 to 1922 unleashed an argument about how to best accommodate Scotland. In the aftermath of the first Irish Home Rule bill in 1886 a Scottish Home Rule Association was founded. This body argued for 'home rule all round', by which was meant the establishment of parliaments in Scotland and Ireland, perhaps also in Wales and even the English regions. Some of the people who argued this were Unionists who saw such schemes as the best way of preserving the Union and reducing the focus on Ireland, which they thought was being rewarded for bad behaviour (Kane 2015). Some Home Rulers of this period developed federalist understandings of the future of the United Kingdom. These were prominent among another Home Rule group, the Young Scots Society. They operated within the Liberal party from the immediate aftermath of the 1900 election and sought to increase the attention paid by the party to Scottish issues, such as home rule and land reform (Kennedy 2013). A significant problem in all of these schemes was how to avoid the difficulties of granting home rule to one part of the United Kingdom, Scotland or Ireland for example, and not to England. The answer to this problem, to grant some form of equality to England in a federal, or quasi-federal structure, brought a whole series of other problems (Kendle 1989). The principal difficulty was how to accommodate one large and three small units in a federal structure. England would dominate and it would be difficult to separate English from British or Imperial issues. One answer would be to regionalise England in some way, but this was difficult to structure. This debate was resolved in what turned out to be a very unsatisfactory way for the history of the United Kingdom: by the partition of Ireland and the creation of a very asymmetric system of devolution, whereby Ulster was the only part of the Union which had a devolved parliament, from 1922 to 1972 (Jackson 2011: 316–31).[4] So, although Scottish politics appears monolithic, in that it appeared to be dominated by the Liberal party, it was pregnant with a range of themes which became important in later periods.

Unionist duopoly?

The second period began in 1918 and lasted until the 1970s. There are ways in which it could be broken down into sub-periods but it has a unity in certain respects. The first point is structural. Further electoral reforms in 1918 extended the franchise to nearly all adult males and to women over the age of thirty, with a fully gender-equal franchise being introduced in 1928. The redistribution of 1918 was very significant. There was an important shift in representation from the rural to the urban, from east to west and from southern and northern Scotland to the industrial Central Belt. This brought representation into line with population to a greater extent than ever before. The western area around Glasgow now had 45 per cent of the seats, compared to only 33 per cent in 1885; on the other hand, rural areas like the Highlands fell from 13 per cent of Scottish seats to 8 per cent and in the Borders and southwest the loss of representation was even more marked, from 13 per cent to 6 per cent (Craig 1974). Although there was an attempt to use arithmetic to equalise the population of seats there was continuing recognition of parliamentary seats as interests or communities of people with similar backgrounds. This is seen most obviously in the creation of the new Western Isles seat, with a relatively small electorate.[5] This redistribution was at least as important as the extension of the franchise because it changed the electoral map of Scotland in a way which favoured the Labour party by extending the number of seats in the geographical area of their greatest strength and diminishing the number of seats in the rural fringes of Scotland where they had little support. The results of this change are seen clearly at the 1922 election. In that contest Labour won nineteen of its twenty-nine seats in western Scotland. Nearly half (48.1 per cent) of the electorate was located there and Labour's share of the vote was 44.1 per cent in this region.

Too much attention has perhaps been given to the extension of the franchise as an agent of political change (Matthew et al. 1976). It was by no means clear in the early 1920s that a majority of the new voters were working class and it is equally dangerous to assume that working-class voters were likely to vote Labour (Tanner 1983). The Unionists certainly believed that they could compete for working-class votes and not just by appealing to an Orange Protestantism, but also by giving priority to important social issues like housing.[6] At least as important as the franchise changes was the establishment of a narrative of politics through the use of political conditions and debates, especially over the housing question, during the Great War. Wartime political conditions worked against the Liberal party, which emerged from the war in a divided and weakened state (Hutchison 1999). The Liberals also seemed not to have the vocabulary to deal with the challenges of the post-war period. Their traditional policies of land reform, free trade and pursuit of peace through international cooperation seemed out of touch with the issues in which the electorate were interested: how to deal with unemployment, industrial depression and a threatening international environment. Further, as their leader pointed out to a party official in the aftermath of the 1935 election, the party was broke, the other parties had tried to 'ground us out of existence' and they had little support in the press.[7]

Politics at both local and national level became increasingly polarised around the threat of socialism. These politics sustained the coalition government in power from 1918 to 1922 and the continued local electoral pacts between Unionists and National Liberals (the term used by those former Coalition Liberals once the coalition had broken up) at the 1923 election and at local government elections. This theme continued throughout the post-war period and works against the idea of a consensus in the 1945-79 period. Although the Liberals rallied in 1923 around the traditional flag of free trade and to a lesser extent in 1929, they were never again the same force as they had been in the pre-1914 period. Principally this was because they could not find the language to communicate their political ideas to the urban core of the Scottish electorate, who were now much more strongly represented. The rural heartlands of the party were decreasingly significant on the electoral map. At the general election of 1945 they lost their last Scottish stronghold when their distinguished leader, Sir Archibald Sinclair was defeated in Caithness and Sutherland (Hutchison 2000). This was an important moment and brings out one of the defining characteristics of this period: its two-party nature.

The domination of Scottish politics by Labour and the Unionists can be seen in the inter-war period, although the creation of the National Government in 1931 disguises it in the 1930s (Hutchison 1998). The creation of the wartime coalition, however, emphasises it and this duopoly was continued until the late 1960s. The domination of this period by Labour and the Unionists is sometimes reduced and over-simplified when the period is characterised as one of consensus – an increasingly contested area – and unionism (Harvie 2000; Toye 2013). To take the latter point as the more interesting from a Scottish point of view: it was the case that, although the SNP was founded in 1934 as the result of a merger between the National Party of Scotland and the more right-wing Scottish party, elections were dominated by broadly unionist parties (Finlay 1994). Nevertheless, the blanket description 'unionist' does a grave disservice to the differing conceptions of unionism that divided Labour from the Scottish Unionist Party. A strong argument in Unionist rhetoric was that Labour's outlook was uniform and centralist to the detriment of the recognition and survival of ideas of Scottishness. The Unionists pushed themselves forward as the party of devolution for Scotland in the

1950s, albeit that it was enhanced administrative devolution that they had in mind. Indeed, they implemented this policy by adding a further minister to the Scottish Office in 1955 and structuring the departments of St Andrews House in 1962. The Unionists contrasted their outlook with that of Labour's policy of nationalisation, which concentrated power in London. Further, the description 'unionist', even in the lower case, simply used to mean that there was no meaningful nationalist alternative in this period, serves to simplify and reduce the richness of what that word could mean. Not only was there a variety of unionisms but there was real depth to what lay behind the doctrine. The place of the Church of Scotland, the legal system and the education system was deeply considered and there was much more to it than simply a Diceyian emphasis on parliamentary sovereignty. Indeed, it might be said to be nationalist in its subtle understanding of the politics of Scottish identity (Kidd 2008). To understand the politics of the post-war period down to the late 1960s it ought to be recognised that it was not a bland and uninteresting period sandwiched between the excitement of Red Clydeside and the Hamilton by-election (Cameron 2010: 263–88).

This period saw important debates about the reconstruction of Scotland's infrastructure after the Second World War. As it had done in the inter-war period, the housing question was the most important aspect of this. Inter-war governments of all stripes had tried to tackle the twin problems of slum clearance and house-building (Glendinning 1995). This was an area of policy that exposed the difficulties in the relationship between central and local government. There was also a debate about economic policy that rested on sharply competing conceptions of the role of the state. This was a constant theme of messages that came from Unionist HQ in the 1950s, especially from the redoubtable party official Colonel P. J. Blair. He reminded candidates and activists of the gulf between Labour and his own party. In a communication of 1959 he felt that the 'myth' of socialist planned expansion ought to be 'exploded'; the difference between 'the "social conscience" which actuates the Unionist Party, and socialism' was to be emphasised at every opportunity. He went on to assert that Unionists should counter the argument that socialists had a 'moral basis for their policies while the Unionist party is merely materialistic'. He wanted his party activists to push the idea that 'Unionist principles and policy recognised the value of human character and to emphasise that the individual has duties to which he owes the community as well as rights due to him by it'.[8] Liberal rhetoric in this period also exemplified the way in which the other parties defined themselves by their opposition to socialism. In 1946, for example, the Liberals resolved that nationalisation of steel would 'inevitably stultify and eventually destroy the spirit of pioneering enterprise which created this great industry'.[9] There was more to this than the narcissism of small differences, and it represented a deeper ideological divide between different conceptions of politics as they related to Scotland.

Nevertheless, towards the end of this period there was a sense in both main parties that the duopoly that had persisted since the 1930s was breaking down. The most obvious symbol of this change was the success of the SNP in the late 1960s, culminating in their good performance in the Pollok by-election of 1966, which the Conservatives (as they were known) won on a minority vote and, sensationally, their victory at the Hamilton by-election in November 1967. Winifred Ewing took Labour's safest seat in Scotland, thereby becoming the SNP's first MP since 1945 (Cameron 2010, 281–6). Although, in retrospect, there were developments in the earlier part of the decade which indicated growing support for the SNP they did not signify the thunderbolt that was the Hamilton result.

Both unionist parties made attempts to explain the changes in the late 1960s that led them to this worrying time. The Conservatives were a little quicker off the mark. Conservative Central Office commissioned surveys of nationalism after the Pollok result. They were aware that there were shifts evident in Scottish politics as they lost four seats in the Highlands and northeast of Scotland at the 1964 and 1966 elections.[10] A more focused study of Hamilton in the run up to the contest revealed that the 'tide of nationalism' was running strongly in Hamilton and the party was prepared for a bad performance. This research revealed terrible image problems for the party in Scotland. They were seen as having little or no connection to Scotland and this encouraged some party officials to reverse the then current opposition to granting more autonomy to Scotland. The fact that this discussion was largely taking place in London perhaps emphasised the problem.[11] The Scottish party felt marginalised when Edward Heath made his 'Declaration of Perth' in 1968, proposing the establishment of an enquiry into the Scottish question with a view to granting some form of devolution. The reaction to this move was widespread criticism of what appeared to be an opportunistic conversion to the merits of a Scottish Assembly. As has been recently pointed out (Pentland 2015), the Conservative mind had been concentrated by electoral losses since 1959. Further, the modest proposals made by Heath at Perth could be seen to be consistent with the party's tradition of recognising Scottish distinctiveness. Heath made some attempt to engage with this history but he had little overall feel for Scotland, even with the grouse moors or deer forests with which his immediate predecessors, Harold Macmillan and Alec Douglas-Home, were so intimately acquainted. For these reasons Heath's proposals came to little. The Commission that he appointed met and produced proposals for a very limited form of devolution but nothing was taken forward before his government lost power and the Scottish political landscape was altered in 1974.[12]

The Labour party was in government when the electoral coherence of this second period began to break down. They were slower to engage with some of the political problems because they had been in the ascendancy at the 1964 and 1966 elections, unlike the Conservatives. Since coming to government they had introduced some striking policies in Scotland, notably the establishment of the Highlands and Islands Development Board in 1965 and the investigation of the economic problems of the industrial areas which led to the Central Scotland plan, but this was not enough to see off a growing feeling that Scotland was being neglected by the central government. It was this perception, which predated the Labour government, on which the SNP was able to capitalise at Pollok, Hamilton and the local government elections in 1968. Labour's initial public response was a classic Wilsonian device – the appointment of a Royal Commission on the Constitution.[13] The Crowther-Kilbrandon Commission did not report until 1973, by which time Labour was out of power. More privately, a ministerial committee on devolution was established in 1968 and included amongst its members the strongly unionist secretaries of state for Scotland and Wales, George Thomas and Willie Ross, as well as Richard Crossman (Tanner 2006). Ross and Thomas saw the problem from the point of view of finding ways to counter Scottish and Welsh nationalism, whereas Crossman argued that 'government should concentrate on attacking the separatist position, but at the same time should carry out proposals … in relation to dispersal, administrative devolution and parliamentary devolution'. Crossman saw the issue as one of general constitutional modernisation which could ultimately be dealt with by a 'federal solution based on regional governments in Scotland, Wales and the English regions, on the analogy of the lander of federal

Germany'.[14] Nationalism was, in this view, of a stripe with the 'frustration and disappointment which results in mass abstentions at English by-elections'.[15] In these elite ministerial conversations in the late 1960s we can see coming to an end the long period of duopoly of the Unionists and Labour since the end of the Great War. We can also see the difficulty that these parties had in understanding the rise of the SNP from a party that was marginal for most of the period since its formation in 1964 but had suddenly made a breakthrough.[16]

The extent to which the political landscape had changed was evident at the general elections of October 1974 and 1983, at which the Labour and Conservative vote fell to 61.0 per cent and 63.5 per cent, compared to 96.8 per cent in 1955. In its first phase this was driven by the remarkable rise of the SNP at the elections of February and October 1974. From a slightly disappointing result in 1970 they advanced to 21.9 per cent and 30.4 per cent of the vote in the two contests of 1974. Important shifts in Scottish society, the expansion of secondary and higher education, the beginning of de-industrialisation, and the improvements in housing had eroded older political loyalties. The SNP was also able to come forward with more convincing economic ideas due to the discovery of oil reserves in the North Sea. Most of the eleven seats won by the SNP in October 1974 were taken from the Conservatives and were beyond the most populous areas of the industrial Central Belt (Jaensch 1976). This geography of representation, however, does not tell the whole story of the effect of the SNP in the politics of the period. The victories were complemented by the fact that the SNP came second in forty-two seats, thirty-five of them Labour-held. In an interesting internal document the Labour party analysed how close it had come to almost complete eclipse in Scotland.[17] The SNP strategy at this point was to claim a mandate by aiming to win a majority of the seventy-one Scottish constituencies. This could be secured on around 40 per cent of the vote. It was concluded, indisputably, that a relatively small further swing to the SNP could put them in a strong position to threaten the integrity of the United Kingdom. For Labour this was a profoundly dangerous moment. The party's weakness was not only electoral but also organisational. The memo reported that there were fewer full-time party agents in Scotland than there were in Norfolk. By contrast, the emboldened SNP was building up its organisation and was making strides among younger voters. An important element of the context of this period was that independence was supported by fewer voters than those who supported the SNP. This allowed Labour to argue that a strong devolution scheme could recover the position (Miller 1981). An attempt was made in the 1970s to bring forward such a scheme. This was seen by its critics, many of them on the Labour back benches, as unnecessary appeasement of the SNP. The opposite view was taken by the author of the memorandum, who argued that only a strong scheme of devolution could prevent the disintegration of the Union. Labour's devolution scheme began with reasonable clarity but got bogged down in detail and parliamentary guerrilla warfare (Cameron 2010: 296–319).[18] The first vehicle, a Scotland and Wales bill, was withdrawn after the failure of a guillotine motion in February 1977, and a Scotland bill reached the statute book but was repealed by the incoming Conservative government in 1979 after failing to secure the support of 40 per cent of the electorate in the referendum of March 1979. These events led to a modest reassertion of 'traditional' two-party politics at the general election of May 1979 when the combined vote of the two main parties rose to 72.9 per cent. After this point it entered a steep decline, with Labour and the Conservatives registering only 64 per cent in 1997 as the Conservative vote collapsed to only 18 per cent. Aside from the SNP, the other force that was present in the breakdown of this duopoly was the Liberal/SDP Alliance at the elections of 1983 and 1987. The SDP had been created in 1982 as a reaction to perceived extremism in the Labour party. As a result of the surge of support for the SDP and the Liberals, who had an electoral pact in 1983 and 1987, the combined Labour and Conservative vote fell again, this time to 63.5 per cent (Aikman 2013).

The principal electoral theme of the remainder of this period is the decline of the Conservative party in Scotland. This was a seemingly unambiguous trend but one which bought complications in its wake and introduced a new element to Scottish politics: a deeper failure to understand how to conduct Unionist politics than at any period, perhaps, since the years between 1707 and 1725.[19] The political and constitutional consequences of this shift were profound. The decline of the Conservative party in the 1980s and 1990s has been seen in terms of the Scottish reaction to 'Thatcherism'. It has been argued that the policies of her governments, especially economic and industrial policy, the National Health Service and education were inimical to Scottish interests and political outlook. In all these areas the Conservative government was alleged to be acting in a way contrary to a supposed Scottish political consensus (Stewart 2009). There were, however, other areas of policy where the Scottish response does not fit this framework. The most obvious of these is housing. After a long period dating back to the early 1920s in which the state sought to invest in public housing, the Conservative government of the 1980s granted the right to sitting tenants to purchase their council houses at substantial discounts. This was not quite a complete reversal of previous policy in that the investment in house building by local authorities and the support granted to them by government for this purpose had been slowing in the 1970s. This was, in the case of the Labour government of the 1970s, as a result of the difficult economic conditions that they were facing: in the case of the post-1979 Conservative government it was an ideologically driven policy (Gibb 1989). As George Younger, the secretary of state for Scotland, argued when he introduced the legislation in January 1980, the motivation for the policy was to give tenants:

> the freedom to choose, the freedom through one's hard work to acquire an asset which can be enjoyed and passed on to one's children, and the freedom to determine one's own way of life. Many of the great reform movements of the past and the present have been associated with these freedoms and with the desire by the people to ensure that property rights become dispersed throughout the community.[20]

The policy was also aimed at trying to add flexibility to the Scottish housing system, which was characterised as almost uniquely rigid because of the very high levels of public housing and, thereby, an inhibition to the mobility of labour. The 'freedom' can be seen in terms of the notion of creating a 'property-owning democracy'. This phrase was coined by Noel Skelton, a leading Conservative thinker and MP from the inter-war period (Skelton 1924; Torrance 2010).[21] The idea, however, of inculcating responsibility and conservatism, if not even Conservatism, in individuals and society through the extension of property ownership was a much older one. It can be seen in policies of the 1890s that sought to give small tenants in Scotland and Ireland the opportunity to buy their land (Cameron 1996). In Scotland in the 1980s the policy had a huge effect on society. From being in 1979 a country where a relatively small proportion of the population owned their own houses Scotland became a decade or so later not dissimilar to England in this respect. A very significant transfer of property, amounting to over 450,000 houses, from the public sector to private individuals took place (Gibb 1989). This can be seen as a policy which had a huge social effect but little political effect, or at least so far as electoral behaviour is concerned. An important political consequence was the change in the relationship between central and local government. The Conservative government also sought to reduce the resources at the disposal of local authorities, which were Labour-dominated in Scotland. This was also an important objective of the reform of local government funding that led to the introduction of the Community Charge, or 'Poll Tax' in 1987 (Butler et al. 1994). In the light of the transformative social implications of her government's housing policy in Scotland, it is difficult to sustain the argument that Scotland engaged in a comprehensive rejection of the ideological tenets of Thatcherism.[22]

There is no doubt, however, that the Conservative government was very unpopular in Scotland and that Mrs Thatcher, despite strenuous efforts, had little feel for the distinctive features of Scottish political culture (Cameron 2010: 320–48). The orthodoxy of Mrs Thatcher as the matriarch of devolution has emerged in the years since her downfall in 1990, and there is no doubt that we are in need of a more nuanced account of the 1980s. There is a danger that we accept the simplistic assumption that a wide range of ills can be placed at the door of Mrs Thatcher without taking into account wider factors. This could form an alternative, and equally simplistic narrative, to that of the inevitable march to devolution and beyond. The global economic forces driving the process of de-industrialisation, the extent to which social and economic change was under way in the 1970s, in the housing market, for example, have not been given sufficient emphasis. An uncritical narrative of the 1980s can become a too handy explanation for much of our recent history, the source of new myths, and risks a narrowing of our political culture. Gerry Hassan (2012: 86) has pointed to a 'set of mobilising myths' about the 1980s that have become important to contemporary Scotland. This requires some discussion.

The decline of the Conservative party in the post-1979 period can be seen in two ways. The first is to emphasise the agency of the anti-Thatcher point of view. This would stress the importance of 1979 as a starting point and point to de-industrialisation and the attempt to reform local government finance. Another way of seeing this change in the political landscape would be to argue that longer-term shifts became sharply evident in the 1980s but had been under way since the late 1950s. This thesis would argue that the Conservatives were the sharper losers in a long-term decline of the two-party system as both the Liberals, in various formulations, and the SNP became more powerful political forces. Some arguments about the longer-term decline of the Conservatives have suggested that they have suffered from the decline of a wider British identity and an erosion of a Scottish protestant identity, both of which were held to have sustained the party in Scotland at the point of its greatest success in the 1950s. There have been important changes in the religious alignment of Scottish voters, especially a notable increase in support for the SNP among Catholics. The narrative of the relationship between the Conservative party and Protestant voters is less clear. The Conservative vote in the 1950s was strongly Protestant but it is not clear that the smaller Conservative vote of more recent times is any less Protestant. The importance of Protestantism in Scottish society has declined, however, as has the importance of religion as a primary reason for voting for a particular party and the rise of other elements of identity, such as nationality. In these ways it might be argued that the large-scale social changes that have taken place in Scotland in the period since the mid-1960s have shifted the electorate away from the politics of the Conservative party. As has been suggested, economics play a very important part in this narrative (Seawright and Curtice 1995). The relatively poor performance of the Scottish economy compared to the rest of the UK, perhaps especially at times of Conservative government, has also played a part in the long-term decline of the party. The very sharp changes that took place during the 1980s bring this period into focus in thinking about the erosion of the Conservative vote in Scotland. Conservative policy in Scotland in the 1980s did little to try to address this matter; indeed, their ideological convictions may have exacerbated the problem. In particular, their willingness to scale back on regional policies was an important change in the attitude of government to the economy in the 1980s. When the Conservative governments of the early 1960s had found themselves in political difficulty in Scotland and they identified economic issues as part of the problem, policies to incentivise more private investment in Scotland was part of their response. This was not so in the 1980s. Regional policy expenditure diminished markedly in the 1980s, from £369 million to £103 million, according to one calculation (Lythe and Majmudar 1982: 119–39; Lee 1995: 186) and the government no longer seemed to be motivated by the political implications of unemployment, as had been the Heath government in the early 1970s or the Macmillan government in the early 1960s.[23] The Thatcher government of the 1980s presided over the closure of most of the monuments to this form of regional policy that had been established by both Conservative and Labour governments in the 1950s and 1960s. This allowed both the Labour party and the SNP to build a narrative that the government was deliberately engaging in the de-industrialisation of Scotland (Kendrick and McCrone 1989). The Conservatives paid the electoral price for the closures themselves and, additionally, for the loss of control of the political battleground in Scotland that led to them fighting on their opponents' terms to a much greater extent than in England. The problem was compounded by rather shallow attempts to try to regain the initiative, such as Mrs Thatcher's speech to the General Assembly of the Church of Scotland in 1988, but they should not be divorced from this wider context.[24]

The longer-term political consequences of this period are quite important for the current state of Scottish politics. Although it was not completely clear at the time, the Conservatives' ceding of the terms of the political debate provided an opportunity for the SNP to begin to establish its own narrative in a more sustained and impressive way than it had been able to do in the 1970s. During that decade when the Labour party put forward a scheme for devolution, it was very clear that the identity of the party was unionist. In the 1980s this was eroded as the Labour party began to use arguments and deploy tactics that were, at least partly, nationalist. This can be seen in the growing prominence of the argument that the Conservatives did not have a 'mandate' to govern Scotland. Although this language became most prominent in the aftermath of the 1987 election, at which the Conservatives lost eleven Scottish seats, it was evident earlier in the decade (Mitchell 1998b). This was an argument that only made sense from a nationalist point of view: in a strict construction of unionism there ought to be no requirement for any party to achieve support in any of the constituent parts of the union so long as they had a parliamentary majority in the union parliament. The matter was not so simple, however. Clearly there were nationalist elements in all of the political parties in Scotland in the sense that they had to be aware of, and cater to, the increasingly prominent Scottish national identity of the electorate (Dickson 1988). This attempted accommodation between unionism and nationalism was possible, as we have seen, in periods when there was little formal nationalist threat, as was the case in the 1950s. By the late 1980s, however, this was no longer the case. Although the SNP did not do quite as well as was expected in the 1987 or 1992 elections there is some evidence that a nationalist outlook was beginning to have a disproportionate effect on the way in which Scottish politics were being discussed. This was evident in the language used in the Scottish 'Claim of Right'[25] by the Scottish Constitutional Convention in the late 1980s and 1990s. The Claim was critical, for example, of the doctrine of parliamentary sovereignty, which could be seen as a nationalist point or as a Scottish unionist point, but it was certainly not in tune with the Unionism emanating from the Conservative government. Although the SNP decried the Constitutional Convention that was established following the publication of the Claim of Right on the grounds that it would not consider independence, the Convention can be seen as evidence of the prominence of the constitutional issue in a way that suited the kind of politics that the SNP wished to conduct. The aftermath of the 1992 election also hinted at the changing landscape of politics in Scotland. Although the Conservatives improved slightly their share of the vote and number of seats in Scotland this was not sufficient for them to regain control of the terms of Scottish politics. The multifarious protest groups that coalesced in the demonstration in Edinburgh in December 1992 during the European summit being held in the city helped to create the context whereby John Smith, the Labour leader, could describe devolution as the settled will of the Scottish people (Marr 1992). The referendum of 1997 and the creation of the Scottish Parliament appeared to demonstrate that this was the case. The politics of the period from the general election of 1997 to the opening of the Parliament in 1999 would repay some careful study. The new prime minister, Tony Blair, honoured the pledge to create a Scottish parliament but, as his memoirs indicate (Blair 2010: 250–3), he was much more towards the unionist wing of his party and he had little feel for Scottish politics or clear understanding of how devolution could fit into his general project. The Scottish Parliament elections have given the SNP the opportunity to create a much more stable base than would ever have been possible in its absence. The voting system for Holyrood, although designed (ineffectually as it turned out) to prevent the SNP from gaining a majority, provided them with the means to increase their number of elected representatives by a considerable degree compared to a system where Westminster elections were the only means to do so. This was the case even in a Scottish election where they did relatively poorly, such as in 2003, and emphatically so in their triumphs of 2007 and 2011 (Cameron 2010: 349–71). So, it can be argued that the experience of the Thatcher years can help to explain the establishment of the Scottish Parliament but it is possible to do this in a slightly more nuanced way than merely to argue that it was a reaction against the anti-Scottish nature of her governments, although this was part of the explanation.

Devolution has had another longer-term political consequence that the architects of the Scotland Act of 1998 could not have foreseen, although there were Unionist warnings that devolution would 'lead', in some undefined way, to independence. This is the way in which the debate about the future of the United Kingdom has not been closed down by the apparent unionist victory in the referendum of 18 September 2014. Many of the points that have been raised in this discussion not only have historical roots and contexts but, more than that, they have been part of the debate about home rule/devolution since 1886. One example of this is the discussion over 'English votes for English laws'. Often presented as a response to the 'West Lothian question' articulated in a particularly effective way by Tam Dalyell, it has deeper roots than that. The Irish

Home Rule bills of 1886, 1893 and 1912 tried to deal with the issue of what happens in the Union Parliament when there is asymmetric devolution and English MPs cannot vote on issues that have been devolved but Irish, or Scottish, MPs can vote on the equivalent English issues. In 1886 there was to be no Irish representation once home rule was granted but in 1893 Irish representation was to continue, albeit at a reduced level, and it was to be reduced further in 1912. The first 'solution' raised the danger of cries similar to the 'no taxation without representation' argument of the American revolutionaries – not a helpful precedent; the second raised the issue later highlighted in the 'West Lothian question'. In 1893 Gladstone did consider trying to identify some parliamentary issues on which Irish MPs would be able to vote and other 'British' issues on which they would not. The practicalities of this were too complicated, even for Gladstone, and the proposal was dropped. The other key issue which has been highlighted by the post-referendum debate is the question of how to fund a devolved settlement. Again this was trailed in the Irish home rule debates of the late nineteenth century. The 1886 bill, for example, proposed to divide powers of taxation; 'domestic taxes' were to be raised in Ireland and used to fund Irish services; Westminster was to retain control of the revenue from customs duties raised in Ireland and the Irish government was to pay a series of charges to reflect continuing unionist responsibilities such as the armed forces and the national debt (Jackson 2011: 67–9, 94–5, 127). Even without Irish home rule the financing of different parts of the United Kingdom has been a complicated matter. The 'Goschen formula' was developed in 1888 by a Unionist chancellor and sought to distribute some areas of expenditure to England, Scotland and Wales according to the proportions 80:11:9 (based on the yields of probate duty from the three nations). This was not applied to all areas of public expenditure, much smaller as a proportion of national income in 1888 than it has become, but was most used in education spending. It survived into the 1950s in some respects although by then it was very outdated.[26] The devolution schemes of the 1970s necessitated the construction of a more up-to-date scheme, which has become known as the 'Barnett formula'. This was based on population shares in the UK and identified Scotland's share of changes to public expenditure in England at 10/85ths (McCrone 2013: 11). This formula is not comprehensive as it does not cover matters not devolved to the Scottish Parliament, or to the Scottish Office prior to 1999, the biggest of which is social welfare, and it is frequently bypassed.

Conclusion

Consideration of the historical context of the current debates about the position of Scotland within the United Kingdom serves two general purposes. The first, as has been shown here, is that there is no single narrative that has brought us to the present moment. A simple story of the decline of the Union to explain the holding of the referendum and the relatively close result is not sustainable. Neither can it convincingly be argued that the Union and Britishness have been consistent in their appeal and that this explains the victory of the No side in the referendum. Above all, however, it is far from clear that the polarity between 'Yes' and 'No' which was enforced by the device of the referendum is a particularly helpful way of understanding Scottish political history. There have been different strands of unionism and nationalism and both themes, as well as others, have been present in all of the main political parties which have traversed the changing political landscape of Scotland since the 1880s.

Notes

1. Edinburgh National Library of Scotland (NLS), Ms 8801, ff. 145–51, Memorandum on the Socialist and Labour movements in Scotland, February 1908.
2. NLS, Acc. 5490(1), f. 32, Joseph Duncan to Mabel, 21 January 1906.
3. I will refer to unionism when writing about general support for the Unions of 1707 and 1800/01 and Unionism when referring to the political parties which used that title.
4. The Liberal cabinet considered these matters in 1910 as they prepared what became the third Irish Home Rule Bill, eventually presented to Parliament in 1912. Winston Churchill was asked to look into the question and a series of papers were written that served to highlight the problems in trying to implement Home Rule All Round or a scheme of federalism; see TNA, CAB37/105/16, Devolution, 24 Feb. 1911 [Winston S. Churchill]; CAB37/105/18, Devolution, 1 Mar. 1911 [Churchill]; CAB37/105/23, Devolution, 9 Mar. 1911 [Courtenay Peregrine Ilbert].
5. PP 1918, XIV [Cd. 8759], *Representation of the People Bill. Redistribution of seats. Report of the Boundary Commissioners (Scotland)*.
6. See the election addresses of Sir John Gilmour in Glasgow Pollok at the contests of 1918 to 1931, Edinburgh, National Records of Scotland (NRS), GD383/15/1–10; Gilmour, it should be noted, was a leading Orangeman.
7. Cambridge, Churchill College, Political Archives Centre, Archibald Sinclair Mss, THRS II 71/2/302, Archibald Sinclair to James Scott, 1 Dec. 1935.
8. Oxford, Bodleian Library, Conservative Party Archive (CPA), Conservative Central Office (CCO) 2/5/20, Area Series File, Scotland, 1958–60, P.J. Blair to Secretaries of Divisional Councils, 7 Dec. 1959.
9. NLS, Acc. 11765/53, Scottish Liberal Party, General Council, 1946–50, 7 Sep. 1946.
10. This was described as a 'concentrated shock', NLS, Acc. 11368/49, Minute Book of the No 4 Area Group (Highland) Executive Committee, 1951–64, 6 Nov. 1964.
11. CPA, CCO 500/50/1, A Survey on The Motivations behind Scottish Nationalism, March 1968.
12. The workings of the commission can be seen in the papers of Lady Tweedsmuir, a member; NLS, Acc. 11884/50.
13. See TNA, CAB130/390 for the minutes of meetings in October 1968 that led up to the establishment of the Royal Commission.
14. TNA, T330/185, f. 71, Devolution to Scotland and Wales, Minutes of a Meeting at 10 Downing Street, 18 July 1968.
15. TNA, CAB164/658, f.1, R.H.S. Crossman to the Prime Minister, 13 November 1967.
16. In some senses there might be some parallels with the current position whereby the Unionist parties struggle to understand and rationalise the success of the SNP in the most recent Scottish and UK elections. The evidenced adduced by Pentland of the Conservatives' perception of an alienation from the political process finding an outlet in the increase in support for the SNP in the late 1960s, matched by my own evidence from Labour ministerial discussions, might be seen to be similar with the current diagnosis that the rise of the SNP in Scotland, UKIP in England, Jeremy Corbyn in the Labour Party and even some presidential candidates in the US, such as Bernie Sanders and Donald Trump, are outbursts borne of frustration with 'conventional politics'. There is also the strand of argument that the SNP seems to be immune from criticism and rational assessment and is in this way akin to a cult (Kidd 2015; McDermott 2015).
17. Entitled 'The political and economic situation in Scotland: a background memorandum', a copy can be found in the papers of John P. Mackintosh in the National Library of Scotland at Dep. 323/143. Its provenance is unclear from this copy but its seems likely that it was received and retained by Mackintosh, rather than authored by that most acute Scottish MP and political scientist. I am grateful to Mr Tam Dalyell for discussing it with me.
18. Just how much detail can be seen in the files in the TNA, CAB198 series. These provide evidence of the depth of thought that went into the scheme and how much official, ministerial and parliamentary time and energy was devoted to it – only for the project to end in failure.
19. This period saw the Union experience deep unpopularity: the economic benefits of the Union were not obvious; patronage was reintroduced in the Church of Scotland in 1712; a vote in the House of Lords almost resulted in an anti-Union majority in 1713; the Hanoverian

succession of 1714 was not conspicuously popular; the Jacobite rebellion of 1715 could, with better leadership, have been a success and increased taxation on malt led to riots in Glasgow, a strongly Whig city, in 1725.

20 *House of Commons Debates*, 14 January 1980, vol. 976, col. 1252.

21 The phrase a 'property-owning democracy', which was taken up by later Conservative leaders as different as Anthony Eden and Margaret Thatcher, has also been referred to by recent 'red Tory' thinkers, such as Phillip Blond, who have seen him as the originator of their line of thinking. Matthew Francis, 'Cameron and the renewal of the "property-owning democracy"', www.historyandpolicy.org/opinion/opinion_25.html.

22 The Right to Buy will be withdrawn from August 2016. Home ownership has increased to 65 per cent of the Scottish housing stock but the policy has also 'depleted the number of houses available to rent from social landlords at a time when there is high demand for affordable housing' according to Linda Nicholson, 'Analysis of Response to the Future of Right to Buy in Scotland Consultation' (Scottish Government, 2012), www.gov.scot/Resource/0040/00408373.pdf.

23 See TNA, BT177/191 for the establishment of the Toothill Committee to look into the problems of the Scottish economy, or TNA, T224/462 for the establishment of a pulp and paper mill at Fort William, both in the early 1960s.

24 NLS, Acc. 11368/39, Minute of the Conservative and Unionist Association Western Divisional Council, 30 Oct. 1959, 27 Sep. 1960.

25 The title 'Claim of Right' had historical echoes and the most modern document to use the title sought to place itself in a tradition of protest against misgovernment. In 1689 the Scottish Convention, essentially the Scottish Estates, or Parliament, meeting without the permission or consent of the king, produced a Claim of Right outlining the misdeeds of James VII and II and outlining why he should be deposed. In 1842 a group of evangelicals in the Church of Scotland also issued a 'Claim of Right' arguing that the state ought not to interfere in the spiritual affairs of the Church; the problems had been compounded in their view by the insensitive policies of a Tory government that seemed not to comprehend the special position of the Church of Scotland within the Union.

26 NLS, Acc. 7656/16/2, W.G. Pottinger to Arthur Woodburn, 1 Aug. 1957; NRS, ED26/1323 contains evidence relating to the application of the formula to education spending as late as the 1969–71 period.

Sources for further reading and study

Books and journal articles

Cameron, E.A. (2010) *Impaled Upon a Thistle: Scotland since 1880*. Edinburgh: Edinburgh University Press.

Cameron, E.A. (2013) 'The political histories of modern Scotland'. *Scottish Affairs* 85: 1–28.

Ferguson, W. (1998) 'Record sources for the electoral history of Scotland, 1707–1832'. *Scottish Archives* 4: 21–31.

Finlay, R.J. (1994) *Independent and Free: Scottish Politics and the Origins of the SNP, 1918–45*. Edinburgh: John Donald.

Hutchison, I.C.G. (1986) *A Political History of Scotland, 1832–1924: Parties, Elections and Issues*. Edinburgh: John Donald.

Hutchison, I.G.C. (2000) *Scottish Politics in the Twentieth Century*. Basingstoke: Palgrave.

Jackson, A. (2011) *The Two Unions: Ireland, Scotland and the Survival of the United Kingdom, 1707–2007*. Oxford: Oxford University Press.

Kidd, C. (2008) *Union and Unionisms: Political Thought in Scotland, 1500–2000*. Cambridge: Cambridge University Press.

Pentland, G. (2008) *Radicalism, Reform and National Identity in Scotland, 1820–1833*. Woodbridge: Boydell.

Stewart, D. (2009) *The Path to Devolution: A Political History of Scotland Under Margaret Thatcher*. London: I.B. Tauris.

Online and web based sources

There are many online resources for Scottish politics, there are fewer that have genuinely historical content: the following provide some information on historical sources for Scottish politics and some routes to finding more material.

The Scottish Political Archive: www.scottishpoliticalarchive.org.uk/wb/.
National Library of Scotland guide to political history topics: www.nls.uk/learning-zone/politics-and-society.
National Records of Scotland guide to records of Scottish government since the union of 1707: www.nrscotland.gov.uk/research/guides/scottish-government-records-after-1707.
The Records of the Parliament of Scotland project: www.rps.ac.uk/static/historicalintro6.html.

References

Aikman, C. (2013) 'The birth of the Social Democratic Party in Scotland'. *Contemporary British History* 27: 324–347.
Biagini, E.F. (1992) *Liberty, Retrenchment and Reform: Popular Liberalism in the Age of Gladstone, 1860–1880.* Cambridge: Cambridge University Press.
Blair, T. (2010) *A Journey.* London: Hutchinson.
Brooks, D. (1985) 'Gladstone and Midlothian: the background to the first campaign'. *Scottish Historical Review* 64: 42–67.
Brown, S.J. (1992) 'Echoes of Midlothian: Scottish Liberalism and the South African War 1899–1902'. *Scottish Historical Review* 71: 156–183.
Burness, C. (2003) *Strange Associations: The Irish Question and the Making of Scottish Unionism, 1880–1912.* East Linton: Tuckwell Press.
Butler, D., A. Adonis and T. Travers. (1994) *Failure in British Government: The Politics of the Poll Tax.* Oxford: Oxford University Press.
Cameron, E.A. (1996) *Land for the People? The British Government and the Scottish Highlands, c.1880–1925.* East Linton: Tuckwell Press.
Cameron, E.A. (2000) *The Life and Times of [Charles] Fraser Mackintosh.* Aberdeen: Centre for Scottish Studies.
Cameron, E.A. (2010) *Impaled Upon a Thistle: Scotland since 1880.* Edinburgh: Edinburgh University Press.
Cameron, E.A. (2013) 'The political histories of modern Scotland'. *Scottish Affairs* 85: 1–28.
Craig, F.W.S. (1974) *British Parliamentary Election Results, 1885 to 1918.* London: Macmillan.
Devine, T. (2014) 'Why I now say yes to independence for Scotland'. *The Conversation.* Available at: https://theconversation.com/tom-devine-why-i-now-say-yes-to-independence-for-scotland-30733.
Dickson, A.D.R. (1988) 'The peculiarities of the Scottish: national culture and political action'. *Political Quarterly* 59: 358–368.
Ferguson, W. (1959) 'Dingwall burgh politics and the parliamentary franchise in the 18th century'. *Scottish Historical Review* 38: 89–108.
Ferguson, W. (1998) 'Record sources for the electoral history of Scotland, 1707–1832'. *Scottish Archives* 4: 21–31.
Finlay, R.J. (1994) *Independent and Free: Scottish Politics and the Origins of the SNP, 1918–45.* Edinburgh: John Donald.
Gibb, A. (1989) 'Policy and politics in Scottish housing since 1985'. In R. Rodger (ed.) *Scottish Housing in the Twentieth Century.* Leicester: Leicester University Press, pp. 155–183.
Glendinning, M. (1995) *Rebuilding Scotland: The Postwar Vision, 1945–1975.* East Linton: Tuckwell Press.
Harvie, C. (2000) 'The moment of British nationalism, 1939–1970'. *Political Quarterly* 71: 328–340.

Hassan, G. (2012) '"It's only a northern song": the constant smirr of anti-Thatcherism and anti-Toryism'. In D. Torrance (ed.) *Whatever Happened to Tory Scotland*. Edinburgh: Edinburgh University Press, pp. 76–92.

Hoppen, K.T. (1985) 'The franchise and electoral politics in England and Ireland, 1832–1885'. *History* 70: 202–217.

Hutchison, I.C.G. (1986) *A Political History of Scotland, 1832–1924: Parties, Elections and Issues*. Edinburgh: John Donald.

Hutchison, I.C.G. (1998) 'Scottish Unionism between the two world wars'. In C.M.M. Macdonald (ed.) *Unionist Scotland, 1800–1997*. Edinburgh: John Donald, pp. 73–99.

Hutchison, I.C.G. (1999) 'The impact of the First World War on Scottish politics'. In C.M.M. Macdonald and E.W. McFarland (eds) *Scotland and the Great War*. East Linton: Tuckwell Press, pp. 36–58.

Hutchison, I.G.C. (2000) *Scottish Politics in the Twentieth Century*. Basingstoke: Palgrave.

Jackson, A. (2011) *The Two Unions: Ireland, Scotland and the Survival of the United Kingdom, 1707–2007*. Oxford: Oxford University Press.

Jaensch, D. (1976) 'The Scottish vote, 1974: a realigning party system?'. *Political Studies* 24: 306–319.

Kane, N. (2015) 'A study of the debate on Scottish home rule, 1886–1914'. Ph.D. thesis, University of Edinburgh.

Kendle, J. (1989) *Ireland and the Federal Solution: The Debate Over the United Kingdom Constitution, 1870–1920*. Montreal and Kingston: McGill-Queens University Press.

Kendrick, S. and D. McCrone. (1989) 'Politics in a cold climate: the Conservative decline in Scotland'. *Political Studies* 37: 589–603.

Kennedy, J. (2013) *Liberal Nationalisms: Empire, State and Civil Society in Scotland and Quebec*. Montreal and Kingston: McGill-Queens University Press.

Kidd, C. (2008) *Union and Unionisms: Political Thought in Scotland, 1500–2000*. Cambridge: Cambridge University Press.

Kidd, C. (2015) 'Non-stick Nationalists'. *London Review of Books* 37(18), 18–24 September: 21–2.

Lee, C.H. (1995) *Scotland in the United Kingdom: The Economy and the Union in the Twentieth Century*. Manchester: Manchester University Press.

Lythe, C. and M. Majmudar. (1982) *The Renaissance of the Scottish Economy?* London: Macmillan.

Marr, A. (1992) *The Battle for Scotland*. Harmondsworth: Penguin.

Matthew, H.C.G., R. McKibben and J.A. Kay. (1976) 'The franchise factor in the rise of the Labour Party'. *English Historical Review* 91: 723–752.

McCrone, G. (2013) *Scottish Independence: Weighing Up the Economics*. Edinburgh: Birlinn.

McDermott, J. (2015) 'A veneer of competence'. *Prospect* 232, July: 32–8.

Miller, W. (1981) *The End of British Politics? Scots and English Political Behaviour in the Seventies*. Oxford: Oxford University Press.

Mitchell, J. (1998a) 'Contemporary Unionism'. In C.M.M. Macdonald (ed.) *Unionist Scotland, 1800–1997*. Edinburgh: John Donald, pp. 117–139.

Mitchell, J. (1998b) 'The evolution of devolution: Labour's home rule strategy in opposition'. *Government and Opposition* 33: 479–496.

Pentland, G. (2008) *Radicalism, Reform and National Identity in Scotland, 1820–1833*. Woodbridge: Boydell.

Pentland, G. (2015) 'Edward Heath, the Declaration of Perth and the Scottish Conservative and Unionist party, 1966–1970'. *Twentieth Century British History* 26: 249–273.

Seawright, D. and J. Curtice. (1995) 'The decline of the Scottish Conservative and Unionist party, 1950–1992: religion, ideology or economics?'. *Contemporary Record* 9: 319–342.

Skelton, N. (1924) *Constructive Conservatism*. Edinburgh: Blackwood.

Stewart, D. (2009) *The Path to Devolution: A Political History of Scotland Under Margaret Thatcher*. London: I.B. Tauris.

Tanner, D. (1983) 'The parliamentary electoral system, the "fourth" reform act and the rise of Labour in England and Wales'. *Bulletin of the Institute of Historical Research* 56: 205–219.

Tanner, D. (2006) 'Richard Crossman, Harold Wilson and devolution, 1966–1970: the making of government policy'. *Twentieth Century British History* 17: 545–578.

Torrance, D. (2010) *Noel Skelton and the Property-Owning Democracy.* London: Biteback.

Toye, R. (2013) 'From "consensus" to "common ground": the rhetoric of the postwar settlement and its collapse'. *Journal of Contemporary History* 48: 3–23.

Whatley, C. (2014) 'Why Tom Devine's switch to Yes is confusing and short sighted'. *The Conversation*. Available at: https://theconversation.com/chris-whatley-why-tom-devine-switch-to-yes-is-confusing-and-short-sighted-30850.

2 How Scotland votes
Elections and electoral behaviour in Scotland

Craig McAngus

Introduction

Voters in Scotland have the opportunity to take part in elections for local councils, the Scottish Parliament, the UK House of Commons and the European Parliament. This chapter will provide an overview of general elections in Scotland and Scottish Parliament elections, as well as assessing why voters behave the way they do.

The chapter begins by outlining how the different electoral systems work. It then provides a detailed overview of general elections in Scotland since 1945, followed by an overview of devolved elections since 1999. The chapter then goes on to assess whether or not elections to the Scottish Parliament can be considered as 'second order', before going on to discuss some of the key driving factors behind voting behaviour in Scotland. The chapter then concludes with some analysis on the effect that the independence referendum has had on elections in Scotland.

Elections in Scotland: plurality and proportionality

There are fifty-nine Scottish seats in the UK Parliament's lower chamber, also known as the House of Commons. These fifty-nine seats represent a corresponding geographic constituency. The majority of constituencies in Scotland are in and around the most populous city in Scotland, Glasgow, with larger constituencies in terms of geographic area located in the north and south of the country. The electoral system in use at the general election, a simple plurality system often referred to as 'First-Past-The-Post' (FPTP), is simple to understand. Voters choose one candidate on their ballot paper, and the candidate who wins the highest number of votes wins the seat and becomes the Member of Parliament (MP) in the House of Commons. The system is often likened to a horse race: regardless whether a horse wins by eight furlongs or by a nose, the winner takes all.

The electoral system used in Scottish Parliament elections is somewhat more complicated. The system in use is known as the 'Additional Member System' (AMS), that uses two ballots which balances off an FPTP constituency vote with a regional vote that introduces an element of proportional representation. There are 129 seats in the Parliament, 73 of which are chosen on the first ballot paper using FPTP, and the remaining 56 members are returned from 8 additional member regions comprised of 7 seats each. Best described as a semi-proportional system, the FPTP contingent of seats outweighs the list seats by 57 to 43 per cent. Although not purely proportional in the sense that a party that does well on the constituency element has a slight advantage, it is still far more proportional than the FPTP system used in UK general elections.

In order to determine the final result of a Scottish election, the results of the FPTP constituencies are required first in order to determine how the regional list will be finalised. In each of the eight regions (for example, North East Scotland, Central Scotland, and Glasgow) there are at least eight and at most ten constituencies. Once the results of these constituency contests are determined by FPTP, and the total votes cast for each party on the regional list are counted, a mathematical formula known as the d'Hondt[1] method is used to determine which of the eight regional seats will go to which party. The formula is as follows:

$$r_n = \frac{v}{(s+1)}$$

The expression r_n refers to each round of seat allocations, of which there are seven in total in order to select all of the list seats in each region. All of the votes cast for each party are counted (v) and divided by the constituency seats won in that region and +1 added on ($s + 1$). This is to ensure that parties who have not won any of the constituency seats do not have their list total divided by zero. Once all of the parties' list totals are divided into by the number of seats plus one ($s + 1$), then the party that has the largest total is allocated the first seat. If, for example, the party which won the first round of list allocations had no constituency seat, then in the next round the list seat it has won is added to its tally of seats so its list total is divided into by two in the next round as opposed to one again.

This system adds proportionality to the electoral system because of the ($s + 1$) element. If for example a party wins all of the constituency seats in a particular region, (which happens to have nine FPTP seats) then their $s + 1$ total will equal ten. Say this party wins 100,000 votes on the regional list, its large denominator of 9 effectively takes its tally to 10,000 and a party which won maybe 50,000 would only get this total divided into by one. Therefore, domination of the constituency seats in a region will count against a party in the list vote. This happened to Labour in the Glasgow region in 1999 and allowed other parties to win the list seats in that region in order to bring an element of proportionality to the overall allocation of seats. Table 2.1 below provides a breakdown of the first three rounds of the North East Scotland region result from the 2011 Scottish election.

UK general elections in Scotland since 1945

Through the 1940s and the 1950s, UK general elections were almost entirely dominated by Labour and the Conservatives. When it came to Scotland, the electoral picture was not very different: as much as 'the United Kingdom has never approximated a classic unitary state, in terms of electoral politics it for a long time looked very much like one' (Wyn Jones and Scully 2006: 115). The once powerful Liberal party had become, largely, an electoral insignificance and the SNP, formed in 1934, existed very much on the fringes of Scottish politics. Despite winning the 1945 general election, a smaller percentage of the Scottish electorate voted for Labour compared to the rest of the UK, and it was the Scottish Unionists (a coalition of Liberal Unionists and Conservatives) that won the plurality of the vote up until 1959, indeed winning 50.1 per cent of the vote in 1955. The Scottish Unionists merged with the Conservatives in 1965, but until then existed as an electoral coalition that encompassed much of the urban middle class,

Table 2.1 First three rounds of the North East Scotland regional list result, 2011 Scottish Parliament election

Party	Constituency seats won in the region(s)	Votes won on the regional list v	$\frac{v}{(s+1)}$	Total votes after formula applied	Seats allocated in this round	Total seats in region after this round (constituency + list)
Round 1 (r₁)						
SNP	10	140,749	140,749/11	12,795	0	10
Labour	0	43,893	43,893/1	**43,893**	1	1
Conservative	0	37,681	37,681/1	37,681	0	0
Liberal Democrat	0	18,178	18,178/1	18,178	0	0
Green	0	10,407	10,407/1	10,407	0	0
Round 2 (r₂)						
SNP	10	140,749	140,749/11	12,795	0	10
Labour	0	43,893	43,893/2	21,947	0	1
Conservative	0	37,681	37,681/1	**37,681**	1	1
Liberal Democrat	0	18,178	18,178/1	18,178	0	0
Green	0	10,407	10,407/1	10,407	0	0
Round 3 (r₃)						
SNP	10	140,749	140,749/11	12,795	0	10
Labour	0	43,893	43,893/2	**21,947**	1	2
Conservative	0	37,681	37,681/2	18,841	0	1
Liberal Democrat	0	18,178	18,178/1	18,178	0	0
Green	0	10,407	10,407/1	10,407	0	0

rural landowners and prosperous farmers, as well as drawing in the 'Orange' Protestant working class who had strong links to Ulster (Wyn Jones and Scully 2006: 117).

By the 1960s, a fragmentation of the party system was in evidence, with the Liberals and the SNP beginning to increase their share of the vote and mount a serious challenge to the dominance of the main two parties. From 1959, the Conservative vote in Scotland fell behind the proportion of the vote it picked up in England, something it has failed to recover to this day (Wyn Jones and Scully 2006: 117–118). Labour benefitted from Conservative decline, becoming the largest party on vote share in Scotland in the 1964 general election and reaching its zenith in 1966 (Hassan and Shaw 2012: 206). It has been argued that modern Scottish politics began in 1967 when Winnie Ewing won Hamilton from Labour in a by-election (Mitchell 2009b). Although the SNP's support would fluctuate quite significantly over the next three decades, it became a permanent feature of Scottish electoral politics from 1967 onwards. The SNP's place in Scottish politics reflected changes in the Scottish economy and society: Scotland was becoming

Table 2.2 Seats won at Scottish general elections, 1945–1970

	1945	1950	1951	1955	1959	1964	1966	1970
Labour	37	37	35	34	38	43	46	44
Conservative	27	31	35	36	31	24	20	23
Liberal	0	2	1	1	1	4	5	3
SNP	0	0	0	0	0	0	0	1

less polarised in class terms than it had been, with heavy industry and manufacturing already declining as a proportion of the Scottish economy, and this facilitated the crumbling of the Labour and Conservative duopoly (Hassan and Shaw 2012: 207).

The SNP did relatively well at the 1970 general election, but it was 1974 when the party made a significant electoral breakthrough. Despite winning 30 per cent of the vote and 11 seats in the October 1974 election, the FPTP system worked against the SNP in the sense that their vote was not as geographically concentrated as Labour's. However, Labour felt acutely threatened given that the SNP had come second in 35 of Labour's 41 Scottish seats, and so proposals to create a Scottish Assembly were drawn up by the government, going to a referendum in 1979. The 1979 referendum returned a slim majority in favour of Scottish devolution but this majority did not represent 40 per cent of the electorate and so the referendum, in effect, returned a 'No' vote.[2] The 1979 general election was held soon after and returned a majority for Margaret Thatcher's Conservatives, despite a higher proportion of Scottish voters backing Labour compared to the Conservatives.

The Conservatives' eighteen-year period in office (1979–1997) resulted in some fundamental changes in electoral politics in Scotland. First, the period saw a steep decline of Conservative electoral presence in Scotland to the point that the party returned no Scottish MPs in 1997. Second, it ushered in a period of Labour electoral dominance in Scotland in terms of seats. Third, the question of democratic legitimacy became an increasingly important part of Scottish politics: how could a party, electorally rejected in Scotland, legitimately continue to impose its policy programme in the absence of any mechanism to defend Scottish interests? Fourth, and related to the third, the 1980s resulted in Labour becoming almost wholeheartedly in favour of devolution, something that was not the case in the 1970s. Significantly, these developments, coupled with the changes to the economy and society that were both accelerated and brought about by Thatcher's government, eventually led to the 'ever looser union' (Mitchell 2009a)

Table 2.3 Seats won at Scottish general elections, February 1974–2015

	Feb. 1974	Oct. 1974	1979	1983	1987	1992	1997	2001	2005*	2010	2015
Labour	40	41	44	41	50	49	56	56	41	41	1
Conservative	21	16	22	21	10	11	0	1	1	1	1
Liberal/ Alliance/ Liberal Democrat	3	3	3	8	9	9	10	10	11	11	1
SNP	7	11	2	2	3	3	6	5	6	6	56

between Scotland and the rest of the UK that has had such an effect on Scottish politics in the twenty-first century.

The 1980s also saw the SDP–Liberal Alliance, which would become the Liberal Democrats in 1988, maintain a sizeable and significant electoral presence in Scotland. The party held its share of the vote comfortably above 10 per cent from 1983 onwards, doing particularly well in 1983 and 2005 by attracting disaffected Labour voters due to, partly, Labour's internal difficulties at the time and the Iraq war respectively. The party was able to make its vote share work more effectively over time, securing at least nine seats from 1987 onwards despite their share of the vote not reaching the heights of 1983. Seats in the Highlands, Aberdeenshire and Edinburgh were considered safe Liberal Democrat territory until 2015 when the party suffered an electoral collapse, losing all but one of its remaining seats (Orkney and Shetland).

The 1997 general election resulted in a landslide victory for Tony Blair's New Labour. In Scotland, Labour won a number of Conservative seats in areas that were not considered traditional Labour areas, in, for example, East Renfrewshire and Edinburgh. The Conservatives lost all of their Scottish seats at the 1997 election, despite winning 18 per cent of the vote. Indeed, first-past-the-post worked against the Conservatives during the 1987 and 1992 elections too, where they won around 25 per cent of the vote but only about 15 per cent of the seats, thus exaggerating their electoral weakness in Scotland (Brown et al. 1998: 153). First-past-the-post continues to work against the Conservatives: the party has only managed to return one Scottish MP at each general election since 2001.

Despite FPTP hampering the Conservatives and, on the surface, hiding a sizeable level of support across Scotland, the fact that Conservative support eventually recovered in England in subsequent general elections after 1997, and indeed in Wales to a lesser extent, leaves Scotland as an outlier in terms of its continued rejection of the Conservatives. Throughout the 1980s and 1990s, survey evidence showed Scotland to be only slightly more left-wing than the rest of the UK (Brown et al. 1998: 164), although Scotland did tend to favour more government intervention in the economy (Bennie et al. 1997: 138). Furthermore, it cannot be said either that the Conservatives only lost support amongst the Scottish working class: their loss of support occurred across all social groups, showing that there was a national dimension, as opposed to a class dimension, to their decline (Brown et al. 1998: 155–156). Despite one of the Conservative's key policies, the right to buy one's council house, having a proportionately higher take-up in Scotland than in the UK as a whole (Torrance 2009), economic gain did not correlate with Conservative support in Scotland (Bennie et al. 1997: 130). By 1997, a majority of the Scottish public was in favour of further social reform, remaining within the EU and creating a Scottish Parliament (Brown et al. 1998: 169), positions that were not forthcoming from the Conservatives and firmly espoused by Labour from the 1980s onwards.

Labour continued to dominate Scotland electorally from 1997 until 2015 despite their share of the vote declining slightly overall. For the 2005 general election, the number of constituencies in Scotland was reduced from 72 to 59. This resulted in a reduction in the number of Labour MPs to forty-one, with the other parties maintaining their seat tally. The 2010 general election saw Labour lose the election to the Conservatives, although the Conservatives fell short of an overall majority and thus formed a coalition with the Liberal Democrats. Despite suffering substantial losses in England, Labour held firm in Scotland and actually managed to increase their share of the vote slightly (Mitchell and van der Zwet 2010). The 2015 general election in Scotland was a different affair, however, with Labour losing all but one of its seats in Scotland, and the Conservatives and Liberal Democrats also winning one seat each. The SNP captured all of the fifty-six remaining seats with 50 per cent of the vote. On the back of the SNP's victory in the 2011 Scottish election and the effect that the independence referendum has had on Scottish politics, it appears that, for the time being at least, a major realignment has occurred in terms of how Scottish voters are prepared to cast their ballots at general elections.

The graph below (Figure 2.1) shows the share of the vote won at UK general elections in Scotland since 1945 by what would now be considered the four 'main' parties. The height of the two-party system occurred in 1955 where Labour and the Conservatives won 97 per cent of the total vote between them. This represented the high point for the Conservatives in Scotland, with their share of the vote declining year on year from that point, with 1979 and 1992 being slight exceptions to that general trend. Labour's peak in terms of share of the vote came in 1966, followed by a sharp decline in 1970 where the party oscillated around the 40 per cent mark until 2015 where they dropped dramatically to 24 per cent and were overtaken by the SNP. The Liberals/Liberal Democrats saw a steady increase in their overall share of the vote, doing particularly well under the auspices of the SDP–Liberal Alliance in 1983 and then again in 2005. However, the party slipped back to pre-1974 levels of popular support in 2015, clearly being punished for its role in coalition government with the Conservatives between 2010 and 2015. The SNP were not a serious electoral force until the two 1974 elections, although the party was beginning to pick up support from the 1964 election onwards. Indeed, four decades would pass before the party was able to register a better result than that of October 1974, with the party winning 50 per cent of the vote in 2015.

Under a proportional electoral system such as Single Transferable Vote (STV), one would expect to see share of the national vote roughly translate into percentage share of seats won. First-past-the-post, however, results in a percentage share of seats won

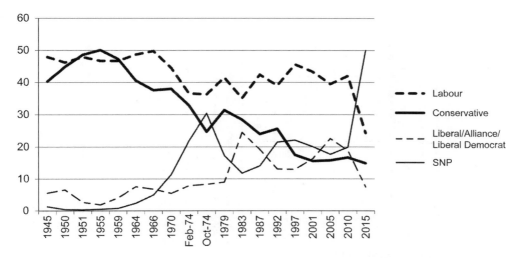

Figure 2.1 Share of the vote won at UK general elections in Scotland, 1945–2015

that does not usually (in this case) or necessarily correlate closely with the share of the vote that a party manages to secure. The graph below (Figure 2.2) shows the percentage of Scottish seats won by each of the main parties at each general election since 1945. Labour's peak in Scottish electoral politics, as mentioned above, came in 1966 when they won nearly 50 per cent of the vote. However, as their vote share dropped to remain relatively stable around 40 per cent from 1970 through to 2010, the party was able to translate this percentage share into comfortably over 50 per cent of the actual seats won. Indeed, 2001 saw Labour win just under 80 per cent of the seats in Scotland despite their share of the vote falling to 43 per cent from 46 per cent in 1997. The reason for this is that Labour's vote has traditionally been very heavily concentrated in Central and Western Scotland and in Glasgow. Other parties, particularly the SNP and the Conservatives, have suffered from having a vote share that is spread out far more evenly across Scotland. It is ironic therefore that the most extreme example of the FPTP effect comes in 2015 with the SNP winning 50 per cent of the vote but securing 95 per cent of the seats in Scotland as a result. The electoral system used in general elections has historically created the illusion of Labour strength in Scotland, whilst the vote share that Labour has been able to achieve has actually fallen quite significantly short of its showing in seats. Therefore, a drop of 18 per cent in 2015 from their 2010 share was enough to allow the SNP to win all but one of Labour's seats and leave both the Conservatives and the Liberal Democrats with one seat each.

Elections to the Scottish Parliament

The first elections to the Scottish Parliament were held in 1999 following the successful passage of the Scotland Act 1998. A two-question referendum had been held in 1997 which asked whether the Scottish electorate, first, wished for a parliament and, second, whether it should have tax varying powers. On both questions a Yes vote was returned (74.3 per cent and 63.5 per cent respectively). After much debate during the 1980s and 1990s within the pro-devolution movement regarding the electoral system, it was

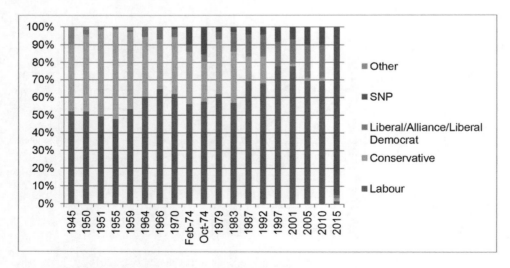

Figure 2.2 Percentage of seats won at Scottish general elections, 1945–2015

decided that an Additional Member System (AMS) would be used. This was a compromise between the Liberal Democrats and Labour, with the former satisfied with a system that introduced an element of proportionality into Scottish elections, and the latter hopeful that such a system would hamper the SNP's capability of being able to secure an overall majority in the Parliament.

The first election to the Scottish Parliament in 1999 saw Labour maintain its presence as the largest party in Scotland, both in terms of seats and vote share, but the nature of the electoral system and a willingness of a larger proportion of the electorate to vote SNP meant that its dominance was far less pronounced than it had been at the 1997 general election. Labour's honeymoon period after 1997 had continued in Scotland, and Donald Dewar proved to be a popular and effective leader of Scottish Labour. Although Labour was comfortably the largest party with fifty-six seats, it was not enough to form a majority government and so the party entered government as part of a coalition with the Liberal Democrats. The SNP, for the first time in its history, took up the position as the largest opposition party, with the Conservatives gaining some consolation from the regional list which, unlike 1997, provided them with a substantial presence in the new parliament.

As the 2003 election approached, there was a discernible sense of disappointment with what the new Parliament had been able to achieve (McCrone 2009). Scotland was not a country transformed as a result of devolution, despite some significant and popular policy developments such as maintaining free personal care for the elderly and the decision not to introduce university tuition fees. The 2003 election saw Labour maintain its lead over the other parties despite falling back slightly, but it was the SNP that was to have the most disappointing election out of the main parties. Internal wrangling over candidate selection on the list for the regional vote had led to serious intra-party tension (Mitchell et al. 2012), and the SNP suffered substantially on the regional vote by the time the election came around. The main winners from this were the minor parties, such as the Greens and the Scottish Socialist Party, leading to the 2003–07 term being dubbed the 'rainbow parliament'.

The 2003–07 period was a critical one in terms of what was to come at the 2007 and then the 2011 election. Despite winning the 2005 general election, it was clear that the Iraq war and Tony Blair's general unpopularity was contributing to Scottish Labour's weakening appeal, as well as general disillusionment with the style of politics that Labour espoused (Hassan and Shaw 2012). The SNP, on the other hand, had gone through a significant period of organisational reform which was designed to assist in making them a credible party of government (McAngus, forthcoming). Scottish Labour and their leader, First Minister Jack McConnell, slipped behind the SNP in the opinion polls and in May 2007 the Scottish electorate returned a result which gave the SNP forty-seven seats ahead of Labour's forty-six. The SNP went on to form a minority government[3] which, against some predictions at the time, endured throughout the 2007–11 Parliament.

With an SNP government, Scotland was now governed by a party that believed that Scotland should become an independent state. After the creation of the Scottish Parliament, the SNP introduced a change to party policy which stated that a referendum ought to be held on the question of independence. This was crucial in that it 'detached' the question of independence from the SNP's drive to promote itself as a credible party of government that could be trusted to run the Scottish Government (McAngus 2015). The issue of Scottish independence naturally climbed up the political and media agenda, with the SNP using government to launch a consultation process known as the

'National Conversation' which was designed to engage the public directly on issues of constitutional change (Harvey and Lynch 2012).

As the discussion of the Scottish Parliament's electoral system outlined, a party that does well on the constituency ballot is penalised on the list. This makes securing a majority of seats in the Parliament difficult and was indeed one of the reasons why the system was chosen in the first place. In 2011, the SNP managed to do what many commentators thought was practically impossible and actually win a majority. Significantly, the SNP won a large number of seats in areas that were considered to be 'safe' Labour areas such as Glasgow, Lanarkshire and Ayrshire. Furthermore, the SNP picked up a number of seats in Edinburgh, a city that the SNP has historically struggled to gain much of a foothold in. The collapse of the Liberal Democrats was a factor in many seats, with previous Liberal Democrat voters either switching to the SNP directly or switching to Labour and replacing some of the voters that had shifted from Labour to the SNP. The scale of the SNP's victory meant that a referendum on Scottish independence was inevitable, and a referendum was indeed held in September 2014, returning a No vote (55 per cent to 45 per cent).

Table 2.4 below shows the results of all four Scottish Parliament elections to date. Labour was comfortably the largest party in 1999 and 2003, with the SNP firmly cementing themselves as the main opposition party. The regional list element of the electoral system was, and continues to be, to the benefit of the Conservatives who have failed to make an impression in constituency contests, and the Liberal Democrats had proved the most consistent party until 2011 with a fairly stable presence in constituencies in Edinburgh, Aberdeenshire and the Highlands and Islands, alongside a modest sum of list seats. The 2003 election saw the SNP lose ten list seats with the main beneficiaries being the Greens and the Socialists who picked up 7 and 6 list seats respectively. However, by 2011, the small parties had largely slipped back in favour of the SNP.

The biggest change in electoral politics since 1999 has been the decline of the Labour party and the success of the SNP in 2007 and then in 2011. These two parties have had their fortunes reversed on the constituency and regional contests: Labour have gone from winning fifty-three seats on the constituency ballot to, in 2011, securing just fifteen, whilst the SNP have seen more than a sevenfold increase in the number of constituency seats they hold. As Figure 2.3 shows, the SNP has managed to increase its share of the constituency vote by nearly 17 per cent, whilst Labour has seen a 7 per cent decline on its share since 1999.

Table 2.4 Constituency (and regional) seats won at Scottish Parliament elections, 1999–2011

	1999	2003	2007	2011
Labour	53 (3)	46 (4)	37 (9)	15 (22)
Conservative	0 (18)	3 (15)	4 (13)	3 (12)
Liberal Democrat	12 (5)	13 (4)	11 (5)	2 (3)
SNP	7 (28)	9 (18)	21 (26)	53 (16)
Green	0 (1)	0 (7)	0 (2)	0 (2)
Various socialist	0 (1)	0 (6)	0 (0)	0 (0)
Other	1 (0)	2 (2)	0 (1)	0 (1)

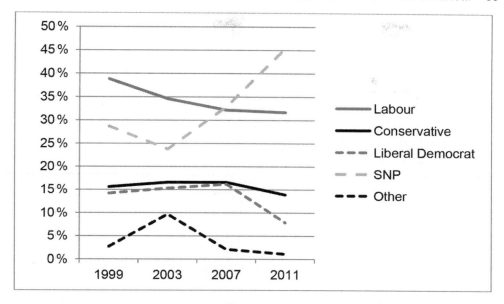

Figure 2.3 Share of the constituency vote in Scottish Parliament elections, 1999–2015

The existence of a second ballot means that voters can split their vote and thus choose different parties on the two different ballots. It also means that voters do not have to vote tactically to the same extent as they may do at general elections, which may indeed be the case in some constituency contests. In terms of the four 'main' parties, the changes in the regional vote over time largely reflect the changes in the constituency vote in terms of share. Figure 2.4 below shows that whilst the Conservatives and the Liberal Democrats (until 2011) have held fairly steady, Labour have dropped just over 7 per cent since 1999, whilst the SNP has increased their share of the regional list vote by almost 17 per cent between 1999 and 2011. Furthermore, their share of the vote in both the constituency and the regional votes more closely match each other (1.4 per cent difference) in 2011 than compared to Labour in 1999 (5.2 per cent difference). This seems to indicate that at the periods when both of these parties have performed best at a Scottish election (2011 and 1999 respectively), it is the SNP that is able to more effectively crowd out the regional vote and thus perform significantly better despite dominating the constituency vote (Johns et al. 2010).

How important are Scottish elections? Are these second order elections?

Elections in Scotland had an element of distinctiveness from the UK-wide picture before devolution in terms of Labour's historic strength and the existence of a popular fourth party in the form of the SNP, but the creation of a devolved Parliament with a new and novel electoral system (at least in the UK context) offered voters the opportunity to make electoral results even more distinctive. Furthermore, it created an institution which resided at the sub-state level which opens up the possibility that elections to the Scottish Parliament may become what's known as 'second order' elections (Reif and Schmitt 1980). If we think of general elections as 'first order' elections, second order

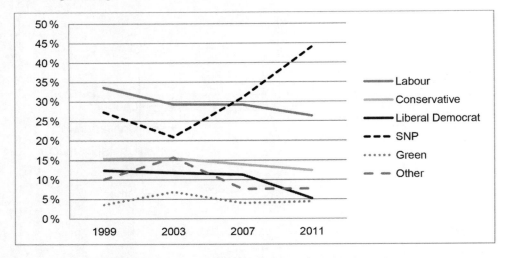

Figure 2.4 Share of the regional vote in Scottish Parliament elections, 1999–2015

elections are seen as less important by voters because they are not considered as influential or crucial. Because these second order elections are seen as having less at stake than first order elections, then the hypothesised effect is threefold:

1   There is lower turnout when compared to a first order election.
2   Smaller parties will gain an electoral dividend from an electorate more willing to experiment and/or register a protest vote.
3   Governing parties will lose support, whilst opposition parties will make gains.

Can we classify devolved elections as second order? If we consider the sequence of general and Scottish elections from 1997 through to 2011, we can clearly see that Labour experiences a UK bonus and a devolution deficit, with the SNP experiencing the opposite. Furthermore, turnout at Scottish elections has been lower than at UK general elections. However, thorough analysis of individual level survey data points to voters wanting 'different things at different elections' (Jeffery and Hough 2009: 234). Even in 1999, when the Scottish Parliament had not even begun deliberating, a Scottish 'arena effect' was noticeable despite the media being dominated by UK political personalities. As Johns et al. (2010: 4) describe, the first election to the Scottish Parliament contained an enhanced Scottish dimension rather than an end to British politics.

Despite there being indications of a second order effect, elections to the Scottish Parliament are better explained by multi-level voting effects; UK issues will continue to have an impact, but there is a recognition that devolved issues are the most important and that devolution is a distinct political arena (Wyn Jones and Scully 2006: 125–129). Indeed, when comparing the 2011 Welsh and Scottish elections, Scully (2013) finds a distinct arena effect in both countries, but that effect is stronger in Scotland due to the fact that UK-wide issues had more impact on voting choice in Wales. This pattern of stronger arena effects in Scotland compared to Wales fits Schakel's (2011) findings, which suggest that in regions where there is a higher degree of self-rule there is more likely to be higher levels of divergence between regional and state-wide elections. Regional elections allow regional concerns to be channelled more directly (Liñeira 2011: 299), and with Scotland receiving a more powerful devolution 'package' in 1999 compared to Wales, the stronger arena effect is therefore in line with theoretical expectations in the literature. Despite this, however, there is evidence to suggest that Scottish voters can and do confuse where particular competences lie and therefore attribute blame and practise accountability incorrectly (Curtice 2009).

Therefore, the weight of evidence points to Scottish parliamentary elections being a distinct arena but not wholly separate from the UK dimension. With the Scottish Parliament's powers comfortably exceeding those of the European Parliament and local councils, typical sites for second order election effects, and many voters regarding devolved elections as more important than general elections, there is strong evidence to doubt the applicability of second order election theory to the Scottish case (Mitchell and Johns 2009: 78). Furthermore, according to Mitchell and Johns (2009: 77), one must appreciate three important differences when comparing Scottish Parliament elections to UK general elections in Scotland: the different, more proportional electoral system; the Scottish-only parties (mainly the SNP) who have been placed in a much stronger position because of devolution; and the different sets of issues and concerns at stake. Indeed, 'Scottish Parliament elections were *supposed* to be different from UK general elections, not because they would be seen as less important, but because they would reflect the Scottish party system and the particular needs and preferences of Scottish voters' (Mitchell and Johns 2009: 82, emphasis added). The potential to engage in 'split ticket' voting where a voter chooses different parties in the constituency and the regional list adds a further element of distinction between UK general elections and Scottish elections (Carman and Johns 2010).

Explaining voting behaviour in Scotland

In many respects, developments in the operation of the British state and society since 1945 would lead one to expect convergence when it came to voting habits and behaviour. Writing in 1975, James Kellas observed that:

> the development of communications, especially the popular press and broadcasting, broke down localism and focussed attention on the capital and British political issues ... the great increase in government power over affairs previously considered local ... drew all the lines of political activity towards the ultimate point of decision, the centre.
>
> (Kellas 1975: 101)

In spite of this, Kellas (1975: 101) went on to observe that:

> If this is so, it is surprising that Scotland can still not be considered fully merged within the British 'norms' of electoral behaviour. The voting figures and opinion survey research indicate that Scotland is a strong 'political region' with its own patterns of voting, and that it has tended to diverge more from the British national average than other regions since 1955.

Attempts to understand the state structures of the UK as 'unitary' do not capture the historical, sociological and institutional characteristics that make Scotland, in a number of respects, 'different' from the rest of the UK (Mitchell 2009a; 2014). This Scottish distinctiveness creates a context whereby the Scottish electorate may process the options available to them on the ballot in a slightly different way. This is not to say that Scottish electoral behaviour is completely different: class identity has played important role in determining how people will vote, and the increase in so-called 'valence' voting (see below) has also become a crucial element in driving electoral behaviour. What makes Scotland different is that Scotland is a nation, it is perceived as such by the vast majority of those living within it, and the majority of its voters possess a fairly strong sense of Scottish national identity. As a result, many in Scotland cast their vote based on which party is best placed to protect and promotes Scotland's interests, whether that be at the UK or the devolved level.

Despite this, many of the ways that voting behaviour has changed have mirrored the changes in voting behaviour in the UK as a whole since the 1960s. British society was far more rigidly defined along class lines, with an industrial, unionised working class making up a far bigger proportion of the population than it does now. This was not only likely to identify a political party, but was more likely to *strongly* identify with one. The February 1974 general election was a key election in the sense that it was the first time that both the Conservatives and Labour suffered concurrent losses since 1922 and, according to Crewe et al. (1977: 132), 'the British pendulum stopped swinging' in the sense that votes were not necessarily moving between Labour and the Conservatives.

The idea that voting behaviour based on class and partisan identity was becoming less and less important in terms of driving voting behaviour is often referred to as 'de-alignment'. In the UK, as well as in other post-industrial states, changing social structures and a growing middle class led to the growth of so-called 'apartisan' voters who, whilst still very interested and engaged in politics, did not take as much of their cues from political parties as those who were closely affiliated with one (Dalton 1984). Although some doubt has been placed on the dealignment thesis, even those sceptical of it state that class–party relationships fluctuate over time (Heath et al. 1995). Indeed, 'dealignment to a degree' (Clarke and Stewart 1984) perhaps sums up how voting has changed given that class will always remain an important predictor for a whole range of human behaviours, not just voting behaviour. However, voting behaviour has become more and more influenced by what is known as 'valence' voting, whereby voters judge a party on its ability to govern well. As parties have ideologically converged over time, it has become more rational and more prevalent to vote on the basis of how well a party is perceived to perform on, for example, running the NHS (Green and Hobolt 2008). Furthermore, with party leaders becoming more and more visible, judgements on a party's competency are in large part down to how 'up to the job' leaders of political parties are perceived to be. Judgements such as these drive the modern British electorate more than partisanship and class (Clarke et al. 2009).

Analysis of voting behaviour at Scottish elections has concluded that valence voting plays an important role in voting behaviour (Johns et al. 2009; 2010; 2013). Although attitudes to constitutional change do have an important role to play for some voters, it is by no means the primary concern for the majority of those who cast their vote at Scottish elections. Despite much of the underlying mechanics of voting behaviour at UK general election being broadly similar to those at Scottish elections and general elections in Scotland, it is important to take into account the specific Scottish dimension when it comes to electoral behaviour in Scotland. This Scottish dimension is not necessarily uniform across different levels of government, given that voters are actually quite aware of what is at stake at general and Scottish elections (Johns 2011).

Why has the SNP been electorally successful?

Scholars of nationalism, regardless of their disagreements on the origin and perpetuation of the nation, will all agree that the nation is an important fact of everyday life which has the potential to affect human behaviour. Reminders of belonging to and identifying with a nation need not necessarily be explicit and forthright, but can indeed be subtle, background and 'banal' (Billig 1995). Scottish identity is thus an important part of Scottish life, but equally so is British identity.

The graph below (Figure 2.5) shows national identity in Scotland from 1999 to 2014. The question used here is known as the 'Moreno question'[4] and asks respondents to place themselves on a scale from 'Scottish not British' through to 'British not Scottish'. As we can see, the vast majority of people in Scotland identify with 'Scottishness' at least equally to 'Britishness'. A small minority (around 10 per cent) identify with being British more than Scottish. However, of the three groups who report being Scottish at least equally with being British, it is only the 'Equally Scottish and British' group that has grown since the advent of devolution. Both 'more Scottish than British' and 'Scottish not British' identifiers have trended downwards since 1999.

Two interesting observations can be drawn from these figures. First, the Scottish public have become more comfortable with Britishness as a key element of their identity. This can partly be explained by the creation of the Scottish Parliament and a sense that, within the UK, Scots have a powerful forum where their interests can be articulated. Second, it is not accurate to say that the electoral successes of the SNP can be explained by a rise in nationalist sentiment. Indeed, one of the sharpest drops in the

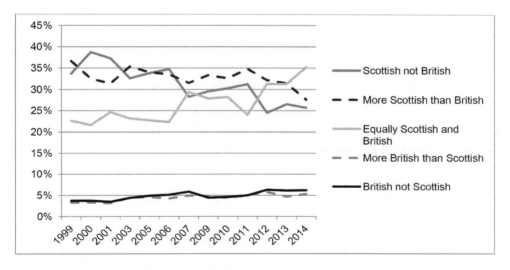

Figure 2.5 National identity in Scotland, 1999–2014

proportion of those saying they were 'Scottish not British' happens between 2011 and 2012, exactly when the SNP won a majority in the Scottish Parliament and a referendum on Scottish independence became practically inevitable. Furthermore, there is a sharp rise in those stating they were 'equally Scottish and British' in that same period. Despite there being a link between national identity and support for the SNP, such a link does not explain the party's electoral fortunes from 2007 onwards, nor does it explain the electoral difficulties faced by Labour, particularly in 2011 and 2015.

Despite exclusive 'Scottishness' declining over time, perceptions about which party is deemed to be 'standing up' for Scotland are an important element of valence voting in Scotland. As Johns et al. (2010: 79–80) argue, the 'Scottish dimension' is itself an issue about perceived competence and a party's discourse on the constitutional question sends out signals, positive or negative, with regards to how well placed they are to stand up for Scottish interests. As Johns et al. (2009; 2010; 2013) have shown using consecutive survey data from the Scottish Election Study, the SNP was significantly ahead of Labour in terms of how well they are perceived to be standing up for Scotland in both the 2007 and 2011 election contests.

Evaluations of political leaders are also an important aspect of valence voting. How a voter perceives a particular individual, especially a party leader, can greatly influence how they decide to vote at a particular election. By 2007, senior figures in the SNP, particularly Alex Salmond, were more favourably rated by the Scottish public than the then leader of Scottish Labour, Jack McConnell. Indeed, substantial numbers of Labour identifiers were undecided between whether or not they rated Salmond or McConnell more highly (Johns et al. 2010: 53), and McConnell was not much more popular than Tony Blair by this stage (Johns et al. 2010: 56). This pattern was repeated at the 2011 election, with the SNP outstripping Labour even more comfortably on leadership perceptions (Johns et al. 2013).

What requires some explanation is the difference in SNP and Labour performance at general elections and Scottish elections. The SNP won the 2007 Scottish election, albeit narrowly, but Labour went on to do remarkably well in Scotland at the 2010 general election in Scotland, outperforming the party in England quite substantially in the sense that it did not incur losses in Scotland and actually managed to increase its share of the vote. The SNP subsequently went on to win a majority at the Scottish election in 2011. As outlined previously, the Scottish electorate is less driven by a second order effect and more engaged in a clear practice of multi-level voting. Different levels have different priorities, and different parties may be best placed to achieve certain ends at these different levels. Therefore, whilst the SNP has been given a boost at the devolved level as it is seen as more relevant at that level in terms of potentially being a party of devolved government, Labour has traditionally received a boost at the UK level in Scotland as it is seen as best placed to represent Scotland's interests in the House of Commons and potentially represent Scotland as part of the UK Government.

The referendum effect

The Scottish independence referendum in 2014 appears to have broken the pattern of Labour dominance at general elections in Scotland and SNP strength at devolved elections. Despite the result of the referendum being the rejection of Scottish independence, and thus a vindication of Labour's position, the vast majority of those who voted Yes in the referendum and subsequently went on to vote in the general election backed the SNP. The SNP won 50 per cent of the vote at the 2015 election, taking 56 of 59 seats. The swings from Labour to the SNP in some seats were huge, and the SNP managed to win seats in areas that have voted Labour for generations.

Two things are worth noting regarding the 2015 general election result in Scotland. The first is that the SNP gains closely reflected many of the gains made at the 2011 Scottish election. Although the Labour vote did hold up better at this election, the SNP still managed to capture a number of seats in and around Glasgow that had historically been Labour strongholds, as well as winning a number of seats in Edinburgh where the SNP had come from third and even fourth place to win. Although the referendum may well have been the catalyst for the 2015 result in Scotland, the 2011 devolved election was certainly a foreshadowing of the electoral effectiveness of the SNP and Labour's weaknesses. The second point is that, with the vast majority of Yes voters backing the SNP, what may well be occurring is some sort of realignment in Scottish politics along nationalist and unionist lines. Whether this holds remains to be seen, and the results of the 2016 Scottish and 2020 general elections will provide the litmus test for such a theory.

Conclusion

This chapter has provided an overview of elections and electoral behaviour in Scotland. It has assessed elections at UK general elections in Scotland and elections to the Scottish Parliament, and provided some explanations as to why voters vote the way they do. The chapter also considered the way in which voters view both elections in terms of importance.

Voters in Scotland do not view Scottish parliamentary elections as second order elections, but rather think about them as being about different issues and concerns than those at a general election. Until 2010, a discernible pattern was emerging: Labour was dominant at general elections in Scotland, whilst the SNP could rely on the more proportional electoral system of Scottish Parliament elections to challenge for and hold governmental office. However, the SNP's majority at the 2011 Scottish election showed that Labour was vulnerable in its traditional heartland constituencies. With the independence referendum campaign persuading many who had previously voted Labour to vote for independence, Labour's vulnerability was brutally exposed at the 2015 general election in Scotland and the party's poll ratings are of no comfort ahead of the Scottish elections in May 2016.

Whether this shift to the SNP represents a long-term realignment in Scottish electoral politics remains to be seen. The independence referendum appears to have structured electoral politics into a division between Nationalism and Unionism. However, the fact that the Scottish public are largely motivated by valence concerns means that voters may well be persuaded away from the SNP should they no longer be considered the most competent party with the strongest leadership and the party best placed to stand up for Scottish interests.

Notes

1 The d'Hondt method refers to Belgian mathematician Victor d'Hondt, who devised a formula that allocates seats in a party-list proportional system. A number of countries around the world use a variant of the d'Hondt formula in their electoral systems.

2 The 1979 referendum was held in order to ascertain whether or not the Scottish public wanted a directly elected Scottish Assembly. Of those who cast a ballot, 51.6 per cent voted Yes, but this result did not represent 40 per cent of the overall electorate and so the referendum effectively delivered a No vote.
3 There was the possibility of an SNP–Lib Dem coalition in 2007 but talks between the two parties broke down, leading to the SNP forming a minority government.
4 The Moreno question refers to the political scientist Luis Moreno who devised this particular question format.

Sources for further reading and study

British Election Study website: www.britishelectionstudy.com/. Homepage of the British Election Study with the latest data available to download and the latest news regarding relevant research.

Carman, C., R. Johns and J. Mitchell (2014) *More Scottish than British: The 2011 Scottish Parliament Election*. London: Palgrave Macmillan. Detailed analysis of the 2011 Scottish election.

Clarke, H.D., D. Sanders, M.C. Stewart and P.F. Whitley (2009) *Performance Politics and the British Voter*. Cambridge: Cambridge University Press. Essential reading on the dynamics of electoral behaviour in the UK.

Bennie, L., J. Brand and J. Mitchell (1997) *How Scotland Votes: Scottish Parties and Elections*. Manchester: Manchester University Press. Excellent book covering elections and voting behaviour in Scotland pre-devolution.

What Scotland Thinks: http://whatscotlandthinks.org/. Excellent website with a frequently updated blog and an interactive feature using opinion poll data.

References

Bennie, Lynn, Jack Brand and James Mitchell (1997) *How Scotland Votes: Scottish Parties and Elections*. Manchester: Manchester University Press.

Billig, Michael (1995) *Banal Nationalism*. London: Sage.

Brown, Alice, David McCrone, Lindsay Paterson and Paula Surridge (1998) *The Scottish Electorate: The 1997 General Election and Beyond*. Basingstoke: Macmillan.

Carman, Christopher and Robert Johns (2010) 'Linking coalition attitudes and split-ticket voting: The Scottish Parliament elections of 2007'. *Electoral Studies* 29(3): 381–391.

Clarke, Harold D., David Sanders, Marianne C. Stewart and Paul F. Whitley (2009) *Performance Politics and the British Voter*. Cambridge: Cambridge University Press.

Clarke, Harold D. and Marianne C. Stewart (1984) 'Dealignment of degree: Partisan change in Britain, 1974–1983', *The Journal of Politics* 46(3): 689–718.

Crewe, Ivor, Bo Särlvik and James Alt (1977) 'Partisan dealignment in Britain 1964–1974'. *British Journal of Political Science* 7: 129–190. Available at: http://goo.gl/uqTtme.

Curtice, John (2009) 'Do devolved elections work?' In Jeffrey, Charlie and James Mitchell (eds) *The Scottish Parliament 1999–2009: The First Decade*. Edinburgh: Luath Press, pp. 85–92.

Dalton, Russell J. (1984) 'Cognitive mobilization and partisan dealignment in advanced industrial democracies'. *The Journal of Politics* 46(1): 264–284.

Green, Jane and Sara B. Hobolt (2008) 'Owning the issue agenda: Party strategies and vote choices in British elections'. *Electoral Studies* 27: 460–476.

Harvey, Malcolm and Peter Lynch (2012) 'Inside the National Conversation: The SNP government and the politics of independence 2007–2010'. *Scottish Affairs* 80: 91–116.

Hassan, Gerry and Eric Shaw (2012) *The Strange Death of Labour Scotland*. Edinburgh: Edinburgh University Press.

Heath, Anthony, Geoffrey Evans and Clive Payne (1995) 'Modelling the class–party relationship in Britain, 1964–1992', *Journal of the Royal Statistical Society. Series A (Statistics in Society)* 158(3): 563–574.
Jeffery, Charlie and Dan Hough (2009) 'Understanding post-devolution elections in Scotland and Wales in comparative perspective'. *Party Politics* 15(2): 219–240.
Johns, Robert (2011) 'Credit where it's due? Valence politics, attributions of responsibility, and multi-level elections'. *Political Behaviour* 33: 53–77.
Johns, Robert, David Denver, James Mitchell and Charles Pattie (2010) *Voting for a Scottish Government: The Scottish Parliament Election of 2007*. Manchester: Manchester University Press.
Johns, Robert, James Mitchell and Christopher J. Carman (2013) 'Constitution or competence? The SNP's re-election in 2011'. *Political Studies* 61(S1), 158–178.
Johns, Robert, James Mitchell, David Denver and Charles Pattie (2009) 'Valence politics in Scotland: Towards an explanation of the 2007 election'. *Political Studies* 57: 207–233.
Kellas, James (1975) *The Scottish Political System*. Cambridge: Cambridge University Press.
Liñeira, Robert (2011) '"Less at stake" or a different game? Regional elections in Catalonia and Scotland'. *Regional and Federal Studies* 21(3): 283–303.
McAngus, Craig (2015) 'Party elites and the search for credibility: Plaid Cymru and the SNP as new parties of government'. *British Journal of Politics and International Relations* (early view) 27 March, doi: 10.1111/1467-856X.12070.
McAngus, Craig (2015) 'Do stateless-nationalist-regionalist-parties differ from other party types? Comparing organisational reform processes in Plaid Cymru and the Scottish national party'. *British Politics* (advance online publication) 2 November; doi: 10.1057/bp.2015.45.
McCrone, David (2009) 'Conundrums and contradictions: What Scotland wants'. In Jeffrey, Charlie and James Mitchell (eds) *The Scottish Parliament 1999–2009: The First Decade*. Edinburgh: Luath Press, pp. 93–104.
Mitchell, James (2009a) *Devolution in the UK*. Manchester: Manchester University Press.
Mitchell, James (2009b) 'From breakthrough to mainstream: The politics of potential and blackmail'. In Hassan, Gerry (ed.) *The Modern SNP: From Protest to Power*. Edinburgh: Edinburgh University Press, pp. 31–41.
Mitchell, James (2014) *The Scottish Question*. Oxford: Oxford University Press.
Mitchell, James, Lynn Bennie and Robert Johns (2012) *The SNP: Transition to Power*. Oxford: Oxford University Press.
Mitchell, James and Robert Johns (2009) 'New parliament, new elections'. In Jeffrey, Charlie and James Mitchell (eds) *The Scottish Parliament 1999–2009: The First Decade*. Edinburgh: Luath Press, pp. 77–84.
Mitchell, James and Arno van der Zwet (2010) 'A *catenaccio* game: The 2010 election in Scotland'. *Parliamentary Affairs* 63(4): 708–725.
Reif, Karlheinz and Hermann Schmitt (1980) 'Nine second-order national elections: A conceptual framework for the analysis of European election results'. *European Journal of Political Research* 8: 3–44.
Schakel, Arjan H. (2011) 'Congruence between regional and national elections'. *Comparative Political Studies* 46(5): 631–662.
Scully, Roger (2013) 'More Scottish than Welsh? Understanding the 2011 devolved elections in Scotland and Wales'. *Regional and Federal Studies* 23(5): 591–612.
Torrance, David (2009) *'We in Scotland': Thatcherism in a Cold Climate*. Edinburgh: Birlinn Limited.
Wyn Jones, Richard and Roger Scully (2006) 'Devolution and electoral politics in Scotland and Wales'. *Publius: The Journal of Federalism* 36(1): 115–134.

3 Quality of Scottish democracy

Thomas Lundberg

Introduction

Between the 1970s and the present day, Scotland undertook a democratic journey. In the late twentieth century, demands for greater autonomy or independence saw the rise of the Scottish National Party (SNP) from little more than a pressure group to a party that had several elected Members of Parliament (MPs). In 1979 a referendum on decentralisation – called devolution in British terminology – resulted in what was effectively a 'No' vote, though support for greater autonomy remained and grew during the 1980s and 1990s. This era of Conservative government at Westminster saw an increase in Scottish alienation from the centre, with opposition to prime minister Margaret Thatcher's policies and her approach to governing Scotland leading to a significant decline in Scottish support for the Conservatives. In opposition, the Labour Party and the Liberal Democrats worked with civil society groups in the Scottish Constitutional Convention on plans for a revival of devolution, coming up with what became much of the blueprint for the Scottish Parliament (often called 'Holyrood' after its location in Edinburgh) that was established after Labour returned to power in 1997.

In 1998 the Labour government charged the Consultative Steering Group, consisting of politicians, civil society figures and academics, with setting out the details of how the Scottish Parliament, elected in 1999, would work. After two Labour–Liberal Democrat coalition governments (for a total of eight years), the SNP formed a minority government in 2007, followed by a majority government in 2011. This SNP majority allowed for an independence referendum to be held in 2014. Thus, Scotland's democratic journey took the nation from being part of a rather centralised United Kingdom to the brink of independent statehood by means of devolution, which one prominent Labour figure, George Robertson, claimed in 1995 would 'kill nationalism stone dead' (Watt 2011). While devolution failed to prevent the independence movement from gaining considerable, though not majority support, one result was a greater level of public engagement with politics, an engagement that has outlasted the referendum campaign (Nicolson 2015).

Enhancing the quality of Scottish democracy appeared to be a significant aspiration for those who devised the blueprint for devolution in the 1990s. Many of those who sought devolution claimed there would be a 'new politics' (Brown 2000) that would differ from the politics of Westminster, which was seen in a negative light. Indeed, one contribution to an edited volume on Scottish devolution published around the time of its enactment was entitled 'Scotland's Parliament: a Mini Westminster, or a Model for Democracy?', implying that the British Parliament was not very democratic (Millar

2000). The use of a proportional electoral system for Scottish Parliament elections was probably the most significant departure from Westminster's procedures, though the apparent goal was to prevent the SNP from winning a seat majority at a future election (Taylor 1999: 57).

While those espousing a new politics were, to some extent, simply reacting to the perceived evils of Westminster (often from a partisan, anti-Conservative perspective – Labour was locked out of power for eighteen years in this era), some of the aspirations for genuine political change invoked themes expressed in the literature on democratic quality. Building on long-standing ideals, literature dating from the 1970s attempted to measure, or at least systematically assess, the democratic quality of political systems around the world. The basic themes of freedom, equality and democratic control are prominent, and these resonate with the aspirations of many of those involved in designing Scottish devolution.

As the following review of the literature on democratic quality will show, some of the complaints about Westminster appear to be more focused on the style, rather than the quality, of democracy. Institutional engineering has its limits; if participants do not want to change established practices, politics will not change. Nevertheless, some complaints about democracy in Britain – and specifically in Scotland – do lend themselves to analysis in the context of the democratic quality literature. Furthermore, much of the debate over Scottish democracy goes beyond the minimalist conceptualisation of democratic quality in the literature, moving into maximalist conceptualisations that are highly contested. This chapter will consider some illustrations of how Scottish democracy in practice relates to the democratic quality literature. While not an exhaustive analysis of the quality of Scottish democracy, these examples reveal a rather mixed record of democratic quality.

Quality of democracy

Democratic quality is not easy to define in detail, let alone critically assess, though much of the scholarly literature on the topic seems to be converging on which basic characteristics of a political system should be analysed. Researchers exploring democratic quality typically focus upon citizen participation and politicians' responsiveness, as well as the linkage between citizens and their state (Dahl and Tufte 1973: 13–15), with more recent research expanding upon this basic approach. Leonardo Morlino focuses on rule of law, accountability, responsiveness, civil rights, and equality (2004: 7). Stein Ringen focuses on 'the security of freedom' (Ringen 2007: 30); his conceptualisation of democracy includes measurements of strength, capacity, security and trust (Ringen 2007: 42). Andrew Roberts cites the linkages between citizens and policy makers, focusing on electoral accountability, mandate responsiveness, and policy responsiveness (2010: 32). The Economist Intelligence Unit focuses on electoral processes and pluralism, functioning of government, political participation, democratic political culture, and civil liberties (2013: 29–39).

The main disagreement in the literature is over whether scholars should focus on simply 'input' – procedures, institutions and institutional rules, and the legal protection guaranteed to them – or also examine 'output' – the outcomes, which could be measured in terms of congruence between what citizens voted for and which policies they got, as well as the level of gender equality in parliaments and cabinets, voter turnout, and even the extent of socioeconomic equality. Some scholars insist on more minimalist perspective of democratic quality. A recent reconceptualisation of democratic quality reviewed much of the literature before concluding that in a democracy, 'the only means of access to government offices' is through elections, which should be 'clean, inclusive and competitive' and allocate seats on the basis of proportional representation in unicameral legislatures where simple majority voting is the rule; furthermore, civil rights ('Freedom of expression, association, assembly, and access to information') are respected and socioeconomic inequality is prevented from turning into political inequality (Munck 2016: 17). The criteria here focus on democratic input, not output.

In this minimalistic reconceptualisation, Gerardo Munck invokes modern classics, like Robert Dahl's *Polyarchy* – much of the above reflects Dahl's (1971: 3) 'Some Requirements for a Democracy among a Large Number of People' – as well as more recent theoretical works, like Anthony McGann's (2006) *The Logic of Democracy*, where the author argues that 'political equality implies majority rule and proportional representation' (McGann 2006: 202) and that 'most institutional features we refer to as checks and balances (bicameralism, presidentialism, federalism, division of power) – violate political equality just as much as explicitly supermajoritarian rules' (McGann 2006: 203). McGann's approach partially contradicts the logic behind Arend Lijphart's preference for the consensus model of democracy, which includes McGann's checks and balances as well as proportional representation, all of which Lijphart sees as dispersing power away from the centre and, as a consequence, working against 'bare' majoritarianism to increase the size of the democratic mandate (Lijphart 2012: 2). Another scholar, Bingham Powell, also argues in favour of something similar to Lijphart's consensus model, what he calls the 'proportional vision' of democracy, finding it to be more congruent with the median voter than the 'majoritarian vision' (Powell 2000).

Lijphart's well-known framework for analysis, which uses the majoritarian and consensus models of democracy as ideal types, is useful for analysing where power lies in a political system. However, the democratic quality of the models, as noted above, may be contentious. Lijphart makes his preference for the consensus model clear in his book *Patterns of Democracy*, stating that 'kinder, gentler' consensus democracies are:

> more likely to be welfare states; they have a better record with regard to the protection of the environment; they put fewer people in prison and are less likely to use the death penalty; and the consensus democracies in the developed world are more generous with their economic assistance to the developing nations.
> (Lijphart 2012: 274–275)

He also points to democratic quality rankings, such as the one developed by the Economist Intelligence Unit, and quantitative indicators, such as the percentage of parliamentarians and cabinet ministers who are female and voter turnout levels, in order to make his case (Lijphart 2012: 276–277).

Munck's literature review takes issue with many of the recent works on quality of democracy, including that of Lijphart. While he does find that most authors he reviews go 'beyond the conventional electoral conception of democracy by including elements about the process of government decision-making', Munck is concerned about how scholars expand the concept of democratic quality into specific outcomes, complaining that 'scholars rarely engage in rigorous theorizing from established general principles' (Munck 2016: 5). Lijphart's conception of democratic quality above calls for the inclusion of data like the proportion of politicians who are female and includes some indicators of the social democratic character of his country cases, using measures of social expenditure (Lijphart 2012: 288–290). Ringen also uses indicators derived from data on child poverty, public health expenditure, confidence in government, 'freedom of choice and control in life', and trust in other people (Ringen 2007: 43–47). These approaches move in the direction of social rights. In response, Munck argues that going too far down the path towards 'the expansive substantive conception of democracy' (particularly when legally mandated) could bring about circumstances such that 'when everything is a right, there is no politics; and when there is no politics, there is no democracy' (Munck 2016: 18).

While Munck makes some valid points about going too far in the direction of democratic outcomes when assessing democratic quality, he approvingly acknowledges the work of Marc Bühlmann, Wolfgang Merkel, Lisa Müller and Bernhard Wessels (Munck 2016: 11). Bühlmann and colleagues propose the 'Democracy Barometer', which conceptualises democratic quality in terms of freedom, control and equality, with freedom composed of individual liberties, rule of law, and the public sphere, control composed of competition, mutual constraints, and governmental capacity, and equality composed of transparency, participation and representation (Bühlmann et al. 2012: 523).

The Democracy Barometer includes something that Munck does not stress – control, or the capacity of government to enact policies decided upon by the legislature (Bühlmann et al. 2012: 522) – thus ensuring that the majority actually gets the policies it prefers. Many other scholars include something similar in their conceptualisations of democratic quality. Policy responsiveness is part of the democratic quality definition used by Roberts (2010: 39), is what Powell refers to as the congruence between citizens and governments (Powell 2000), and is alluded to by Dahl's requirement for 'Institutions for making government policies depend on votes and other expressions of preference' (Dahl 1971: 3). Responsiveness is linked to accountability, which 'influences the degree to which citizens will be satisfied with the performance of democracy and view it as legitimate' (Diamond and Morlino 2004: 27). With so much of the literature seeing accountability, responsiveness or at least some kind of linkage between what the public wants and what it gets as essential to a high quality democracy, Munck's refusal to include this concept is a significant omission.

There is, therefore, a disagreement in how far to go when considering democratic quality. Munck prefers a more minimalist conceptualisation, while others prefer a more maximalist one. A middle ground appears to exist in the form of the Democracy Barometer, which allows for Munck's definition based on freedom and equality, with the addition of the control concept, which the barometer's authors have fleshed out to include an explicit recognition of horizontal and vertical accountability, competition and responsiveness (Bühlmann et al. 2012: 522). This chapter will consider the Democracy Barometer's conceptualisation of democratic quality, with some input from Munck's reconceptualisation, to be the minimalist definition, while conceptualisations used by scholars like Lijphart (2012), which expand upon the minimalist definition in the area of equality, will be considered part of the maximalist definition. These conceptualisations are summarised in Table 3.1.

Both minimalist and maximalist conceptualisations of democratic quality have been referred to in the Scottish case, and some examples will be analysed in the next section. Before that, however, another aspect of the democratic quality literature that has relevance to Scotland should be brought up. Some research has recently considered the

Table 3.1 Conceptualisations of democratic quality

Minimalist

- Freedom (civil rights: freedom of expression, association, assembly, and access to information; rule of law)
- Equality (clean, inclusive and competitive elections by means of proportional representation; unicameralism and simple majority decision-making procedures; equal participation – socioeconomic inequality prevented from turning into political inequality)
- Control (accountability; competition; responsiveness)

Maximalist

All of the above plus:

- Equality (high levels of participation; gender equality in political representation; entitlements to high levels of social benefits; 'kinder, gentler' policies)

Source: Bühlmann et al. 2012; Lijphart 2012; Munck 2016.

relationship between size and democratic quality, arguing that 'the social system in small states, which alters the environment in which the political and economic systems operate' affects democracy (Ott 2000: 9), and that where states are not small, decentralisation can enhance democratic quality (Diamond and Tsalik 1999). At the elite level, Dana Ott argues (2000: 195) that due to the relatively small number of elite political actors, who are likely to know each other well and interact closely, cooperation in small states is more likely than in larger states and this example can have a positive impact on the wider society. In some small states, such as New Zealand, leaders cultivate a sense of closeness to their people, at least appearing to be accessible and down-to-earth (Miller 2015: 24).

On the other hand, some research rejects the notion that smaller is better (Erk and Veenendaal 2014; Newton 1982), and quantitative research examining large data sets yields mixed results using Freedom House and Polity IV datasets (Högström 2013: 214). The work by Dahl and Tufte (1973) was not very conclusive regarding the relationship between size and democracy. Noting how 'intensely personalized' politics can be in small polities, Wouter Veenendaal and Jack Corbett point out that there are both good and bad aspects of such personalisation (2015: 541). Therefore, small size may not be the most important factor associated with high-quality democracies; indeed, other variables, like wealth and education, may be more important. Yet even among wealthy countries with highly educated populations, the smaller states come out ahead in recent democratic quality rankings. As Table 3.2 shows, relatively small countries dominate the top ten on each list.

For some supporting Scottish independence, the appeal of small, highly democratic states, many of which fit into Lijphart's consensus model, is apparent. The SNP has stated its admiration for Scotland's wealthy neighbours, like Ireland, Iceland and Norway, with former first minister Alex Salmond approvingly referring to an 'arc of prosperity' (*Scotsman* 2006). The (SNP) Scottish Government's White Paper on independence also argued that small neighbours like Norway and Denmark 'enjoy an independence bonus that allows them to deliver fairer societies' (Scottish Government 2013: 59) and that residents of an independent Scotland could avoid British levels of economic inequality, pointing to Norway and Sweden, which 'have demonstrated that fairness and prosperity are part of a virtuous circle, reinforcing each other and delivering a range of benefits for society as a whole' (Scottish Government 2013: 152). While the literature on small states and democratic quality does not appear to be conclusive about the role of population size in enhancing democracy, the SNP seemed to be mainly concerned during the referendum campaign about preventing Scotland's small size from deterring voters from supporting independence.

Table 3.2 also shows that the United Kingdom (UK) comes in below the top ten states in two democratic quality rankings. While not at the bottom of the list of states that are considered to be democratic, the UK's rather mediocre performance in these rankings underscores the criticisms that are often made of British democratic quality, some of which could be heard during the period before devolution. In the years since devolution, the rhetoric surrounding the democratic character of Scottish politics has echoed both minimalist and maximalist conceptions of democratic quality.

The blueprint for devolution

The Consultative Steering Group (CSG), set up in November 1997 by the Labour government after the successful referendum on Scottish devolution, comprised

Table 3.2 Democratic quality rankings

Economist Intelligence Unit, 2012
1 Norway
2 Sweden
3 Iceland
4 Denmark
5 New Zealand
6 Australia
7 Switzerland
8 Canada
9 Finland
10 Netherlands
16 United Kingdom

Global Democracy Ranking, 2014
1 Norway
2 Switzerland
3 Sweden
4 Finland
5 Denmark
6 Netherlands
7 New Zealand
8 Germany
9 Ireland
10 Belgium
13 United Kingdom

Source: Campbell et al. 2014; Economist Intelligence Unit 2013.

members from the political world – from the four main Scottish political parties at the time (Conservative, Labour, Liberal Democrat and SNP) – the academic world, and Scottish civil society. Its remit was the following:

> To bring together views on and consider the operational needs and working methods of the Scottish Parliament; to develop proposals for the rules of procedure and Standing Orders which the Parliament might be invited to adopt; to prepare a report to the Secretary of State by the end of 1998, to inform the preparation of draft Standing Orders.
>
> (Consultative Steering Group 1998: 3)

Building upon a 1997 White Paper, the CSG used the following 'key principles' throughout its work:

- The Scottish Parliament should embody and reflect the sharing of power between the people of Scotland, the legislators and the Scottish Executive.
- the Scottish Executive should be accountable to the Scottish Parliament and the Parliament and Executive should be accountable to the people of Scotland.
- the Scottish Parliament should be accessible, open, responsive, and develop procedures which make possible a participative approach to the development, consideration and scrutiny of policy and legislation.
- the Scottish Parliament in its operation and its appointments should recognise the need to promote equal opportunities for all.

(Consultative Steering Group 1998: 6)

The CSG notes that these principles are reminiscent of the Scottish Constitutional Convention and aim to overcome 'a great deal of cynicism about and disillusionment with the democratic process' that its members had seen among the public (Consultative Steering Group 1998: 6).

The CSG's key principles echo much of what scholars examine when studying the quality of democracy. The minimalist conceptualisation of democracy (Table 3.1) appears frequently, particularly when it comes to equality and control. The key principle calling for accountability on the part of the Scottish Parliament and Executive (now called the Scottish Government) falls under the concept of control, as does responsiveness. Equal opportunities are demanded in the fourth principle; this shows up potentially under both minimalist and maximalist conceptualisations of democratic quality (Table 3.1). The first key principle calls for power sharing, which is favoured by Lijphart in his advocacy of the consensus model of democracy, where power is to be shared between parties in broad coalition cabinets and between the cabinet and the legislature (Lijphart 2012: 33–35).

The CSG's plans for devolution built upon work carried out by the Scottish Constitutional Convention and the Scottish Constitutional Commission shortly before Labour came to power. A major institutional component that these bodies decided upon was the electoral system. With the agreement of Labour and the Liberal Democrats, a proportional electoral system was devised for the Scottish Parliament in the 1990s. Called the additional member system in Britain, the system is more widely known by political scientists worldwide as the mixed-member proportional (MMP) system and is based upon the proportional representation (PR) system used in

Germany since the late 1940s. The term MMP, adopted by New Zealand which introduced the system for elections in 1996, comes from the fact that representatives are elected via single-member constituencies and party lists (with voters normally having a vote in each type of contest), yet the overall result in partisan terms is proportional to the party vote because party list representatives are added in a way that compensates for most of the deviation from proportionality that can occur from plurality ('first-past-the-post') elections in single-member constituencies (Lijphart 2012; Reynolds et al. 2005; Shugart and Wattenberg 2001).

In its report, the Constitutional Convention criticised the system used to elect the House of Commons for allowing an MP 'to be returned with little more than one third of the votes cast' and creating a situation in which 'Mrs Thatcher has dominated for a decade although in the most respectable of her three election victories her Party polled only 42 per cent of the vote and a very much smaller share of the qualified electorate' (Scottish Constitutional Convention 1992: 91). This complaint shows that members of the Constitutional Convention saw the single-member plurality electoral system as unfair. This criticism of a core element of Lijphart's (2012) Westminster model was accompanied by what appears to be a belief in the power of electoral systems to influence politics, a view consistent with Giovanni Sartori's argument that the electoral system is 'the most specific manipulative instrument of politics' (1968: 273). The Constitutional Convention called for a Scottish Parliament electoral system that would encompass six criteria:

> that it produces results in which the number of seats for various parties is broadly related to the number of votes cast for them; that it ensures, or at least takes effective positive action to bring about, equal representation of men and women, and encourages fair representation of ethnic and other minority groups; that it preserves a link between the member and his/her constituency; that it is as simple as possible to understand; that it ensures adequate representation of less populous areas; and that the system is designed to place the greatest possible power in the hands of the electorate.
> (Scottish Constitutional Convention 1992: 91–92)

The Constitutional Convention's criteria are not easy to maximise simultaneously (see, for example, Reynolds et al. 2005). The first criterion implies a form of PR and in order to achieve gender balance, a closed-list PR system would be most effective, provided that parties agree (or are compelled by law) to alternate men and women and include minorities on their lists. Preserving a (presumably individual) link to constituencies, however, may be more difficult when you use multimember constituencies electing many representatives, which is necessary for a high level of proportionality. MMP can reduce this problem with its single-member constituency element, but there will still be several representatives elected on a regional or national basis to ensure proportionality on a partisan basis, and their constituency role may not be clear. Another PR system, the single transferable vote (STV), can be used with relatively few representatives elected per constituency (three to five in Ireland's parliament), but this was not chosen.

As far as the Constitutional Convention's simplicity criterion is concerned, the logic of PR is simple enough – that parties win seats in proportion to their vote share – but the mechanism, especially in systems like MMP or STV, which allows voters to express candidate preferences, may not be so easy to explain to the public. Regarding the criterion of 'adequate representation of less populous areas', this would be a problem in most electoral systems, especially if you want a 'link' between representatives and constituents – it is difficult and costly for elected representatives to maintain regular personal contact with constituents spread across a large, lightly populated area. The final criterion, placing 'the greatest possible power in the hands of the electorate', is not very clear; it could imply increasing intra-party democracy by requiring parties to hold primary elections for candidate and party list selection, or it could be a reference to a preferential electoral system like STV.

The Constitutional Convention's support for PR is consistent with the equality concept under the minimalist conceptualisation of democratic quality. With a PR system, voter equality is more likely than with a majoritarian electoral system because PR more faithfully reflects the electorate's intentions on a partisan basis, and the Constitutional Convention noted that this was the 'decisive factor' in its support for PR (Scottish Constitutional Convention 1992: 91). Scottish devolution's blueprint also called for a unicameral parliament, so this characteristic also fits into the minimalist equality concept. Referring back to high-quality democracies (Table 3.2) according to the Economist Intelligence Unit (2013) and the Global Democracy Ranking (Campbell et al. 2014), the former includes six countries with unicameral legislatures in the top ten (indeed, the top five all have unicameral legislatures), while the latter includes five in its top ten.

Under the maximalist equality concept is gender equality. This was important to the Constitutional Convention when it developed its plan for the Scottish Parliament's electoral system. The Constitutional Convention noted its 'particular and pressing concern' about what it called 'the failure of the British political system to face the issue of women's representation' and stated:

> The new Parliament provides the opportunity for a new start and the Convention is determined that positive action will be taken to allow women to play their full and equal part in the political process. The principle of equal representation for women in a Scottish Parliament has been agreed. The Convention is committed to securing a mechanism to achieve this in further consultation and discussion about the electoral system.
>
> (Scottish Constitutional Convention 1992: 91)

Because the commitment to equal representation did not become a statutory requirement, the onus was on the parties to take their own actions to increase the number of women elected. Since MMP has both a single-member constituency ('first-past-the-post') and a party list component, this meant that different strategies would be needed.

The record since devolution

Ultimately, the Constitutional Convention was aiming for the introduction of a 'new politics' that would bring about a significant change from Westminster. The Scottish Parliament would stand apart from its counterpart in London, with the Constitutional Convention insisting that it would 'not be a pale imitation of Westminster' and would instead 'encourage an open, accessible and democratically accountable government and a participatory democracy' (Scottish Constitutional Convention 1992: 92). Here, the Constitutional Convention invokes democratic conceptualisations in a way similar to that of the CSG a few years later, and some of these resonate with minimalist and maximalist conceptualisations seen in Table 3.1.

The aspiration to a new politics, however, sometimes refers more to a change from Westminster-style politics than to a particular level of democratic quality. There were calls for a more consensual style of governing during debates on devolution (Mitchell 2000: 617) indicating a dislike for the adversarial style of British politics that can be associated with Lijphart's majoritarian model (Lijphart 2012: 15). The 1997 devolution referendum debate saw Labour and the SNP cooperate, though these parties were normally very much at odds over the question of Scottish independence (Mitchell 2000: 617).

Whether Scotland has actually experienced a new politics since devolution has been explored in the academic literature. One of the most damning verdicts on the question of Scotland's divergence from Westminster comes from James Mitchell, who argues that 'Holyrood is very much the child of Westminster', with its electoral system constituting one of the few differences (Mitchell 2010: 98–99). Referring to what he calls 'a narcissism of small differences', Mitchell disputes how different Holyrood and Westminster actually are in response to David Steel's 'dozen differences' between the two bodies, saying that many of the differences between them are minor and have been exaggerated (Mitchell 2010: 107–110).

On the matter of accountability, part of the minimalist conceptualisation of democratic quality ('Control' in Table 3.1), the CSG does mention 'scrutiny of policy and legislation' in its key principles (Consultative Steering Group 1998: 6). While a powerful role for committees was anticipated by those involved in the design of the Scottish Parliament (Brown 2000), critics reject the idea that the Holyrood's committees are in any way remarkable. 'The view that the Scottish Committee system is superior to that [of] Westminster has become commonplace but the evidence is far from obvious', Mitchell claims (2010: 110). He notes that Westminster has attempted to improve its committee system, with the creation of a Scrutiny Unit, as well as allowances for committee chairs, and concludes that Holyrood's committees 'are effective but no more so and possibly less so than the Westminster Committees' (Mitchell 2010: 111). In a similar vein, Paul Cairney argues that Holyrood's committees 'did not provide the "motor of a new politics"' (Cairney 2011a: 53–54) largely due to its lack of resources and the fact that committees were meant simply 'to hold ministers and civil servants to account, to make sure they consult properly (i.e. they do not undertake large consultations themselves) and to initiate legislation as a last resort if MSPs believe that government policy is inadequate', so committees were never meant to challenge the government's ability to govern (Cairney 2011a: 53).

Regarding one of the areas where there is agreement that devolution has brought about a significant change – the introduction of a proportional electoral system – observers of post-devolution Scottish politics could be forgiven for thinking that in some ways, things have not changed very much from the adversarial norm. While Holyrood election results do reflect how Scots have voted, on a partisan basis, in a much more accurate way than Westminster results show, the rather combative nature of party politics remains the same. As Mitchell states above, Labour and the SNP strongly disagree over a core issue dimension in Scottish politics – the constitutional question (Mitchell 2000: 617). This issue, coupled with the SNP's courting of the working-class vote, has resulted in an intense rivalry between the two parties (Lynch 2009). The use of the particular version of PR chosen for Scottish Parliament elections, as well as a recent election outcome – minority government – have demonstrated that the attempt to engineer a significant change from Westminster-style politics has not been entirely successful.

The MMP electoral system is characterised by the election of candidates in two different ways – from single-member constituencies, as well as from multimember regions, in which representatives typically (but not always) come from closed party lists. In the process, MMP allows for dual candidacy, where parties may nominate the same candidates both for constituencies and for the party lists in the regions in which the constituencies are located, meaning that if a candidate loses in a constituency contest, the candidate could enter the Scottish Parliament via the regional party list if he or she is placed high enough on the list. While this practice is the norm for parties in MMP-using Germany and New Zealand, Labour was very hostile to dual candidacy in Scotland and Wales and actually banned the practice for elections to the National Assembly for Wales; critics argued that Labour was unhappy with the competition it was facing (often for the first time) in what used to be safe constituencies for the party (Lundberg 2007).

After eight years of Labour–Liberal Democrat coalition government, the SNP formed a minority government in 2007. During this time, relations between the SNP and Labour remained tense, with the latter party still displaying hostility towards the equality of constituency-elected and regional list-elected Members of the Scottish Parliament (MSPs) by opposing the equalisation of office allowances and rewording the code of conduct (Lundberg 2014). Poor relations between the parties made things difficult as the SNP tried to run its minority administration, with the SNP actually having better luck working with the Conservatives (Cairney 2011b). As the then Liberal Democrat leader Tavish Scott put it, 'there is a level of visceral hatred between the Nationalists and Labour to this day. So, it just transferred from London to Edinburgh' (quoted in Lundberg 2013: 622).

The adversarial relationship between Scottish parties, particularly the SNP and Labour, shows that while institutional engineering should, in theory, promote a more consensual politics, the politicians themselves may not respond in the anticipated way. Nevertheless, the use of PR does meet the minimalist conceptualisation of democratic quality. A related goal – the presence of more women in Scottish politics – meets the maximalist conceptualisation of democratic quality and here, Holyrood has easily surpassed the House of Commons, which reached its highest female proportion of MPs, 29 per cent, in 2015 (Bengtsson et al. 2015). Table 3.3 shows the percentage of MSPs who were women at the time of Scottish Parliament elections from 1999 to 2011.

Labour was most willing to take action to increase the number of female MSPs, using 'twinning', defined as 'pairing up constituency seats on the basis of "proximity" and "winnability", with a male and female candidate selected for each pair of seats'

Table 3.3 Female membership of the Scottish Parliament (percentages) at each election, 1999–2011

Election year	Female membership, %
1999	37.2
2003	39.5
2007	33.3
2011	34.9

Source: Scottish Parliament 2015; McMillan and Fox 2010.

(McMillan and Fox 2010: 9). Due to the party's strength in the constituency contests of the first MMP elections, this was likely to be more effective than the 'zipping' strategy used by Plaid Cymru in the first National Assembly for Wales elections, where the party alternated female and male candidates on regional party lists, an approach rejected by the SNP (Bradbury et al. 2000: 61).

Looking at the wider role of women in the Scottish Parliament, there have been several female party leaders: Wendy Alexander, Johann Lamont and Kezia Dugdale for Labour; Annabel Goldie and Ruth Davidson for the Conservatives; and Nicola Sturgeon for the SNP, who became Scotland's first minister after Alex Salmond's resignation in 2014, right after the independence referendum. Sturgeon's first cabinet had an equal number of women and men, with the first minister saying that 'this government will work hard in all areas to promote women, to create gender equality and it sends out a strong message that the business of redressing the gender balance in public life starts right here in government' (BBC News 2014).

The referendum

The final example of democratic quality in Scotland could be seen as both a failure of devolution and also as an opportunity for the enhancement of democracy. The independence referendum, held on 18 September 2014, was the fulfilment of the SNP's promise to legislate for the vote if it won the 2011 Holyrood election. After obtaining the agreement of the UK government to honour the result, the Scottish Government agreed a clear yes-or-no question with the UK Electoral Commission, and this was put to the Scottish electorate. Before the referendum, however, supporters of each side campaigned actively, with the campaign in favour of independence spawning a social movement that has persisted since the referendum. The extent of public participation, though door-to-door canvassing and social media, plus the very high level of voter turnout, revealed a deeper level of democratic engagement than is otherwise the norm.

The fact that the referendum was held at all is remarkable; the UK government reserves constitutional matters to itself, and most countries do not want to get smaller as a result of secession. UK prime minister David Cameron responded to questions about why he allowed the referendum like this, invoking minimalist democratic conceptualisations: 'The Scottish people elected in 2011 a Scottish National Party government in Edinburgh with Alex Salmond at its head. One of their policies was to have a referendum on the future of Scotland being a part of the UK' (Watt 2014). Cameron's conclusion was that he was doing the right thing, despite the risk to the future of the Union.

The UK government allowed the Scottish Parliament a lot of control over the process, including the date, franchise, question wording, campaign finance, and other rules involved in the referendum (Scottish Government 2012). Perhaps most significantly, the UK government did not insist upon obstacles like a supermajority requirement. This decision is in line with the minimalist conceptualisation of democratic quality – a simple majority is all that was required for Scottish independence. As Stephen Tierney argues, 'there seems no obviously principled alternative to simple majority, since any threshold requirement will be arbitrary to some extent' (Tierney 2012: 294). Indeed, a supermajority requirement would privilege the minority of the population by allowing it to block the will of the majority (McGann 2006: 89).

Questions of democracy formed part of the referendum debate. During the referendum campaign, the Scottish Government frequently invoked a democratic argument.

An example can be found early in the White Paper, *Scotland's Future: Your Guide to an Independent Scotland*, with the Scottish Government arguing that with a Yes vote to the question of independence, 'Scotland's future will be in Scotland's hands' and that with a No vote, 'Decisions about Scotland would remain in the hands of others' (Scottish Government 2013: i). Alex Salmond, Scottish first minister and SNP leader at the time, argued that his party's proposals in the White Paper were only one vision of an independent Scotland and that other visions were possible; 'That is the real democratic value of independence – the people of Scotland are in charge. It will no longer be possible for governments to be elected and pursue policies against the wishes of the Scottish people ... Independence will put the people of Scotland in charge of our own destiny' (Scottish Government 2013: xi).

The Scottish Government also pointed to Westminster's democratic deficiencies: 'One of the arguments for independence is that the Westminster system is not democratic enough', noting 'failures' where 'for 34 of the 68 years since 1945, Scotland has been ruled by governments that were elected by fewer than half of Scottish constituencies'; 'in only two of the 18 elections since 1945 (October 1964 and February 1974) – would the largest party in the UK Parliament have been different if Scotland had been independent and not returned MPs to Westminster'; the House of Lords is not elected; 'the first-past-the-post electoral system ... does not fully reflect the voting intentions of the people'; and Westminster 'is based on the principle of unlimited power, usually referred to as Parliamentary sovereignty' which could 'repeal the Human Rights Act or abolish the Scottish Parliament' (Scottish Government 2013: 548–549).

Other aspects of democracy, particularly those that characterise the maximalist conceptualisation of democratic quality, could also be seen in the referendum debate. The White Paper cited many examples of how an independent Scotland, if governed by the SNP, could enhance social equality: 'A transformational extension of childcare'; 'Abolition of the "bedroom tax"'; 'A halt to the rollout of Universal Credit and Personal Independence Payments in Scotland allowing future Scottish governments to develop reforms to our welfare system that meet our needs'; 'The first steps towards a fairer tax system by ensuring that basic rate tax allowances and tax credits rise at least in line with inflation'; 'Pensioners' incomes protected'; 'A Fair Work Commission and a guarantee that minimum wage will rise at least in line with inflation' (Scottish Government 2013: xiii).

Campaign groups organised around each side in the referendum, with some of those involved in the Yes campaign arguing that independence could lead to a more socially equal Scotland. The Radical Independence Campaign pointed out in a brochure how Scottish independence could solve a variety of social problems, including fuel poverty, child poverty, pensioner poverty, infant mortality, regional inequality, and 'a wealth gap twice as wide as any other EU country' (Radical Independence Campaign 2014). Another group, Women for Independence, includes the following objective in its constitution: 'To campaign for fair and equal gender representation in public and political life in Scotland, and for other causes likely to further the interests of women in Scotland and enhance democracy' (Women for Independence 2015). Both groups have continued to pursue their objectives after the referendum, reflecting a legacy of maximal democratic quality (Table 3.2).

Another aspect of maximal democratic quality arising from the independence referendum is that of greater political participation in the form of voter turnout. Scottish Parliament elections display rather lacklustre turnout figures, dropping from a high of 58 per cent at the first election in 1999 to around 50 per cent at the other three that

Table 3.4 Voter turnout (percentages) at Scottish Parliament elections, 1999–2011

Election year	Voter turnout, %
1999	58.2
2003	49.4
2007	52.4
2011	51.1

Source: Scottish Parliament 2015.

occurred before the referendum (Table 3.4). Voter turnout at the independence referendum, however, was 84.6 per cent, the highest for any election held in Scotland since universal suffrage (Electoral Commission 2014: 1). Turnout at the May 2015 House of Commons election from Scotland was 71.1 per cent, the highest of any nation in the UK (BBC News 2015). These voter turnout figures, coupled with the huge increase in membership of parties supporting independence, with the SNP reaching 100,000 in March 2015 (Duncanson 2015), indicate that Scottish political participation is at record heights.

Conclusion

This chapter explored the academic literature on democratic quality, distinguishing between minimalist and maximalist conceptualisations. Both have been used in the debates over Scottish democracy since devolution. Scotland's post-devolution democratic record may look disappointing in some respects, but this observation could be more of a reaction to the adversarial behaviour among politicians and the presence of contentious issues, like the question of Scottish independence, rather than a reflection of how the literature views democratic quality. Post-devolution Scotland meets the minimalist conceptualisations of democratic quality and improves upon the UK's record for equality by virtue of having a PR electoral system and a unicameral parliament.

The question of equality, particularly in regard to its maximalist conceptualisation, has been the focus of recent developments in Scottish democracy. The significant increase in public participation, the greater representation of women in political life, and the intense debate over social welfare all indicate that Scotland has moved on, even without independence, into a deeper level of engagement with democracy. The maximalist conceptualisation of democratic quality, however, is contentious among scholars and will undoubtedly be contentious among the Scottish public. Many will argue that political (or social) outcomes should not be considered indicators of democratic quality. This debate has been running in the academic literature for decades and it is likely that it will run in Scotland for some time, particularly as the stakes get larger in the form of greater autonomy – or eventual independence.

Further reading

Bühlmann, Marc, Wolfgang Merkel, Lisa Müller and Bernhard Wessels (2012) 'The Democracy Barometer: A New Instrument to Measure the Quality of Democracy and Its Potential for Comparative Research'. *European Political Science* 11(4): 519–536.

Dahl, Robert A. (1971) *Polyarchy: Participation and Opposition*. New Haven, CT: Yale University Press.

Economist Intelligence Unit (2013) *The Economist Intelligence Unit's Index of Democracy 2012*. Available at: www.eiu.com/public/topical_report.aspx?campaignid=DemocracyIndex12.

Lijphart, Arend (2012) *Patterns of Democracy: Government Forms and Performance in Thirty-Six Countries*. New Haven, CT: Yale University Press.

McGann, Anthony J. (2006) *The Logic of Democracy: Reconciling Equality, Deliberation, and Minority Protection*. Ann Arbor: University of Michigan Press.

References

BBC News (2014) 'Nicola Sturgeon Announces New Scottish Cabinet'. 21 November. Available at: www.bbc.co.uk/news/uk-scotland-scotland-politics-30138550.

BBC News (2015) 'Results: SNP Surges to Scottish Landslide'. Available at: www.bbc.co.uk/news/election/2015/results/scotland.

Bengtsson, Helena, Sally Weale and Libby Brooks (2015) 'Record Numbers of Female and Minority-ethnic MPs in New House of Commons'. *The Guardian*, 8 May. Available at: www.theguardian.com/politics/2015/may/08/record-numbers-female-minority-ethnic-mps-commons.

Bradbury, Jonathan, David Denver, James Mitchell and Lynn Bennie (2000) 'Devolution and Party Change: Candidate Selection for the 1999 Scottish Parliament and Welsh Assembly Elections'. *The Journal of Legislative Studies* 6(3): 51–72.

Brown, Alice (2000) 'Designing the Scottish Parliament'. *Parliamentary Affairs* 53(3): 542–556.

Bühlmann, Marc, Wolfgang Merkel, Lisa Müller and Bernhard Wessels (2012) 'The Democracy Barometer: A New Instrument to Measure the Quality of Democracy and Its Potential for Comparative Research'. *European Political Science* 11(4): 519–536.

Cairney, Paul (2011a) *The Scottish Political System Since Devolution: From New Politics to the New Scottish Government*. Exeter: Imprint Academic.

Cairney, Paul (2011b) 'Coalition and Minority Government in Scotland: Lessons for the United Kingdom?' *The Political Quarterly* 82(2): 261–269.

Campbell, David F.J., Paul Pölzlbauer, Thorsten D. Barth and Georg Pölzlbauer (2014) *Democratic Ranking 2014*. Vienna: Democracy Ranking. Available at: http://democracyranking.org/ranking/2014/data/Scores_of_the_Democracy_Ranking_2014_a4.pdf.

Consultative Steering Group (1998) *Shaping Scotland's Parliament: Report of the Consultative Steering Group on the Scottish Parliament*. London: Scottish Office. Available at: www.scottish.parliament.uk/PublicInformationdocuments/Report_of_the_Consultative_Steering_Group.pdf.

Dahl, Robert A. (1971) *Polyarchy: Participation and Opposition*. New Haven, CT: Yale University Press.

Dahl, Robert A. and Edward Tufte (1973) *Size and Democracy*. Stanford, CA: Stanford University Press.

Diamond, Larry and Leonardo Morlino (2004) 'An Overview'. *Journal of Democracy* 15(4): 20–31.

Diamond, Larry and Svetlana Tsalik (1999) 'Size and Democracy: The Case for Decentralization'. In Larry Diamond (ed.) *Developing Democracy: Toward Consolidation*. Baltimore, MD: Johns Hopkins University Press, pp. 117–160.

Duncanson, Hilary (2015) 'Boost for SNP as Membership Hits 100,000 Mark'. *Scotsman*, 22 March. Available at: www.scotsman.com/news/uk/boost-for-snp-as-membership-hits-100-000-mark-1-3725308.

Economist Intelligence Unit (2013) *The Economist Intelligence Unit's Index of Democracy 2012*. Available at: www.eiu.com/public/topical_report.aspx?campaignid=DemocracyIndex12.

Electoral Commission (2014) *Scottish Independence Referendum: Report on the Referendum Held on 18 September 2014*. Available at: www.electoralcommission.org.uk/__data/assets/pdf_file/0010/179812/Scottish-independence-referendum-report.pdf.

Erk, Jan and Wouter Veenendaal (2014) 'Is Small Really Beautiful? The Microstate Mistake'. *Journal of Democracy* 25(3): 135–148.

Högström, John (2013) 'Does the Choice of Democracy Measure Matter? Comparisons between the Two Leading Democracy Indices, Freedom House and Polity IV'. *Government and Opposition* 48(2): 201–221.
Keating, Michael and Malcolm Harvey (2014) *Small Nations in a Big World: What Scotland Can Learn*. Edinburgh: Luath Press.
Lijphart, Arend (2012) *Patterns of Democracy: Government Forms and Performance in Thirty-Six Countries*. New Haven, CT: Yale University Press.
Lundberg, Thomas Carl (2007) *Proportional Representation and the Constituency Role in Britain*. Basingstoke: Palgrave Macmillan.
Lundberg, Thomas Carl (2013) 'Politics Is Still an Adversarial Business: Minority Government and Mixed-member Proportional Representation in Scotland and in New Zealand'. *British Journal of Politics and International Relations* 15(4): 609–625.
Lundberg, Thomas Carl (2014) 'Tensions Between Constituency and Regional Members of the Scottish Parliament Under Mixed-member Proportional Representation: A Failure of the New Politics'. *Parliamentary Affairs* 67(2): 351–370.
Lynch, Peter (2009) 'From Social Democracy Back to No Ideology? – The Scottish National Party and Ideological Change in a Multi-level Electoral Setting'. *Regional and Federal Studies* 19(4–5): 619–637.
McGann, Anthony J. (2006) *The Logic of Democracy: Reconciling Equality, Deliberation, and Minority Protection*. Ann Arbor: University of Michigan Press.
McMillan, Joyce and Ruth Fox (2010) *Has Devolution Delivered for Women?* London: Hansard Society and British Council Scotland.
Millar, David (2000) 'Scotland's Parliament: A Mini Westminster, or a Model for Democracy?'. In Alex Wright (ed.) *Scotland: The Challenge of Devolution*. Aldershot: Ashgate, pp. 14–26.
Miller, Raymond (2015) *Democracy in New Zealand*. Auckland: Auckland University Press.
Mitchell, James (2000) 'New Parliament, New Politics in Scotland'. *Parliamentary Affairs* 53(3): 605–621.
Mitchell, James (2010) 'The Narcissism of Small Differences: Scotland and Westminster'. *Parliamentary Affairs* 63(1): 98–116.
Morlino, Leonardo (2004) '"Good" and "Bad" Democracies: How to Conduct Research into the Quality of Democracy'. *Journal of Communist Studies and Transition Politics* 20(1): 5–27.
Munck, Gerardo L. (2016) 'What Is Democracy? A Reconceptualization of the Quality of Democracy'. *Democratization* 23(1):1–26.
Newton, K. (1982) 'Is Small Really So Beautiful? Is Big Really So Ugly? Size, Effectiveness, and Democracy in Local Government'. *Political Studies* 30(2): 190–206.
Nicolson, Stuart (2015) 'The Birth of Scotland's "New Politics"'. *BBC News*, 15 September. Available at: www.bbc.co.uk/news/uk-scotland-scotland-politics-34226810.
Ott, Dana (2000) *Small Is Democratic: An Examination of State Size and Democratic Development*. New York: Garland.
Powell, G. Bingham (2000) *Elections as Instruments of Democracy: Majoritarian and Proportional Visions*. New Haven, CT: Yale University Press.
Radical Independence Campaign (2014) 'New RIC campaign: "Britain Is for the Rich: Scotland Can Be Ours"'. 26 February. Available at: http://radicalindependence.org/2014/02/26/new-ric-campaign-britain-is-for-the-rich-scotland-can-be-ours/.
Reynolds, Andrew, Ben Reilly and Andrew Ellis (2005) *Electoral System Design: The New International IDEA Handbook*. Stockholm: International Institute for Democracy and Electoral Assistance.
Ringen, Stein (2007) *What Democracy Is For: On Freedom and Moral Government*. Princeton, NJ: Princeton University Press.
Roberts, Andrew (2010) *The Quality of Democracy in Eastern Europe: Public Preferences and Policy Reforms*. Cambridge: Cambridge University Press.

Sartori, Giovanni (1968) 'Political Development and Political Engineering'. In James D. Montgomery and Albert O. Hirschman (eds) *Public Policy*, vol. XVII. Cambridge, MA: Harvard University Press, pp. 261–298.
Scotsman (2006) 'Salmond Sees Scots in "Arc of Prosperity"'. 12 August. Available at: www.scotsman.com/news/salmond-sees-scots-in-arc-of-prosperity-1-1130200.
Scottish Constitutional Convention (1992) 'The Final Report of the Scottish Constitutional Convention'. In L. Paterson and D. McCrone (eds) *The Scottish Government Yearbook 1992*. Edinburgh: Unit for the Study of Government in Scotland, University of Edinburgh, pp. 84–97.
Scottish Government (2012) *Agreement between the United Kingdom Government and the Scottish Government on a referendum on independence for Scotland*. Edinburgh. Available at: www.scotland.gov.uk/About/Government/concordats/Referendum-on-independence.
Scottish Government (2013) *Scotland's Future: Your Guide to an Independent Scotland*. Edinburgh: Scottish Government.
Scottish Parliament (2015) 'The Electoral System'. Available at: www.scottish.parliament.uk/visitandlearn/Education/30313.aspx.
Shugart, Matthew Søberg and Wattenberg, Martin P. (2001) 'Mixed-Member Electoral Systems: A Definition and a Typology'. In Matthew Søberg Shugart and Martin P. Wattenberg (eds) *Mixed-Member Electoral Systems: The Best of Both Worlds?* Oxford: Oxford University Press, pp. 9–24.
Taylor, Brian (1999) *The Scottish Parliament*. Edinburgh: Edinburgh University Press.
Tierney, Stephen (2012) *Constitutional Referendums: The Theory and Practice of Republican Deliberation*. Oxford: Oxford University Press.
Veenendaal, Wouter P. and Jack Corbett (2015) 'Why Small States Offer Important Answers to Large Questions'. *Comparative Political Studies* 48(4): 527–549.
Watt, Nicholas (2011) 'Tony Blair's Scottish Nightmare Comes True as Alex Salmond Trounces Labour'. *The Guardian*, 6 May. Available at: www.theguardian.com/politics/wintour-and-watt/2011/may/06/snp-alexsalmond
Watt, Nicholas (2014) 'David Cameron Defends Decision to Allow Scottish Independence Vote'. *The Guardian*, 8 May. Available at: www.theguardian.com/politics/2014/may/08/david-cameron-defends-decision-scottish-independence-referendum.
Women for Independence (2015) 'Constitution'. Available at: www.womenforindependence.org/constitution.

4 Political parties in Scotland

Duncan McTavish

Introduction and background

From 1945, through the 1950s and 1960s, the Labour and Conservative parties dominated the political landscape in Scotland. The Conservatives' vote share between 1945 and 1970 varied between 38 and 41%, achieving just over 50% in 1955 (against 40–46% at UK level); that of Labour 44–49% (42–48% at UK level); the Liberals from 2% to 7%. A Scotland-only dimension barely registered until the by-election victory of the SNP in Hamilton in the mid-1960s. In the 1970 general election the SNP won over 11% of the popular vote. Since then the SNP has had a fluctuating presence among political parties in Scotland.

Supporting foundations of Scotland's main political parties

The political party environment post 1945 and into the 1970s and beyond has been likened by some to a semi-pillarization model (see Devine 2013) with class and religion and the associated organizational and group structures forming the key mainstays of support for the main parties. The Conservatives received significant class based support from middle-class voters as well as a bedrock of Protestant working-class voters often with strong connections to church (Church of Scotland) membership. Labour's pillars of support were class based too (urban working class) with work based trade union networks, but this conflated with the very large numbers of Labour voters, especially in west and central Scotland, adhering to the Roman Catholic church and its social and communal structures – this conflation of course makes it difficult to determine the most important vote determinant, class or religious faith. Another pillar of support was provided through the large densities of council housing built after the Second World War, often by Labour councils, to alleviate congestion, overcrowding and otherwise inadequate housing. Although rather broad-brush (since for example there were strong areas of Orange-Protestant tradition consistently voting Labour as well as leading Protestant church figures prominent in the Labour party), this characterization has some analytical value in explaining the foundational supports of the main political parties in Scotland at the time.

Largely missing from political party discourse was a Scottish-national dimension. (See Chapter 1 for an analysis of the historical context of this.)

Labour

Labour in Scotland in this period has been characterized as relatively low key ('docile' – see Cameron 2010: 268), with considerable breadth but little depth of support: having strong bases in councils, trade unions, parliamentary representation and so on, but contributing little heft to the party UK-wide, either in terms of personalities or leading thinkers. The party had a lower membership base population pro rata than Britain-wide Labour as a whole. Despite earlier commitment by the party to Scottish home rule, final movement towards support for devolution was simply a response to a threat from the Scottish National Party. Labour prime minister Harold Wilson set up the Kilbrandon Royal Commission on the Constitution in 1969 in the wake of rising support and by-election victories for both Scottish and Welsh nationalists (both the Report and Dissenting Memorandum of Kilbrandon made some very prescient comments and recommendations[1]). Progress towards devolution was either imposed by the UK leadership (instanced at a special party conference in Glasgow 1974), or was supported by those who if not quite outsiders were not quite among the party's leading or mainstream figures (e.g. Richard Crossman; Scottish MP John MacKintosh). When in 1972 a Scottish Assembly was organized to discuss the implications of the UCS crisis and home rule it was convened not by Labour but the Scottish Trades Union Congress, with strong representation from civic Scotland as well as business interests. Labour's position did change after the 1970s when the party found itself in opposition at Westminster, with some leading Labour personalities from Scotland becoming both major contributors to UK Labour and also serious proponents of devolution: figures such as John Smith, Gordon Brown and Donald Dewar. Smith and Brown both became party leaders; Brown was the UK prime minister and Dewar was the first Scottish first minister. However, even then it was a party still with a strong UK focus in its commitment to UK-wide tax and welfare spend uniformity and UK-wide party organizational structure.

Conservatives

The Conservatives' position on Scotland was rather different, superficially at least, with something of a Scottish tone. The First World War and the period up to World War II in 1939, illustrated the extremely close nexus between major business figures and interests in Scotland, the Conservative Party and the British state. Lord Weir (of the Weir engineering business) was wartime air minister, Sir James Lithgow (of Lithgow Shipbuilding) wartime controller of shipbuilding and later adviser to the Bank of England, Lords MacLay and Inverforth were wartime controllers of shipping, Sir Andrew Duncan was wartime controller of steel and a Bank of England adviser; and Sir Eric Geddes, with extensive railway interests, was a key figure in post-World War I governments (Foster 2001). So even if unionism was in the party's DNA (in fact it was formally the Unionist Party until 1965 when it joined with the Conservatives in England and Wales), this Scottish-unionist context provided the logic behind a semi nationalistic antipathy from some leading Scottish Tories, bemoaning the post-war Labour government's nationalization programme as a form of Whitehall centralism not attuned to Scottish needs. This view was voiced by leading Conservatives in Scotland, though of course such complaint did not extend to a commitment to home rule (Cameron 2010).

In policy terms, many aspects of the party's programmes in government were part of the mainstream, shared with Labour, on economic and social reconstruction in the 1950s and 1960s, particularly in the field of social (mainly council owned) housing growth, but in other aspects of welfare state and public sector growth too. Yet, like Labour, policy commitment was through a strong UK prism. This was typified, rather ironically, through the evolution of regional economic development policy. Here there were two broad imperatives. The first was the long term structural decline in the heavy engineering, steel, mining and shipbuilding bases of the Scottish economy. Although some of these industries were remarkably resilient in the post-World War II reconstruction period, many (e.g. shipbuilding) were increasingly uncompetitive against new foreign industry entrants. And these sectors still employed significant numbers at a time when the political salience of unemployment – and policies to keep this low – was high amongst the main political parties. The second imperative was the wider concern of UK governments and macroeconomic policy. Britain's new industries were overly concentrated in the Midlands and Southeast of England and expansion was threatened by overheating of the economy there, largely due to inflationary and cost pressures caused by labour supply shortages. Governments therefore favoured a dispersal programme with Scotland as a prime candidate for industrial relocation. Both these drivers – Scotland's reliance on economic sectors in long term decline and overheating elsewhere in Britain – provided the key motivation for regional development policy. Policy was clearly driven from UK central government, though often implemented through the Scottish Office Development Department. New growth and development areas were established (initiated by Conservatives but expanded dramatically by Labour to include all of Scotland, except Edinburgh, at a cost of £600 million), and the creation of a strip mill at Ravenscraig (funded through a £50 million subsidy to Colvilles) built to provide steel for a newly built car production plant at Linwood (to produce for Rootes) and a British Motor Corporation truck plant at Bathgate. These projects (in particular Ravenscraig and Linwood) involved interventions at the most senior level of British government, and in the case of Ravenscraig against the commercial judgment of the company.

As the Scottish dimension to politics surfaced from the late 1960s, the Conservatives' approach was in some senses similar to Labour's, that is a reaction to a perceived political threat, driven not by the party in Scotland but from the UK party. The 'Declaration of Perth' at the Conservatives' Scottish conference led to the creation of a constitutional committee, but this was very much a creation of the leader, Ted Heath, and resented by many in the party. And under Margaret Thatcher's leadership from the mid-1970s (with the party still in opposition) there was a firming up of an anti-home rule stance, sparking two major resignations – from Malcolm Rifkind and Alick Buchanan Smith – but no serious support for, nor any realization of the need to address the devolution issue. This starts to indicate differentiation from Labour's position. The Conservatives could be depicted above all else as a party of unionism with little to say about devolving power to Scotland.

Scottish National Party

Previous to the 1970s, the Scottish National Party (SNP) was a sideshow to the two-party political system in Scotland. It had no significant presence in democratic representation or in political institutions at local or central government level. It was essentially a small extra-parliamentary party with few financial resources, no full time employees (see Mitchell et al. 2011) and episodic successes, mainly at by-elections, for example in 1962 in West Lothian (gaining almost a quarter of the vote) and most notably a victory at Hamilton in 1966. It was outwith the mainstream in some other senses too: given the salience of class identification in politics in 1970, an activist survey in that year saw a very high proportion of activists not identifying with any class (internal SNP document, cited in Mitchell et al. 2011); even until well into the period when the SNP was part of the Scottish political firmament (i.e. the late 1990s), its hostility to Westminster and lack of a strategy for representation there set the party aside from the Scottish political mainstream until the mid-1970s, with little electoral or strategic focus. In the 1974 general election the party won eleven seats (30.4% of the vote), in effect keeping a minority Labour government in power then withdrawing that support when the government did not pursue legislation following a narrow Yes majority in the referendum (the majority gained was not sufficient after the insertion of an amendment in the referendum legislation). The party lost all but two of its seats and its vote share dropped to 17%. In many ways this was a junction for the SNP and the national chairman's (Billy Wolfe) report on the 1970s provided the explanatory framework for the position the party was in. He believed the Parliamentary group had 'reduced us to fundamentalist nationalist image – we have lost the social-democratic middle ground, and both of the main parties can point to us and say that we are either anti-Tory or anti-Labour' (Wolfe 1979, cited in Mitchell et al. 2011); he also cited the lack of discipline and behaviour of SNP MPs, strategic and political incoherence, and a lack of proper communication and structures between MPs and the party's National Executive Committee. In other words, it was not really a major force, lacked sufficient political credibility, had organizational and structural limitations and could be squeezed by the main political parties.

Change and new political opportunity structures

Major structural, societal and institutional change radically disturbed and altered the underpinnings of the political party system as outlined above. Change was not symmetrical in terms of timing and impact. Arguably the Conservatives were affected over a longer time period while the changing landscape for Labour was masked by its electoral showing in Scotland during the years of Conservative governments at Westminster in the 1980s and 1990s (see Table 4.1), and the SNP's increasing salience not becoming apparent until the creation of a devolved Parliament at Holyrood.

Scottish Conservatives

The Protestant working-class element of the Conservative vote declined from the 1960s, as did church membership and religion as an identifier in voting behaviour more generally (though not quite as quickly with the working-class Roman Catholic voter). Much of the leadership base of the Conservatives in Scotland had been industrially based and this gradually disappeared (along with the significance of the business

Table 4.1 UK general elections 1979–1997: party representation from Scotland

Year	Conservative	Labour	SNP	Liberal
1979	22	44	2	3
1983	21	41	2	8
1987	10	50	3	9
1992	11	49	3	9
1997	0	56	6	10

empires they represented), replaced by a leadership considered as 'anglicised lairds and aristocrats' (see Devine 1999) and out of touch with modern political reality for most in Scotland. In addition the housing estates created on the periphery of Scotland's major cities were foundations of Labour's support, while new suburban population clusters had a bigger impact in eroding urban support for the Conservatives rather than adding to the stock of new Conservative voters (ibid.). The strong Liberal presence (albeit with relatively few seats) in many parts of rural Scotland meant such areas were also off limits for the Conservatives. These contours of change to the Conservative's detriment were well in place – we now know – by the mid-1960s. As Table 4.1 shows, the Conservatives, while in power at Westminster from 1979 to 1997, were in serious decline in Scotland. Not surprisingly then, the party in Scotland exhibited two broad trends from the late 1970s. The first was a strand redolent of the Conservatism of the 1950s and 1960s, that is symbolism of an industrial base and the use of the Scottish Office to extract support for sectors under pressure from economic restructuring and deindustrialization. The Tory secretary of state for Scotland, George Younger, made it clear that the closing of Scotland's strip steel facility at Ravenscraig was a no-go area, for him a resigning matter. In a private interview with a journalist after demitting office he said:

> I don't actually recall saying that [about the Ravenscraig closure as a resigning matter] to Mrs Thatcher's face but it was clear to everybody ... the reasons for the closure of Ravenscraig were wrong ... this was the last bit of the true west of Scotland indigenous home based industry and it had to be preserved if possible.
> (Interview with Arnold Kemp, 1993, cited in Kemp 1993: 59)

As the 1980s progressed economic developments placed the Conservatives in a no-win situation (see Chapter 1). Interestingly, after Younger left government he joined the board of the Royal Bank of Scotland (RBS) and became chairman. His very proactive support of the bank's growth strategy was influenced by his pro-Scottish business inclinations, in many ways reminiscent of the Scottish Conservative–Unionist business nexus of the past, though we now know that much of RBS's growth was certainly not built on secure foundations (Fraser 2014).

The second trend, the converse of the 'symbolism of the past', the 'death of the old Tories' was the attempt to plot a new path forward for the Tories by the strong supporter of Margaret Thatcher, Michael Forsyth – to transplant Thatcherite networks into the Conservatives' Scottish operation. This was initiated with the appointment of Forsyth as chairman of the Scottish Conservative Party when he was a junior minister and Malcolm Rifkind as Secretary of State for Scotland – somewhat destabilizing since the Junior Minister was known as a strong Thatcher supporter (more unequivocally than Rifkind) and with back channel access to her (Kemp 1993). Forsyth became secretary of state for Scotland in 1995 but the party's fortunes declined even further and it was out of tune with wider political feeling in Scotland. Move forward a few years and any new opportunities created by the devolved Scottish Parliament were unlikely to prove advantageous for the Conservatives: of all the main parties in Scotland, they alone were against devolution and campaigns for constitutional change by the Scottish Constitutional Convention and others in the 1980s and 1990s; the party was out of sync with public opinion in the 1997 devolution referendum. Subsequently the Conservatives have found it difficult to find a meaningful voice in Holyrood. This has barely altered in the sixteen years since the Parliament's creation. Current Scottish leader Ruth Davidson's 'line in the sand' speech during her campaign for party leadership, arguing against any increased devolved powers, was dramatically reversed after the independence referendum. Currently the party is lagging behind the public mood, its stance on the Scottish national question contributing to its worst ever Scottish vote at the 2015 general election, winning one seat and throughout Scotland gaining only 14.9% of votes cast, almost 2% below its 2010 result. More recently it gained c. 22% of votes cast in the 2016 Holyrood election, though still less than half the MSPs of the leading party.

Scottish Labour

Labour's changing landscape and the undermining of its support has been explained by the diminution of its traditional bases of support, that is the loss of its industrial, trade union class base (with some commentators also accentuating the loss of working-class Catholic support), the demise of its council housing fiefdoms, the ending of the party's power base in local councils. The first of these is neither new nor unique to Labour in Scotland. Throughout the UK, working-class voters have loosened ties to Labour. In 1966, 69% of manual workers voted Labour, by 1985 only 45% did; between 1945 and the end of the 1950s, around 60% of skilled manual workers supported Labour but by the mid-1980s only 34% did (Crewe 1986) – this was temporarily and partially reversed for a short period under New Labour from 1997 to 2005.

The decoupling of working-class voting and Labour in Scotland is evident. In the 2011 Holyrood election Labour trailed the nationalists by 14% among Scots who identified themselves as working class (and 19% by those who qualified as working class by official criteria); the SNP was the party of choice for trade unionists too (Maxwell 2013). Those identifying as Catholics (especially working-class), a strong bedrock of Labour voting up to the 1980s (see Devine 2013) were also voting SNP in 2011 (Maxwell 2013), though this is conflated with decoupling of working-class voting and Labour more generally. Added to this of course has been the long term decline of industrial and engineering sectors, where traditionally trade union density and institutional linkages to Labour have been close. While this trend occurred throughout Britain, deindustrialization was more intense in Scotland and here it was accompanied by the beginning of serious pressure for devolution and the perceived failure of London governments, especially in the 1980s, to address or deal with the consequences (Philips 2008); interestingly such pressure was initially led not by Labour but by the trade unions, especially the Scottish Trades Union Congress, typically well ahead of Labour in arguing the case for devolution. At present, the trade union–UK Labour link has loosened somewhat in Scotland with unions in the areas most likely to be unionized (in the public sector); for example the Public and Commercial Services Union in the Scottish Government and Unison in the NHS have devolved structures and Scottish-level bargaining units, leaving open the possibility of developing links with the SNP.

The dramatic and rapid growth of social housing in Scotland from the 1950s, the vast majority of this under democratically, politically controlled councils, was important for Labour. Although this growth was strongly supported by Conservative governments too, it was local councils which controlled the publicly subsidized development and were responsible for building, allocation, management and maintenance of the housing stock. Given Scotland's housing need this presented a strong power base for Labour, a significant force in local government, particularly since it was in largely Labour controlled urban areas where council house building was proportionally most significant. The scale of council house building in Scotland was substantial. From 1945 to 1980, 518,000 houses were completed by the public sector (overwhelmingly councils) in Scotland, against 2,720,000 in England and Wales. The Scottish figure was significantly higher relative to population than in England and Wales (English 1983). Some 86% of all houses built in Scotland between 1945 and 1965 were in the public sector (Devine 1999). Given such a scale, it is logical and natural to assume that the sale of council stock to sitting tenants introduced in the 1980s, thereby removing council control, would weaken this power base; this has been a key argument of some writers on Labour's decline in Scotland (e.g. Hassan and Shaw 2012). The sale of council housing was as popular in Scotland as elsewhere in the UK, with the largest sales of houses in the period 1980–2005 in Glasgow (42,000), Fife (30,000), South Lanarkshire (30,000), Edinburgh (25,000), Aberdeen (17,000), and Falkirk (15,000). However, perhaps this loss of power base argument should not be over-stressed. A significant stock of housing remained in council hands, often in Labour's heartlands. The proportion of stock sold was 26% in Glasgow; 50% in South Lanarkshire; 48% in South Ayrshire; 48% in East Dunbartonshire; 47% in West Lothian; 46% in Fife; 40% in East Lothian; 38% in Edinburgh; and 38% in Renfrewshire. And while some of the remaining stock was subsequently lost to council control due to stock transfer to housing associations (e.g. in Glasgow), this was not universal practice (Scottish Executive 2006).

With regard to local government, Labour's power base was still substantial at the end of the twentieth and into the early years of the twenty-first century. In 1999 it had overall control of fifteen councils (out of a total of thirty-two); in 2003, thirteen. But this was based on the disproportionate first-past-the-post-voting system: in 2003, Labour held 51% of all council seats on only 33% of the popular vote. The introduction of a proportional representation system (the Single Transferable Vote, STV), agreed by Labour as part of its coalition agreement with the Liberal Democrats at Holyrood, altered this completely and irreversibly. The first election using STV saw Labour with an overall majority in only two councils, increasing to four in 2012.

What these explanations don't address is why, given the party's significant position at the start of devolution in Scotland, was there no narrative of renewal or regrowth? An obvious explanation can be found in Labour's early success in electoral terms in post-devolution Scotland: the creation of the Scottish Parliament, a job achieved, rewarded by electoral success.

The first Holyrood election saw Labour as the dominant party, winning fifty-six seats overall (fifty-three constituency seats based on 38.8% of the vote and three regional seats on 33.6%), with its nearest rival the SNP on thirty-five seats (seven constituency seats on 28.7% of the vote and twenty-eight regional seats on 27.26%) (see Table 4.2).

Labour had achieved a devolved parliament and was in a leading position there, mirrored by their Scottish performance in Westminster elections, perhaps contributing to a mind set that believed there was no need for change. The Westminster election in 2001 almost mirrored their 1997 triumph, winning fifty-five seats (down one from 1997) with 43.3% of votes cast (against 45.6% in 1997). Every Holyrood election since then has seen Labour's position weaken. The most recent in 2016 saw Labour pushed into third place.

In Scotland there was little appetite for much of the Brown–Blair New Labour agenda implemented at Westminster, especially marketization. There were no Foundation Hospitals, little of the competition and choice model in health introduced in England, and the use of league tables in schools was much lower key in Scotland;

Table 4.2 Scottish parliamentary election 1999: main parties' constituency and regional representation

Party	Central Scotland	Glasgow	Highlands and Islands	Lothians	Mid-Scotland and Fife	Northeast Scotland	South Scotland	West Scotland
Labour	9(c)	10(c)	1(c) 3(r)	8(c)	6(c)	4(c)	6(c)	9(c)
Total	9	10	4	8	6	4	6	9
SNP	5(r)	4(r)	2(c) 2(r)	3(r)	2(c) 3(r)	2(c) 4(r)	1(c) 3(r)	4(r)
Total	5	4	4	3	5	6	4	4
Cons.	1(r)	1(r)	2(r)	2(r)	3(r)	3(r)	4(r)	2(r)
Total	1	1	2	2	3	3	4	2
Lib Dem	1(r)	1(r)	5(c)	1(c) 1(r)	1(c) 1(r)	3(c)	2(c)	1(r)
Total	1	1	5	2	2	3	2	1

Note: (c) = constituency seat; (r) = regional seat.

Scotland retained comprehensive education within local authority control to a much greater extent than England. But nor was there much in the way of renewed political or policy initiative as an alternative to the New Labour agenda. It has been suggested that key figures in Labour with strong Scottish connections (mainly Gordon Brown) only pushed for minimal adoption of the New Labour agenda on the Scottish party, but the 'deal' was that Labour in Scotland would refrain from seeking change in the constitutional relationship between the party in Scotland and at UK level – though the evidence of any motivation to alter the party's state-wide/sub-state regional structure is somewhat patchy (Hopkin and Bradbury 2006). There was a perception that Labour in Scotland had difficulty mapping out areas of policy distinctiveness which were both popular and seen as independent of UK Labour's preferences. The eventual adoption of two headline policy initiatives, which have subsequently become distinctive to Holyrood, highlights the difficulty of setting a path different from UK Labour. These are the abolition of higher education fees and the introduction of free personal care.

Scottish Labour and higher education fees

The Blair government introduced fees for higher education students in 1998, i.e. prior to the establishment of Holyrood, so wholly applicable in Scotland. The Liberal Democrat partner in the coalition with Labour in Edinburgh had a policy of no higher education fees and indicated this was a coalition deal breaker (somewhat ironic in light of Conservative–Liberal Democrat coalition government policy on this after the 2010 UK election). The Cubie report commissioned by the government in Edinburgh recommended a student endowment rising to £3,000, but not being paid upfront, rather collected after the student was in employment and earning over £25,000 p.a. After much to-ing and fro-ing between Holyrood and New Labour at Westminster a much lower employment earnings figure was accepted (£10,000).

Scottish Labour and introduction of free personal care

The second policy initiative was free personal care, that is personal residential care for the elderly without means testing and with no personal charge being incurred. This policy was recommended by the Sutherland report (the Royal Commission on Long Term Care, chaired by Sir Stewart Sutherland) and rejected by the UK government. However, Scotland's first minister Henry McLeish was a supporter, and in 2001 the Scottish Executive's support for the policy was announced. McLeish faced resistance from Labour colleagues in Westminster. This was highlighted by emails later released under Freedom of Information. For example the Care Development Group, the body set up to plan the policy's implementation, required statistics from the UK Department of Social Security (DSS), but the request was rejected. An email between officials inside the Scottish Executive noted: 'I think it is fair to assume that if they are not prepared to co-operate on paper the chances of DSS sending someone to Edinburgh to give us a presentation must be slim. Politics appear to be key here' (www.heraldscotland.com/secret-files-reveal-bitter-labour-infighting-over-flagship-policy-on-free-personal-care-1.828849 (accessed 13/6/2015).

Labour MP Alistair Darling withheld £23 million in attendance allowance (a reserved benefit), thereby forcing the Holyrood government to meet this from their own funds. This provoked a letter from McLeish to Darling:

> Our opponents will say this is £23m taken from Scotland and spent on increasing benefits to people in England. ... would give [comfort] to those who oppose the devolution settlement ... or who argue that conflict between Westminster and Edinburgh is inevitable within the current settlement.
> (www.heraldscotland.com/secret-files-reveal-bitter-labour-infighting-over-flagship
> -policy-on-free-personal-care-1.828849)

In reality, policy implementation was more complex. There were senior figures within the Holyrood government who had doubts about the policy on grounds of cost and the issue of universalism versus targeting greatest need (e.g. health minister Susan Deacon and environment minister Sam Galbraith), but it was to prove a popular policy and the government's opponents in Holyrood could label this as an obstacle from a UK Labour government placed in the way of a Scottish (Labour) initiated policy, with little in the way of reply from Scottish Labour.

Scottish National Party

Devolved institutional governance has created a political opportunity structure for the SNP. That a Scottish legislature within a devolved UK state should present opportunities for a sub-state party like the SNP is hardly surprising. Although the party had a locus in Westminster, the Holyrood Parliament was clearly its main arena. The six SNP MPs elected to Westminster in 1997 all stood as candidates in the first Holyrood election, were elected there, and five of them stood down at the Westminster election in 2001 – in contrast, very small proportions of Labour MPs (or Lib Dem MPs) stood for the Scottish Parliament. This should be viewed alongside the SNP's clearer policy commitment to the devolved legislature in the late 1990s – in contrast to the bruising experience of the 1979 referendum when the party toyed with some forms of civil disobedience, had internal dissent on an organized basis around some aspects of policy (from the 79 group), and did not participate in the cross-party Campaign for a Scottish Assembly in the 1980s (seeing this as a diversion from the aim of independence). But after a period of leadership under Alex Salmond the party shifted to support the cross-party devolution campaign in the wake of the upcoming referendum following Labour's election victory in 1997 (Mitchell et al. 2011; Lynch 2002). Coupled with the earlier support for 'independence in Europe', it was now less easy to portray the SNP as a narrow nationalist party outwith the political mainstream. The electoral system for the devolved Parliament (additional member system, with a number of MSPs elected Westminster-style by first-past-the-post in constituencies, the others on a regional list basis, thereby giving some proportionality to the system) established the SNP with a national representation base which would have been impossible on a constituency-only vote (see Table 4.2).

An important aspect of the ability to capitalize on the new opportunities created was the professionalization of the party (well documented by Mitchell et al. 2011). Traditionally the party's branch structure was the basis of its membership growth in the 1960s, helping strengthen the party on the ground (as distinct from 'the party in central office' or the 'party in power' according to Mair's classification [Mair 1994). Yet, the dynamic of gaining an electoral power base helped stimulate internal party reforms (spearheaded by the leader John Swinney after a disappointing performance in the second devolved parliamentary election in 2003) and this represented a definite shift towards an electoral professional party defined as: greater influence of personalized leadership; reduced role for party members; less of an ideological definition of political purpose (Panebianco 1988). The reforms included a reduction in the size of the National Executive Committee (NEC), the introduction of one member one vote (OMOV) for leader, deputy leader and candidate selection (though the latter was increasingly centralized in terms of who could be approved to stand), the creation of a party leader rather than national convenor, and the appointment of a business convenor not from the NEC but by the party leader. This gave power to 'non aligned party members' less likely to be associated with particular tendencies (see Mitchell 1990; Rose 1964). It could be argued that prior to post-2003 reforms the reduction in ideological commitment was already in evidence in the pragmatic gradualism under Salmond's leadership, culminating in support for a devolved legislature though without altering the long term aim of independence. Many of these reforms were not always universally accepted or popular, but the professionalization and central party discipline has been a feature of the SNP since, though much of this may be due to the seeming rewards resulting in electoral success from minority government at Holyrood in 2007, to majority in 2011, and spectacular success at the 2015 UK general election. It is unknown whether a severe or sustained downturn in support would question the trend towards the electoral professional party underpinned by central party discipline.

A profile of Scotland's main political parties

Members and elected representatives

Membership levels

Accurate membership counts of political parties are not always easy or straightforward to determine. For obvious reasons, parties will wish to minimize the publicity attached to declining numbers. There are also difficulties with the official reporting of membership. While the Political Parties, Elections and Referendums Act (2002) requires registered parties to submit financial statements to the Electoral Commission, not all submit membership statements on a regular basis; membership numbers based on financial returns may be inferences. There may also be complications when assessing how up to date parties' own figures may be – e.g. there may be a time lag between lapsed members' direct debit termination and the members disappearing from the membership lists and so on. There is also the conflation of social club membership and political membership, where the inclusion of the former would give an unrealistic inflation of party members – in Scotland this would apply mainly to Labour. More recently, parties are offering a special membership category (registered supporter status) mainly for leadership or candidate selection. It remains to be seen if such supporters convert to increased membership numbers or longer standing support. Finally, recent research on party membership has been produced by the House of Commons Library and though it includes information on SNP membership, it does not disaggregate the main state wide parties' data for Scotland (Keen 2015).

Membership of Scottish Labour has not been officially released by the party since 2008. In that year it was reported at 17,000, down from a peak of 30,000 immediately prior to the 1997 UK general election (BBC 2008). The decline of Labour membership in Scotland is particularly significant given its generation-long political dominance in the country. Detailed research of UK Labour membership has shown that the average size Constituency Labour Party (CLP) was lowest in Scotland (ranked last throughout UK) with 385 members in 1997, reducing to 223 in 2010 (Pemberton and Wickham-Jones 2013). However, the latter figure may have been inflated: in that year, just over 13,000 ballot papers were issued for the (UK) leadership election to Scottish members but some members could receive several ballot papers (e.g as parliamentarians, members of trade unions, etc.) so this figure would probably be an overestimate. Other estimates have put the figure at around or under 10,000. During the 2015 election campaign, the leader of Scottish Labour claimed 'around 20,000'. One of the candidates for leader (Kezia Dugdale) in June 2015 claimed 15,000 (*Sunday Herald*, 21/6/2015), though whether this includes social club affiliations (who do not have membership or voting rights) is not stated. UK Labour experienced a significant increase in membership after the 2010 general election and especially during the period leading up to the election of a new leader and deputy leader (along with the introduction of a low cost 'registered supporter' category specifically for voting in the leader and depute leader elections).

Similarly, the Conservatives in Scotland do not officially publish membership figures. In 2012, a membership of 12,000 (this is roughly a Scottish-UK population pro rata figure based on the published UK Conservative membership figure of that year – see Keen 2015) was claimed (www.opendemocracy.net/ourkingdom/adam-ramsay/quick-note-on-party-memberships-in-uk (accessed 20/6/2015). However, the Conservative's Scottish Policy Forum, resurrected in 2012 as part of the Scottish Conservatives' policy review process, produced 'monthly consultation papers on a range of devolved and reserved topics which we send to a 1200 strong database of members' (www.scottishconservatives.com/policy/scottishpolicyforum (accessed 20/6/2015). Information received in interview with a former party chairman and Scottish Office minister puts membership higher than this but considerably below the 12,000 figure: 'When I was party chairman [in the mid-1990s] we created the first data base and the membership figure then was 20,000. It is tiny now, I would estimate about one fifth of that' (Personal interview A, February 2015). This would give a membership figure of around 4,000.

The Liberal Democrats in Scotland claim to have 'around 3,000 members' (cited in Ramsay 2015), which is population proportionate to figures cited for UK Liberal Democrat membership (Keen 2015).

The two parties which have seen the largest rise in membership have been the Scottish Greens and the SNP, both of which are non-unionist and supported the Yes campaign in the 2014 referendum. Both of these parties publish membership figures. The Scottish Greens claim a current membership of 8,000, up from around 2,000 before the September 2014 referendum, itself an advance on the 2013 figure of 1,200. The SNP membership in 2002 was 16,000; it dipped to 9,500 after the 2003 Scottish election and has risen every year since, reaching 24,000 in 2012. Post-referendum it increased substantially, standing at 93,000 in January 2015 (Keen 2015), increasing to 100,000 prior to the 2015 UK general election (*Scotsman* 2015).

Members' motivation

In terms of what motivates people to become party members, there is clearly a requirement for empirical research on Scotland's political parties, particularly in the context of the SNP and Green membership increases. The literature and thinking on membership motivation focuses on the incentives and benefits which people perceive or expect to derive from party membership. Incentives include the desire to seek office or other aspects of career advancement or the desire to share an ideological or values space with like minded people; altruistic or some form of emotional attachment (see e.g. Whiteley et al. 2006; Whiteley and Seyed 2002; Seyed and Whiteley 1992). Research on SNP membership indicates the ideological driver (of seeking independence as well as the advancement of other Scottish interests) to be a strong motivator as well as the idea of pursuing this within a collective network. The existence of a devolved Parliament in Scotland may also provide a context-specific environment giving an institutional presence ('tangible localism') and greater proximity to political activity, consistent with other desired outcomes and incentives. Research on party activists also indicates that holding office in the party is considered a discrete category of activism representing a somewhat different dimension to other forms of activity like campaigning or attending party meetings (Mitchell et al. 2011). This raises the possibility that some activists may well have the key focus of office-seeking as their main membership motivation. While there is little empirical research on Labour and Conservative members in Scotland, interviews with senior party figures do tend to indicate what the key motivations may be. According to a senior Labour Party member and activist:

> I would say that individual members [i.e. distinct from affiliated members – trade unionists mainly] have become younger – their principal purpose in joining is to follow a professional career in the party – many have a university background. They are the modern activists. Activists used to be working class. Over the last ten years there has been a major shift from working class activists.
> (Personal interview B, March 2015)

In interview with a former Scottish Conservative Party chairman and Scottish Office minister, different motivations were evident:

The members' key interest is who is in control not at Holyrood but at No. 10 [Downing Street] – members that is, but leaders [in Scotland] different. Supporters and members have no input on policy. Only real thing members do now is candidate selection. Generally members are less active than in the past. Media events are important. Now for Conservative voters the postal vote is huge, so candidates don't need members any more. There are big fund raising events, so there the membership base is not important either.

(Personal interview A, February 2015)

Composition of party members

Beyond these figures some general comments can be made about party members. There is some research on party membership internationally, on a UK basis too, and some of this is of relevance to Scotland. The most up-to-date extant research on the Scottish context relates to the SNP, the most recent of which is Mitchell et al. (2011). These sources are used, as is material gained from a small number of private interviews with leading members of the main parties in Scotland.

In general, members of political parties tend to be more middle class, older and more male dominated than the population as a whole – research indicates this to be an international phenomenon (Young 2013; Scarrow and Gezgor 2010). All the parties in Scotland have over a long time period seen the age profile of their membership become older, not younger. Mitchell et al. (2011) show that the SNP's membership average in 1997 was older than Labour's in Scotland. The demographic skewing towards older age groups appears to apply to all political parties in Scotland. What is less clear (at least until the recent surge in SNP membership post referendum) is whether this is newer recruits being older – Mitchell et al. raise this possibility given the increased membership of the SNP since 2003, though a rather different interpretation of the Conservatives' membership profile was given in a private interview:

It seems to me that membership of the Tory Party in Scotland ... has continuities with my time there [i.e. the mid-1990s] ... anecdotally, but I observe this too ... many of the current members were members when I was there, a bit younger then obviously.

(Personal interview A, February 2015)

The SNP with its post-referendum surge in membership claimed that under-30s make up 21% of members in December 2014 (before the referendum the figure was 10%) (www.snp.org/media-centre/news/2014/dec/new-snp-members (accessed 14/1/2015).

Gender and party membership in Scotland

In terms of gender balance of party members, research indicated that in 2008 the SNP had amongst the lowest ratio of female-to-male members of the main political parties in Scotland, with males outnumbering females by 2 to 1 (Mitchell et al. 2011). By 2014, males still accounted for two thirds of party members. Reasonably up-to-date figures show almost 40% of Conservative members are female, with 31% for Labour and just under 30% for the Liberal Democrats (Keen 2015). The SNP claims that its post-referendum membership increase saw, by December 2014, females representing 44% of total party membership (www.snp.org/media-centre/news/2014/dec/new-snp-members (accessed 14/1/2015).

Representing and giving voice to members: the case of female elected representatives

Promoting member representation and voice is generally considered positive and progressive, enhancing party democracy. This can present some complexities in terms of broader systemic representation, which can be highlighted by the case of gender representation. Female under-representation among the main parties' elected representatives is well documented. Women have accounted for a reducing proportion of MSPs in the Scottish Parliament over time, currently standing (2015) at under 35% of the total. There are significant variations between parties, with women accounting for 27% of SNP MSPs, while the figures are 47% for Labour, 60% for the Conservatives, 80% for the Liberal Democrats and 50% for the Greens. The latter two have small numbers of MSPs (five and two respectively), so few conclusions can be drawn. At the 2015 general election in Scotland, 36% of SNP candidates were women, with Labour at 27%, the Conservatives 15%, the Liberal Democrats 27%, the Greens 42%, and UKIP 7%. Currently 34% of Scottish MPs are women, all of them SNP (Kenny et al. 2015). Finally, less than 25% of all councillors in Scotland in 2012 were female (Denver et al. 2012).

However, attempts to address female under-representation through membership democracy and voice mechanisms can have unintended consequences for political parties when seen through broader representation parameters. Party members and activists in most parties are more likely to be male – and this is an international phenomenon (Young 2013). Arguably, this may build in a bias when candidate selection occurs; if membership supply (the candidate selection supply pool) is not gender balanced, then the outcome, i.e. candidate selection, is likely to reflect this. Giving greater member influence may not address this imbalance, leading to a 'representation deficit': candidates offered to the electorate as a whole may not reflect voter composition, which is broadly 50–50 female to male.

Women's under-representation concerns all the main parties in Scotland. All have various initiatives to encourage more women candidates and leaders, with the Conservatives and Liberal Democrats at the 'softer' end of support (e.g. leadership and development programmes). Labour, the SNP and the Greens are more inclined to have 'harder' positive action initiatives (e.g. rules and procedures on gender balance among candidates for selection). Yet, addressing the issue via internal party member democracy may be ineffective, given that members and activists are more likely to be male. This can lead to party leaderships taking direct action over the heads of party members to achieve more equal representation outcomes. Scottish Labour has traditionally led the way here with the use of all-women shortlists and other measures (including 'twinning' of constituencies to ensure male and female candidates within geographical and constituency boundaries), and this was highly effective in increasing the proportion of women MSPs in the first Scottish Parliament in 1999. The SNP was somewhat laggard in this regard when the party conference in 1999 rejected a leadership attempt to move in this direction. More recently, the party has taken major steps to promote more female representation. Soon after her election as party leader and first minister, Nicola Sturgeon, in a high-profile move, gender-balanced her Cabinet. At the party's spring 2015 conference it voted in favour of empowering the NEC to introduce all-women shortlists for a 2016 Holyrood election constituency seat where the sitting candidate stands down, and introduced balanced regional lists to ensure equal numbers of male and female candidates on these lists. But the party leadership and NEC backed off from requiring regional lists to be 'zipped' (i.e. the alternation of males and females on the list as followed by Scottish Greens), leaving the possibility of party membership ranking women in lower positions on the list. This may indicate the leadership's inability to gain support for this firmer equality proposal – interestingly party officials did not disclose voting numbers and the debate was held in closed session with media excluded (Carrell 2015). Nonetheless, 46% of SNP constituency candidates and 45% of regional list candidates for the 2016 Holyrood election were female (www.holyrood.com/articles/inside-politics/snp-releases-candidate-lists-ahead-2016-election (accessed 21/10/15). Added to the Scottish Labour leader's commitment that at least 50% of Labour candidates for Holyrood 2016 will be female (www.scotsman.com/news/politics/top-stories/labour-seeks-gender-balance-in-2016-candidates-1-3865800 (accessed 21/10/15), it was anticipated that the proportion of women MSPs from 2016 will be higher than the 35% in the 2011–16 Holyrood Parliament. However the post 2016 Scottish Parliament's proportion of female MSPs remains the same as 2011, due to the relative success of the Conservatives who had low numbers of women candidates.

Are elected representatives, politicians, a class apart?

A broader aspect of the representativeness of elected politicians is the extent to which their background reflects and represents the experiences of the general voting public. That elected representatives are not a cross-section of the population they serve has long been recognized. Although much Labour and Conservative parliamentary representation in Scotland from 1945 to the 1980s followed class stereotypes (that is, more working-class representation among Labour, more business and farming amongst Conservative MPs) for both parties the largest single category of occupational background prior to election was professional. Although there have been significant changes in the past three or four decades, MPs are more highly educated than the population as a whole, come from professional socio-economic groups, and are more likely to be white and male.

There are similar trends in the Scottish Parliament (Keating and Cairney 2006), though some substantial differences: for example, unsurprisingly, Oxbridge educated representatives are not significant (nor have they been for Scottish MPs since 1945). Glasgow University, followed by Edinburgh University, is the most commonly cited university among MSPs with degrees (70% have degrees) (Scottish Parliament Information Centre – SPICe 2011).

More recently another form of unrepresentativeness has been the subject of study and concern, that is the rise of the 'professional politician'. This is someone who has his or her main career background and experience in 'political employment', that is as a party researcher, policy adviser, party official, employment in politically connected think tanks or research organizations, etc., prior to becoming an elected representative. While there is a growing body of research measuring this development and studying the impacts (which this chapter draws upon and updates with the most current data from the 2015 general election), there is relatively little explanation why this development and growth has taken place.

The rise of the professional politician would appear to be linked to the shifting nature of the main – mass – political parties. As the links between political parties and their societal-organizational bases have fractured, then these bases are no longer capable of providing a supply chain of candidate material to the same extent as previously. Added to this, catch all and cartelization of parties (see below) has narrowed the range of ideological and policy differences so it has been argued the goals of politics become self-referential, professional and technocratic (Mair 2013). The professional politician has come to typify this, certainly among many commentators (e.g. McKinstry 2014; Groves 2012; Wright 2012; Oborne 2007; Aaronovitch 2004). Neither the uniqueness nor the novelty of this should be overstated. The concept was well known to Weber in his distinction between those who live *from* politics as distinct from those who live *for* politics (Gunlicks 1978); it exists in most advanced democracies though looks very different from country to country (Borchert and Zeiss 2003).

It also begs a question. Why should politics be different from other aspects of occupational and professional life? Many areas of activity have been professionalized as economies develop and career paths are formed (Perkin 1988). It is also recognized that there may be democratic value in the professional political class. Although unrepresentative in descriptive terms, the professional political class may improve substantive representation (that is, representing the interests of certain groups in society if they possess policy or political processing, advocacy or other skills (Riddell 2011; HC 239 2010; Saward 2010). So there has been the emergence of a sizeable grouping among elected representatives who could be termed professional politicians by their experience and personal profile gained prior to election.

The current position in Scotland, in terms of occupational background can be seen below. The data are provided for current MEPs, MSPs, candidates and elected MPs for Scottish constituencies at the 2015 Westminster general election (see Table 4.3); figures are also given for each party (Table 4.4). A slightly different categorization has been used from previous studies. The 'political/political friendly' category has not included some occupations present in extant studies, for example journalist, unless the individual's journalism was directly related to a political party; 'manager' has not

Table 4.3 Scotland 2015: background of MEPs, MSPs, candidates for Scottish seats in the UK election, and MPs elected

Occupational background	MEPs (2015)	MSPs (2015)	General election 2015 candidates	MPs (2015)
Political/friendly career[1]	3 (50% of total)	34 (27%)	41 (14%)	12 (20%)
Professional[2]	1 (16%)	37 (28%)	65 (23%)	17 (29%)
Business owner/director/ business consultant	2 (34%)	11 (9%)	35 (12%)	6 (10%)
Manager		10 (7%)	30 (10%)	7 (12%)
Council officer		7 (5%)	5 (2%)	1 (2%)
Third sector		8 (6%)	26 (9%)	6 (10%)
Journalist		6 (5%)	12 (4%)	4 (7%)
Other[3]		16 (12%)	74 (26%)	5 (8%)
Total	6	129	288 (+20 unknown)	59

Source: Party and individual candidates's websites; local press; Scottish Parliament elected members information.

Notes: [1]This category includes political researcher, full time party worker including employed election agent, full time councilor.
[2]Includes lawyer, teacher or lecturer, medical professional, social worker, civil servant.
[3] Includes police officer, member of armed services, fire fighter, farmer, fisherman, student, manual worker.

distinguished between public and private sectors, since this was not the purpose of the exercise; 'third sector' was included as a category since a significant number fall into this specific occupational area; 'other' is broader than some previous categorizations used – this is justified since the purpose is to indicate the extent of representation from a broad range of occupational backgrounds rather than, for example, the somewhat dated and ill defined 'blue and white collar'.

The figures in Table 4.3 illustrate very few differences in the % categories for MEPs, MSPs, candidates for Westminster and elected MPs, except that the 'political/friendly' category is lower and 'other' higher for Westminster candidates. Arguably this could indicate less willingness by those in the professional politician category to stand for unwinnable seats. For successful candidates at all levels the 'political/friendly' category is significant at 20% for MPs, 27% for MSPs and 50% for MEPs, though with the low number of MEPs – only 6 – caution is required with this figure. The largest category for all representatives and candidates is 'professional'. Those with a business, managerial or third sector background are also significant and broadly similar across MSPs, candidates and MPs (from 9–12%). 'Others' are lower for MPs than MSPs, perhaps showing a greater occupational diversity for the latter.

There are differences between the parties as shown in Table 4.4. The aggregated figures for MEPs, MSPs, Westminster candidates and MPs indicates 'Political/friendly' is significant for all the main parties, but there is a substantial difference between the SNP at 17%, Labour at 34% and the Conservatives at 11%. An explanation for this difference may be that Labour has until recently been the party of incumbency in Scotland, therefore offering more career opportunities for career politicians – by this reasoning if the SNP's progress since forming a government in 2007 was to continue,

Table 4.4 Scotland 2015: background of MEPs, MSPs, candidates for Scottish seats at UK election by party affiliation

	SNP	Lab.	Cons.	Lib Dem	Greens	UKIP
Political/friendly career	21 (17% of total)	33 (34%)	8 (11%)	6 (9%)	1 (3%)	1 (4%)
Professional	37 (31%)	25 (26%)	23 (31%)	10 (16%)	7 (22%)	1 (4%)
Business owner/director/ business consultant	12 (10%)	5 (5%)	18 (24%)	7 (11%)	2 (6%)	4 (17%)
Manager	18 (15%)	7 (7%)	5 (7%)	8 (13%)	1 (3%)	1 (4%)
Council officer	5 (4%)	6 (6%)	1 (1%)	0	0	0
Third sector	9 (7%)	7 (7%)	0	11 (17%)	6 (19%)	0
Journalist	8 (7%)	4 (4%)	3 (4%)	2 (3%)	1 (3%)	0
Other	11 (9%)	11 (11%)	17 (23%)	20 (31%)	14 (44%)	16 (70%)
Total	121	98	75	64	32 (+11 unknown)	23 (+9 unknown)

Source: Party and individual candidates's web sites; local press; Scottish Parliament elected members information.

then its numbers from this background would increase. Conversely, the relatively low figure for Conservatives may reflect the lack of prospects for the party in Scotland for some time now. Unsurprisingly, the three main parties have high proportions of professionals, though at 26% for Labour this is overshadowed by the percentage of their representatives and candidates from the 'political/friendly' category. From a business background, the Conservatives have the highest figure (24%), reflecting the party's traditional base; the comparable Labour and SNP figures here are 5% and 10% respectively. Of SNP representatives, 15% are from a management background, significantly higher than Labour and the Conservatives (7% for each). 'Other' is relatively low for SNP and Labour – 9% and 11% – but substantially higher for all other parties, again showing greater occupational diversity and/or lack of an opportunity structure therefore disinterest from those with a political career backdrop.

Party type

Mass, catch-all and cartel parties

The 'ideal' mainstream party type in a democracy has long been considered the mass party, with a large and relatively open membership base, leadership accountable and responsive to that base and internal party democracy. There is also a normative aspect to this, as found in some intergovernmental and supranational codes of practice and guidelines as well as in a range of development programmes. For example:

- 'Venice Commission' – European Commission for Democracy's Code of Practice in the Field of Political Parties (www.venice.coe.int/docs/2009/cdl-ad%282009%29021-e-pdf);
- Parliamentary Assembly of the Council of Europe (PACE) (http://assembly.coe.int/main.asp?Link=//documents/workingdocs/doc10/edoc12107.htm);
- USAID (http://serbia-montenegro.usaid.gov/code/navigate.php?Id=23).

(All accessed 27/3/2015)

However, if we look at the electoral purposes of parties, changing links between leaders, members and representation over the last thirty years or so, and relate these to political parties in Scotland, it can be seen that this ideal type is, at least in part, out of step with some developments on the ground. In advanced industrial democracies the mass political party (with as the name implies a large membership base) has been a key instrument of democratic representation, aggregating and articulating the interests of broadly identified groups and individuals in society. Typically, left of centre social democratic parties have an interest and support base clustering around organized labour and working-class interests; conservative parties around those identified as belonging to higher socio-economic categories, property owning, etc. (Webb et al. 2002). This of course does not exclude an appeal to articulating the interests of groups and categories of voters outwith this core. Though this is a somewhat crude categorization, it can be observed to a large extent in the positioning of Scotland's main political parties at least until the 1970s (see above). But over a period of time, the mass party in Scotland (as in other advanced democracies) has been undermined by various developments on the ground, most obvious of which is the decline in party membership (van Biezen et al. 2012).

Development of catch-all and cartel parties

Beyond membership decline, two broad dimensions to this undermining can be seen. First has been the development of the 'catch-all' and 'cartel' party types, and second the relationship between party members and leaders. The catch-all party concept is attributed to Kirchheimer (1966), who indicated that the mass parties formerly held together by economic class or religious denomination transformed themselves into a new party type, the catch-all party. Occurring in the context of changing social conditions (accompanied by post-industrialization) such parties are characterized as mainstream, pursuing votes at the expense of ideology with centrist (and often inconsistent) programmes designed to appeal to ever widening audiences, levelling out to the 'median voter'; and they are often elite-driven (see also Williams 2009).

The cartel party goes beyond this. According to the cartel party concept, the strong attention paid to the median voter (and the ability of modern marketing and campaigning techniques to aid this), downplays the social identity and definition of the mass party, leading to a decline in grass roots activity. There is a trend to policy congruence following the median voter (which may become even smaller in size – e.g. the focus of parties on key demographics in swing seats at elections), and parties become part of the state through a process of 'public brokering': that is they aggregate electoral desires to the state but act as agents of the state in defending policy. The state funding of parties – required increasingly with the decline in party members – further intensifies party–state relationships and the main political parties collude in this system (hence the term cartel), since they receive funding and resources from the state when outwith power. Arguably too, the reliance on corporate funding adds a complementary dimension and strengthens the party–state–corporate interest nexus (Katz and Mair 1995).

Evidence of the catch-all party in operation amongst the mainstream players in Scotland is not difficult to find. Much of Labour's development UK-wide (especially under New Labour) saw it reach beyond its core constituency; and while the New Labour programme was never accepted by Labour in Scotland with the same zeal or comprehensiveness as it was by the UK party leaders, there was enough policy convergence between Labour at UK and Scottish levels to make the catch-all label common to both. Catch-all can also be applied to the SNP over a significant time period. Arguably, nationalist parties with an overriding aim of enhanced autonomy or independence – if not premised on linguistic, ethnic or cultural identity – will wish to present themselves as catch-all, appealing to a broad spectrum of support within the nation's boundaries. The SNP falls into this category. While it currently has a left, social democratic centre of gravity in policy terms, there is plenty of evidence over the medium term of catch-all policies, transgressing traditional left–right core political constituencies. For instance, in the SNP minority government from 2007 to 2011, decreased business rates especially on small business (as part of the council tax freeze) were passed every year in the budget, made possible by support from Conservative MSPs after scrutiny by the Parliament's Finance Committee; a reduction in corporation tax as a 'business friendly' policy was advocated by the SNP until fairly recently; Green MSPs and their core constituency were targeted by the Climate Change Act passed in 2009, ahead of England.

The cartel party concept applies directly in post-devolution Scotland in terms of: electoral strategy; decline in grass roots activity; decline in the party's social identity and a strong dependence on professional party organization. Dependence on state funding is evident: financial assistance is given to non-executive parties in the Scottish Parliament (over £0.5 million per annum). The SNP raises some interesting issues too. Although not a state-wide party, its participation in Westminster elections qualifies it for financial support given to non-governmental parties, its recent success at the 2015 election in winning all but three Scottish constituencies giving access to about £1 million per annum. Policy congruence with others on the party's key aim seems unlikely, rendering this aspect of a cartel arrangement somewhat meaningless, yet its behaviour in government indicates a form of 'public brokering' between electoral demands and key actors in the Scottish sub-state polity – for example in the governance arrangements with local government and other institutional players – often downplaying the role and impact of directly elected parliamentary representatives (see Chapter 12 on Scottish policy style). But unlike the cartel model, the party's grass roots activity seems particularly vibrant since the referendum, although whether this is sustainable remains to be seen. Despite the large membership base the party is professionally driven with a strong centrally directed policy on a range of activities where members have a strong locus, most evident around aspects of candidate selection.

Party members and leaders

The second broad dimension is the changing relationship between party members and leaders. The mass party conception of democracy is about competition between collections of citizens who share common beliefs, with parties being the organized expression of this. Party members and leaders are key and conventionally their relationship has been expressed as a principal–agent one. Members play a key part in providing and mobilizing party support. In this context, leaders (the agents) are accountable to the membership (the principals) for a range of party matters. Members have a key role in leadership selection, have a strong influence on policy formation and on internal party governance procedures. Forms of internal party democracy govern how this operates (Katz and Cross 2013). Actual relationships between leaders and members can be somewhat removed from this idealized type. In the face of declining membership and/or electoral performance parties have blurred the boundaries between members and supporters. Labour, Conservative and Liberal Democrat parties, UK-wide and in Scotland have for some time enabled supporters to join on-line networks and contribute policy and other ideas (e.g. through the Labour Supporters Network, Friends of Conservatives, or Friends of Liberal Democrats); how significant these have been is difficult to say, but such initiatives do alter the principal–agent relationship, the bottom-up transmission via members–branches–party policy. The use of such techniques as open primaries (allowing non-party members to vote) for candidate selection (piloted in a constituency in Scotland by the Scottish Conservatives in 2015), or the enabling of registered supporters (for a small fee) to vote in leadership elections (used by Scottish Labour and Labour at UK level in 2015) is intended to involve more of the population in party processes, but this does of course 'dilute' member control, altering somewhat the principal–agent relationship between party member and elected representative.[2] Scottish Labour's outgoing leader in 2015 presented proposals for open primaries in every constituency for the 2020 UK general election. In the wake of the 2014 independence referendum and prior to the 2015 general election, the SNP considered the idea of fielding 'sympathetic' candidates who were not party members, but this came to nought.

Party policy has also been an area where a link between party members and policy (often via party policy debates) has been disrupted and/or redefined. The Conservatives 'resurrected' the Scottish Policy Forum in 2012 'as part of the Scottish Conservatives' policy review process and is now the most direct way for our supporters to get involved in policy development' (www.scottishconservatives.com/policy/scottish-policy-forum (accessed 4/3/2015).

The sixteen policy papers created through this process have all been produced by Conservative MSPs and the input or involvement of party members in the process is unknown, though likely to be minimal (Personal interview A).

Labour has over a number of years broadened its policy formation from one focused on conference delegate–leadership dialogue and debate, to a policy making system which is largely centralized around the leadership (diluting the role of the party's National Executive Committee) and based on a series of Policy Commissions inviting contributions from members, branches and supporters, feeding into a National Policy Forum (there is a Scottish Labour Policy Forum based on this model). The significance and extent to which this forum actually involves members and/or supporters is questionable. In the opinion of one senior party member in Scotland:

> Policy forums ... have meant discussion to try to reach consensus, using outside advisers. Sometimes the trade unions are taken out of the process and consulted separately ... [my] constituency and many others I know of spent time submitting a position paper, but then nothing happens, little is taken into account, no feedback.
> (Personal interview B, March 2015)

That said the current Labour leader, elected UK-wide in 2015, aims to abolish the National Policy Forum and re-establish the importance of conference as a policy-making body.

For the SNP, the context has been different. The party traditionally has placed importance on its branch structure – in fact until the party reforms implemented by John Swinney in the early 2000s, the party had no central membership list. Ever-increasing party membership since 2003 (dramatically so since 2014) makes the SNP unique amongst Scotland's main political parties. However, like other parties' initiatives to broaden policy discourse, the SNP has also gone down this road. In 2007 it launched a 'conversation' ('Choosing Scotland's Future') with website, encouraging comments from members of the public rather than SNP members/supporters or other interest groups. Unlike other parties' initiatives, this was presented as a White Paper: it was issued by the SNP government and first minister of Scotland rather than a party document – 'a nation in waiting' as it were rather than a party policy consultation. But like the other parties' initiatives discussed, the aim was to reach beyond traditional party membership forums and channels to elicit support. Nonetheless, despite this extended reach and although considerable streamlining in party and policy making structures (including stage managing of conferences) has taken place, some insist there is still the possibility that membership quiescence cannot be guaranteed. A senior party member, now an MP, and who has held senior party positions, has insisted:

> Neither the leader nor NEC can be sure to get their way with conference – conference is the key policy making body in the party – the popular sovereignty idea still carries weight, that is the membership rather than party leader holds sovereignty. There's an element of risk but that's the price you pay. Local branch members can

mandate how the branch votes at conference, the MSPs or candidates carry no particular weight.

(Personal interview C, March 2015)

The closely fought proposal and resulting debate on an independent Scotland's membership of NATO at the SNP conference in 2012, perhaps provides some supporting evidence.

Scotland's political parties from 2015

The factors which have framed the political environment in Scotland are, first, the continued increase in support for the SNP (through the referendum and into the 2015 UK general election) and second, the 2016 Scotland Bill/Act devolving more powers to the Scottish Parliament. This legislation devolves to Scotland setting the bands and rates of income tax, not taxation on savings and investments; and leaves levels of national insurance, national minimum wage and national living wage to the UK government. Tax credits will not be devolved. The first 10% of VAT will be assigned to Scotland; air passenger duty will be totally devolved; corporation tax, duty on fuel and alcohol, oil and gas tax revenues remain at UK level. It is estimated that around 40% of tax take in Scotland will be under the control of Holyrood, along with around £2.5 billion of welfare spend currently controlled by the UK government. Universal credit welfare benefits set at UK level will require co-ordination/compliance between UK and Scottish governments.

Devolution to this extent raises a number of political and policy complexities which will affect the main political parties. For instance, if increased responsibilities in specific welfare areas are not well aligned with appropriate fiscal packages, then the increase in autonomy will be somewhat limited and if implemented may be destabilizing, either in terms of Scottish–UK government relationships and/or relationships between parties within the Scottish polity. This must be considered a possibility, given the need for intergovernmental negotiation which will be required in the context of cuts to UK government welfare budgets. More generally, resource flows (a form of redistribution from richer to poorer regions) are normally required in decentralized governance. This is a difficult political issue even in properly designed federal arrangements (which the UK is not), where more prosperous 'contributing' regions, states or provinces often kick back against such resource reallocation. This is complex in the UK, due to the existing basis of funding devolved institutions – the Barnett formula – not being needs-based but determined by historical spending patterns, further complicated by the Smith Commission's 'no detriment' principle (that is, neither Scotland nor the rest of the UK should be adversely affected by further devolution of powers underpinnig the Scottish–UK Government's fiscal framework for the coming years). In addition, devolving a range of fiscal and welfare powers may be welcomed by autonomist (or nationalist) parties but may be feared by state-wide parties as a race to the bottom, since welfare and other public services and social supports have often been guaranteed at state-wide level. However, practice does not always justify this fear. For instance, a study of Germany's 2006 federalism reforms which transferred a range of competences to the *Länder* in areas of prison reform, regulation of care homes, and pay and conditions for large groups of public sector workers, found more evidence of upward pressure on standards rather than a race to the bottom (Turner and Rowe 2015); neither has Quebec shown much evidence of racing to the bottom vis-à-vis other parts of Canada (Noel 2013).

It is interesting to consider the response and strategies of the political parties in the post-2015 environment. It is conceivable that much of this will continue to reflect the binary position of the referendum campaign and beyond with the pro-unionist parties forming positions around an independence/referendum oppositional position and the SNP around creating an opportunity structure for another independence referendum. While this may account for much of the parties' headline statements, the actual activities of the main parties are likely to be more nuanced and complex. It is worthwhile considering how the parties' strategies may play out in reality.

Scottish Conservatives

The Conservatives are likely to experience their core difficulty in Scotland as an inability to speak to the (Scottish) national question. Most centre-right parties articulate around a patriotism of sorts, certainly a vision of the nation. For the Conservatives in Scotland this is a British form of patriotism. Murdo Fraser's attempt at the time of his leadership campaign to create an independent Scottish party with a credible view on home rule has gained no traction subsequently. The political salience of centre-right parties in other devolved countries is not feasible for the Conservatives in Scotland for the foreseeable future. For example, in Catalonia a centre-right government led by Artur Mas and the pro-nationalist, pro-autonomist Convergencia i Unio (CiU) has led the government there; even in the Basque Country the state-wide conservative right-of-centre party (Partido Popular) has held the mayorship of the city of Vitoria for the last thirty years. This is a stark contrast to the Scottish Conservatives' isolation from power in the devolved politics of Scotland. Significantly the uplift in the Conservative vote at 2016 election was based on presenting an effective opposition to the SNP, not a narrative for Scotland. However, there is a piece of speculation which can be made. Traditionally the Conservatives UK-wide have practised 'statecraft' in centrally organizing and driving government – that is, political management from the (UK) centre (Bulpitt 1983). So although the party was initially hostile to devolution, the actual devolved settlement as implemented in the late 1990s was not incompatible with that centre-dominant approach, since key fiscal, economic and foreign policy areas were reserved for the centre (i.e. the UK government) and not devolved; in reality the Conservatives have permitted more autonomy over devolved policy to the Scottish leadership than Labour has. While the Scotland Act 2016 may start to dilute this notion of central management combined with local permissiveness, it is the case that UK Conservatives are not dependent in any way on Scotland for achieving the party's key aim, which is always to gain a UK governing majority; this superordinate priority may allow a free hand to the leadership in Scotland to pursue policies perceived as more robustly 'Scottish'.

Nonetheless a range of evidence suggests this hypothetical scenario is not very likely to occur. The shifting of Scottish leader Ruth Davidson's famous 'line in the sand' in 2011 indicating there should be no more powers for the devolved Parliament, towards a position of support just three years later for devolution of income tax powers, is hardly a Damascene conversion, more an outplaying of the unionist parties' 'vow' in the final days of the referendum campaign to deliver more devolved powers if the electors voted no to independence. In the Scotland Bill 2015 discussions, outwith the devolution of income tax powers, the Scottish Conservatives were generally supportive of tax 'assignment', that is allocating to the Scottish Government a proportion of taxes collected across the UK, thereby maintaining UK tax integrity. And much of the Conservative narrative with regard to enhanced devolved powers is about accountability for taxes raised, with much talk of reduced taxes and the possibility of a Scottish Conservative low tax manifesto commitment for Holyrood elections, rather than the consideration of Scottish public policy outcomes in the new tax-and-spend environment. This all sounds like a UK Conservative prism.

Scottish Labour

In contrast to the Conservatives, Labour does require Scottish representation at Westminster to enhance its chances of forming a UK government. Prior to its 2015 losses, Labour consistently returned forty-plus seats from Scottish constituencies. The loss of these seats, when added to around another 30–50 estimated losses in England due to boundary changes by 2020, illustrates the importance of Scotland to Labour state-wide.

Labour's seeming inability to address the national dimension of politics in Scotland (ironically after playing a key role in delivering a devolved Scottish Parliament in 1999) also has some resonance in other devolved countries. In Spain, the state-wide social democratic Socialist Workers Party (PSOE), traditionally well supported in Catalonia and under the leadership of Zapatero, agreed with the Catalan authorities to a revised Statute of Autonomy guaranteeing more autonomy to Catalonia. But this was struck down by the Constitutional Court in 2010, and the very visible way in which the PSOE backed down in the aftermath of the decision has created immense problems for the party ever since in Catalonia: it is unable to reconcile on the one hand conservatives within the party who wish to resist further autonomy for Catalonia and, on the other, support for enhanced autonomy and self-determination in Catalonia (and elsewhere); its previously fruitful relations with the Catalan Socialists (PSC, Socialist Party of Catalonia) has been fractured, since it appears unable to address the Catalan autonomy issue. The PSOE's inability to address this in Catalonia is in effect making it very difficult for the party to command national power at state level (Teruel 2014).

It would therefore seem imperative for Labour to address the national question in Scotland. Responses to this so far have been about party structures and decision making processes. Not atypical of those in Labour trying to address this problem is the following comment from former Scottish party leader and first minister, Henry McLeish:

> A new relationship between Scottish and UK Labour is also required. This ... is long overdue ... Labour in Scotland needs political freedom ... The idea ... is about strengthening the party in the UK and making it more relevant and credible to the different nations and electorates it seeks to serve ...
>
> (McLeish 2015)

There are considerable practical difficulties in such a move. It is clear the party has a low membership base and little independent resourcing in Scotland, so its current organizational and financial links with UK Labour remain crucial. Party employees are employed not by Scottish Labour but UK Labour. In such circumstances autonomy may be difficult to achieve. Furthermore there is pressure in some trade unions currently affiliated to Labour to devolve political funds, raising the possibility of disrupting the trade union–Labour financial link.

Labour's position has shifted from an initially very cautious approach to income tax devolution, proposing to the Smith Commission devolution of only a proportion of income tax with particular restrictions on movement of the upper bands of income tax (and these only upward from UK level). Labour also had proposals for some devolution to local government, bypassing the Scottish Parliament (e.g. devolution of the Work Programme to councils). It has been shown that state government bypassing the sub-national government in this way can often be used (by design or otherwise) to undermine the sub-national government's policy capacity – examples of this are found in Spain, Italy and France (Keating 2015). While this may or may not have been Scottish Labour's intention at the time, it has not been pursued; nor has any sustained thinking on devolution powers to local government taken place.

For Scottish Labour to map out a feasible political presence and position in Scotland over the short-to-medium term will be challenging. While an oppositional stance to the UK Conservative government may be possible, this is extremely limited by the presence of only one MP in Scotland and a significantly stronger SNP presence both in Westminster and Holyrood.

Scottish Liberal Democrats

In some senses the Scottish Liberal Democrats' position is puzzling. The party (and its predecessor Liberal Party) had a strong and fairly sustained commitment to home rule (see Chapter 1). The party was in coalition government for the first two Scottish Parliaments, playing a particularly strong role in initiating and supporting some distinctive policies there (e.g. major voting reform in local government, restructuring of student funding, free personal care, and the smoking ban). Of all the UK parties, the Liberal Democrats have the strongest commitment to federalism, and the party has a federal structure giving considerable autonomy to the party in Scotland. The Liberal Democrats' Commission in 2007 (Steel Commission 2007) proposed a strong commitment to the Scottish Parliament raising the bulk of taxes to finance expenditure in Scotland along with a UK-wide fiscal equalization (fiscal federalism). Although restated by the party's Home Rule Commission in 2012, no specific strategies were developed to take this forward. Severe losses in the 2011 Holyrood elections (seen as related to the party's decision to enter coalition government with the Conservatives at Westminster) and a virtual wipeout at the 2015 general election make it unlikely the party will be in a position to advance on this front any time soon. The Liberal Democrats' position on the Smith Commission has shown little difference from that of the Conservatives (though arguing for some tax assignment from corporation tax). Lib Dem focus has been on the increased accountability dimension of devolved powers (Jeffery 2015).

Scottish National Party

Of significant interest in the coming period will be the SNP's position in Scottish politics. Since the party forms the Scottish Government, was on the losing side in the independence referendum but has subsequently won 56 of the 59 UK parliamentary constituencies in Scotland, its actions will have significance for Scottish politics. Like most electorally successful parties it is part of the mainstream (in Scotland) and as shown previously this is reflected in party organization and structures. It is fairly clear from both electoral studies and analyses of Scottish social attitudes surveys that the rise in SNP support since it formed a minority Scottish Government in 2007 has not been based on national identity or a rise in nationalist sentiment. Until about 2006 around one in five respondents rated 'Scottish and British equally' as their preferred identity; this has increased steadily to one in three in 2014. At the same time SNP voting has been increasing consistently (Eichhorn 2015). Study of the 2011 Scottish election resulting in an SNP majority government was based largely on positive perceptions of the minority SNP administration's salience and competence in government (Carman et al. 2014). It is therefore reasonable to project that SNP political strategy is likely to follow the 'normal' mainstream party route, that is about quality and competence of governance, policies and service delivery rather than focusing on identity and nationalism; albeit that the party has a unique aim among mainstream parties, namely independence for Scotland.

The SNP will of course try to map out major differences with other political parties in Scotland. Whereas the pro-union parties' submissions and responses to the Smith Commission have been about increased powers and the mechanisms for accountability of decision making and governance, the SNP's attention has been on use of powers to promote economic competitiveness, growth and management – in the context of this as a second best to independence (Jeffery 2015).

There are other areas where it will be interesting to see if the SNP attempts to craft significantly 'Scottish' policy positions. One such is in the area of immigration. Increased immigration featured in the Scottish Government's White Paper as an economic growth lever, on the grounds of Scotland's needs due to population demographics along with greater capacity to increase immigration vis-à-vis the rest of the UK (Scotland has a pro rata immigration rate of about half the level of the UK). Although immigration is a matter reserved to Westminster, the area of migrant rights is less clear and there is some precedent of specific Scottish policy initiatives here (e.g. the Fresh Talent Initiative). Evidence taken by the Scottish Parliament's European and External Relations Committee suggests that the UK Government's focus on migrant rights as part of the negotiation of Britain's EU membership may present opportunities for a specific Scottish Government policy response (Scottish Parliament 2015). A second area where there may be a specific SNP Government approach is in the devolved areas of welfare. Though this will be a somewhat fraught area, given UK welfare cuts (and consequent fiscal knock-on effects for Scotland) and in certain areas limited opportunities to deviate from UK approaches, nonetheless the smaller population base in Scotland and the ability to shape the newly devolved powers (over for example attendance allowance, disability allowance, carers' allowance and the Work Programme) with existing health and social care competences may enable the shaping of distinctive policies with less bureaucratic delay and complexity for benefit recipients (McEwan 2015). Finally, the SNP may adopt some distinctiveness and novelty in approach. It launched a National Conversation, a consultation exercise on how the new powers in the Scotland Bill/Act can be used in a range of ways to reduce poverty and inequality, improve educational attainment and address mental health, for example. It has also undertaken a similar exercise on the NHS/health care in Scotland led by the Cabinet secretary for health and well being. There may be a degree of scepticism, indeed cynicism about such initiatives; they may be tokenistic or exercises in delay and shuffling around difficult and controversial decisions; it may have some small wins (likely) and it may change perhaps modestly the tone of how politics, policy and government takes place. Only time will tell.

Conclusion

An appreciation of both long-term and more immediate trends is valuable to an understanding of the current position of the main political parties in Scotland. The decline of the Conservatives as a major force can be seen from the 1960s, accelerating during the years of Conservative governments at Westminster in the 1980s and 1990s. Scottish Labour's current position of decline – in opposition at Holyrood and with only one MP – appears more dramatic, since it was the biggest party in the first two Scottish parliamentary elections and held about two thirds of Scottish seats at Westminster until 2015. But relative decline occurred over the longer term too, with reduced support at each devolved election since 1999 and reduced vote share at Westminster elections from 2001, added to which were consistently reducing numbers of party members. Whether Labour will bounce back remains to be seen. The dramatic rise in SNP support, from majority party at Holyrood in 2011 to winning almost all Scottish seats at Westminster in 2015, also has longer term antecedents: the slow rise in support at by-election victories in the 1960s and 1970s, fluctuations in support at UK elections in the 1970s and then a significant presence in the Scottish Parliament leading to single largest party and government formation at Holyrood in 2007.

How active – in terms of membership – and how representative are the main parties in Scotland? Most parties have experienced a long term decline in membership. The SNP (and amongst smaller parties the Scottish Greens) are the exceptions, with substantial increases since the referendum. In representation terms parties (may) experience a number of tensions. In the case of the SNP, its significantly increased membership since the 2014 referendum may be a force pushing the party to call for another referendum, arguably creating tensions for the leadership, which will wish to represent members but be cautious on the issue – as one would expect from a catch-all party – if a pro-independence vote is far from guaranteed. Of course the motivations of the membership are assumed and have yet to be tested by empirical research.

Party representation and gender provide an interesting case. All parties have an espoused desire for greater female representation, yet the operationalizing of this may run counter to efforts at greater representation rights for party members as a whole – if (as is the case) party members and membership structures are skewed towards males. Another aspect of representation is the extent to which party members who hold elected office are broadly representative of the electorate. Primary research shows that the parties in Scotland follow trends elsewhere in the dominance of 'professionals' amongst elected members at parliamentary levels, with a significant number of 'professional politicians' holding or attempting to hold office. There are, however, some significant differences between the parties in Scotland – for example, Scottish Labour has more 'professional politicians' while the SNP has more 'managers' from both business and public sector backgrounds.

Consistent with international trends in most democracies, parties in Scotland have shown a shift from the mass party ideal type to cartel and catch-all parties – perhaps more accurately in reality, hybridized forms of all three types. Much of the party professionalization that goes along with this (e.g. increased power to party leadership and bureaucracy) is likely to remain, since parties will wish to remain as election-winning machines. But a key question for the future – requiring primary research – is the extent to which substantial numbers of new members will accommodate to this, whether passively or actively. A related question is how the new category of 'registered supporter' will fit into membership structures, disappear or convert to membership, and if the latter will act as a driver for more direct member involvement.

Finally, in the short-to-medium term there are two broad areas which will affect and be affected by the political parties in Scotland. The first concerns the terrain of Scottish politics and where the mainstream will lie. With increased powers going to the Scottish Parliament, will political debate be structured around tax-and-spend policies and will this be a crucial area for political positioning? This appears to be a key desire of the Scottish Conservatives who wish to position themselves as a low tax party. Or will the focus be on governmental competence, which has been the focus and strategy of the SNP-led Scottish Government since 2007? Alternatively, political narratives may form around accountability of government, where parties outwith government will try to engage the electorate.

Second is where the post-referendum and post-2015 and 2016 election environment will take political thinking and action in Scotland. Much was made of the inclusiveness and energizing impact of the referendum in 2014 (with a very high turnout of 86%), involving groups of the population in forms of political activity rarely seen in conventional political events. This was lauded by all political parties and had impact on the 2015 UK election in Scotland, not only in terms of result but also turnout (which was almost ten percentage points above turnout in England). Yet the post-referendum consultations on new powers were conducted in largely 'conventional' ways with relatively limited input from civic Scotland or non-aligned individuals. Beyond this, the extent to which specific Scottish political and policy positions and outcomes can be crafted and implemented within the enhanced devolved powers and financial envelope of the Scottish Government will be of major significance to the political parties. So too will be the position adopted by them on discussions, negotiations and dealings with the UK Government. In the case of Scottish Labour, its ability and willingness to have distinctive policy and organizational frames for Scottish politics will be particularly important.

Notes

1 The main report (Kilbrandon Report 1973a) pretty much mirrored much of the initial devolution settlement in 1999. The minority dissenting report (published in a separate Memorandum of Dissent by Lord Crowther-Hunt and Professor Alan Peacock (Kilbrandon Report 1973b) called for elected regional assemblies for Scotland and Wales. In addition it called for five elected regional assemblies for England taking over much of the machinery of central government in their areas and each with its own civil service. These would replace regional health authorities in England, have supervisory control over water and gas and have significant economic and social development powers.
2 There are interesting examples of parties enabling supporters to vote in elections. This has long been the case in the USA, with registered supporters able to participate in primaries. There is also an 'open access' model where, for example, the Progressive Party in Alberta (Canada) permits citizens to pay $5 on the day of the leadership election to qualify for a vote (Young 2013). Considerable numbers of registered supporters paid £3 and voted for the UK Labour leader and deputy leader in 2015. There is very little evidence, though, of a similar pattern in the same year under the same rules for Scottish Labour's leadership election.

Sources for further reading and study

Books

In addition to Cameron (2010), Hassan and Shaw (2012) and Mitchell et al. (2011) all cited and referenced below, there is Torrance, D. (2012) *Whatever Happened to Tory Scotland?* Edinburgh: Edinburgh University Press.

Journals

Publius, the Journal of Federalism: Oxford Journals.
Regional and Federal Studies: Taylor and Francis.
Scottish Affairs: Edinburgh University Press.

Websites

www.bbc.co.uk/news/correspondents/briantaylor
www.bellacaledonia.org.uk
www.centreonconstitutionalchange.ac.uk
www.devolutionmatters.wordpress.com
www.scottishconstitutionalfutures.org

References

Aaronovitch, D. (2004) 'Talking dirty to woo the voters'. *The Guardian*, 16 June. Available at: www.theguardian.com/politics/2004/jun/16/elections2004.comment.
BBC News (2008) 'Labour's foot soldiers falling away'. 29 March.
Borchert, Hans and Jurgen Zeiss (eds) (2003) *The Political Class in Advanced Democracies: A Comparative Handbook*. Oxford: Oxford University Press.
Bulpitt, J. (1983) *Territory and Power in the United Kingdom*. Manchester: Manchester University Press.
Cameron, E.A. (2010) *Impaled Upon a Thistle: Scotland Since 1880*. Edinburgh: Edinburgh University Press.
Carman, C., R. Johns and J. Mitchell (2014) *More Scottish than British? The 2011 Scottish Parliament Election*. London: Palgrave Macmillan.
Carrell, S. (2015) 'SNP vote in all-women and 'balanced' shortlists for next Holyrood election'. *The Guardian*, 29 March. Available at: www.theguardian.com/uk-news/scotland-blog/2015/march/29/snp-vote-all-women-shortlists-zipping-holyrood-elections (accessed 5 May 2015).
Crewe, I. (1986) 'On the death and resurrection of class voting: some comments on how Britain votes'. *Political studies* 34(4): 620–638.
Denver, D., H. Bochel and M. Steven (2012), 'Mixed messages for (some) parties: the Scottish council elections of 2012'. *Scottish Affairs* 80: 1–12.
Devine, T.M. (2013) 'For the good times'. *Scottish Review of Books* 8(4). Available at: www.scottishreviewofbooks.org/index.php/back-issues/513-for-the-good-times-thomas-devine (accessed 3 April 2015).
Devine, T.M. (1999) *The Scottish Nation*. London: Penguin.
Eichhorn, J. (2015) 'Votes for the SNP are not votes for independence'. University of Edinburgh Centre on Constitutional Change. Available at: www.centreonconstitutionalchange.ac.uk/blog/votes-snp-are.not-votes-for-independence (accessed 12 June 2015).
English, J. (ed.) (1983) *The Future of Council Housing*. London: Croom Helm.
Foster, J. (2001) 'The twentieth century 1914–1979'. In R.A. Houston and W.W.J. Knox (eds) *The New Penguin History of Scotland From the Earliest Times to the Present Day*. London: Allen Lane.
Fraser, I. (2014) *Shredded. Inside RBS: The Bank That Broke Britain*. Edinburgh: Birlinn.
Groves, J. (2012) 'Increase in "professional politicians" means 1 in 7 MPs have never done a real job'. *Daily Mail*, 19 July.
Gunlicks, A.B. (1978) 'Max Weber's typology of politicians: a reexamination'. *The Journal of Politics* 40(2): 498–509.
Hassan, G. and E. Shaw (2012) *The Strange Death of Labour in Scotland*. Edinburgh: Edinburgh University Press.

HC 239 (2010) *Speaker's Conference (on Parliamentary Representation), Final Report*. London: Stationary Office.

Hopkin, J. and J. Bradbury (2006) 'British statewide parties and multilevel politics'. *Publius: The Journal of Federalism* 36(1): 135–152.

Jeffery, C. (2015) 'Tax and welfare devolution: how did we get here?' In *Future of the UK and Scotland, Beyond Smith: Contributions to the Continuing Process of Scottish devolution*. University of Edinburgh Centre on Constitutional Change.

Katz, R.S. and W. Cross (2013) 'Problematizing intra-party democracy'. In W. Cross and R.S. Katz, *The Challenges of Intra Party Democracy*. Oxford: Oxford University Press.

Katz, R. and P. Mair (1995) 'Changing models of party organization and party democracy: the emergence of the cartel party'. *Party Politics* 1(1): 5–25.

Keating, M. (2015) 'Debates on additional devolution. What is happening elsewhere?' In *Future of the UK and Scotland, Beyond Smith: Contributions to the Continuing Process of Scottish devolution*. Edinburgh: University of Edinburgh Centre on Constitutional Change.

Keating, M. and P. Cairney (2006) 'A new elite? Politicians and civil servants in Scotland after devolution'. *Parliamentary Affairs* 59(1): 43–59.

Keen, R. (2015) *Membership of UK Political Parties*. London: House of Commons Library.

Kemp, A. (1993) *The Hollow Drum: Scotland Since the War*. Edinburgh: Mainstream Publishing.

Kenny, M., J. Swann and F. Mackay (2015) 'Women and the 2015 general election: fractures in the glass ceiling?' Available at: www.centreonconstitutionalchange.ac.uk/blog/women-and-2015-general-election-fractures-glass-ceiling (accessed 29 May 2015).

Kilbrandon Report (1973a) *Royal Commission on the Constitution 1969–1973, Volume 1*. Cmnd 5460. London: Stationery Office.

Kilbrandon Report (1973b) *Royal Commission on the Constitution 1969–1973, Volume 2*. Memorandum of Dissent by Lord Crowther-Hunt and Professor A.T. Peacock. Cmnd 5460. London: Stationery Office.

Kirchheimer, O. (1966) 'The transformation of the Western European party systems'. In J. LaPalombara and M. Weiner, *Political Parties and Political Development*. Princeton, NJ: Princeton University Press.

Lynch, P. (2002) *SNP. The History of the Scottish National Party*. Cardiff: Welsh Academic Press.

Mair, P. (2013) *Ruling the Void: The Hollowing of Western Democracy*. London: Verso.

Mair, P. (1994) 'Party organisation: from civil society to state'. In R.S. Katz and P. Mair (eds) *How Parties Organise: Change and Adaptation in Part Organisations in Western Democracies*. London: Sage.

Maxwell, J. (2013) 'Scotland special: what's wrong with Scottish Labour?' Available at: www.totalpolitics.com/articles/427917/scotland-special-whatand39-wrong-with-scottish-labour.thtml (accessed 3 April 2015).

McEwan, N. (2015) 'Devolving welfare. University of Edinburgh Centre on Constitutional Change. Available at: www.centreonconstitutionalchange.ac.uk/blog/votes-snp-are.not-votes-for-independence (accessed 12 June 2015).

McKinstry, L. (2014) 'Our political class is utterly out of touch with voters'. *Daily Express*, 19 June. Available at: www.express.co.uk/comment/columnists/leo-mckinstry/483342/Leo-McKinstry-on-Britain-s-political-class.

McLeish, H. (2015) 'A new relationship between Scottish and UK Labour is required'. *Holyrood Magazine*, 7 July. Available at: www.holyrood.com/articles/comment/henry-mcleish-new-relationship-between-scottish-and-uk-labour-required (accessed 8 July 2015).

Mitchell, J. (1990) 'Factions, tendencies and consensus in the SNP in the 1980s'. In A. Brown and R. Parry (eds) *Scottish Government Yearbook*. Edinburgh: Edinburgh University Press, pp. 49–61.

Mitchell, J., L. Bennie and R. Johns (2011) *The Scottish National Party: Transition to Power*. Oxford: Oxford University Press.

Noel, A. (2013) 'Quebec's new policies of redistribution'. In K. Banting and J. Myles (eds) *The Fading of Redistributive Policies: Policy Change and Policy Drift in Canada*. Vancouver: University of British Columbia Press.
Oborne, P. (2007) 'The establishment is dead. But something worse has replaced it'. *Spectator*, 12 September. Available at: www.spectator.co.uk/features/162011/the-establishment-is-dead-but-something-worse-has-replaced-it/.
Panebianco, A. (1988) *Political Parties: Organisation and Power*. Cambridge: Cambridge University Press.
Pemberton, H. and M. Wickham-Jones (2013) 'Labour's lost grassroots: the rise and fall of party membership'. *British Politics* 8: 181–206.
Perkin, H. (1988) *The Rise of Professional Society*. London: Routledge.
Personal Interview A (2015) Former Scottish Conservative MP, Party Chairman in Scotland, Minister, Scottish Office, 2 February.
Personal Interview B (2015) Senior Scottish Labour Party Member and Constituency Party Chairman, 9 March.
Personal Interview C (2015) Senior SNP member, former SNP National Voice Convenor, 15 March.
Philips, J. (2008) *The Industrial Politics of Devolution: Scotland in the 1960s and 1970s*. Manchester: Manchester University Press.
Ramsay, A. (2015) 'A note on party memberships in the UK'. *Open Democracy*. Available at: www.opendemocracy.net/ourkingdom/adam-ramsay/note-on-party-memberships-in-uk (accessed 25 August 2015).
Riddell, P. (2011) *In Defence of Politicians in Spite of Themselves*. London: Biteback.
Rose, R. (1964) 'Parties, factions and tendencies in Britain'. *Political Studies* 12: 33–46.
Saward, M. (2010) *The Representative Claim*. Oxford: Oxford University Press.
Scarrow, S.E. and B. Gezgor (2010) 'Declining memberships, changing members? European political party members in a new era'. *Party Politics* 16(6): 823–843.
Scotsman (2015) 'Boost for SNP as membership hits 100,000'. 22 March. Available at: www.scotsman.com/news/uk/boost-for-snp-as-membership-hits-100-000-mark-1-3725308.
Scottish Executive (2006) 'Right to Buy in Scotland: pulling together the evidence. Available at: www.gov.scot/publications/2006/2009/26114727/5.
Scottish Parliament (2015) 'The UK's future relationship with the EU'. Written evidence from Dr Eve Hepburn and Dr Daniel Kenealy. Scottish Parliament European and External Affairs Committee, 10th Meeting (Session 4), 4 June.
Seyd, P. and P. Whiteley (1992) *Labour's Grass Roots: The Politics of Party Membership*. Oxford: Clarendon Press.
SPICe (2011) 'Background of MSPs'. LG (2011) Paper 046, 24 October. Available at: www.scottish.parliament.uk/parliamentarybusiness/research/backgroundofMSPs_LG__paper046_scottish_parliament_s4_demographics (accessed 7 March 2015).
Steel Commission (2007) *Moving to Federalism: A New Settlement for Scotland*. Available at: www.scotlibdems.org.uk/files/steelcommission.pdf (accessed 7 March 2015).
Sunday Herald (2015) 'UK Labour takes over Scottish recruitment'. 21 June.
Teruel, J.R. (2014) 'Spain's Socialist Party must carefully balance competing pressures over its policy on Catalan independence'. Available at: http://blogs.lse.ac.uk/europpblog/2013/10/31/spains-socialist-party-must-carefully-balance-competing-pressures-over-its-policy-on-catalan-independence/ (accessed 2 June 2015).
Turner, E. and C. Rowe (2015) *A Race to the Top, Middle or Bottom? The Consequences of Decentralisation in Germany*. Manchester: Institute for Public Policy Research, IPPR North.
van Biezen, I., P. Mair and T. Poguntke (2012) 'Going, going – gone? The decline of party membership in contemporary Europe'. *European Journal of Political Research* 51(1): 24–56.
Webb, P., D. Farrell and I. Holliday (eds) (2002) *Political Parties in Advanced Industrial Democracies*. Oxford: Oxford University Press.

Whiteley, P. and P. Seyed (2002) *High-Intensity Participation: The Dynamic of Party Activism in Britain*. Ann Arbor: University of Michigan Press.

Whiteley, P., P. Seyed and M. Billinghurst (2006) *Third Force Politics: Liberal Democrats at the Grassroots*. Oxford: Oxford University Press.

Williams, M.H. (2009) 'Catch all parties in the twenty first century? Revisiting Kirchheimer's thesis 40 years later: an introduction'. *Party Politics* 15: 539–541.

Wolfe, B. (1979) 'Comment on SNP results and on matters affecting them'. SNP Internal Memorandum. Edinburgh: Scottish National Party.

Wright, A. (2012) *Doing Politics*. 'London: Biteback.

Young, L. (2013) 'Party members and intra-party democracy'. In W.P. Cross and R.S. Katz, *Challenges of Interparty Democracy*. Oxford: Oxford University Press.

5 Corks on a beach?
Finding a hard budget constraint for the Scottish Government

Paul Hallwood and Ronald MacDonald

Smith Commission and enhanced devolution

The 2014 Smith Commission Report[1] was agreed between the main Scottish political parties, immediately becoming the basis for further fiscal reform in Scotland. This of course followed from the independence referendum and a 'vow' promised by the unionist parties to increase powers to the Scottish Parliament should Scotland vote 'no'. However, in a very different political environment all of its main tax provisions, at least in outline and sometimes in detail, had been proposed ten years earlier.

In 2004, a high profile group (including a Nobel laureate) was brought together by Labour MSP Wendy Alexander (who subsequently became Labour leader in Scotland). The proceedings of this group, resulting in a book on the future of Scotland, included some thinking on fiscal powers and the devolved Scottish Parliament.[2] The proceedings also included comment and reflections, such as:

> We will have succeeded if we have redefined the terms of debate on this [tax] issue away from political rhetoric towards a focus on the real choices, the comparative experience of other nations, and the economic evidence.
> (Hallwood and MacDonald 2004: 64)

There followed the Calman (2009) and Smith (2014) Commissions, the Scotland Act of 2012, and the Scotland Bill of 2015. All of these set out what they considered to be the 'real choices' of what tax devolution should be.

Our earlier discussions in 2004 were concerned with the lack of a hard budget constraint on spending by the then Scottish Executive, because with virtually all of its spending financed by a block grant it had no need to be concerned with the tax costs of financing that spending:

> Rational decisions are much more likely to be made when people in a 'benefit region' have to pay the costs as well as enjoying benefits of public expenditure.
> (Hallwood and MacDonald 2004: 22)

> the appropriate institutional framework has to include a willingness of the local politicians to abide by the rules of a *hard budget constraint*.
> (Italics added, Hallwood and MacDonald 2004: 30–31)[3]

Though Calman and the Scotland Act 2012 had not, Smith seemingly adopted the principle of a hard budget constraint:

> the revised funding framework should result in the devolved Scottish budget benefiting in full from policy decisions by the Scottish Government that increase revenues or reduce expenditure, and the devolved Scottish budget bearing the full costs of policy decisions that reduce revenues or increase expenditure
>
> (Smith 2014: para. 95(2))

Smith, however, went on to fudge (or 'politically manage') the issue of a hard budget constraint, because it continued:

> The Barnett Formula will continue to be used to determine the remaining block grant. New rules to define how it will be adjusted at the point when powers are transferred and thereafter will be agreed by the Scottish and UK Governments and put in place prior to the powers coming into force. These rules will ensure that neither the Scottish nor UK Governments will lose or gain financially from the act of transferring a power.[4]
>
> (Smith 2014: 4)

'Thereafter' is the operative word: both Calman and the Scotland Act (2012) had the same sort of wording – amounting to 'leave it to the politicians at the UK level' to agree a hard budget constraint; or not. The likelihood of a hard budget constraint being set does not seem great because the UK political parties are wedded to keeping Scotland in the Union and a hard budget constraint is unlikely to be consistent with that priority.

Indeed, the Scotland Act (1998) created the Scottish Consolidated Fund into which funds are transferred from the UK's Consolidated Fund and the only limits on these transfers are political. The Scotland Bill of 2015 did not change this arrangement, which in effect leaves the Scottish Government and Parliament as a client of the Westminster government, and leaving the former without the discipline of a hard budget constraint – something that truly independent governments face. Because the design of a fiscal system for Scotland is still incomplete, and setting aside Independence, it is quite possible that the Scotland Bill 2015 will be superseded by at least one more Act that is better designed with a hard budget constraint in mind.

It is worth emphasizing that earlier work (Hallwood and MacDonald 2004) on this topic did not rule out the need for a block grant in a devolved system of taxes and revenue for Scotland (indeed the key element a block grant would play in any system which pools and shares risks was recognized). Crucially, however, in a hard budget constraint system the block grant should be unrelated to any fiscal imbalance that arises from the decision making of the Scottish Government. Barnett itself does not satisfy this criteria since its operation is clouded in a lack of transparency (see Heald 2003), and other proposals that include a Barnett component (specifically Calman and Smith) will fall foul of this issue too.

There are other comparisons between our considerations in 2004 and what Smith recommended in 2014. It is instructive to list some of these:

Income tax

Hallwood and MacDonald proposed devolution of income tax as well as minor taxes (Hallwood and MacDonald 2004: 57). Smith recommended in 2014 that the Scottish Parliament should have the power to set the rates of income tax and the thresholds at which these are paid for the non-savings and non-dividend income of Scottish taxpayers (Smith 2014: para. 76). Smith also recommended all other aspects of income tax should remain reserved to the UK Parliament, including the imposition of the annual charge to income tax, the personal allowance, the taxation of savings and dividend income, the ability to introduce and amend tax reliefs, and the definition of income (Smith 2014: para. 77).

North Sea oil tax revenues

Hallwood and MacDonald recommended against devolution of oil tax revenue (Hallwood and MacDonald 2004: 57). Smith concluded in 2014 that aspects of the taxation of oil and gas receipts remain reserved (Smith 2014, para. 83).

Value added tax

Similarly it was recommended that VAT should be assigned revenue rather than seen as a devolved tax (Hallwood and MacDonald 2004: 57). And Smith in 2014 recommended that the receipts raised in Scotland by the first ten percentage points of the standard rate of Value Added Tax (VAT) be assigned to the Scottish Government's budget (Smith 2014, para. 84).

Minor taxes

In keeping with the 2004 recommendation of the devolution of minor taxes, Smith devolved Air Passenger Duty and Aggregates Tax 2004. The recommendation was 'consideration of the devolution ... of a package of minor taxes' (Hallwood and MacDonald 2004: 57; Smith 2014: para. 89).

Borrowing

Finally, Smith recommended some additional borrowing powers (Smith 2014: para. 95); this was also part and parcel of our 2004 analysis (Hallwood and MacDonald 2004: 33).

Macroeconomic stabilization

A continuity of thinking is also evident in macroeconomic management, with the centrality of the UK government emphasized: 'The high regional business cycle correlation in the UK suggests that the role of macroeconomic stabilization should largely be left to central government' (Hallwood and MacDonald 2004: 28). And in 2014, Smith's position was: 'the UK Government should continue to manage risks and economic shocks that affect the whole of the UK. The fiscal framework should therefore ensure that the UK Government retains the levers to do that ...' (Smith 2014: para. 95).

Corporation tax

This tax was not specifically ruled out or ruled in for a devolved Scottish Parliament in 2004 but it has been successfully devolved in other devolved fiscal systems and it is the key tax that the SNP has repeatedly said they would like to use (with the devolution of this tax to the Northern Ireland assembly and proposed further devolution to the English regions, the time would seem to be ripe for the devolution of this tax). But in 2014, a more definitive view was taken by Smith: 'All aspects of Corporation Tax will remain reserved' (Smith 2014: para. 82).

Thus, seven suggestions for devolved taxes made a decade ago in 2004 were incorporated into Smith – income tax, VAT assignment, oil taxes, minor taxes devolved, macroeconomic stabilization retained at the Treasury, borrowing capacity, and at least lip service to a hard budget constraint. The link between policy ideas, policy formation and implementation is complex and the processes involved not always linear, but, metaphorically, if seven corks were floated out on a turbulent sea (of political argument), and ten years later they were found together on the same beach, somebody might think this an enormous coincidence, or, there is a link between ideas expressed in 2004 and those suggested for legislative enactment in 2014.

A further idea expressed in 2004 was an emphasis on appropriate decision-making being made at the margin – the so-called marginal tax rule. That is, given a hard budget constraint is in place that increased expenditure over and above assigned taxes and grants be financed either by a reduction in spending in another category, or an increase in taxes, or if the cost is reasonable, by an increase in borrowing (Hallwood and MacDonald 2004: 56). In this regard we had in mind especially if, say, the tax on capital is reduced (by a reduction in corporation tax) it would be possible to raise another tax – income tax – to counter this. However, the 2015 Scotland Bill rules out such tax changes, so there is no link there between earlier ideas and current legislative intent.

Scotland's political parties and hard budget constraint

We continue in the rest of this chapter with a discussion of the fiscal proposals made by the leading Scottish political parties immediately prior to the September 2014 referendum. We will assess each of them against the standard of a hard budget constraint (HBC) – a constraint that would force the Scottish Government to compare the benefits and costs of its spending decisions. We will argue that the Scottish National Party and the Scottish Conservatives went furthest down the road of a HBC. Scottish Labour was hopelessly adrift with no apparent appreciation of the concept.

Hardness of suggested budget constraints

The budget constraints either in effect (Barnett) or suggested for the Scottish Government prior to the 2014 referendum are listed below – we include the Holtham Committee even though it relates to Wales because it suggested something close to a workable hard budget constraint:

1   Continuation of the Barnett formula
2   Calman Commission and the Scotland Act, 2012
3   Scottish Labour Devolution Commission (2014)

4   The Holtham Commission (2010) on Wales but could be extended to Scotland
5   Scottish Liberal Democrats (2014)
6   Scottish Conservatives (2014)
7   The Scottish Green Party, 2014 (Harvie and Chapman 2014)
8   The SNP, 2014 and continuing (Scottish Government 2014)
9   The Scotland Bill 2015

The large literature on the financing of sub-central governments establishes the principles that for fiscal efficiency – in both spending and taxing, as well as in accountability to the voters, the budget constraint under which political decision-makers operate is hard.[5] This means that decisions taken by the Scottish Government have real costs: that increased government spending out of gross domestic product means that taxes – the burden on the taxpayers – have to go up to finance it. In general, voters and citizens at the sub-central level have to understand that what public spending they vote for has real costs to them.

With a soft budget constraint, public sector decision-makers do not have to make hard choices trading off greater public spending with greater tax burdens on the population that gets to enjoy that greater level of public spending.

The four desirable effects of a hard budget constraint (HBC) on sub-central government (SCG) are:

i   It aligns the policies offered by SCG with what the voters at that level are willing to pay for. This is not inconsistent with equalization payments between regions of a country, but these would be expected to flow to low-income-per-head regions.
ii It creates incentive alignment between SCG and central government (CG) – the former does not spend funds allocated to it wastefully. This is a misuse of funds, or moral hazard, issue.
iii It is time consistent in the sense that SCG should not expect to be bailed out by CG if it mismanages the level or allocation of its spending. Finally,
iv It should prevent adverse selection by voters at the SCG level when voting for their SCG. That is, the political parties should be unable to make promises that they know, or, should know, are un-financeable out of local sourced revenues in the long run.

1 The Barnett formula

The Barnett formula as of 2016 still governs public spending by the Scottish Parliament – and was proposed to continue by the Smith Commission and it is in the Scotland Bill, 2015. In the pre-referendum documents of the Scottish Labour Party it would do so into the indefinite future. However, the Scottish Liberal Democrats foresaw the Barnett formula being used only for a short while after budget reform before being phased out. The SNP said that the Barnett formula should be kept in any arrangement short of full fiscal autonomy. In a failed proposal to amend the Scotland Bill in June 2015, the SNP wanted a commitment to phase in full fiscal autonomy so phasing out Barnett funds – that are transferred through the Scottish Consolidated Fund to the Scottish Government and Parliament – but only when Scottish own-sourced funds were sufficiently large. It is also worth noting that in the so-called 'vow', the prime minister David Cameron, ex-prime minister Gordon Brown and shadow chancellor Ed Balls also stated that Barnett should be kept in a new devolution settlement.

The Barnett formula per se (i.e. as the sole means of funding) is an extreme example of a soft budget constraint (SBC). Under its rules, established by the Labour government in 1978, Scottish Government spending, S, equals the difference between taxes raised in Scotland, T_S, less taxes, T_{-W}, 'sent to Westminster', plus Barnett funds, F, transferred to Scotland. Or:

$$(1) \qquad S = T_S - T_{-W} + F$$

Thus, under Barnett all income and expenditure taxes, as well as some other taxes (such as betting tax) collected in Scotland (T_S) are transferred to Westminster, meaning that Scottish Government spending is financed just by the Barnett block grant. The so-called 'tartan tax', the ability to change the basic rate of income tax in Scotland by plus/minus 3 per cent, was never used.

It is the absence of tax issues in Scottish Parliamentary deliberations that makes Barnett a soft budget constraint. Thus:

a   With Barnett, as the Scottish Parliament does not have to be concerned with tax policy at all, questions that are the essence of fiscal policy and tough decision-making never come up. The Scottish Parliament never has to ask: 'Is it worth raising more taxes to finance more government spending?', or, 'Is it worth cutting Scottish public spending to be able to cut Scottish taxes?' But with a HBC these are real questions with politicians having to make decisions involving very real trade-offs between: (i) more spending and the political cost that comes with it – more taxing; and (ii) the political benefit of less taxing with the cost of less spending.
b   With Barnett it is not in the Scottish political domain that the size of the Scottish tax base (from which taxes are collected) matters for the long-run prosperity of Scotland and thus the future levels of public spending. No thought has to be given by the Scottish polity to whether tax policy can be used to promote work incentives or entrepreneurship. The size of the Scottish tax base needed to finance increased spending in the future is neither here nor there.
c   With Barnett, if taxes raised in Scotland happen to fall, the Scottish polity does not have to be concerned with balancing the budget by cutting the level of public spending.
d   With Barnett, the Scottish polity does not have to risk the wrath of voters by raising tax rates (rather than cutting its spending).
e   With Barnett, the Scottish polity does not have to think about increasing its borrowing by issuing tradable securities against future tax revenues.

It is for all of these reasons that under the Barnett block grant system the Scottish Government is most unlikely ever to have to worry about the balance of public and private spending in Scotland both in the present or over time – the size of the Scottish tax base from which tax revenues are drawn just doesn't matter to politicians who can only be elected and re-elected on what the voters think of their spending choices.

So it is that the absence of an HBC for the Scottish polity also means that there is the same absence for the voters. All the voter has to decide on is which politicians offer them the best spending policies. This is not a proper fiscal system in which politicians have to offer a combination of spending and taxing policies.

The hardness of the budget constraint, and the advantages it brings for taxpayers across the UK, is increased the smaller is the block grant relative to own-sourced taxes.

2 The budget constraint proposed by the Calman Commission (2009) and in the Scotland Act, 2012

The Scotland Act, 2012, retained the mechanism of the Scottish Consolidated Fund into which Westminster at its discretion pays in funds for use by the Scottish Parliament – is clear about what it wanted to achieve with respect to income taxes. Paragraph 26 (2B) says that (from April 2016), the basic rate, higher rate and additional rate for a tax year on the non-savings income of a Scottish taxpayer is to be found as follows. Step 1: Take the basic rate, higher rate or additional rate determined [by Westminster]. Step 2: Deduct ten percentage points. Step 3: Add the Scottish rate (if any) set by the Scottish Parliament for that year. Then the Scottish Government obtains for its own use the taxes gathered from the Scottish income tax rate as determined by Step 3. These are 'own-sourced taxes' and they are expected to increase fiscal discipline as the Scottish Government's spending is now linked to the discipline of raising taxes from Scottish taxpayers.

However, the Scotland Act, 2012 left undefined what was to happen to the block grant – the words 'block' and 'grant' do not appear in the legislation. This is as in the Calman Commission (2009) proposals that underpinned the 2012 Act. The Calman Commission said that what would happen to the block grant was beyond its remit.

However, Recommendation 3.4 of the Calman Commission reads:

> The block grant, as the means of financing most associated with equity [between regions in the UK], should continue to make up the remainder [i.e. 83 per cent] of the Scottish Parliament's Budget but it should be justified by need. Until such times as a proper assessment of relative spending need across the UK is carried out, the Barnett formula should continue to be used as the basis for calculating the proportionately reduced block grant.

The UK Office of Budget Responsibility (2012) underlined this lack of commitment to a new policy on the block grant, noting that the eventual decision on the method for adjusting the block grant will be a matter for the UK and Scottish governments (paragraph 1.8).[6] This moment arrived with the May 2015 Scotland Bill that we discuss below.

It is really quite odd that, despite this lack of clarity over the future of the block grant, the Calman Commission claimed that: 'we are clear that real financial accountability is achieved' (paragraph 3.181). This was an unjustified claim because no policy was set on what would happen to the block grant if and when Scottish own-sourced taxes rose or fell.

Thus, would fiscal failure (e.g. spending own-sourced taxes in a way that reduces work incentives) be rewarded by a larger block grant (apparently, yes, if the 'needs' referred to in Calman didn't also happen to fall)? Alternatively, would fiscal success be rewarded by a smaller block grant (again, possibly, yes, if 'needs' remain unchanged and Scotland was able to finance an increasing proportion of these needs out of own-sourced taxes)?

Under these circumstances – tax policy success rewarded with a lower block grant and tax policy failure with a larger block grant – in terms of equation (1), the only difference that Scottish own-sourced taxes would make is that Scottish taxes transferred to the Consolidated Fund, T_W, would be reduced alongside an equal reduction in block grant funds, F, transferred into Scotland.

If this was the case there is no incentive for the Scottish Government to worry about tax policy or the tax costs of its spending policies. Only if the Scottish Government got to enjoy incremental net revenues would it have any real interest in using tax policy to benefit the Scottish economy; similarly, an HBC would require that any failure on tax policy not be automatically offset by a larger block grant.

3 Scottish Labour Devolution Commission proposals

The Scottish Labour Devolution Commission (2014) opened by noting that it is impossible to close the fiscal gap to zero unless Scotland were independent. So they are about balancing the accountability of the Scottish Parliament to its voters so that they have a stake in the success of the Scottish economy – i.e. to get the extra revenue if it successfully grows the economy. Scots should also share in the rest of the UK resources so that all could enjoy similar levels of prosperity and be guaranteed the same rights such as free health care at the point of need. Scottish Labour proposed giving the Scottish Parliament powers to raise around £2 billion more in revenues in addition to the Scotland Act (2012), so raising about 40 per cent of its budget from its own resources. Thus there would be a 60–40 per cent split between, respectively, a block grant and own-sourced taxes (Scottish Labour Devolution Commission 2014: 65–66).

The main way own-sourced taxes would be increased is by widening the variation of income tax by half (relative to what is in the Scotland Act, 2012) from 10 pence to 15 pence so that three quarters of basic rate income tax will be under the control of Scottish Parliament.

Scottish Labour also proposed introducing a Scottish progressive income tax rate in the higher income tax rate bands, but there would be no powers to reduce those rates relative to what was already set by Westminster.

Scottish Labour also said that VAT, national insurance contributions, corporation tax, alcohol, tobacco and fuel duty, climate change levy, insurance premium tax, vehicle excise duty, inheritance tax, capital gains tax and tax on oil should remain 'reserved' – they would continue to be set at Westminster.

As to the block grant from rest of the UK (rUK) the Scottish Labour Devolution Commission planned to keep the Barnett formula, saying:

> the Barnett formula should remain as the funding mechanism for public services in Scotland. Under our proposal, the grant will be reduced to take account of the fact that the Scottish Parliament will have a revenue stream of its own … principally Scottish income tax payers.
>
> (2014: 16)

Scottish Labour went on to argue that these proposals would ensure the appropriate balance between fairness, accountability and efficiency.

SCOTTISH LABOUR AND THE HBC

Scottish Labour proposals did not address the issue of the HBC. At best, the matter is fudged. They repeatedly (but implicitly) implied that the budget constraint would be soft: if own-sourced tax funding plus the block grant became inadequate to finance Scottish public spending it would be made good by increased funding from the rUK.

For example, they asserted that the UK is a 'sharing union', with economic, social, and political aspects, in which risks and rewards are collectively pooled (11). Later they asserted that welfare benefits are the key instrument of social union (136); that Barnett provides stability in levels of public funding, and so public services (139); that a tax programme should include constancy in fiscal-policy making and the way fiscal policy impacts the economy (141); and that there is a need to retain a shared taxation base with the UK to ensure social solidarity and a minimum level of public service provision across the country (146–147).

It is easy to see that the 2014 Scottish Labour proposals were not a design for an HBC but an outline of a social programme – the Scottish tax system should 'support aspirations', 'promote a green economy', and have 'flexibility to fund public expenditure' (146–147).

Nor was any consideration given to using the tax system to raise the tax base by promoting economic growth; rather it was repeatedly asserted that tax competition is a bad thing – especially in rates of corporation tax and at the higher rates of income tax.[7]

4 The Holtham Commission

One year after the Calman Commission made its recommendations the Holtham Commission (2010) made recommendations for tax devolution to Wales. Its deliberations are relevant to the Scottish case given that the Scotland Act, 2012, Scottish Labour's proposals, and the Scotland Bill, 2015 have so many unresolved issues in terms of HBC.

Like the Calman Commission, the Holtham Commission emphasized a needs-based funding regime (para. 2.19, p. 12) for the Welsh Assembly Government.

Yet the Holtham Commission also set the principle that 'the Welsh budget should *not* be protected from Welsh *policy risk*, i.e. changes to the tax-base arising from decisions of Welsh Ministers should have their budgetary impact in Wales' (para. 5.8, p. 47). This means that the Welsh Assembly Government would keep for its own purposes 100 per cent of any extra tax revenues it generated from changes in its tax rates with no reduction in the block grant. Also, any reduction in tax revenues due to a reduction in its tax rates relative to those in England would also be borne by Wales with no increase in the block grant.

The policy of a needs based fiscal regime and Wales bearing its own policy risk are conflicting because if Welsh own-sourced taxes fell Wales would not be able to meet its 'needs' – assuming them to be unchanging – out of the sum of block grant and own-sourced taxes. But Holtham has a very neat answer to this – as we are about to see.

Similarly, an increase in Welsh Assembly Government revenues relative to needs may also be problematic because English taxpayers could well ask why they should pay the same block grant to Wales when the Welsh Assembly Government had more than sufficient revenues to meet Welsh needs.

It is arguable therefore that the proposed policy of tax revenue changes due Welsh Assembly Government tax policy being incident on Wales is a politically non-viable. Rather, if needs are emphasized, lower Welsh tax revenues would be offset by larger block grants.

In fact, the Holtham Commission brilliantly recognized that its two priorities – financing of 'needs' and the effects of Welsh tax policy being incident only on Wales – were contradictory; to have one is not necessarily to have the other. The Holtham Commission resolved this contradiction by recommending infrequent changes in the size of the Welsh block grant – every 12 or 15 years, irrespective of whether the Welsh tax base was growing or shrinking. This is the 'Holtham interlude'.

Under such a regime, should Welsh own-sourced taxes fall they would not be immediately balanced by an increase in the block grant and Welsh citizens would suffer the consequences. And should Welsh own-sourced taxes increase, the block grant would not be immediately reduced and Welsh citizens would enjoy enhanced levels of public spending.

The most important aspect of this arrangement is that, at least during the 12- or 15-year interval, it amounts to an HBC with the needs principle effectively sacrificed to the 'Welsh tax policy incident on Wales' principle. The social solidarity so evident in the proposals of Scottish Labour is there, but in the long run.

5 The Scottish Liberal Democrats Commission

The Scottish Liberal Democrats Commission (SLDC) on devolution built on the 2006 Steel Commission report. They proposed a version of home rule for Scotland within a reformed, federal United Kingdom. By home rule they meant that the Scottish Parliament would have control over most aspects of Scottish domestic affairs, including responsibility for raising the finance for the greater part of its own spending, but with welfare and pensions (as well as defence) provided by Westminster.

To quote from the SLDC's document:

> The plans would allocate permanently to the Scottish Parliament control of the rates and bands of income tax, capital gains tax, inheritance tax and air passenger duty. Together with the proceeds from corporation tax this would give the Scottish Parliament the authority over 60 per cent of what it spends.
> (Scottish Liberal Democrats 2014: 7)

The SLDC rightly saw this as a radical transfer of powers in a new system of fiscal federalism within the UK which would keep intact the UK single market and the 'social welfare union' and 'open up choices to be made in Scotland about the kind of country we should be' (2014: 7–8).

THE SCOTTISH LIBERAL DEMOCRATS' PROPOSED BUDGET CONSTRAINT

Under the Scottish Liberal Democrats' proposals the budget constraint faced by the Scottish parliament would have become:

$$(2) \qquad S = T_S - T_{-W} + F + B$$

where B is borrowing (set at a maximum aggregated limit of £1 billion) to be used to cushion spending in a cyclical downturn, that is, to maintain S even as T_S falls. The other terms have the same meaning as before. The share of own-sourced taxes in Scottish Government spending $(T_S - T_{-W})/S$ would be about 55 per cent or so. This was a good deal higher than that of Scottish Labour, set at about 40 per cent. Also, fiscal transfers from Westminster, F, would ultimately change from being set by the Barnett formula to being 'needs based'.

How hard would the SLDC's budget constraint have been, what incentives would it have given to Scottish voters to elect Scottish governments committed to adopting policies to raise the Scottish tax base by promoting economic growth; and what incentives does it give to MSPs to offer such growth promoting policies?

As all income tax collected in Scotland is to be retained there and that income tax is the largest single source of tax revenue, it offered a strong incentive to grow the income tax base as it could lead either to greater public spending in Scotland or to lowered income tax rates.[8] Moreover, the Scottish Liberal Democrats referred favourably to the Holtham Commission, and as we have seen the latter suggested a 12–15 year HBC. That is, any adverse consequences of Scottish fiscal spending or taxing policies would not be bailed out by the rUK immediately, and SCG would have to bear the policy risk for that extended period of time.

What was not absolutely clear in the Scottish Liberal Democrats' recommendations was how the needs assessment would operate. If the rUK were to finance 100 per cent of these needs that would mean that the Scottish Government would have little fiscal interest in adopting policies to reduce them – which would mean that the rUK would bear the policy risk for policies it was not responsible for. The important thing here is how much of its 'needs' would Scotland have to finance out of its own-sourced taxes. If it was a high percentage it would incentivize the Scottish Government both to adopt policies aimed at reducing the 'needs' as well as policies aimed at raising the tax base to make them easier to finance.

The opposite would be true if Scotland was required to finance only a small percentage of its needs, as it would not benefit fiscally from reducing them and would not have the incentive to grow its tax base to finance them. The SLDC really should have offered more detail on these matters.

6 The Scottish Conservatives

The Scottish Conservative Commission (Scottish Conservatives 2014) (known as the Strathclyde Commission) identified a fiscal gap (or vertical imbalance as defined in the literature on public finance) and noted (see also Hallwood and MacDonald 2009) that this was large in the Scottish context since, although the Scottish Parliament and Government have control over more than 60 per cent of identifiable public spending, they are responsible for only raising a small fraction of that amount. Closing the fiscal gap through fiscal devolution, they argued, would create a more responsible polity. Their main proposal was that the Scottish Parliament should be responsible for setting the rates and bands of personal income tax in Scotland. Income tax on investment and savings should remain in the UK to safeguard the integrity of the UK's single market in financial services. The personal allowance should be set for the whole of the UK.[9]

THE SCOTTISH CONSERVATIVES' PROPOSED BUDGET CONSTRAINT

The proposals of the Scottish Conservatives (2014) were clearly informed by the idea that tax systems are about the revenue side of government policy while commitments to public spending programmes are on the other side of the ledger. With this clarity they called for an HBC on spending by the Scottish Government. Thus:

> we need to ensure that devolved policy choices have a direct link to the money available to the Scottish Exchequer ... otherwise all efforts to establish fiscal accountability are wasted ... any further fiscal devolution [should] demonstrate a clear link between Scottish fiscal policy choices and expenditure in Scotland.

This statement came close to a 'no bailout clause'. Scottish governments could enjoy higher tax revenues if they could create them; but if they adopted policies that weakened the Scottish tax base then they would suffer the consequences. This, of course, is the nature of an HBC.

However, the Scottish Conservatives did imply that block grants could be adjusted, but only after a delay during which the consequences of tax policy were felt. This idea squares with the 'Holtham interlude'. The Scottish Conservatives' proposal had the attractive feature of combining an HBC in the medium term with maintenance of the 'welfare union'.

The Scottish Conservatives were also in agreement with the Scottish Liberal Democrats in that:

> the Scottish Parliament should be responsible for setting the rates and bands of personal income tax in Scotland.
>
> (2014: 13)

It also concluded that pension and social security financial provisions would remain at the UK level. If Scotland wants to be more generous than that, it should finance them itself.

7 The Scottish National Party.

The SNP's proposed fiscal powers (Scottish Government 2014) for the Scottish Parliament were contained in four key points. The Scottish Parliament should have 'full fiscal responsibility' in that all tax revenues should be retained in Scotland unless there is a particular case for continued reservation. In their view, the Scottish Parliament should have full fiscal autonomy with control over income tax, national insurance, corporation tax, capital gains tax, fuel duty, air passenger tax and inheritance tax. Under EU legislation, VAT and some excise duties would be reserved taxes. However, although such taxes would not be devolved, the SNP favoured 100 per cent assignment of such reserved taxes.

Additionally, the SNP proposed that the Scottish Parliament should be responsible for all domestic expenditure, including welfare spending, and would only make payments for reserved matters (defence and foreign affairs) to the UK government. They also argued that to have a sustainable framework for public finances would require the 'necessary borrowing powers'. In any agreement which falls short of full fiscal responsibility, the SNP argued that the Barnett formula should continue to be used to determine Scotland's resources during any transitional period[10] and that the formula should be adjusted appropriately according to the actual degree of fiscal responsibility.

THE SNP'S PROPOSED BUDGET CONSTRAINT

Comparing all the proposals prior to the 2014 referendum, the SNP's budget constraint was the hardest of all – all spending to be financed out of own-sourced taxes. And after a phase-in period their proposals did not allow for a welfare union because transfers from Westminster would be phased out. Moreover, it was made clear to the SNP by, for example, the Bank of England, that an independent Scotland within the sterling area could have only limited borrowing powers, meaning that this particular shock absorber would not be available.

It is interesting to note that the SNP emphasized the macroeconomic framework in which their policy would be embedded. Specifically, it would be embedded in the sterling zone monetary union with exchange rate and interest rate setting being reserved matters; and financial stability would also continue to be delivered across the United Kingdom by the Bank of England. Most tellingly, the SNP noted that: 'Scotland would use its greater tax, spending and borrowing powers within a sustainable overall fiscal envelope guaranteed by clear rules and procedures to ensure affordability' (Scottish Government 2014).

However, it is hard to see how the full fiscal autonomy option would work in practice, absent political independence, since there is no historical precedent for such a devolved system working within a nation state anywhere in the world. Such a system would presumably require unlimited borrowing powers for the Scottish Government for both current and capital spending and there would always be the risk (to the rest of the UK) that Scotland would have to be bailed out since borrowing, say to meet a shortfall in the oil revenues, would probably be unsustainable (given the Scottish electorate would not be prepared to accept the consequences for taxes and their expenditure) and this would threaten the stability of the UK-wide financial system. One could of course argue that the recent Eurozone experience represents an example of the kind of issues that could arise if Scotland had full fiscal autonomy (i.e. no fiscal union) whilst remaining part of the sterling monetary union, although of course the countries comprising the Eurozone are politically independent.

8 The Scottish Greens

In general terms the Scottish Green Party (Harvie and Chapman 2014) argued that the Scottish Parliament and local authorities should have the powers to design and raise the majority of their own taxes and therefore fund the majority of their own spending. More specifically, the SGP argued for the devolution of taxes which can easily be made progressive, those based on immovable assets, such as land and property, and those which are intended to achieve behavioural changes such as environmental and resource taxes. The Greens argued for the full devolution of income tax in terms of rates, band reliefs and personal allowances. Taxes levied at a flat rate such as VAT and corporation tax should not in their view be devolved but could have a percentage of the revenue assigned. The Greens recognized the importance of the pooling and sharing of resources stressed by the Better Together campaign during the referendum campaign. They suggested the block grant should be retained and set by a yet to be agreed formula.

With respect to borrowing powers, the Scottish Greens argued that the Scottish Parliament needed the freedom to make its own borrowing decisions, without the need for approval given or limits set by the UK Government. However, the Bank of England during the referendum campaign said that the latter could very well be inconsistent with macroeconomic policy set for the whole of the UK. If the Scottish Parliament insisted on it there would have to be a credible 'no bailout' clause so that financial markets in no way came to believe that the rUK would come to the rescue in the case of default.

9 The Scotland Bill (2015)

The strictness of the rules governing the financing of Scottish Government expenditures through own-sourced taxes and a continuing block grant did not and do not set a strict, or inelastic limit on the amount of funding that would or could be available for spending. The Scotland Act (1998) created the Scottish Consolidated Fund (section 64(1)) allowing 'The Secretary of State [for Scotland] shall from time to time make payments into the Fund out of money provided by [the Westminster] Parliament of such amounts as he [sic] may determine' (64(2)). In this sentence money 'provided' means money 'voted'.

The implication is that the amount of funding available to the Scottish Parliament can be changed by Westminster – a political decision made at the UK level. By way of example, if the amount of own-sourced taxes and existing block grant became insufficient to meet Scottish Government spending needs – perhaps because not enough had been done to increase the Scottish tax base – more funds could be made available to Scotland through a vote in Westminster. This would be more likely, we think, if the political party in power at Westminster wanted to win more votes in Scotland. Crucially, there is nothing in the Scotland Bill (2015) that sets limits on this extra, and elastic, source of funding.[11] The implication of the foregoing is, then, that the Scottish Parliament does not necessarily face a hard budget constraint on its spending even after 'tough rules' have been set on Scottish tax sources and residual Barnett block grant; there is always the possibility of a 'bailout' via increased funding from Westminster.

Conclusion

This chapter considered the devolution of more fiscal powers to the Scottish Parliament and Government. The argument builds on policy ideas aired by us a decade ago played out in the context of the current political environment in Scotland.

We have argued that a soft budget constraint (SBC) would continue to allow the Scottish Parliament and Government to spend without having to consider all of the tax and, therefore, political consequences in Scotland, of that spending.

There is a need to consider the continuing financial relationship between the Scottish Consolidated Fund and the Westminster Treasury's Consolidated Fund: unless legislation was put in place tying the hands of the Westminster Parliament – which the Scotland Bill 2015 does not do – it would remain the case that if 'needs be' – a political advantage could be gained – extra funding could be made available to the Scottish Parliament and Government. Such SBC would effectively continue the current situation where the incentives to promote economic growth through Scottish fiscal policy – on both the tax and spending sides – are weaker than they otherwise could be. This is what the Scotland Act 1998, the continuing use of the Barnett block and the Scotland Bill 2015, granted to Scotland.

Other budget constraints have been suggested: those of the Calman Commission (2009) and the Scotland Act (2012), as well as by the Smith Commission (2014) and the ones offered in 2014 by the various political parties – Scottish Conservatives, Scottish Greens, Scottish Labour, Scottish Liberal Democrats and the Scottish Government (SNP). There is also the budget constraint designed by the Holtham Commission (2010) for Wales that could be used in Scotland.

We've examined to what extent these offer the hard budget constraint (HBC) that would bring tax policy firmly into the realm of Scottish politics, asking the Scottish electorate and Parliament to consider the costs to them of increasing spending in terms of higher taxes; or the benefits to them of using public spending to grow the tax base and own-sourced taxes.

The hardest budget constraint of all is offered by independence but, as is now known, a clear majority of those who voted in the referendum did not vote for this form of budget constraint. Rather they voted for a significant further devolution of fiscal powers while remaining within a political and monetary union with the rest of the UK, with the risk pooling and revenue sharing that this implies.

It is not surprising therefore that none of the budget constraints on offer, apart from the SNP's, are the same as the HBC of independence. Although the Scotland Bill 2015 does offer a harder budget constraint than its predecessors there is still the issue, raised in this chapter, that it may not be quite hard enough due to the Barnett legacy. However, the so-called 'no-detriment' clause, which has created much heat and not perhaps much light, is a means of addressing this at least in part. To quote Smith: 'the Scottish and UK Governments' budgets should be no larger or smaller simply as a result of the initial transfer of tax and/or spending powers, before considering how these are used'. So in the first year the block grant will be cut by an amount equal to the amount raised in new taxes, thereby maintaining the same budget in Scotland and in the rest of the UK – so neither Westminster nor the Scottish Parliament suffer detrimental consequences of the new devolved powers. And, similarly, the block grant should be enhanced in any initial settlement to reflect any further devolved spending to the Scottish Parliament. In moving away from the initial devolved settlement Smith envisages the growth of the block grant being indexed to an external factor such as, perhaps, the growth of UK tax revenue. In this way the Scottish Government could grow its overall budget if it introduced 'growth friendly policies'. In terms of the latter, the majority of this leverage can only come from income tax changes. The marginal tax rule, for example, suggests that a more powerful devolution settlement would trade off changes in one major tax – say corporation tax – for changes in another – income tax.

Notes

1 *Report of the Smith Commission for Further Devolution of Powers to the Scottish Parliament*.
2 *New Wealth for Old Nations*, ed. Diane Coyle, Wendy Alexander and Brian Ashcroft, Princeton, NJ: Princeton University Press, 2005.
3 In the same vein we wrote: 'The principle of equalisation, effected by a bloc grant, raises the "moral hazard" issue caused by the lack of a hard budget constraint on public spending in Scotland' (pp. 22–23) ... 'At issue is how to align more closely the decisions of politicians and civil servants (the agents) with those of the electorate (the principal)' (p. 23) ... '[Scottish] politicians have little incentive to spend much of the [Barnett financed] budget on goods and services which might raise economic growth [in Scotland] since the benefits of improved growth, in terms of increased tax revenue, accrue to the exchequer in London' (p. 30).
4 That neither the Westminster nor Scottish governments will lose nor gain from the transference of further powers is captured by the no-detriment clause, discussed further below.
5 In particular see Oates (2004).
6 Office of Budget Responsibility, *Forecasting Scottish Taxes*, March 2012. Available at: http://budgetresponsibility.org.uk/wordpress/docs/Forecasting-Scottish-taxes.pdf.
7 How much difference would it have made that the proposed block grant would drop from 100 per cent of spending to 60 per cent? Since Scottish Labour said nothing about this, and especially not with respect to an HBC, here are some scenarios that illustrate what a mix-up Scottish Labour was presenting: (1) If Scottish Labour meant what it said, that 'the Barnett grant will be reduced to take account of the fact that the Scottish Parliament will have a revenue stream of its own', then the incentives to take measures to increase the Scottish base and increase taxes collected in Scotland would have been weak because each extra pound of tax revenue would be offset by one less pound of block grant. To make the incentives sharper what was needed was a clear statement – which was not made – that each extra pound of tax revenues collected in Scotland would remain with the Scottish Government for the financing of extra spending or reduction in Scottish tax rates. (2) It was never made clear by Scottish Labour what it meant when it referred to a 60–40 per cent split between block grant and

own-sourced taxes. If they meant that it is to hold through time then there would be a perverse incentive to increase the Scottish tax base and taxes collected in Scotland, as that would mean larger block grants! It is hard to believe that anybody would have argued for that, not least because it ran against the grain of the 'welfare union' – a Scotland that anyway starts off with relatively high per capita income in the UK would be in receipt of larger and larger block grants financed by the rUK. (3) While the latter is too extreme to be realistic – it is just an example of Scottish Labour's lack of clarity – under the Barnett formula, Scotland would anyway be receiving ever larger block grants as public spending in the rUK increased. Thus, it could be that if the Scottish Government took measures successfully to increase the Scottish base and tax collections, this source of public funding would be supplemented by a growing block grant. This too seems to run against the grain of a 'welfare union' for the reasons just stated. Moreover, better than risk some future less favourable block grant formula, it is quite easy to imagine that Scottish Governments would not risk taking measures to raise the Scottish tax base and tax collections. That is, as under the Barnett formula, even as adjusted in the Scottish Labour document, there is a strong incentive not to introduce growth-promoting fiscal policies. These would be risky as they might not pay off and could be politically unpopular – and if they did work, could end up being rewarded with a smaller block grant.
8 To be given 'powers over income tax, bands and rates' (2012: 10). Recommendation 15: Income tax paid by Scottish taxpayers should be almost entirely the responsibility of the Scottish Parliament.
9 In more detail, the Scottish Conservatives argued that a 'share' (left undefined) of VAT should be assigned to Scotland. National insurance (both employees' and employers' contributions) should not be devolved if the social security system was to continue to operate at a UK-wide level and provide the same benefits to all. Corporation tax should not be devolved since it relates to activity that can easily be transferred across borders and it is highly volatile and does not give a reliable yield. Capital gains and inheritance taxes are not high-yielding taxes and they are seen as not being suitable for devolution. Smaller taxes bundled, such as air passenger duty, climate change levy, excise fuel and vehicle duties, etc., were also considered but these totalled less than 10 per cent of UK tax revenue; some also relate to activities that are highly mobile (e.g. fuel duty and betting duties) and so should not be devolved. Air passenger duty should be devolved. The Scottish Conservatives Commission noted that the volatility of North Sea oil revenues – £10 billion in 2011/12 to £5.5 billion in 2012/13 – mean that this is better smoothed by the whole of the UK and so it is unsuitable for devolution.
10 The SNP accepts that the transition to full fiscal responsibility will take some years to complete, as implementation of the Scotland Act 2012 has demonstrated.
11 H.M. Government (2015) refers to the Scottish Consolidated Fund only to say that a share of Scottish VAT and some minor revenues will be paid into it – 2.13.3, 4.23.3, and 5.5.7. The Scotland Bill (2015) and Scotland Bill Explanatory Notes refer to it in the same contexts.

Sources for further reading and study

Gruber, J. (2010) *Public Finance and Policy*, 3rd edn, especially Chapter 10, 'State and Local Government Expenditures'. New York: Worth Publishers.

Oates, W.E. (1999) 'An Essay on Fiscal Federalism'. *Journal of Economic Literature* 37, September: 1120–1149.

Oates, W.E. (2005) 'Towards a Second Generation Theory of Fiscal Federalism'. *International Tax and Finance* 12: 349–373.

References

Calman Commission (Commission on Scottish Devolution) (2009) *Serving Scotland Better: Scotland and the United Kingdom in the 21st Century*, June. Available at: http://news.bbc.co.uk/2/shared/bsp/hi/pdfs/15_06_09_calman.pdf.

Carney, M. (2014) 'The Economics of Currency Unions'. Speech given at the Scottish Council for Development and Industry, 29 January, Edinburgh.

Hallwood, C.P. and R. MacDonald (2004) *Fiscal Federalism*. Allander Series, Scotland's Economic Future, no. 8. Glasgow: Fraser of Allander Institute.

Hallwood, C.P. and R. MacDonald (2005) 'The Economic Case for Fiscal Federalism'. In Diane Coyle, Wendy Alexander and Brian Ashcroft (eds) *New Wealth for Old Nations*. Princeton, NJ: Princeton University Press, pp. 96–118.

Hallwood, C.P. and R. MacDonald (2006a) 'A Restatement of the Case for Scottish Fiscal Autonomy (or, the Barnett Formula – a Formula for a Rake's Progress)'. *Quarterly Economic Commentary* 31(2), October. Also published as University of Glasgow, Department of Economics, Discussion Paper 2006–2014. Available at: www.gla.ac.uk/departments/economics/research/discussion_papers/2006.html.

Hallwood, C.P. and R. MacDonald (2006b) *The Economic Case for Scottish Fiscal Autonomy: with or without Independence*. Pamphlet, May. Edinburgh: Policy Institute. Available at: www.policyinstitute.info/AllPDFs/MacDonaldApr06.pdf. And in I*nternational Conference: Basque Economic Agreement and Europe*, Proceedings of the International Conference of December 2006, ed. Eduardo Alonso Olea. Ad Concordiam Association and the Basque Institute of the University of Deusto. ISBN: 978–984–612–0302. Translated into Spanish and Basque.

Hallwood, C.P. and R. MacDonald (2006c) 'Fiscal Autonomy for Scotland? Yes Please! A Rejoinder'. Department of Economics, University of Glasgow, Discussion Paper 2006–14. Available at: www.gla.ac.uk/departments/economics/research/discussion_papers/2006.html.

Hallwood, C.P. and R. MacDonald (2009) *The Political Economy of Financing Scottish Government*. Cheltenham: Edward Elgar.

Harvie, P. and M. Chapman (2014) 'Scottish Green Party Submission to Smith Commission on Devolution'. Available at: www.scottishgreens.org.uk/wp-content/uploads/downloads/2014/10/SGP-submission-to-Smith-Commission.pdf.

Heald, D. (2003) 'Fiscal Transparency: Concepts, Measurement and UK Practice'. *Public Administration* 81(4): 723–759.

H.M. Government (2015) *Scotland in the United Kingdom: An Enduring Settlement*. Presented to Parliament by the Secretary of State for Scotland, January, Cmd 8990. London: Stationery Office.

H.M. Treasury (2013) *Scotland Analysis: Macroeconomic and Fiscal Performance*, September, Cmd 8694. London: Stationery Office.

Holtham Commission (2010) *Independent Commission on Funding and Finance for Wales, Final report: Fairness and Accountability: A New Funding Settlement for Wales*. Crown Copyright. London: Stationery Office. Available at: http://gov.wales/funding/financereform/reports/?lang=en.

Jones, P. (2014) 'SNP Plans for Increased Powers at Holyrood Represent Independence by Stealth and Would Make the UK Unworkable'. *Scotsman*, 14 October.

Oates, W.E. (2005) 'Towards a Second Generation Theory of Fiscal Federalism'. *International Tax and Finance* 12: 349–373.

Scottish Conservatives (2014) *Commission on the Future Governance of Scotland*. Edinburgh. Available at: www.scottishconservatives.com/wordpress/wp-content/uploads/2014/06/Strathclyde_Commission_14.pdf.

Scottish Government (2014) *More Powers for the Scottish Parliament: Scottish Government Proposals*, Ch. 4, 'Scotland's Economy and Public Finances'. Edinburgh. Available at: www.gov.scot/Publications/2014/10/2806.

Scottish Labour Devolution Commission (2014) *Powers for a Purpose: Strengthening Accountability and Empowering People*. Edinburgh. Available at: http://b.3cdn.net/scotlab/26e0eb4bdf4c775d14_ram6b81bk.pdf.

Scottish Liberal Democrats (2014) *The Report of the Home Rule and Community Rule Commission of the Federalism: The Best Future for Scotland*. Edinburgh. Available at: http://worldofstuart.excellentcontent.com/repository/CampbellIIreport.pdf.

Smith, R. (Baron Smith of Kelvin) (2014) *Report of the Smith Commission for Further Devolution of Powers to the Scottish Parliament*. Available at: www.smith-commission.scot/wp-content/uploads/2014/11/The_Smith_Commission_Report-1.pdf.

6 Scottish local government
Past, present and futures

Colin Mair

Introduction: devolution and subsidiarity

'Devolution' and 'subsidiarity' have been a central focus within the Scottish political narrative over the last few years. This has been substantially driven by the independence referendum in 2014, and the subsequent Smith Commission report on further devolved powers for the Scottish Parliament. However, as Lord Smith noted in the preface to his report, devolution within Scotland warranted the same critical attention as devolution to Scotland (Smith 2014).

It was, at the least, ironic that during the run through to a referendum built around the subsidiarity principle, single national police and fire services were created by simply removing these services from local government control and at the same time, local councils were obliged to 'freeze' the level of local taxation, or face grant penalties equivalent to the increase they levied. As the Scottish Government grant now accounts for over 80 per cent of local government income, councils have little choice but to comply with this requirement.

This is not a particular critique of the current SNP Government in Scotland: all the major parties, with the exception of the Green party, advocated the freezing of local taxes at the 2011 Scottish Parliament elections and most favoured taking major services away from local government (police, fire and rescue, care services) by creating national agencies. That freezing a local tax featured in major parties' manifestos for a national parliamentary election sums up an attitude of mind: better to have such decisions made nationally than leave them to the vagaries of local choice. Whatever else this represents, at minimum, it suggests considerable ambivalence about subsidiarity within Scotland, and about the role of local government as part of that.

Nor is this new: it reflects a much longer term trend that we examine below. Between 1974 and 1996, Scotland went from having over 200 elected local governments to having 32. Across the period since 1974, responsibility for public health, community health care, further education colleges, water and sewerage services, police and fire services have all been removed from local democratic governance in Scotland. At the same time, half of the local fiscal base was removed from local control by removing the setting of business rates from councils, though more recently the Scottish Government has eased this and permitted councils to reduce business rates to stimulate economic and business activity and retain the revenue locally.

We can find no comparable erosion in the number of local governments, the role of local government and the fiscal base of local government in any other European country in the post-Second World War period. The scale of change points to systemic issues that we will tease out below. The key introductory point is simply that the recent past is in line with a much longer trend.

This chapter explores what has happened to local government over the last fifty years, why it happened and the future(s) for local government that may imply. It must be acknowledged, however, that commitment to decentralisation and subsidiarity need not and, recently, has not focused on the role of institutional local government and local representative democracy. 'Participative democracy' and 'community empowerment' have recently been emphasised: getting beyond and below the institutional structures of government and local government to enable citizens and communities to be truly in control of their own opportunities and outcomes in life (e.g. The Community Empowerment Scotland Act, 2015).

If 'subsidiarity' should not stop at the Scottish Parliament, then presumably it should not stop at the council chamber either. It could potentially imply decision making at community level or even household level, rather than by local government. These tensions between 'representative' and 'participative' democracy, between local government and community governance, will be explored in the final section of the chapter that looks at the potential futures of local government in Scotland. The potential links between current advocacy of alternative approaches to local democracy, and the longer term trend of rationalisation and (de)localisation of local government are explored in that context.

Across the chapter, three key narratives are identified as shaping thinking about local government in Scotland across the last fifty years. There is a strong technocratic narrative that has focused on the proper planning and delivery of services: the achievement of economies of scale and skill, identifying efficient modes of specialisation, and ensuring local government was an effective vehicle for the delivery of national policy. This narrative generates a 'delivery system' view of local government and sees the public as consumers of services, rather than citizens within an active local democracy.

The second narrative is substantially a response to the perceived defects of the first. Large scale corporate structures tend to become remote and bureaucratic, and struggle to respond effectively to the diversity of communities, cultures and contexts in Scotland. Corporate bodies focus on their own distinct roles, responsibilities and accountabilities at the cost of a 'joined up' approach to households and communities. Strict demarcation of roles and responsibilities leads to fragmentation: a focus on services, not outcomes. Finally, not all 'consumers' are equivalently empowered, and corporate public services have worked least well for the most vulnerable households and communities. They have tried to do things to such communities, rather than working with them to improve their lives and opportunities.

The third narrative has developed around 'devolution' of powers within the UK and, more recently, has emphasised 'subsidiarity' in the form of 'devo max', 'full fiscal autonomy' and 'independence'. While 'devolution' implies an empowered superior level of government that delegates some of its powers to a subordinate level of government, 'subsidiarity' asserts a much stronger claim: that citizens and communities have the right for decisions affecting them to be made as close to them as is possible, and the right to be actively involved in them. The confused and contentious discussion following the independence referendum reflects the gap between 'devolution' and 'subsidiarity': devolution is 'top down' and subsidiarity is 'bottom up'.

Although the focus has shifted around between 'devolution' and 'subsidiarity', the locus remains the Scottish Parliament, and its powers. That an equivalent case for devolution and subsidiarity could be made within Scotland is evident, but is either ignored or sequenced: the Scottish Parliament can only be truly empowering if it itself becomes fully empowered.

These narratives have had serial impacts on local government, as we explore in the following sections. They evolved at different points in time, but elements of previous narratives continue to have influence even when new narratives develop. All of these narratives contain valid points, albeit in an overly accentuated way. The chapter explores the extent to which they can be reconciled and integrated to provide a more coherent framework for reform.

From evolution to revolution: towards technocracy, service delivery for central government – rather than local democracy

In the 1960s and early 1970s, Scotland had 206 elected local authorities, county councils, city corporations, new town development corporations, town councils and burghs. These bodies had a diverse array of distinctive powers and functions and often overlapping jurisdictions. However, the larger councils, counties and cities, had responsibility for major services such as education, public health, community health and care, and child protection, which were clearly statutorily prescribed and related to national rights and entitlements locally delivered. The smaller councils delivered services that were seen to be more reasonably open to local choice, or were discretionary in character (e.g. waste collection, leisure and recreation, local planning and licensing).

The system was closer to other Northern European countries in terms of number and diversity of councils than it is now, but was seen as seriously problematic. It had evolved rather than been designed; was highly fragmented and deemed confusing for the public; required substantial duplication of political and management resources; was subject to 'turf wars' with overlapping jurisdictions; and characterised by very low electoral turnouts and uncontested elections, particularly for the smallest councils.

It was ripe for review, and was reviewed in the late 1960s. The Wheatley Commission reported in 1969, and fundamentally transformed the local government landscape (Wheatley 1969). The Commission's conclusions and recommendations were driven by a number of key assumptions that have had influence on the subsequent history of local government. These are:

1. 'Form follows function': the structure of local government should be driven by the scale and capacity necessary to deliver the services it is charged with. Different types of services required different scales and capacities.
2. 'Technocratic imperatives override democratic imperatives': getting the right scale and capacity, and economies of scale and skill, was necessary even if that eroded the true 'localness' of local government in Scotland. In the Commission's work, 'local' rapidly becomes simply 'sub-national' and it is no accident that one of its core recommendations was for 'regional' councils, one of which covered around 50 per cent of the Scottish population.
3. 'Self-sufficiency': by getting the scale and capacity right, councils should be self-sufficient in delivering their functions rather than dependent on others or interdependent with others.

The effect was revolutionary. There would be a two-tier system of local government in Scotland. 'Regions' would be responsible for services that required a large scale and capacity, and therefore a large population catchment. The major services would be education, social work and social care, roads and strategic planning. 'Districts' would provide more local services such as leisure and libraries, parks and open spaces, waste collection and management that could be provided with smaller scale and capacity. The Shetland and Orkney Islands were seen as impossible to fit to this model because of their remoteness and small populations so they would be 'unitary' councils, i.e. responsible for all services.

The Commission recommended seven regions, thirty-seven districts and the two unitary councils. The regions were defined geographically to be broadly equivalent in territorial scale, albeit completely different in population scale given the uneven population distribution in Scotland. The Commission's recommendations were seriously challenged through consultation, and throughout the legislative process that followed, largely on issues of historical and geographical identity. The end result was nine regions, rather than seven, with Fife and Borders becoming regions in their own right. The thirty-seven districts became fifty-three, and the two unitary councils become three with the Western Islands being added to Orkney and Shetland.

The Commission, its reception and the subsequent legislation provide an instructive case study of reform. Big ideas tend to refute themselves in practice. Despite differentiating services and functions in terms of their necessary scale and capacity for delivery, one 'region' ended up serving over 2 million people (Strathclyde) and another had a population of 131,000 (Borders). Furthermore, some districts (e.g. Glasgow, Edinburgh, Aberdeen) were much bigger than some regions in population served, budgets and staffing levels. If scale and capacity were the criteria, Glasgow, Edinburgh and Aberdeen made much more sense as education authorities than Borders or Central regions.

As importantly, the response to the report and the legislation that followed indicated that local identity could not be easily suppressed by rationalistic design. The powerful assertion of the Kingdom of Fife, and Borders, as regions in their own right reflects this, as does the painstaking (re)negotiation of the number and boundaries of district councils. Both were attempts to retrofit historical and cultural identity to the rational planning approach adopted by the Commission. That frustrated localism partially explains the response to the dissolution of the Wheatley system twenty years later, whereby regional level infrastructures and capacities were deconstructed rather than protected.

Finally, and characteristic of public service reform in Scotland, a completely separate review of the Health Service recommended that public health and community health care should be taken from councils, and merged with the then Hospital Boards to form 'Health Boards'. There would be fifteen Health Boards. Non-clinically based social care would be located within Regional Councils. This tendency to review sectors separately and atomistically has remained characteristic, and created the major fault lines that still bedevil the public service system in Scotland.

Three wider points are also worth noting. First, that a national government with a majority could simply abolish over 200 local governments by a vote in Parliament without any special constitutional procedure, or a referendum, expresses a very distinctively British, rather than European, understanding of local government. Local government is seen as a delivery system for national government rather than as an expression of the democratic will and 'self-determination' of local populations. It also points up the subordinate status of local government and its lack of constitutional protection.

The second point follows from the emphasis on services and service delivery in the Commission's work. The population served moves from being seen as 'citizens' within a local democracy to being seen as recipients and 'consumers' of services. This 'consumerist' view implicitly underpins the delocalisation of local government the Commission proposed: as long as services were well planned and delivered, it did not matter that they were provided by a remote authority over which very little local control could be exercised at all. Local democratic accountability was a secondary concern.

The final point is that the Commission's recommendations were tailored to the political landscape that confronted it: a unitary state with no devolved parliaments or assemblies. The Regions were regions of the UK under a UK government. It is inconceivable that a region as big as Strathclyde, covering 50 per cent of the Scottish population, would have been created if a devolved parliament existed. Had the regional dispensation not been abolished prior to devolution, it would have had to be abolished as part of devolution.

The revolution continues

Although the Commission had meticulously planned a system to be fit for purpose across fifty years, it was reviewed and abolished within twenty. The seeds of its demise were built in from the outset. Once delocalisation is achieved, it is hard to maintain emotional and cultural identification with public authorities. Two tiers of local government are in principle easier to coordinate than five, but regions and districts often operated autonomously and in parallel rather than together. Services that needed to work together, e.g. social work, social care and housing, often struggled to do so in an integrated way.

Regions, as corporate bodies, quite rightly adopted the strategic planning approach the Commission recommended but, because of the scale and diversity of the populations they served, this often resulted in a redistributive approach that alienated more affluent, 'lower needs' areas. The Regions often exhibited diseconomies of scale, very elaborate expensive management structures and corporate services arrangements, and the smaller districts struggled to achieve economies of skill or scale at all.

It was, however, the political context that eventually led to its dissolution. Most of the period of the region/district system was under Conservative governments that did not command majority support in Scotland. Large Labour-controlled regions, particularly Strathclyde, became major sources and focal points for Scottish opposition to UK government policy, and were very effective at doing so (with respect to the treatment of mining, shipbuilding and steel industries, privatisation and competition, the poll tax, etc.).

The UK Government undertook a review of Scottish local government in 1992/93 (see Midwinter 1992). As the then prime minister had defined a region the size of Strathclyde as 'monstrous' at the outset, there was little surprise in the review, but the conclusions quite subtly unpicked the threads of the Wheatley Commission. The aggregated scale and capacity necessary for regional services was rejected, partly by reference to the utter inconsistency of the system that evolved: very small as well as very large regions, and district councils that were bigger than most regions.

The unitary approach, previously restricted to the Islands councils, was advocated for all. Rather than a complicated two-tier system, have all local services under one democratic authority. This meant that the new councils would have to have reasonably large population catchments: smaller than some regions but bigger than most districts. Unitary councils would allow rationalisation of management arrangements and costs. Communities that had been governed remotely by the large regions would go back to a more locally controlled arrangement.

The legislative outcome was for the thirty-two unitary councils we now have in Scotland: twenty-nine mainland councils and the three island councils. The boundaries determined were controversial: particularly a single unitary council for what was previously the Highlands region, covering a land area the size of Belgium, and the removal of affluent suburbs from cities and their location within neighbouring suburban councils. The diversity of population coverage, and geographical coverage, of the new councils make it hard to discern coherent principles in their design, with the exception that all 'local' services would be integrated under single governance and management.

There are continuities with Wheatley. A substantial scale was assumed to be necessary for services such as education, social work and social care, and a number of previous 'regions' simply directly became unitary councils (Fife, Scottish Borders, Highland). As with Wheatley, there was huge variation within the system. The average population covered is 170,000 but the ten largest councils have an average population coverage of over 320,000 and the smallest ten have an average coverage of under 80,000. Ignoring the politics of particular boundaries, this illustrates the dilemma that any top-down system design approach will face in accommodating population distribution in Scotland (the need to accommodate distinctive Highland and Island patterns; the concentrations of populations in cities and the growing suburban/semi-rural drift).

The second continuity is the predominance of technocratic concerns in the reform: this is about the integration of the governance and management of services, not 'localism' or democracy. Again, it is about the sub-national and not the local in the proper sense of 'close to where people live'. The whole approach was top-down, and devoid of any coherent reflection on subsidiarity at all. Again, it progressed by majority decision of the UK Parliament, not a plebiscite of those affected. It is a government tidying up its own delivery system, and again the public are implicitly conceptualised largely as consumers rather than as participants in local democracy.

The final continuity with the 1970s is that again local health services were simply, and contradictorily, excluded from consideration. If the key principle was of all local services under a single democratically elected authority, it is very hard to see why public health and community health services were not included in this integrative vision. The hospital sector is nationally planned for very large population catchments, but the public and community health sector have a localised and targeted focus that links closely to the child care and adult care responsibilities of councils. Ironically, much of the subsequent period has seen serial attempts to achieve better inter-agency collaboration between community health and social care services.

The system of local government we have now is the product of a critical period from the Wheatley Commission to the dissolution of its work in 1996. The predominant mindset was technocratic rather than democratic, with local government seen functionally as a 'delivery system' and citizens as recipients of services. 'Localness' in any meaningful sense was a secondary consideration, and subsidiarity no real consideration at all.

In comparative terms, Scottish local government ends up being scarcely 'local' at all. For example, in France the average local government covers 15 square miles, in Germany 52, in Denmark 450 and in Scotland 2,449 square miles. This is forty-five times the European average. Across Europe, the average local government population scale is

20,000: in Scotland it is 170,000 or eight times greater. Equally, the average local government in Europe raises over 50 per cent of its own income locally: the comparable figure for Scotland is under 20 per cent (COSLA 2014).

Present tensions in local government

Much has changed since the new unitary system was created in 1996, not least the creation of the Scottish Parliament in 1999 and recession, depression and public sector 'austerity' since 2008. The former indigenised the typical tensions in central/local relations to Scotland, and the latter has exacerbated the pre-existing challenge of meeting demand growth driven by demographic change and embedded inequalities in Scotland. We look at both in turn.

The Scottish Parliament and local government

Some quite gloomy prognostications were made about the future of local government with the advent of the Scottish Parliament: a view that, denied macro-economic and fiscal policy, foreign affairs and defence, Scottish governments would spend their time micro-managing councils and other local public services (Midwinter 1997). In reality, relations have been much more varied over time: periods of substantial tension over finance, top-down prescription, and removal of powers and functions, but equally periods of genuinely creative partnership. Local government has had substantial involvement over time in national policy development and reform initiatives, and policy communities around education, planning, social care, roads, etc. continued to cut across a simple national/local divide (Cairney 2013).

The view that Scottish governments would simply use their legislative and resource power to 'steamroller' local government has not been vindicated either. The atmosphere has been more of trading and compromise, than imposition. For example, local government has not supported the council tax freeze since 2007, but they have not frustrated it either. As long as the Scottish Government 'paid' for it, they could have it. The Scottish Government wanted the integration of health and social care, probably into health boards or through a national agency. Local government rejected the loss of a major service. The compromise was the creation of Health and Social Care Partnerships at arm's length from both councils and health boards under an 'Integration Joint Board'. These compromises sometimes have a lowest common denominator feel, nobody getting what they want, and have led to a proliferation of 'partnerships' in Scotland.

The major exceptions were the removal of police and fire services from local control and the creation of 'Police Scotland' and the 'Scottish Fire and Rescue Service'. Local government was opposed to this but it was simply imposed. Even here, care was taken to make provision for local scrutiny of these services through councils. The local government budget has also been relatively protected as a percentage of Scottish public spending since 2010, in comparison to the substantial reductions elsewhere in the UK (Keep 2015).

Some of this has to do with circumstances. Until the present Scottish Government, all were either coalitions or minority governments and that made imposition harder to effect. With only thirty-two councils, Scottish local government was more competent at maintaining a disciplined collective voice than its English counterpart. Because of the Barnett formula, and the higher percentage of devolved Scottish expenditure on health and education, financial pressures have been less severe than elsewhere in the UK.

However, it is also to do with a recognition that local government is a democratically elected tier of governance in Scotland, and a proper reticence about simply imposing on it (Scottish Government 2007). Circumstances and ethos interact, however, and this view is not immutable.

Fiscal constraint and the new reform agenda

Rising demand and increasing financial constraint are combining to create severe challenges for Scottish public services. Current service models are accepted to be unsustainable against future pressures and significant, consensual effort has gone into 'public service reform' over the last five years. The key focal points for reform are:

1. Recognition that a lot of demand within the system is because it is reactive. Bad things happen in people's lives and then public services react, often expensively. It would be cheaper and better to prevent the bad things happening in the first place. 'Shift to prevention' becomes a key reform motif.
2. To do that, the focus needs to shift from service activities and outputs, to the impact of services on people's lives and opportunities in life: focus on 'outcomes', not services, is a second key motif.
3. As life outcomes are shaped by a variety of social and economic factors, no public service or intervention in isolation can deliver improved outcomes. For example, housing and health services may be as critical to a child's educational achievement as the school they attend, and all these services need to work in a joined up way to have optimum impact. 'Partnership', 'joint working' and 'integration' are the third key reform motif.
4. A further key insight is that public services cannot 'do' outcomes to people and that communities' own capacity and behaviours are critical to better outcomes. This has led to an emphasis on building 'community capacity' and 'social capital', community participation and, more generally, working with communities rather than doing things to them. 'Coproduction' and so called 'asset based' approaches exemplify this fourth reform motif.
5. The final recognition, massively statistically documented, is that life outcomes cluster at community level, and communities with very good outcomes in one aspect of life (health, educational achievement, employment, etc.) tend to have good outcomes across the range and, vice versa, other communities have poor outcomes across the range. Communities with better outcomes tend to be effective consumers of public services and get good value from them: communities with poorer outcomes tend to struggle with public service structures and cultures and get poor value from them (Scottish Government 2011). The key expression of this final motif is commitment to 'reducing inequality of outcomes'.

The last ten years have developed a new narrative of enhanced local democracy, outcomes, place, empowerment and reducing inequalities, and is in part a critique of the failure of the technocratic model that had dominated the previous period. It had not worked and it had specifically failed the communities most dependent on public services. However, this new emphasis did not wholly replace the older narrative and they continue to interact in interesting ways.

Thus the 2007 SNP Scottish Government agreed a 'concordat' with local government that made them fully partners in policy making and removed many of the national restrictions on local choice about priorities and resource use: very 'new' narrative. The same Government, however, proposed the removal of police, and fire and rescue services from local government control on the basis of essentially technocratic arguments about economies of scale and standardisation.

More recently, the Scottish Government has passed the 'Community Empowerment Scotland Act' which strengthens communities' rights to challenge local public services, to seek transfer of assets and services to community management, and to be active participants in local decision making. At the same time, and with no apparent sense of paradox, the same government continued the 'top-down' freeze on local taxes and 'ring-fenced' pupil/teacher ratios. Communities should have the right to choose, but not in areas where the Scottish Government has already made up its mind.

This is often linked to the advocacy of 'devo max' and 'fiscal autonomy'. If the Scottish Parliament itself had appropriate empowerment, these restrictions on local government would be unnecessary. However, given the Parliament's limited fiscal powers, UK decision making constrains the Scottish Government and that inevitably passes down to local government in turn. There is an element of truth in this. For example, if the Parliament had more or, at least, more usable tax powers, it would probably have shown less interest in local tax decisions. Equally, as a substantial proportion of council income is from within the Scottish Departmental Expenditure Limit (D.E.L.), if the Scottish D.E.L. is cut by Westminster, cuts to the local grant automatically follow.

However, choices have been made. Freezing council tax since 2007 has resulted in a cumulative £2.7 billion of income foregone, assuming that an average 2 per cent per annum increase would have been expected across the period. The freeze was intended to mitigate the effects of declining real wages in Scotland, and support disposable household incomes, in the absence of any Scottish control of the wider fiscal system. However, the mitigation was very limited, benefited most those with high value housing, and denied public services a major financial resource. Most importantly, if subsidiarity was the key principle, local communities should have had the right to decide the balance of tax and spending in their area.

Future perfect

The local government system that now exists in Scotland embodies the unresolved tensions of the last fifty years of development. Tensions between scale and standardisation and localism and diversity; between specialisation around services and integration around outcomes; between a 'delivery system' view and an emphasis on local self-determination; between 'representative' and 'participative' democracy. Overarchingly, it embodies a tension between local government as a sector and 'subsidiarity' and 'localism' as whole system characteristics. What follows builds on the key insights of the past, and the practical exigencies they capture, but with a view to seeing whether they can be better integrated to provide a platform for the future.

(i) Scale, capacity and localism

Given the combination of financial constraint and demand growth faced across the foreseeable future, any sustainable system will have to be capable of economies of scale and skill. This has been assumed to require aggregation of services scales and population catchments that are inimical to localism. However, this has gone along with fragmentation: multiple large scale service organisations with separate governance and management arrangements delivering local services separately to the same communities. This is very resource intensive, and attempts to overcome fragmentation by creating additional partnership vehicles that patch across the core structures require further layers of governance and management (e.g. community planning partnerships, health and social care partnerships, community justice partnerships, etc.).

The alternative route to economies of scale, capacity and resilience could be through local integration, rather than service aggregation. If a single body was responsible for the whole range of local services, economies of scale would be achievable with much smaller territorial and population coverage. At minimum, it is certainly worth considering whether service and sectoral fragmentation have been the key factors in creating tension between economies of scale and localism.

(ii) Outcome and service focus

The current public service reform agenda in Scotland strongly emphasises an outcome focus: prevention of negative outcomes, improvement in positive outcomes and reduction of inequalities of outcome. The strong emphasis is on service integration around families and communities. This is not necessarily incompatible with an emphasis on service quality and specialisation. These characterise inputs to the system, not outputs or outcomes. An integration agenda only makes sense if the quality of input necessary to achieve outcomes is maintained and deployed in a creative fashion.

If an integrative localism was adopted, through a single responsible body, specialists would be deployed as part of multi-disciplinary services and the balance and level of specialisation necessary to achieve outcomes could be fully explored. The key point is that the need for specialised expertise does not imply the need to build corporate structures around service speciality, rather than around place, people and outcomes.

(iii) 'Delivery system' and subsidiarity

All public service bodies are 'delivery systems' in an obvious sense: they deliver services. Where services relate to national or human rights, national governments necessarily have a substantial role in defining these rights, and ensuring they are consistently respected. They do this through legislation and by establishing regulatory and inspection regimes. None of this is antithetical to subsidiarity as long as the universality of rights and entitlements is not confused with standardisation and uniformity of provision.

Any truly universal system would have to have the capacity to accommodate and respond to the diversity of community cultures and circumstances it encounters. A standardised, uniform system that suited some communities more than others would not be 'universal' at all. Concerns with 'postcode lotteries' often confuse 'rights', and local decisions about the best way to deliver rights under specific local circumstances (e.g. a child's right to education confused with a specific teacher/pupil ratio).

Equally, subsidiarity does not imply that all decisions about policy and services should be taken at local level. It implies solely that those that can be, should be. This fully allows that some cannot, and should be taken at higher levels of the system. 'As local as possible' is clearly a contestable criterion but is not, in principle, opposed to consistency of rights and entitlements.

(iv) 'Representative' and 'participatory' democracy

The advocacy of participatory democracy emerges partly as a critique of representative democracy (remoteness; political party domination; voter disillusion, etc.) and partly as an advocacy of citizens being actively engaged with issues and decisions that affect their lives. The 'participative' element is clear enough but why this is a form of 'democracy' is not self-evident. For example, a group of parents protesting the closure of a local primary school are using a right to protest guaranteed in most democracies, but that does not confer democratic legitimacy on the particular case they make.

They may simply be self-interested, and not at all representative of the wider community or accountable to it. By definition, this type of participatory democracy is about (self) selective issues and interests. The articulation/advocacy of selective issues and interests is often seen to be essential to developing and clarifying policy choices in a democracy but this view precisely presumes some form of representative democracy is in place to adjudicate and prioritise between them.

To this extent, 'representative' and 'participative' local democracy are interdependent: any case for 'representative' local government presumes openness to local people and communities, and any case for 'participative' democracy presumes some democratic process for reconciling selective and collective values and interests. If representative local government becomes 'scaled up' to the point of not being really local at all, managing these interrelationships becomes more difficult and a gap develops between representation and participation. This makes it more likely that participatory democracy is seen as an alternative to representative democracy, rather than complementary to it.

(v) 'Sectoral' or 'whole system' focus

The foregoing points taken together flag up a more fundamental issue: whether local governance is seen as a thing, a sub-sector of the public sector, or as a principle that should be characteristic of the whole public service system. Why some local services should be governed by elected local politicians and others by nationally appointed boards, some locally accountable and other nationally accountable, is hard to explain. It seems at minimum unhelpful from a reform perspective, and requires substantial duplication of governance and management resources. It also produces absurdities: for example, multiple public authorities, elected and appointed, to provide services to the 21,000 people in the Orkney Islands.

The 'community planning' system in Scotland, which tries to bring together all the public services in each council area, is necessary precisely because the core sectoral architecture of public services fragments them. As an integrative device, it struggles with the different boundaries of different partners: thirty-two councils, fourteen NHS health boards, one police service and one fire and rescue service. These different geographical scales create understandably different priorities, and are complicated by some services being accountable nationally, and some locally. (The largest Health Board participates in twelve Community Planning Partnerships but its key performance requirements and accountabilities are set by the Scottish Government!)

The current sectoral structure was based on professional and service specialisation but, as noted above, this is about inputs, and could be accommodated within a more holistically integrated public service system. At minimum, if the end aim (now enshrined in law) is to improve outcomes, reduce inequalities, and empower community participation, the current sectoral structure of Scottish public services does not help practically or democratically (COSLA 2014).

Future options

These tensions within the system need to be addressed in a practical way: taking full account of the proper role of the Scottish Parliament, taking full account of the wider public service reform agenda, and taking account of the acute finance and demand pressures that Scottish public services will face. The discussion above suggests they can be balanced on a more creative basis and that core points on all sides can be accommodated.

This can only happen, however, if it is accepted that fundamental reform is necessary and there is clarity about the priorities for reform. Two factors potentially mitigate against this. First, the continued focus on independence/further devolution makes it tempting to leave reform within Scotland until that is settled. The disruptive impact of major reform may be seen as an unnecessary and potentially contentious diversion.

Second, past experience of reform, particularly structural reform, is often off-putting. Significant costs of change are incurred, performance and discipline drops in the transition, and new arrangements often take time to bed in satisfactorily. This explains the emphasis on 'partnership' as an alternative to structural reform over the last few years. However, as noted above, the proliferation of partnerships is itself costly and disruptive, and leaves a flawed core architecture in place.

The solution may be to recognise that any intelligent, evidence-based and participative review process will take time, and that substantial further time would be necessary for legislation and then implementation. If begun in the next Scottish Parliament, it would certainly not be implemented until well into the next. A review looking at future arrangements for governance and public services in Scotland is quite compatible with continued interest in further devolution and/or independence. Both are about the 'Scotland we want'.

Any review would need to have clear principles and priorities built into its remit. This itself would require careful thought but should reflect a national emphasis on subsidiarity and the reform agenda already agreed. It should also take account of the finance and demand pressures that the Scottish public services will face for the foreseeable future. In that context, key requirements of the review would probably include:

a   A requirement to focus on the whole public service system, its structure and governance, with a strong emphasis on local integration and minimising duplication of governance and management arrangements.
b   A presumption in favour of elected local governance and local accountability as the default position for local public services, unless compelling reasons exist against this.
c   A requirement that the economies of scale achievable through integration, replacing multiple public authorities with a single integrative authority, are identified and fully scoped.
d   A requirement that economies of scale through shared service arrangements that could support 'local' authorities are identified, scoped and built into any proposed arrangements at the outset.

e A requirement that any proposed reforms create authorities that are demonstrably 'as local as is possible' while meeting other requirements.
f A requirement for specific proposals to enhance public participation in and influence on local public service decision making, linked to the duties of any new public authorities proposed.
g A requirement that the role(s) of the Scottish Parliament and Government vis-à-vis local public service authorities are specified, and limited to respect subsidiarity.
h A requirement that the financial and fiscal powers and responsibilities of local authorities are specified and are sufficient to enable responsiveness to local preferences for the balance of taxation and spending.

No such holistic review has ever been undertaken in Scotland: previously different parts of the system have been reviewed in isolation. It leaves entirely open the extent of subsidiarity and local democratic control that is feasible, but requires it to be examined seriously. It allows economies of scale through both integration and aggregation to be explored.

As an illustration, assume the outcome was that the core of the future system was a single, elected public service authority for each part of Scotland. To promote localism and participation, further assume 70 to 100 such authorities. The option would remain for a 'regional' type tier to oversee services benefiting from a larger scale of organisation but this would need to be thought through carefully: a focus on precise service functions rather than whole service areas. For example, learning support rather than the whole of education or serious crime investigation rather than the whole of policing.

As service levels and standards are the critically local decisions, local authorities could commission or take a range of services and support services from larger scale delivery organisations. Some services would probably not fit a localist model at all: hospital services, prevention and detection of cybercrime, major roads and infrastructure, etc. but they could be part of a regional tier. As hospitals function on an interdependent network basis, and are largely nationally planned, it would be possible to eliminate the fourteen Health Boards by creating a single National Acute Services Board and integrating public health and community health care into local authorities. This would also allow the elimination of thirty-two Health and Social Care Partnerships.

Although purely illustrative, these examples show that an integrative localism is not incompatible with economies of skill and scale, and could enable substantial rationalisation of the public service landscape in Scotland. It would also strengthen interest in local democracy: an empowered authority responsible for all major local services might be more worth voting for than the current system. Finally, much more local 'local government' would make it more feasible to bridge the gap between representation and participation.

An analysis of Eurostat data for the 'Commission on Strengthening Local Democracy' in 2014 makes the point clearly. It suggests three linked points:

i The most localised local government systems in Europe not only have the highest electoral participation but also have the highest participation in NGOs, civic organisations, etc.
ii The most localised systems have the highest belief among citizens that voting in local elections allows them to shape outcomes; and
iii The highest belief that participation in NGOs, civic society organisations, etc. helps shape local outcomes.

In contrast, more centralised systems, such as the UK's, have citizens with the lowest confidence in their ability to shape local outcomes through electoral or civic participation. Decentralisation and subsidiarity appear to provide a locus, a focus and a sense of empowerment/confidence with respect to control of outcomes that is missing in more centralised dispensations.

There is related UK evidence that confidence in one's ability to shape one's own outcomes is central to expectations and aspirations with respect to education, health and wellbeing. There is also evidence that the most deprived communities have the lowest confidence in their ability to control their own destiny, potentially resulting in 'low aspirations', 'fatalism' and lack of interest in electoral or civic participation. Centralised government and local governments that seem large-scale, remote and bureaucratic are at minimum unlikely to help. Smaller, more local governments, closer to these communities would potentially improve contact, relationships and sense of empowerment.

Conclusion

Local government has been serially reformed in the last sixty years in Scotland, largely in isolation from the rest of the public sector. These reforms have reduced the number of councils and reduced the function of councils while scaling them up to a point when they are scarcely local at all. The driving ideas have been technocratic rather than democratic, and links with historical and cultural identities have been broken. In a globalised and corporatised world, this might simply accepted as inevitable. The problem is that it has not worked in terms of outcomes and inequalities in Scotland.

Most past reforms of local government have lasted about twenty years. The current dispensation of thirty-two unitary councils is coming up to its twentieth birthday and faces severe challenges to its resilience due to rising demand and falling income. If a technocratic and sectoral view continues as the default position, another reform is likely soon and it would be likely to further reduce the number and the functions of councils, and even further delocalise the local government system in Scotland. At that point it would be questionable why an elected local government system was worth the effort.

The only coherent alternative is a much more fundamental 'whole system' review of the governance and management of local public services in Scotland that treats local governance as a cross-cutting principle, rather than a sector. Proper technocratic concerns with scale, capacity, efficiency and resilience should be part of the review but the default position would be more local, fully integrated, democratically elected and accountable public service authorities for each part of Scotland. This could generate substantial economies of scale through integration and allow substantial rationalisation of the wider public service landscape of appointed public bodies and partnerships.

This approach has a clear affinity with national (re)negotiation of subsidiarity within the UK, links to the consensually agreed and legislated national reform agenda, and addresses the flawed core architecture of public services in Scotland. The paradox of local government in Scotland at present is that it is neither local nor empowered governance. If this is not addressed, it will continue to lose capacity and legitimacy.

Sources for further reading and study

For excellent overviews of the institutional, political and policy context of local government in Scotland, see:

Keating, M. (2010) *The Government of Scotland*, Edinburgh: Edinburgh University Press.
Cairney, P. and N. McGarvey (2013) *Scottish Politics*, Basingstoke: Palgrave.

For a recent exploration of a technocratic perspective on local government reform, see:

Reform Scotland (2012) *Reviewing Local Government*. Reform Scotland.

For a range of materials from a subsidiarity/democratic perspective see:

www.localdemocracy.info.

References

Cairney, P. (2013) 'Territorial Policy Communities and the Scottish Policy Style: The Case of Compulsory Education'. *Scottish Affairs* 82: 10–34.
COSLA (2014) *Effective Democracy. Reconnecting with Communities*. Report of the Commission on Strengthening Local Democracy. Edinburgh. Available at: www.localdemocracy.info/wp-content/uploads/2014/08/Final-Report-August-2014.pdf.
Keep, M. (2015) 'Scotland: Public Spending and Revenue'. House of Commons Library Briefing Paper, no. 06625.
Midwinter, A. (1997) 'Local Government in a Devolved Scotland'. *Scottish Affairs* 18: 24–35.
Midwinter, A. (1992) 'The Review of Local Government in Scotland – A Critical Perspective'. *Local Government Studies* 18(2): 44–54.
Scottish Government (2011) *Renewing Scotland's Public Services. Priorities for Reform in Response to the Christie Commission*. Edinburgh: Scottish Government.
Scottish Government (2007) 'Concordat between Scottish Government and Local Government'. Edinburgh: Scottish Government.
Smith (2014) *Report of the Smith Commission for Further Devolution of Powers to the Scottish Parliament*. Available at: www.smith-commission.scot.
Wheatley (1969) *Report of the Royal Commission on Local Government in Scotland*. Cmnd 4150-1. Edinburgh: HMSO.

7 Civil service and machinery of government

Richard Parry

The pace of evolution of governmental institutions is not necessarily the same as that of party political institutions. After three devolved Scottish Parliaments, things have changed unimaginably in the party and electoral landscape. In contrast, the landscape of government is much the same. There are still thirty-two single-tier local authorities, fourteen out of fifteen area health boards (Argyll and Clyde failed financially and was merged with neighbours without fuss), public corporations like Scottish Water and Calmac, and state-funded universities. Audit Scotland, an important creation of devolution, audits the entire system. The main obvious changes – a Scottish Government (SG) without departments in place of a Scottish Executive with them, and all-Scotland police and fire services – have been natural non-partisan developments. The one major accretion of a policy area has been of railways infrastructure and franchising in 2005.

Is this because devolution has imposed constraints on institutional change? Or have all parties in office approved of the arrangements they encountered? Or perhaps they have not cared greatly and devoted their political energies to higher constitutional issues? This chapter will argue that the explanation is more subtle than that. A preserved version of the British state inherited in 1999 suits most Scottish political interests, including the Scottish National Party (SNP). It embodies resistance to the more extreme version of new public management found in England. It avoids disturbing interest groups whose consent to the devolved system needs to be secured. And it promotes the 'gaming' of the UK system in favour of Scotland, the traditional role of the Scottish administration.

At the start of the Scottish devolved system in July 1999, in most respects devolved meant derivative. Public sector structures were based on decades of UK norms about, for instance, what was a civil servant, a local authority or a public corporation. The administrative machine of the Scottish Office was integrated, long standing and readily detachable from the UK Government and transferable to the control of devolved institutions. What was transferred was not just law and administration, but also sociology and anthropology.

This derivate nature initially applied to the party systems as well. Labour in particular remained a branch of the British party organisation, and UK elections secured higher turnouts and attention than Scottish ones. Then everything changed. In 2007, the SNP secured entry to government as a minority party in a way last seen in the UK in the short-lived Labour government of 1924. But its statecraft was far more successful than Labour's. After the SNP consolidated its position at Holyrood (in 2011) and Westminster (in 2015), Scotland made a decisive political break with its progenitor system. And yet in myriad ways Scotland's machinery of government remains tied into UK processes of public sector financial and personnel management.

The SNP has in general preserved and promoted UK administrative styles that were current before radical public sector management took hold. Scotland has resisted the UK Government's approach (radical contracting-out of departmental functions; further privatisation of public services; a search for 'leaders' in Whitehall unlike old-style administrators; final ministerial say in top appointments; promoting city regions rather than a uniform structure of local government). Instead, the SNP has promoted older practices such as the selective use of contracting; a stable and joined-up civil service machine; 'partnership' between the centre and a uniform structure of local government and the NHS; and the maintenance of public corporations in industries that might have been privatised, notably Scottish Water.

The SNP had a political need after 2007 to consolidate its position among various Scottish elites that had not previously been prominent as a source of support (like education and the law) or had become accustomed to a UK connection (like business and the Civil Service). New SNP ministers seemed genuinely uncertain about whether they could work with an official machine that was part of the Home Civil Service, but found they were receiving the loyal support accorded to any elected administration (even one in a parliamentary minority). At the top, SNP ministers have resisted picking top officials standing in an insurgent relationship to the UK similar to their own. The permanent secretary they inherited, Sir John Elvidge (2003–10) asserted the right of ministers to be advised on reserved matters, including promoting and planning for independence. Such was the SNP's confidence that they were prepared to import a Whitehall permanent secretary, Sir Peter Housden, as their top official on the basis of shared interest in better and more integrated public service delivery. On 1 July 2015 Leslie Evans took over as the third consecutive non-native Scot to be permanent secretary; her background is in local government, joining the Scottish Executive post-devolution and having latterly been director-general for learning and justice.

The chapter will convey some detail on the machinery of government in Scotland that is important to understanding the operation of the devolved system and the practicalities of proposals for further transfers of powers. But it will also discuss the personalities and politics around an approach to public bureaucracy that almost has the flavour of 'traditional best of British' and is one element of the SNP's remarkable construction of its base of public support and confidence.

The Scottish machinery of government

The best way of understanding government in Scotland is through the employment and accountability position of those who might be regarded as being in the public sector workforce. This indicator has been defined and understood better by UK national statistics in recent years and has also become more politically salient. Quarterly data are published at UK and Scotland level. Previously excluded staff in state-owned companies have been brought within the count to reflect their effective control and financing by government (Lloyds Banking Group has come and gone from state control while RBS remains) but comparable self-employed health practitioners and university staff (both under devolved control) remain excluded.

Table 7.1 shows that the devolved system accounts for 89 per cent of public sector workers in Scotland but that the core Civil Service working for the Scottish Government is a tiny 1 percent of this (though numbers expanded from 4,300 to 5,700 in the first two years of SNP government). Sixty per cent of civil servants in Scotland work

Table 7.1 Public employment in Scotland, 1999 and 2015

'000s, headcount	1999 Q2	2015 Q2	% change
DEVOLVED	470.9	487.5	+3.5
Scottish Government core	14.6	5.2	+21.2
Civil service agencies		12.5	
NHS	129.1	160.6	+24.4
Local government, police and fire	293.5 (including 25.3 police and fire)	274.0 (including 28.3 police and fire no longer in local government)	−6.6
Further education	15.7	13.9	−11.5
Public corporations	9.5	7.1	−25.3
RESERVED	74.7	58.1	−22.2
Civil Service	33.8	26.3	−22.2
Armed forces	14.9	9.4	−36.1
Public corporations	20.2	12.7	−37.1
Public bodies	5.8	9.7	+67.2

Source: Public Sector Employment Statistics for 2nd Quarter 2015 (Scottish Government online, 16 September 2015).

for the UK Government, down from 70 per cent in 1999. Health and local government workers are a solid block of devolved staff, and justice-related civil servants are also significant. Many parts of the devolved workforce – especially in health – have a professional or trade union orientation to the British level. Data on private staff performing public functions under contract are less clear; much of that industry would also have a British orientation, and employment law around the transfer of undertakings is the same.

The present trend is for the devolved workforce to get relatively bigger. This is because staff in Scotland under the policy control of the UK Government are concentrated in functions bearing the brunt of cuts in running costs – defence, social protection and tax collection. Employees in state-controlled banks, a temporary boost to public sector numbers after the financial crisis of 2008, are also being wound down.

Beyond the numbers, the modalities of the categories of public employment are similar. Partly through rules of government accounting and UK company law, there is a common structure of civil services, government departments (ministerial and non-ministerial), public corporations, local authorities, non-departmental public bodies and companies limited by guarantee. As parliamentary auditors have found, this structure is complex and inconsistent and it is necessary to chase down the circumstances in which government provides the money or appoints the directors. Even if it had legally been able to do so, the Scottish Government has shown no inclination to create its own architecture of public administration. Not least, the daunting complexity of reconciling terms and conditions of employees involved in changes make it an unrewarding task. To understand how we reached this point, it is necessary to mention some aspects of the historical legacy of devolution.

126 Richard Parry

The inherited legacy of Scottish government

The Act of Union of 1707 was a pre-modern construct. It preserved some things that existed in 1707 – Scottish courts and laws, the church, the structure of school education, the existence and privileges of burghs and parishes – but it could not anticipate the development of the state in the nineteenth and twentieth century. New institutional forms of civil administration at central and local level in Scotland were created from London, including the Scottish Office in 1885 that thereafter consolidated itself from previously distinct Scottish boards and departments in the 1930s and 1970s. These forms also had financial implications, including the rate-levying powers of local government and capital financing of public corporations. These sustained a network of procedures for accounting and authorisation, the timetable of the financial year, and the lack of relationship between tax revenue raised and public money spent in Scotland.

The Scottish system after 1999 was free to pursue its own policies in devolved areas, but was not necessarily free to replace the mechanisms and processes it inherited. This happened on the technical level of government accounting and public expenditure management, but also on a psychological level. As well as inertia and lack of interest in 'boring' public administration, there was also a lack of intellectual engagement with the agenda of new public management that took hold in Whitehall in the 1980s. This was based on theories of institutional economics, and rational, 'rent-seeking' behaviour by public employees. The answer was seen to lie in the use of internal and external contracts for public employees, performance-related pay, the demarcation of agencies within the public sector that could be monitored through targets, restriction of the revenue-raising powers of local government, and the privatisation of tasks not seen as intrinsic to government. This entire agenda has in some form been adopted by Scottish government before and after devolution – after all, it is a worldwide agenda – but full intellectual assent to it has been lacking.

The professions and public sector trade unions in Scotland reinforce this conservatism. Those organised in distinct Scottish institutions – most notably the teachers – resist threats to their working conditions on the grounds of their previous success and esteem. Those who are part of British institutions – Unite, Unison, civil service unions, doctors, nurses and social workers – see Scotland as more benign arena for the pursuit of their wider agenda.

As is well known, the civil servants of the Scottish Executive remained in 1999 as members of the Home Civil Service, and no attempt has been made to change this position even when a statutory opportunity presented itself in the Constitutional Reform and Governance Act 2010. But two particular aspects of this situation deserve emphasis. The first is that civil service standards, ethics and practices do not rest on being part of the Home Civil Service. The 2010 Act lists other services – including the Diplomatic Service, the Northern Ireland Civil Service and the Security Service – which offer one another mutual recognition as merit-based, ministerially accountable services of the state. Transfer between them – though possibly constrained by collective agreements – does not in principle require re-certification.

The second is that Home Civil Service membership, while retained as symbolic, involves in substance the reservation of civil service management to Westminster. This includes the distinction between the Senior Civil Service, managed centrally, and their grades which are devolved to departments (including for this purpose the Scottish

Government's A, B and C bands). It also includes professional streams like economists, researchers and statisticians. This means, for instance, that the annual publication on *Government Expenditure and Revenue in Scotland* ('GERS') is 'kitemarked' as a National Statistics publication and is hard for either government to challenge methodologically. Officials who are administrators giving policy advice can also look to heads of profession channels in Whitehall. Networks of mutuality are brokered by think-tanks like the Institute of Government, which sponsors seminars and research projects and has taken an interest in intergovernmental working (Paun and Munro 2015).

The 1999 Concordat between the Cabinet Office and the Scottish Executive foresaw Scottish participation in civil service-wide management initiatives under the 'Modernising Government' brand. Over the next decade the Cabinet Office lost interest in monitoring the devolved administrations. There was also no direct Treasury control of running costs as long as they could be accommodated within assigned budgets. Various UK efficiency and public expenditure plans included lines for Scotland. Some compatible policies were applied by the SG, including 'Workforce 2015' with its cut of 25 per cent in the senior staff paybill, but generally Scotland was shielded from direct Treasury action on running costs (Hood and Dixon 2013). The result has been unexpected: a symbolic issue that seemed controversial, membership of the Home Civil Service, has caused no difficulty and mechanisms that might have asserted substantive Whitehall control over public sector management in Scotland have withered through indifference.

The civil service role in the devolved system

The first two first minsters, Donald Dewar (1999–2000) and Henry McLeish (2000–01), had got to know officials when ministers in the pre-devolution Scottish Office. Much of the early attention to civil service matters was on special advisers like John Rafferty who navigated the roles of press briefer and leaker, chief of staff and strategic thinker. Public administration as such attracted little attention. The first devolved permanent secretary, Sir Muir Russell (1998–2003) also came from the pre-devolution milieu and was careful to maintain his attendance at Whitehall permanent secretary meetings. Their longer-serving successors Jack McConnell (first minister 2001–07) and John Elvidge (permanent secretary 2003–10) were more clearly products of devolution. Elvidge had been McConnell's lead official at Education in the early days of devolution and outflanked several more senior colleagues to get the top job. Together, they started exploring how the Executive could address a wider range of economic and social issues in Scotland rather than confined itself to public service delivery of non-cash devolved services to the citizen. The 'Futures Project' of 2006 (i.e. before the election of an SNP Government) brought together data that compared Scotland with independent countries, and was a natural but accidental bridge to the SNP's approach. The saltire alone flew at St Andrew's House even before the SNP took office.

Russell and Elvidge promoted tartanised versions of the UK agendas of modernising government and civil service reform – 'Twenty-First Century Government', 'Changing to Deliver' and 'Shaping Up'. They generated much activity around the themes of joined-up government and serving ministers better. Within government, clarity and impact was less. 'Taking Stock', an external review in 2006 (similar to the capacity reviews being undertaken of Whitehall departments at the time) revealed some lack of internal understanding and communication. Elvidge responded by tightening his Management Group (now called the Strategic Board) and for a time not including some directors-general. By the 2007 Scottish election, the devolved system, a junior adjunct to Blair's Britain, was looking tired. The advent of the SNP to government transformed the political context in a way that required a stable organisational context and provided an opportunity for officials to deploy their skills in managing regime change.

Relating to nationalists in government

UK constitutional theory has emphasised the principle that officials serve ministers and discharge their function by doing so to the best of their ability while being able to offer a similar service to another administration. This requires impartiality between political parties; but does it require impartiality between fundamental ideas about the state? This is the question that faced the two partners thrown together in 2007. It was a journey into unknown territory for both. SNP politicians had never been in ministerial office and were committed to overturning the devolution settlement of which they were now a central part. Officials had similarly scant knowledge of their new ministers and were faced with the need to develop new constitutional protocols about the advice they would give on independence.

The 'odd couple' of a nationalist political party and a civil service that had operated within a unionist consensus found that they had more in common than they imagined. The key to this link is the fusion of clarity of political mandate (maximising Scottish interests and exploring the fullest nature of devolved powers) with bureaucratic notions of serving ministers and advancing their interests. Alternative conceptualisations – that the SNP would disrupt intergovernmental relations, or that civil servants would promote an allegiance to unionism or distaste for supporting 'separatists' – have not been substantiated.

It was implicit in the devolution settlement in 1998 that those without a UK state allegiance would come into government. Northern Ireland's compulsory coalition meant that some ministries, and their statutory executive power, would go to Sinn Fein. In Wales, the red–red coalition of Labour and Plaid Cymru was always plausible in programmatic terms and was in place from 2007 to 2011.

By entering office, nationalists embraced a mechanism for doing business in government. They may have been rejecting the British nation, but were they rejecting the British state and its practices? SNP and Plaid Cymru politicians had sat in the House of Commons for years and absorbed the sociology of parliamentary accommodation and performance. The notion of parliamentary officials serving all parties was familiar to nationalists, but relating to departmental civil servants who had been writing the lines for unionist political opponents was not. But once they did enter government, nationalists benefited from the loyalty that officials show to ministers.

The notion of exclusive loyalty (set out in the Civil Service Code, now with a Scottish version, and enacted in the Constitutional Reform and Governance Act 2010) was of great benefit to the SNP when they entered government in 2007. They were a minority in the Parliament, but they were the sole party in government and the sole source of executive power. When it became apparent that the new ministers were generally moderate, pragmatic, competent and courteous, the stage was set for an 'old public administration' relationship. The SNP even included concepts from the Civil Service Code in clause 16 of their draft interim constitution for an independent Scotland (Scottish Government 2014).

From the start of devolution in 1999, Scottish officials had assumed the near-certainty of coalition government, and so their pre-election analysis of possible outcomes required two level of analysis: of party positions, but also the compatibility of positions between parties. By 2007 they were on the third post-devolution election, and four practices had become set:

i teams of officials scrutinising the policy positions for each party to allow post-election briefing on their implementation;
ii 'gaming' of possible coalitions on the basis of compatibility of party programmes – these probably tended to downplay the possibility of the SNP entering government;
iii the offer of meetings with officials to opposition parties on the Westminster model; in this case John Swinney was the key SNP contact;
iv the offer of post-election facilitation of coalition formation, with premises and officials made available, the objective being the drafting of a 'Programme for Government' that was the operational form of the manifestos of the governing parties (in other words, the parties' own text of legitimacy was superseded by one drafted with civil service advice).

John Elvidge has described in some detail (2011: 18–20) how this played out, with initial contact with the SNP made very quickly and outgoing first minister Jack McConnell showing no desire to intervene as the SNP were rejected as coalition partners by the Liberal Democrats, struck a limited deal with the Greens, and then became a minority administration as the other parties declined to vote down Alex Salmond as first minister.

Before long, there was a 'Scottish Government'. Under the Scotland Act, there was no clear term for the executive branch – Scottish Administration was probably the most technically correct – but 'government' was denied and the term 'Scottish Executive' was adopted, redolent of a subordinate status. But, unlike the 1978 devolution proposals, the new system included the heavily symbolic judicial administration apparatus (the Crown Office, Scottish Courts Service, Scottish Prison Service and Lord Advocate's Department) that was a bridge back to pre-Union days. The enshrining in law of 'Welsh Assembly Government' in 2006 was a bridgehead for the 'G' word, but it was still a skilful operation when the old 'Scottish Executive' signs were taken down unannounced over a weekend in September 2007 and 'The Scottish Government' substituted. Although Whitehall resisted the term in its own usages, it declined to make a big issue over it and conceded the title legally in the Scotland Act 2012.

Having (unusually) set out a proposed revised structure of departments in the devolved executive its 2007 manifesto, the SNP was persuaded to go along with Elvidge's wish to abolish them, thus completing the process of creating an administration without ministries that had started in 1939. The SNP also signed up in 2007 to the structure of fifteen (later sixteen) National Outcomes and fifty National Indicators set out under the 'Scotland Performs' rubric that does not mention nationalism at all.

Here we must address the personality of SNP ministers in relations with their officials. Sir John Elvidge, appearing on a television documentary on Salmond's first 100 days in August 2007 (itself significant) signalled his willingness to advise on all matters ('all governments are entitled to set out their policies; I don't think that policies on constitutional change are different to anything else'). Of Salmond, he said 'he's demanding but professional. He's courteous, he's focused on the substance of the issue and wanting to find a way forward' (quoted by Torrance 2010: 288). Elvidge later wrote 'I do not think it is a contentious judgement to opine that Alex Salmond is a dominating political figure. In a Cabinet context, he chairs meetings forcefully' (Elvidge 2011: 25). The reversion to 'Sir Humphrey' prose, and the use of loaded adjectives, speaks volumes.

Salmond had been a civil servant, an economic adviser at the Scottish agriculture department from 1978 to 1980 (Torrance 2010: 49–51). In this kind of post briefing is driven by data, not political nuance, and Salmond's wish was for evidence new to him which he could fit into a political framework himself; he did not want to be 'advised' about a policy line in the classic ministerial sense (there may be some resemblances here to former Scottish Labour leader Wendy Alexander).

Salmond's successor in November 2014, Nicola Sturgeon, inherited in great measure Salmond's positives but not his negatives. Sturgeon has proved to be a remarkably adept and successful minister. Her professional background is in the most classic kind of political formation, the law, with its twin skills of advocacy and absorption of briefs. As health minister, she balanced official advice and political sense to stay out of trouble with facility. One theme we can discern is Sturgeon's awareness of gender issues – Salmond had created a gender balance of Cabinet secretaries in 2014 by promoting two junior ministerial portfolios to the status and Sturgeon maintained the practice. Taking advantage of a power secured by UK ministers, Sturgeon was able to let it be known that she had chosen Leslie Evans as the Scotland's first female chief civil servant, the official wording in the press announcement of 20 May 2015 being 'the competition was conducted by the First Civil Service Commissioner in accordance with the Civil Service's recruitment principles, which provide for an open competition on merit, with the First Minister invited to choose between those candidates deemed suitable for appointment'. Originally the UK prime minister had been required to confirm such an appointment; that means of control was now gone.

An important adjunct to Sturgeon's political leadership has been the role of John Swinney, since 2007 finance secretary and since 2014 deputy first minister. Skilful at his brief, thoughtful to civil servants, much liked, Swinney has become the chief operating officer of the Scottish Government machine for spending and managing public resources, requiring constant interaction with the Treasury. Like Sturgeon, Swinney has been immersed in the SNP since his teens, after the point when the party had become a central rather than a fringe force in Scottish politics – and his degree from Edinburgh University is in politics.

Kenny MacAskill and Mike Russell, long-serving Justice and Education secretaries until 2014, and Alex Neil (a former rival of Salmond's, brought in to run Housing and later Health and Social Justice) were also big personalities at the Cabinet table. Successful junior ministers like Michael Matheson, Keith Brown, Angela Constance and Shona Robison rose to the Cabinet. Special advisers have been used as in previous administrations: warranting special mention are Kevin Pringle, chief special adviser from 2007 until leaving to join the referendum campaign in 2013, and Elizabeth Lloyd, Nicola Sturgeon's chief of staff, whose background is in research rather than activism for the SNP. Taken as a whole, Salmond, Sturgeon & Co. have probably given us the highest level of ministerial calibre and general statecraft skills seen in UK devolved systems, and this has been the bedrock of their relations with officials.

The Civil Service and the independence referendum

The ability of the Civil Service to manage its position in the independence referendum of 2014 derived from the way the issue had been handled in 2007 when the Scottish Government set out, under civil service advice, a position on the legitimacy of an independence referendum different from that later articulated by the UK Government (which was that the referendum was about promoting independence, which was about repealing the Act of Union, and hence was reserved).

The SNP's proposed referendum wording in their first White Paper (published on 14 August 2007, three months after taking office, and launching the 'National Conversation') was 'The Scottish Government should negotiate a settlement with the Government of the United Kingdom so that Scotland becomes an independent state' (Scottish Government 2007: 35). The underlying argument – and the basis for the whole history of civil service support for the constitutional project – was set out as follows:

> At present the constitution is reserved, but it is arguable that the scope of this reservation does not include the competence of the Scottish Government to embark on negotiations for independence with the United Kingdom Government. Legislative action at both Holyrood and Westminster would be required to effect independence for Scotland or to transfer substantive responsibility for reserved matters.
> (Scottish Government 2007: 35)

A great deal rested on the single word 'arguable'. In the end, the point became moot once the UK Government decided to give the Scottish Parliament power to call a single-question referendum. Further, by attending St Andrew's House in person to sign the 'Edinburgh Agreement' in October 2012, David Cameron imparted an intergovernmental, flags-on-the-table character to the negotiations, and undermined the earlier Whitehall approach that the correct grade equivalent to the first minister was the secretary of state for Scotland. The placing of Cameron opposite a political map of Scotland with swathes of yellow SNP constituencies was a piquant detail.

Before that, important issues had arisen for the Civil Service about the giving of advice on reserved functions by devolved officials. There are inevitable overlaps with devolved areas and decisions, and ministers have to be briefed on UK and international matters raised in the Parliament. But there was a contention in the air that it was impermissible to ask officials to do planning work on what would happen after a Yes vote to independence or in a future independent Scotland. This was articulated most fully in the Labour Party's proposals for further devolution in 2014:

> we do have considerable concerns about the way SNP ministers have used their position of influence to force officials into often uncomfortable choices between adhering to the Civil Service Code and serving the Scottish Government loyally. The SNP have questions to answer on the appropriateness of using civil servants in overtly political projects like the National Conversation and the White Paper on Independence.
> (Scottish Labour Party 2014: 113)

This expressed a common complaint of the No campaign, not a surprising one as many SG officials would surely have a unionist mentality or indeed have been attracted to the Civil Service before 2007 because of it.

Scotland's Future, the Scottish Government's statement of its case in November 2013, was often described as a 'White Paper', though there is no such clear demarcation in SG publications (whereas at the UK level, the denomination and numbering of a 'paper presented to Parliament by command of Her Majesty' is clear). *Scotland's Future*, with its extensive discussion of polices that would be pursued by the SNP after independence, its hundreds of questions and answers resolving any doubts, its assertions that transitional matters could be negotiated successfully, took the genre to a controversial level. It was UK precedent on White Papers that were a complete puff for government achievements, or mentioned long-term plans running beyond the next general election, that enabled Scottish officials to stave off alleged breaches of impartiality.

Under promptings from the No campaign, the House of Commons Public Administration Committee undertook an investigation into *Civil Service Impartiality in the Scottish Referendum*, with hearings in mid-2014 but no report until after the poll. Oral evidence from Sir Bob Kerslake, then head of the Civil Service, and Sir Peter Housden played a straight bat: officials advised their own ministers, no improper pressure was applied by ministers, there was no problem. In their view, civil service advice on text about what would happen after independence was analogous to a UK Government's long-term plans beyond the next general election. The pursuit of, in Scottish Labour's wording, 'overtly political projects' cut both ways.

Permanent secretaries: the importation of the 'foreign manager'

SG budget management has involved constant interaction with Whitehall, especially with the Cabinet Office and the Scotland Office over constitutional matters and the Treasury over the working-out of the Barnett formula and major capital projects like the second Forth crossing. In this context, the importation of Peter Housden as SG permanent secretary in 2010 from the UK Department of Communities and Local Government made sense. The only group that could be considered without a competitive advertisement for the post were existing permanent secretaries in Whitehall. As with the succession to Muir Russell in 2003, the natural internal constituency was the existing directors-general. There was also an external constituency of public sector leaders in local government, education and the health service, and senior figures in industry and finance who might plausibly have filled the post. The SNP avoided them. When itemising his relocation expenses under a freedom of information request, the SG said that 'Sir Peter Housden transferred to the Scottish Government at the request of the Cabinet Secretary and under arrangements agreed with the Chief Secretary to the Treasury and Minister at the Cabinet Office' (www.scotland.gov.uk/About/FOI/Disclosures/2011/09/RelocationExpenses).

Low-profile media reporting of the announcement was telling:

> Mr Salmond – who must rubber-stamp the decision made by the civil service on Sir John's replacement [not quite accurate] – welcomed Mr Housden, with a government source indicating he remained unconcerned by news that Scottish civil servants had been overlooked. 'The fact that, for the first time, this job will be filled by somebody who is already a permanent secretary shows the increased status that the role now has,' they said.
>
> (*Scotsman*, 22 May 2010)

Housden's appointment facilitates the role of the official as a fixer and a technocrat. The idea of the foreign manager brought in as a 'best of breed' for the post in question is familiar from sports coaches (especially Fabio Capello as England football manager), commercial bank chiefs and the governor of the Bank of England, Mark Carney. What is being acquired is not just competence but contacts and credibility among international peers, and perhaps also a sense of dispassion. Housden professed no prior relationship with Scotland (and his blog to staff on his arrival revealed a sense of a neophyte's discovery of matters as diverse as the Scottish landscape and housing market).

Housden fitted in successfully as a loyal official whose main focus was on service delivery rather than the constitution. Gus O'Donnell, as head of the Civil Service, regularly had to fend off opposition accusations that the Civil Service was planning independence. The tone of some of Housden's internal communications was also criticised. O'Donnell's response, in letter to opposition leaders (most fully quoted in www.holyrood.com/articles/2011/10/07/odonnell-letter-clears-housden-over-biasallegations/) set out the ground rules that officials play for their team:

> Within Scotland there is an elected Government with a policy programme for, amongst other things, very significant constitutional change. The UK Government takes a different view on some of these issues. It is right and proper that civil servants working to their respective administrations undertake the relevant work to support Ministers to pursue their aims, whether or not those aims are the subject of political controversy ... a key duty for senior civil servants is to explain the government's policy to staff. Peter Housden's reported comments were set within the context of an internal staff communication designed to stimulate engagement and whilst the language is informal it is explaining the views of Scottish Ministers ...

The issue had arisen over the appointment of a new director-general for strategy and external affairs, condemned by opposition parties as a post designed to plan independence. In the event the person appointed (the acting incumbent) was Ken Thomson, the director-general with the most classic administrative civil service background, having been private secretary to Donald Dewar during the devolution transition. In return, Salmond said: 'I have always regarded Sir Gus O'Donnell as a model civil servant, who has been extremely fair in recognising and respecting the democratic mandate of the Scottish government' (BBC News website, 'Sir Gus O'Donnell Warns over Independence Challenge', 22.12.11).

The impact of Leslie Evans remains to be assessed. In a lecture on leadership at an Institute of Directors event in Inverness in March 2011 (htpps://vimeo.com/21337297) Evans shows herself to be a systematic thinker with an interest in personnel development (recalling how in her early civil service days a memo from her starting 'I was somewhat surprised ...' seemed to be interpreted by an old-timer as so harsh as to be almost a call for resignation, and noting the dangers of poor but over-confident male leaders). The other directors-general include two woman (Sarah Davidson, always tipped for the top after surviving the highest-profile of roles as the project leader of the Holyrood Parliament Building, and finance director Alyson Stafford) and seasoned St Andrew's House veterans. Various other officials are playing (in 2015) connective roles as they move between governments, but with exclusive loyalty to their minister of the moment: Philip Rycroft, second permanent secretary in the Cabinet Office in charge of the UK Governance Group, used to be a director-general in the SG, and Francesca Osowska, head of the Scotland Office, had been Alex Salmond's principal private secretary. In general, though, for reasons probably most to do with the practicalities of career planning, transfers have dried up despite their ease of processing within the Home Civil Service (Parry 2010: 264).

Analytical work on independence and the reinforcement of the government machine

Official work on independence has had lasting significance and has built upon the largely technocratic approach to policy development taken by the SNP since 2007. Published economic commentary established a genre of analytical but SNP-friendly approaches set out in annual reports of the Council of Economic Advisers the SG established, and especially in the Fiscal Commission Working Group, whose membership includes the marquee names of Nobel prizewinners James Mirrlees and Joseph Stiglitz (Scottish Government 2013a). A statutory Scottish Fiscal Commission is being legislated in 2015–16. Relating to these arguments about economic potential is easy for the Civil Service and is a point of contact with international research on the use of devolved public bureaucracies in nation-building projects.

On planning in policy areas, as with the referendum wording, the nature of the legal and political advice the SG received has attracted much attention. Our understanding of advice has been bedevilled by the political attraction of using freedom of information norms to expose government action that might be contrary to what officials are advising. The SNP Government has been prepared to use legal resistance to the disclosure of advice even when endorsed by the Information Commissioner (unsuccessfully so in the case of council tax issues). Alex Salmond and Nicola Sturgeon had protracted political trouble in 2012–13 over whether legal advice had been received on EU membership after independence. The SNP has been ready to shore up the now crumbling UK conventions about the impermissibility of revealing both the existence and the content of advice.

In 2012 the SG had promised to 'publish a comprehensive white paper setting out full details of the offer to the people of Scotland' (Scottish Government 2012: 5) after the Referendum Act received royal assent. Sixteen workstreams were set up in the SG to draft the White Paper, but it was a delayed 'big bang' whose publication required the SNP to state its position on many matters it may have been reluctant to clarify. Once completed, the work had lasting value as a store of expertise on reserved functions. An important initial deployment was in SG evidence to the Smith Commission.

In contrast, the UK Government began issuing its 'Scotland Analyses' series of papers earlier in 2013, covering international matters (issued by the Cabinet Office), currency, financial services and macroeconomic trade (all by the Treasury) and cross-border commerce (by the Business Department). Others followed in 2014. The Treasury papers had the most evidence-based analysis and revealed a strong distaste for sharing any control of the currency and monetary policy. The Treasury reinforced its position in February 2014 in the form of a striking intervention by its permanent secretary Sir Nicholas Macpherson. With the chancellor's agreement, Sir Nick published his official advice against a currency union, partly on the grounds of his examination of the SNP's post-independence fiscal strategy. In later public statements his pro-Union views were made even more explicit. By these actions the Treasury made it somewhat easier for Scottish officials to justify their approach – for if it was permissible for UK officials to promote such an agenda, Scottish officials' much more discreet advice on the SNP's case was surely underwritten. John Elvidge's initial decision in 2007 not to demarcate programme and constitutional advice was of great importance, as it halted any attempt to set up the whole Home Civil Service as a unionist force.

The most visible workstream was that on welfare. Well before the referendum an expert advisory report was issued setting out what a 'Scottish welfare system' might look like (Scottish Government 2013). The paper also clarified the extent of cross-border administration of pensions and benefits. This work was precipitated by the UK Welfare Reform Act 2012 that required the SG to take a position on benefits issues raised by the introduction of Universal Credit and Personal Independence Payments. Because the interface of welfare reforms with housing, local taxation, disability and mental health policy was much more than technical, a consensus developed in 2011 that a Scottish-grown response was preferable to taking order-making powers under the UK Act with a legislative consent order. The result was Scottish legislation in 2012 and a new Welfare Reform Committee of the Parliament to monitor it.

The expert group report staked out a cautious report that usefully delineated the cross-border traffic on social security administration (benefits for Scottish claimants being processed in England, and vice-versa) but seemed overly influenced by pro-welfare groups and the protection of beneficiaries. Its calls for a wider national conversation on the principles that might underlie a Scottish welfare state and led to a second expert group established in 2013 that reported in 2014 and promoted a vision of a participative, bottom-up welfare system closer to Nordic norms that might reverse UK cutbacks (Scottish Government 2014a). It is less clear how this vision could be achieved through variable policies within UK norms and structures, the approach pioneered in the Scottish Rate of Income Tax (SRIT) and eventually adopted in the report of the Smith Commission.

Consolidated administration and networks without reorganisation

The SG has been consolidating an extensive but incomplete administrative apparatus that could take on wider tasks, and as a matter of policy some of it has been located outside Edinburgh. For instance, in a low-rise building near the terminus of the new Borders Railway in Tweedbank, the Scottish Public Pensions Agency administers the occupational pension of a range of retired Scottish public servants, including teachers, health service workers, police officers and firefighters. Many others, including devolved civil servants, receive their pensions from UK schemes run from English locations, with administration typically contracted-out to private providers.

Alongside this, throughout its life the devolved system has responded to perspectives on the machinery of government set by the UK centre. This is partly because of Barnett consequentials of reductions in running cost budgets, but also from a genuine technocratic interest in efficiency and 'improvement' (the concept embodied in the title of the 'Improvement Service' for local government). The NHS in Scotland is now firmly run from the centre, with management and policy fused, in a way similar to Whitehall. The Labour/Liberal Democrat coalition in 2001, and the SNP in 2008, produced plans for 'quango-culls', now known as 'simplification' and tracked on the SG website (Parry 2009; 2010).

Administrative change has been facilitated by the Public Services Reform (Scotland) Act 2010, which allows administrative reorganisation to be done by secondary legislation, even when a body may originally have been created by primary legislation. Its passage caused controversy because at the time it seemed more permissive of rapid reorganisation than the Westminster equivalent. This strategy is typical of the second term strategy of the SNP, somewhat less protective of well-established and local interests. The SNP completed a messy, half-completed merger of the Scottish Arts Council and Scottish Screen into Creative Scotland, and has concentrated its 'culling' efforts on smaller advisory bodies. A notable merger in 2015 is of Historic Scotland, a civil service agency, and the long-established Royal Commission on the Ancient and Historical Monuments of Scotland, into Historic Environment Scotland. The general UK trend to put such bodies under boards outside the Civil Service is being followed.

The 'big bang' reorganisations have been of a single Police Scotland and a single Scottish Fire and Rescue service in April 2013. The underlying problem went back to local government reorganisation in 1975 when the small regions of Central and Dumfries and Galloway, and their police and fire services, were created adjacent to Strathclyde. Some rationalisation was always likely; the political decision was to override local interests and have a national service under effective SG control. The political risk was the old contention that devolved Scotland would be 'Strathclyde writ large', especially when Strathclyde chief constable Sir Stephen House was given the Scotland job. He lasted only two years amid suggestions that an alien style of policing was being imposed on the quieter areas of Scotland. Centralisation of the force implied centralisation of political attention and responsibility when anything went wrong at the operational level anywhere in Scotland. The issue remains in play and is not resolved by the SNP's approach of not rationalising the local government structure but depriving it of the ability to raise council tax or business rate levels.

One further theme of Scottish devolved practice has been the promotion of networks without reorganisation of structure. This has been made possible by the overarching nature of the 'Scotland Performs' objectives, set out with accompanying indicators of success on a Scottish Government website. 'Community Planning', made mandatory for all local authority areas in the Local Government in Scotland Act 2003, seeks to bring together all public services, including reserved ones, in a mechanism of joint meetings. 'Single Outcome Agreements' with local authorities, the most recent in 2013, seek to align local action with the SG's National Objectives. These agreements are typical of the non-binding concordats fashionable in UK government that summarise aspirations better than impelling action. More potent has been the network of senior officials in the SG, local authorities and health boards who meet in the Scottish Leaders Forum.

The most concrete action has been in the area of health and social care – more precisely, creating some mechanism for using NHS money to support clients in more cost-effective settings outside hospitals. In 2015–16, a network of Integration Joint Boards of local councillors and health board members came into being. Typically, they have a combined budget for adult social care, primary health care, general hospital services and substance abuse services. The NHS retains control of acute hospital services and surgery, and social work departments retain children's services and criminal justice.

The catch – shared with the devolved 'powerhouses' being created in England by the UK government – is that existing institutions and employment relationships remain. The boards have a highly-paid chief officer, often coming from senior NHS or social work roles in the locality, but staff continue to work for either the local authority or the NHS as previously. This allows a potentially significant change to be bound by inertia to as much of the present budgetary lines and delivery patterns as becomes politically necessary.

Further devolution: the Smith Commission and the machinery of government

Lord Smith's commission produced on a rapid timescale in October–November 2014 an attempted reconciliation of party positions on further devolution within the UK – almost by definition, a lowest common denominator of what parties could support. It was about policy, not machinery. The status of the Civil Service was long dead as a topic for controversy. The Smith proposals did venture into a major system design area: the proposed right of the Scottish Parliament by a two-thirds majority to amend its composition, method of election and frequency of its terms. These powers, subsequently offered to the National Assembly for Wales by the St David's Day Agreement of 2015, mark the moment when the Westminster mentality moved from devolution as power retained to self-government as power renounced.

At the operational level, Smith implicitly promoted the concept of a fused administration seen in the Scottish Rate of Income Tax (SRIT). The devolution of the land and buildings transactions tax from 2016 has brought into being a small new agency, Revenue Scotland, but the much more significant SRIT is being managed by H.M. Revenue and Customs, who are working closely with the Scottish Government and will report for audit purposes direct to the Scottish Parliament.

Under Smith's proposals, the money-transferring agencies – both H.M. Revenue and Customs and the Department for Work and Pensions – will manage variables rates within the tax and benefits system and allocate citizens authoritatively between England and Scotland on the basis of predominant residence. There was much surprise at Smith's retention of Universal Credit as a structure for organising working-age income transfers. But from the UK point of view, insisted upon to Smith, the indivisibility of work sanctions and income tests is vital. The Scottish Government can pay for more generosity within the system, but not change its framework. As the DWP pointed out in its evidence to Smith, UC technology has been built to be territorially variable (because of non-uniform level of housing benefit) and is much more adept at accommodating rate changes than the systems it replaces. Much of the academic debate about Smith was on how far it was reined in at the last minute as UK interests took fright. More to the point is that the mechanisms of extended devolution are now in solid shape and are based on similar, compatible processes and organisations.

Conclusion: the Scottish model of government reassessed

John Elvidge's *Northern Exposure* set out his view of the 'Scottish model of government' that underlay his approach as permanent secretary under both Labour and the SNP. It is a technocratic model of evidence-based performance measurement of progress towards stated socio-economic objectives. The model is facilitated by an integrated approach to the organisation of government in which deliberate horizontal and vertical disarticulation is built in order to avoid the emergence of silos. This was made possible by the pre-1997 tradition of the Scottish Office and the integration of its finance and personnel functions in the 1970s. The objectives belong to a competition state view of Scotland, one that is not owned by any political party and does not require independence to be moved forward.

Elvidge does not touch directly on UK variables, but as UK civil service reform unfolded uneasily it became clear that Scottish developments represented a contrasting model that was much more consonant with traditional minister–official norms. Whereas UK ministers seemed frustrated with the policy advice and delivery success they were getting, SNP ministers expressed no reservations about the balance of responsibilities between ministers, private office, special advisers and policy officials. Arrangements within the Home Civil Service seemed to be giving them all the flexibility they wanted. Whatever their private thoughts, Scottish officials were lined up behind Scottish ministers, just as they had been for the Conservatives from 1979 to 1997 – with the change that, practically and intellectually, officials had no need to accommodate UK interests.

Elvidge states that:

> it would be a bold hypothesis to connect the success of the Scottish National Party in winning an overall majority of seats, an outcome previously considered unachievable for any political party, to their adoption and successful deployment of the Scottish model of government.
>
> (Elvidge 2011: 37–38)

But he does not dissuade us from making the hypothesis. The indefinable change of atmosphere during the 2011 election campaign in 2010–11, during which opinion swung from Labour to SNP, might have found a parallel in swings in elite thinking about the success and competence of present and past ministers in meeting the governmental challenges that fell to them.

The 'odd couple' are providing a lively input into commentaries about the decline of the Whitehall model (Page 2010) and the public service bargain in the UK (van Dorpe and Horton 2011). Canadian political scientist Peter Aucoin (2012), in an article published after his death, showed how a defence and reconstruction of the old approach to public administration in Whitehall-derived systems could be made. It is rare for politicians and officials to find a mutual interest in the old model – but in Scotland we have seen it.

From a constitutional perspective, whether or not Scotland is independent might seem a totally overwhelming first order issue. But, like a change of ownership of an established business, or a new rail or broadcasting franchise, the inherited activity goes on. EU law on employee rights when undertakings are transferred ('TUPE') gives us a model of 'everything changing but everything staying the same'. In the end, things do change, but some of the forces impelling this will be deep, international, and regime-unspecific. A putative independent Scotland would start life in substantial continuity with devolved Scotland, which in turn was shaped by the nineteenth- and twentieth-century British state.

Sources for further reading and study

Books

Work on the politics and financial arrangements of the devolved Scottish system has tended to treat administrative and machinery issues only tangentially. Useful material can be found in:

Cairney, P. (2011) *The Scottish Political System since Devolution* (Ch. 4). Exeter: Imprint Academic.

Keating, M. (2010) *The Government of Scotland* (Ch 5). Edinburgh: Edinburgh University Press.

Reports and websites

Audit Scotland (2013) *Scotland's Public Sector Workforce*. Available at: www.audit-scotland.gov.uk/2013/nr_131128_publi_sector_workforce (accessed November 2015).

Beyond Smith: Contributions to the Continuing Process of Scottish Devolution (2014). Available at: www.centreonconstitutionalchange.ac.uk/beyondsmith (accessed November 2015).

Elvidge, J. (2011) *Northern Exposure. Lessons From The First Twelve Years of Devolved Government in Scotland*. Institute for Government. Available at: www.instituteforgovernment.org.uk/publications/northern-exposure (accessed November 2015).

References

Aucoin, P. (2012) 'New political governance in Westminster systems: impartial public administration and management performance at risk'. *Governance* 25(2): 177–199.

Elvidge, J. (2011) *Northern Exposure: Lessons from the First Twelve Years of Devolved Government In Scotland*. London: Institute for Government.

Hood, C. and R. Dixon (2013) 'A model of cost-cutting in government? The great management revolution in UK central government reconsidered'. *Public Administration* 91(1): 114–134.

Page, E. (2010) 'Has the Whitehall model survived?'. *International Review of Administrative Sciences* 76(3): 407–442.

Parry, R. (2007) 'Public service reform and the efficiency agenda'. In Keating, M. (ed.) *Scottish Social Democracy: Progressive Ideas for Public Policy*. Brussels: P.I.E. Peter Lang.

Parry, R. (2009) 'Quangos, agencies and the Scottish Parliament'. In Jeffery, C. and Mitchell, J. (eds) *The Scottish Parliament 1999–2009: The First Decade*. Edinburgh: Luath Press.

Parry, R. (2010) 'Reshaping structures of government across the UK'. In Lodge, G. and Schmueker, K., *Devolution in Practice 2010*. London: Institute for Public Policy Research.

Paun, A. and R. Munro (2015) *Governing in an Ever-looser Union: How the Four Governments of the UK Co-operate, Negotiate and Compete*. London: Institute for Government.

Scottish Government (2007) *Choosing Scotland's Future*. Edinburgh.

Scottish Government (2012) *Your Scotland, Your Referendum*. Edinburgh.

Scottish Government (2013a) *Fiscal Commission Working Group, First Report: Macroeconomic Framework*. Edinburgh.

Scottish Government (2013b) *The Expert Working Group on Welfare May 2013 Report*. Edinburgh.

Scottish Government (2014a) *Re-thinking Welfare: Fair, Personal and Simple (Expert Welfare Group, 2nd Report)*. Edinburgh.

Scottish Government (2014b) *The Scottish Independence Bill: A Consultation on an Interim Constitution for Scotland*. Edinburgh.

Scottish Labour Party (2014) *Powers for a Purpose: Strengthening Accountability and Empowering People*. Edinburgh. Available at: http://b.3cdn.net/scotlab/c07a7cdb97a522f4c5_h1m6vwh8l.pdf.

Torrance, D. (2010) *Salmond: Against the Odds*. Edinburgh: Birlinn.

Van Dorpe, K. and S. Horton (2011) 'The public service bargain in the United Kingdom: the Whitehall model in decline'. *Public Policy and Administration* 26(2): 233–252.

8 Social policy in a devolved Scotland
Different, fairer?

Kirstein Rummery

Introduction

> Social justice and fairness are the hallmarks of Scottish Society.
> Donald Dewar, (Labour) first minister at the first session of the Scottish Parliament, May 1999

> An independent Scotland could be a beacon of progressive opinion – addressing policy challenges in ways which reflect the universal values of fairness.
> Alex Salmond, (SNP) first minister, addressing the Scottish Parliament in January 2012

Scotland has long laid claim for a different national identity to the rest of the UK, and that its society is inherently based on notions of fairness, social justice, and egalitarianism (Keating 2009). The rhetoric of social justice holds a particularly powerful sway in the way Scotland perceives its approach to social policy. The quotes above show that this perception crosses party lines and is a powerful rhetoric when making arguments for Scotland-centred social policy development: whether that is for devolution, increased policy capacity, or full independence. The political map of Scotland looks very different from the 1999 Parliament: the Labour party suffered its biggest historical electoral defeat in Scotland in 2011 (mirrored later in the general election of 2015) where it lost substantial support to the SNP. Contemporary Scottish citizens appear to politically support a party at both Holyrood and Westminster that favours maximum control over Scottish social policy to rest with the Scottish Parliament.

Prior to the 1999 devolution settlement, Scotland already had a different legal and education system incumbent since the Act of Union in 1707, with the result that criminal and education policy were already significantly different from the rest of the UK. The Scottish Office, established in 1885, gave an institutional home for this difference in social policy, and it oversaw the majority of Scottish social policy apart from macro-economic policy, taxation and social security (Keating 2010; Mitchell 2014). The Scotland Act 1998 devolved to the Scottish Parliament all legislative powers not reserved to Westminster,[1] meaning that these social policy powers were exercised by a legislature elected by, and accountable to, the Scottish electorate rather than the whole of the UK. Indeed, the Scottish parliament has been argued to be largely a social policy making body. Although different in structure and voting systems, the Scottish Parliament arguably has a very similar policy 'style' to Westminster (Cairney 2008). However, an analysis of its first term indicated that from an early stage, the Scottish Parliament opened itself up to working in co-operation with civic society and allowed relatively easy access for interest groups to policy (Shephard and Cairney 2005) at multiple points (Cairney 2014).

This opening up of policy spaces reflects the fact that until the SNP won an overall majority in 2011, the Scottish Parliament had been ruled by coalition or minority governments. This meant that in order to push through social policies, ministers usually had to gain cross-party consensus, and apart from the SNP which had little Westminster focus for its policy platform, the Labour, Conservative and Liberal Democrat parties in Scotland had no particular incentive to deviate substantially from the policy platform held by their Westminster counterparts. Moreover, the general population is not always fully aware of the extent of social policy power held at Holyrood versus Westminster (or at local authority level) and so electoral campaigns on specific social policy issues tend to have little effect if that policy issue is not one already associated in the public's mind with a particular political party.

This led to a certain degree of path dependency on the part of some of the main political parties, with the result that their social policies did not deviate significantly from the rest of the UK. Conversely, where there is pressure from grassroots campaigners, civic society and the third sector to develop policies that do deviate from the UK norm, a majority government is under less pressure to cater to non-political pressure because it has the power to push through social policies without working in co-operation. Nevertheless there has been some acknowledgement on the part of the Scottish Government that many of the issues Scotland faces are 'wicked issues' in social policy terms – complex, multi-faceted, and outside the scope of any one agency to tackle on its own. Partnership and co-production are in some ways easier in the Scottish context because of scale – as Cairney (2014) points out, the key stakeholders in any particular social policy issue in Scotland would fit easily around a negotiating table. In tone if not in substance there are numerous spaces for different voices to be heard in the policy process, and this gives rise to some scope for policy deviation and experimentation.

The foundations of the UK welfare state lie in the 1942 Beveridge Report, which identified five giant 'evils' in society which post-war social policy should attempt to address: squalor, ignorance, want, idleness, and disease. The remainder of this chapter will be structured around these five social policy areas, critically examining where Scotland has shown policy deviation from the rest of the UK, and discussing whether that deviation demonstrates a more solid commitment to fairness and social justice than the rest of the UK, looking particularly at the outcomes along social divisions. The penultimate section will examine the options for social policy in Scotland under further devolution of welfare powers under the Scotland Act (2015) and reflect on whether Scottish social policy really can lay claim to being different and fairer to the rest of the UK.

Tackling squalor: Scottish housing policy

Prior to devolution, Scotland had already begun to deviate in some substantial ways in its housing policy from the rest of the UK: for example, by continuing to invest in social housing at a time when policy priorities elsewhere were supporting owner-occupation and the development of a private rented sector. Although the 1980s Right to Buy policy extended to Scotland, favourable terms for Registered Social Landlords meant that access to social housing did not decline as significantly as in the rest of the

UK (Pawsin and Mullins 2010), and most social landlords in Scotland are small community organisations governed by residents (SHR 2010). This means that one in four Scots currently live in social housing, and in some cities like Glasgow this rises to 40 per cent (Wilcox, 2007). Moreover in 2010 the SNP government introduced the Housing (Scotland) Act which effectively ended the Right to Buy.

The tenant involvement in the governance of housing associations provides an accessible and legitimated route to citizen engagement in social policy development for members of the community who would otherwise be fairly inaccessible to statutory planning. So for example, housing associations regularly send representatives to Community Safety Partnerships to plan the development of policing and other services, and are often involved in planning community care services with local authorities, particularly if they have a high number of older and disabled tenants. This is helped by the fact that unlike in the rest of the UK, both local authority and housing association tenants have a single secure tenancy under the Housing (Scotland) Act 2001, and a single regulatory framework under the Housing (Scotland) Act 2010, which provides security of tenure and monitoring of housing quality across the whole of Scotland.

In addition to an investment in social housing that is at odds with the rest of the UK, Scottish citizens also benefit from homelessness social policies which are arguably more progressive than the rest of the UK. Although the Housing (Homeless Persons) Act 1977 applied in Scotland prior to devolution, this focussed on 'priority need' – i.e. offering accommodation only to those who were considered to be vulnerable, rather than a universal provision. This had the result of making social housing the norm for low income, vulnerable households rather than for a mix of social classes – the residualisation of social housing (King 2010). One of the first acts of the 1999 Scottish government was the creation of a Homelessness Task Force which included representation from social landlords, the third sector and the public as well as local and national statutory bodies. It recommended the abolition of priority need with the eventual aim of providing universal access to social housing. In addition the Housing Act (Scotland) 2001 gave a legal duty to Registered Social Landlords to comply with local authority requests to house unintentionally homeless people, indicating that the Scottish Government was willing to create tensions with powerful vested interests in order to achieve social policy objectives.

Perhaps the most radical social policy development to deviate from the rest of the UK is the commitment, under the Housing (Scotland) Act 2003, to end homelessness by a specified date (2012). This has been heralded internationally as one of the most progressive housing policies in Europe (Anderson 2009) and added additional obligations to the Housing (Scotland) 2001 Act to provide temporary accommodation to all homeless people waiting for permanent accommodation – including the 'intentionally' homeless. However, the target has not quite been met due in no small part to a failure to invest in building new social housing to meet demand, creating tensions between the Scottish government, local authorities and registered social landlords. Nevertheless, one of the biggest homelessness charities has praised the sea-change in policy and practice that has resulted from the commitment and asserts that it remains achievable within the foreseeable future (Shelter 2014).

However, this commitment to ending homelessness is not a commitment to universal access to affordable housing – and it has been asserted that unlike other universal services like the NHS and education, housing policy in Scotland has had the effect of widening inequalities between higher income owner occupiers who have an investment in a capital asset and social housing tenants who don't (Malpas 2010). Moreover, in the absence of long-term care insurance in Scotland, housing remains the primary asset that is used to contribute to the costs of social care in later life, which further exacerbates inequalities accumulated over the lifecourse. Despite a rhetorical commitment to universal tenancy, in reality the concentration of social housing on the poorest and most vulnerable means that poverty and deprivation have a geographical concentration of disadvantage. Over a third of households in the social rented sector are unemployed, and nearly 17 per cent are retired, and over two thirds rely on housing benefit (SCORE 2010). This concentration of deprivation also leads to concentrations in social problems such as crime, drug and alcohol abuse, and anti-social behaviour, making it difficult for tenants to protect their communities and creating tensions between landlords, long-term and vulnerable tenants, with racist, sectarian and disablist hate crimes particularly prevalent in deprived areas (Kintrea 2006; Anderson 2009). This is in contrast to the 1970s and 1980s where social rented housing was the norm across different social groups, the focus on maintaining it for the most vulnerable has stigmatised and removed social cohesion. Moreover, key policy levers that could be used to address these issues, such as housing benefit, tax credits and social security, lie outside the scope of the Scottish government to address (Kintrea 2006).

The housing budget has never been a protected area like health and education, and there never has been a full scale commitment to universal social or affordable housing from the Scottish government. Social policies designed to achieve a mix of housing within the same community to support social cohesion have been piecemeal at best, with limited obligations on new build housing developments to provide a mix of rented and owner occupied housing. Some effort has been made to improve access to low-cost home ownership through shared equity schemes, which are cheaper for the public purse than social housing and do provide access to capital assets for low-income groups (McKee 2010). However, this focus in a time of economic hardship and austerity policies that, no matter how unpopular they are in Scotland do restrict significant parts of public investment, is a significant issue in social policy. The need for social housing, particularly amongst growing numbers of older, disabled and low income people, is going to grow, not decline. Moreover, older and unemployed people (including significant numbers of disabled people) are excluded from owner-occupation and the opportunity to accumulate capital assets. A social policy that is both a significant departure from the rest of the UK and focused on being fairer is, arguably, widening social divisions and inequality in Scotland.

Fighting ignorance: social justice and education policy

Scotland's historically 'different' education system and policy is arguably an important part of its national identity and a distinctive part of why Scotland maintains a rhetoric of 'fairness' and difference in social policy (Keating 2010). The first minister, Alex Salmond, summarised this Scottish view of its education policy neatly at the 2011 SNP conference:

> This nation pioneered free education for all, which resulted in Scots inventing and explaining much of the modern world. We called this the Scottish Enlightenment. Out of educational access came social mobility as we reached all the talents of a nation to change the world for the better ... the rocks will melt with the sun before

I allow tuition fees to be imposed on Scottish students ... This is part of the Scottish Settlement, our social contract with the people.

The Act of Union in 1707 maintained Scottish control over education (along with the church and law). For example, reforms designed to introduce marketised performance measures into education were resisted, even when both Westminster and Holyrood had Labour governments intent on pursuing them (Croxford et al. 2002). Although recent educational reforms such as the Curriculum for Excellence do link educational performance to employment and economic growth objectives, the creation of an internal market in education based on competition over performance has never become a key part of Scottish education policy in the way it has in the rest of the UK under Labour, the coalition and the present Conservative administrations, providing further evidence for the Scottish rhetoric of a fairer, egalitatarian education system (Grek et al. 2009). Scotland's view of itself as the keeper of a 'Scottish Enlightenment' in education is backed up by its focus on higher education: there are nineteen university and higher education colleges in Scotland (for a population of 6 million) compared to ninety-one in England (for a population of 53 million), making the Scottish institutions nearly twice as powerful in civic society as their English counterparts. The strength of the higher education sector and the control over its institutions gave Scotland important policy levers to resist unpopular changes in education policy designed by the Westminster government. The ongoing resistance of the Scottish government to university fees, in the face of the failure of the Liberal Democrats to abolish them as part of the 2010–2015 UK coalition government, is often held up as further proof of a uniquely Scottish commitment to egalitarianism and fairness through education policy.

However, when the *outcomes* of social mobility through the education system in Scotland versus the rest of the UK are compared, the evidence that the Scottish system is 'fairer', more egalitarian and meritocratic and leads to greater social mobility does not stand up to scrutiny. There are seventy-two private/independent schools in Scotland, educating less than 5 per cent of Scottish pupils (compared to 7 per cent of English pupils who go to private schools) and 69 per cent of their pupils attained grade As in the new National 5 level exams in 2015, compared with 37.5 per cent nationally. As entrance to university in Scotland and the rest of the UK is determined by exam performance it is clear that the wealthy elite who can afford to pay for private school fees have a significant advantage in access to higher education than those attending free state schools. As state school pupils routinely outperform those from private schools in the attainment of final university degrees (82 per cent of state school pupils graduated with a first class or 2:1 degree in 2014, compared to 73 per cent of private school pupils). Although 56 per cent of state school leavers and 60 per cent of private school leavers go on to university, pupils from private schools are more than twice as likely to attend the 'Russell Group' of universities than their state educated counterparts; it is clear that privilege rather than merit is the overwhelming factor in gaining access to elite higher education.

Moreover, although on the face of it a fair, universal social policy that should aid social mobility, the refusal to impose fees in Scottish universities for Scottish students in fact has the opposite effect. The structural advantage enjoyed by higher income pupils which means they are more likely to gain access to university, and in particular 'elite' universities, than lower income pupils is not compensated for by free university tuition. Although overall, 70 per cent of Scottish graduates entered employment shortly after graduating in 2014 (compared to 65 per cent of graduates in England and Wales) and commanded slightly higher starting salaries than the rest of the UK, these differences disappear when analysed by type of university, with graduates from elite institutions commanding salaries nearly one third higher than those graduating from other universities: Scotland's disproportionately higher employment and salary rates for graduates is down to its disproportionately high numbers of students attending elite institutions, not because of a 'Scottish effect', and we have already established that attendance at these institutions is dominated by higher income students. As Scottish graduates are graduating without having to repay fees, they are in effect the beneficiaries of state subsidy of the higher earnings capacity of higher income groups, and do not have to repay this benefit in the form of increased taxation or repayment of fees. In addition, one of the conditions of being able to impose higher fees placed on elite institutions in England is that 'fairer access' for lower income and marginalised groups of students must be supported. This has the effect of obliging institutions to offer incentives and financial support to these groups, with the result that the proportion of state school entrants, ethnic minorities and disabled pupils has risen in elite English institutions whereas in Scottish ones it has remained the same. In addition, funding for further education (which has a higher proportion of entrants from state schools and lower income groups) has been cut in favour of preserving funding for higher education, further exacerbating the divide between access to high income graduate jobs between pupils from higher and lower income backgrounds.

So, it can be argued that if it were serious about 'fairness', Scotland would arguably enable its elite institutions to charge fees on the same (or even more punitive in terms of widening access) basis as English institutions, and use the income gained to invest in further, not higher, education. However within the current political climate this is a highly unlikely policy scenario: Scotland's elite jealously guards its 'world class' universities and even the SNP favours investment in higher, rather than further education. Moreover, research on educational policies indicates that income/class are better predictors of social outcomes than educational attainment, and it is possible to fairly accurately predict a child's outcome at 18 by the time they are 5 years old. In order to address social inequalities through education, the focus should therefore be on Early Years (3–5, and in some cases even younger – comparative research shows that all children benefit from formal intervention from age 2), rather than post-18 education (by which point privilege and inequality have become structurally embedded). Comparative research and that of others indicates that where local authorities have to provide universal access to high quality pre-school care and education (full time), this has the dual effect of raising the educational attainment of low income pupils, and of enabling parents in low income families to work and raise the family income: a double attack on inequality which is far more effective at achieving egalitarian outcomes over the lifecourse than investing in the supply side or private sector provisions (Rummery and McAngus 2016).

However there are significant cultural, social, political and structural barriers to be overcome before investment in early years and further education takes priority over attainment in secondary and higher education. Until those barriers are overcome in Scotland it is likely there will continue to be significant gaps between the educational attainment and outcomes of higher income versus lower income and marginalised pupils and students.

The end of want? Anti-poverty strategies

Relative poverty in Scotland has been falling steadily since devolution, and falling slightly faster than in the UK as a whole, as Figure 8.1 shows over the same period, income inequalities in Scotland have reduced, although they have remained the same in the UK (see Figure 8.2).

Over a similar period child absolute poverty dropped from 30 per cent to 15 per cent, but relative poverty only dropped from 30 per cent to 22 per cent – the proportion of

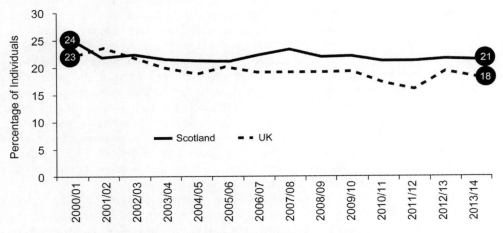

Figure 8.1 Relative poverty after housing costs, Scotland and the UK
Source: Scottish Government 2015.

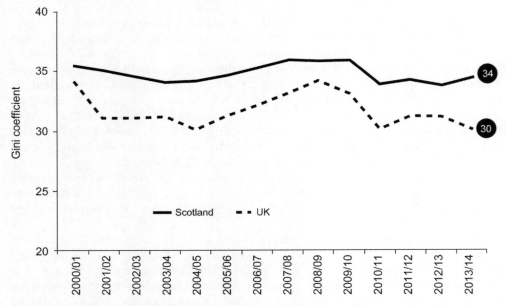

Figure 8.2 Equality of household income, as measured by the Gini coefficient, Scotland and the UK
Source: Scottish Government 2015.

children on a low income fell from 26 per cent to 17 per cent: overall this compares favourably to, for example, London, which has seen a decrease from 34 per cent to 27 per cent, and the West Midlands which has seen a rise from 27 per cent to 28 per cent (Family Resources Survey 2013).

So how, in the absence of control over macro-economic and welfare policy, did Scotland achieve this success? First, it should be noted that the first decade saw a time of UK-wide economic growth and a rise in incomes, as well as growth in employment rates for women. One of the surest ways to address child poverty is to improve mothers' access to work, and in this period female employment rates rose and the gender wage gap narrowed. These trends were not particular to Scotland. Second, Scottish social policy concentrated on addressing social inclusion, rather than simply income poverty. This meant that policies were focussed on the multi-dimensional nature of social exclusion, including access to training, education, improving skills, childcare provision, improving access to work, investing in regeneration and in social services, and improving household finances. Measures to reduce fuel poverty, abolishing prescription charges, free personal care, the council tax freeze, and assistance with early years intervention all improved access to resources for low income families (particularly low income families in work) all contributed to the success. Third, the co-operative approach to policy making used by the Scottish government is a clear example that this can work successfully: many policy initiatives came out of work with groups such as the Poverty Alliance and the Poverty Truth Commission, which places people and communities with direct experience of poverty at the heart of their consultation process (Poverty Truth Commission 2011).

Finally, it should be noted that Scotland only looks successful when compared to the most deprived areas in the rest of the UK (particularly London and the West Midlands): it is London's failure, rather than Scotland's success that makes the figures look so positive (Sinclair and McKendrick 2012). When compared with broadly similar countries internationally, Scotland does not look so successful. One in five Scottish children are living in poverty, compared to one in ten Danish children. There has been no systematic investment in early years education, care and maternity and paternity leave: these are the key tools needed to address women and children's poverty (Rummery and McAngus 2016). Moreover there have been few efforts to engage with business to tackle issues such as zero hours contracts and a living wage, or to shift funding away from the NHS towards preventative services that might tackle the causes of health inequalities (for example worklessness, drug and alcohol abuse, mental health issues, high dependence on family and informal care, food poverty, gender-based violence and abuse, child neglect, social isolation, chronic ill health, and other issues). It would appear that greater difference and policy divergence is needed for Scotland to address poverty and social exclusion successfully.

Idleness: work, employment and social exclusion

Despite high levels of poverty and inequality, Scotland currently has the highest employment rate of the four countries in the United Kingdom.

Even after the 2008 recession, unemployment in Scotland has remained lower than the rest of the UK and well below EU averages. Historically, Scotland has relied on agriculture and heavy industry such as shipbuilding, coal and engineering, but the decline of these in the 1970s coupled with the Conservative government's dismantling

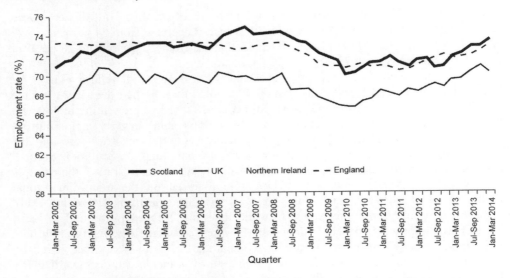

Figure 8.3 Employment rates (16–64) in the four countries of the UK, Q1 2002–Q1 2014
Source: ONS, Labour Force Survey 2014.

of key industries meant that Scotland was suffering from mass unemployment in the 1980s (Knox 1999). Many (predominantly) male workers also suffered long-term ill health and disability which had been hidden by high levels of employment, and so Scotland still has higher than average levels of unemployed people on disability-related benefits (Alcock et al. 2003). Like other areas of the UK, the manufacturing industry never recovered, and job growth in the late 1980s was largely due to a rise of employment in the service sector, banking, and health and social care provision (Futureskills Scotland 2009). A combination of proliferation in low quality, insecure jobs, a decline in trade union strength and social security changes have meant that the expectation of full-time employment for life is out of reach for most Scots.

Access to employment also has a geographical dimension in Scotland, with differences between patterns of paid work in urban and rural areas. Whilst the rural labour market has remained relatively stable, transport, infrastructure and access to training and childcare remain challenging, particularly in the Highlands and Islands with very dispersed populations. This means the labour market is very segregated along both income and gender lines, with poorer and women workers in particular finding the costs of accessing work far higher than their urban counterparts, and jobs being concentrated in the agricultural and service sectors, both of which are seasonal, low paid and relatively low skilled (de Lima, 2008). There is also a higher demand for migrant labour than the rest of the UK, due to declining birthrates, net emigration and an ageing population (de Lima and Wright, 2009).

As in the rest of the UK, the Scottish labour market is very segregated along gender lines, with 40 per cent of women working part-time, compared to 9 per cent of men, but the gender pay gap is smaller, with Scottish women working full-time earning 12 per cent less than their male colleagues, compared to 17 per cent less in the UK as a whole (for part-time workers the gender pay gap is 33 per cent and 38 per cent respectively) (EOC 2006). In part this is due to overall wages being lower in Scotland,

and a greater proportion of the workforce in the public sector (particularly health and social care, and education) where gender pay gaps are lower than the private sector (13 per cent compared to 23 per cent).

Scotland lacks control over macro-economic and social security policy (although see below on the coming devolution of further social security powers), which means it does not have access to the social policy levers to effect significant change in its labour market. In terms of unemployment it has weathered the current recession better than the rest of the UK, although further cuts to public sector funding will affect the block grant it receives from Westminster and therefore its ability to maintain the current levels of public sector employment. Since 1997 the Westminster government has instigated a long programme of 'welfare reform', encompassing changes to social security designed to move people off sickness-related benefits and into more punitive, time limited unemployment benefits. This policy direction continued under the 2010 coalition and 2015 Conservative governments at Westminster. The Scottish Government lacks significant policy levers to create more high quality accessible jobs or to make out-of-work benefits fairer, and this has a significant impact on unemployed Scots.

'Work' (as in not being idle) does not only consist of being in paid employment, and this has a gendered dimension. Women's roles as parents and carers means that they are less likely to be employed in the labour market (and when employed are more likely to be working part-time), and they therefore feel the impact of the withdrawal or reduction of state benefits more acutely than men. For example, 92 per cent of lone parents are women, and 95 per cent of lone parents dependant on income support are women; 74 per cent of people claiming carer's allowance are women and they make up around 60 per cent of unpaid carers (Carers UK 2014). Unpaid carers save Scotland around a third of its health and social care budget, but carer's allowance is currently only 25 per cent of the minimum wage. Moreover, the development of universal credit, designed to make work pay and encourage more people into the workforce, did not take childcare issues into account. As a result of changes to child benefit, the childcare element of working tax credit and income support, low income women with very young children were forced into looking for work, women with high income partners lost what was often their only independent source of income, all women lost some income that was the only source targeted directly at children, and access to childcare was reduced for low income families, particularly lone parents (Poverty Alliance 2013). All of these changes were outside the control of the Scottish Government.

Disease, ill-health and disability: a fairer approach to health and social care?

Scotland famously suffers from persistent health inequalities, both in mortality and morbidity, compared to the rest of the UK, as Figure 8.4 shows.

Moreover, these inequalities are particularly noticeable across different local authorities, and persist even when you compare mortality rates for the same diseases: the so-called 'Glasgow effect'.

Moreover, as general life expectancy has risen, these inequalities have widened: the average life expectancy of a man in Glasgow is currently 71.6 years – nearly seven years below the national average of 78.2 years and well below the highest life expectancy in East Dunbartonshire of 80.1 years (Graham 2009; Karlsen and Nazroo 2010). These patterns can also be found in morbidity rates across Scotland (Shaw et al. 2007).

150   Kirstein Rummery

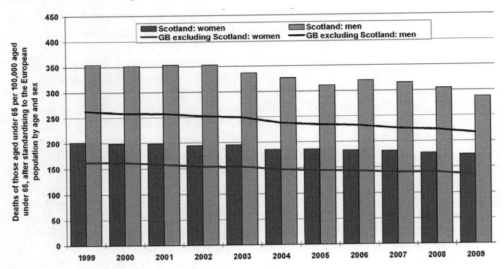

Figure 8.4 Throughout the last decade the rate of premature deaths in Scotland has been much higher than in England and Wales.
Source: The Poverty Site 2015.

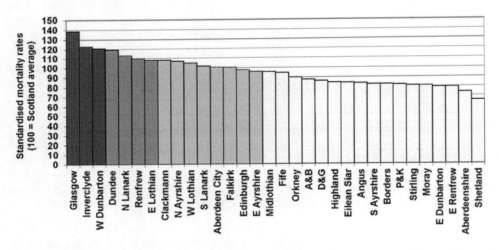

Figure 8.5 The standardised mortality rate for stomach cancer, lung cancer and heart disease in Glasgow is almost twice as high as that in the best areas.
Source: The Poverty Site 2015.

Most health sociologists argue that access to material, social and cultural resources shape and determine patterns of life expectancy and population health risks (Abel 2008). However – perhaps not surprisingly, given that engaging constructively with improving access to those resources would be a complex, lengthy and resource-heavy task – Scotland's key health policy makers have chosen to take a much narrower approach. Policy makers consistently refer to the evidence base on inequality, access to resources and health (see for example the 2000 report *Our National Health*, and more recently the Health and Sport Committee report of 2015 which included evidence on this from noted health sociologists Kate Pickett and Clare Bambra). However, the 2005 White Paper on 'Delivering for Health' neatly sums up the disconnect between the evidence base and the policy approach adopted in Scotland:

> The most significant thing we can do to tackle health inequalities is to target and enhance primary care services in deprived areas. Strengthening primary care teams and promoting anticipatory care in disadvantaged areas will reduce health inequalities by targeting health improvement action and resources at the most disadvantaged areas ... this approach will ensure that the people at greatest risk of ill health are actively identified and offered opportunities for early detection, advice and treatment.
>
> (Scottish Executive 2005: 24)

In other words, the focus is not on tackling material deprivation or inequality, but on providing better access to health services. This approach does make political sense: the NHS is consistently a key factor in elections, its universality creates social cohesion and solidarity, and voters, particularly middle-class and elderly voters (who benefit disproportionately from its services) always prioritise it in deciding which way to vote. Scotland has, along with the other devolved administrations, consistently opted to ring-fence and protect spending on the NHS (and in the current wave of cutbacks in public spending even the UK Conservative government has done the same). Arguably, no political party that wanted to gain, or keep, power would argue for diverting resources away from the NHS towards anti-poverty and equality programmes that would benefit the poor more than the middle classes and elderly (Cairney 2015).

Much of health policy in Scotland is driven by a normative and ideological framework that is a rejection of the neoliberal values of marketisation and private sector involvement, and a framing that is more in line with mutualism, co-production and valuing the health workforce (Birrell 2009). There has been rejection, for example, of changes to NHS structures designed to promote managerialism, performance management and the internal market in England in favour of collaboration with NHS professionals (Keating 2009). Moreover, 'universal' and 'fair' policy initiatives such as free personal/nursing care, free eye tests, free dental checks and free prescriptions actually serve to widen health inequalities (because very low income people would have been entitled to these anyway, and so the real benefits are felt by higher income patients, particularly wealthy elderly patients who do not have to use their assets to purchase personal/nursing care). Some elements of managerialism in health care – particularly the setting of performance standards and targets – have been enthusiastically adopted by the Scottish NHS (see for example Audit Scotland 2009). Other public health initiatives – e.g. public smoking bans, alcohol pricing, investment in sports policies, free school meals – are also embraced, often giving Scotland the opportunity to be a trailblazer for health policy – so long as these are seen as medically modelled, health-driven solutions. However, there remains a huge reluctance to embrace the diverting of resources away from the NHS towards tackling material deprivation and access to cultural and social capital.

In contrast to health policy, Scotland's distinctiveness and claim to fairness in social care is based on the idea that the foundation of social services in Scotland under the 1968 Social Work (Scotland) Act created a framework and a set of principles to drive social work to tackle disadvantage and inequality. This is often argued to demonstrate a substantial policy divergence from the rest of the UK which has seen a move towards marketisation, resource capping and new public managerialism in social work services, leaving disabled people increasingly at the mercy of service cutbacks and welfare sanctions (Ferguson 2008). However, this has arguably been a difference more rhetorical than substantive. The 1968 Act gave local authorities the power to make cash payments to tackle poverty and deprivation, which was illegal in England and Wales. Nevertheless, the development of direct payments (whereby disabled people were given cash to manage their own support in lieu of directly provided care services) was a policy development that was instigated in England (where it was technically illegal and had to be done via third party trusts) and not in Scotland (where it was actively resisted, particularly by the unions).

'Scottish self directed support' is the latest in a series of policies including the Community Care and Health (Scotland) Act 2003, which placed a duty on local authorities to offer 'Direct Payments' (DP) in lieu of standard community care services. The local authority made the payment to the individual (or representative) to arrange the services they were assessed as needing, which for some users improved the choice and control they could exercise over their services. Scottish local authorities (in line with English and Welsh local authorities) have a duty to offer eligible people Direct Payments. From April 2005 the first non-disabled user groups became eligible: parents of disabled children and older people (aged 65 and over) who have been assessed as needing care services due to infirmity or age. Under the 2013 Act all Scottish local authorities would have to offer service users the option of directing their own support, which can take various forms including Direct Payments. Users will still need to undergo an assessment to see if they have needs which services could meet.

Take-up, at both institutional and individual level, has varied considerably across the UK: rates of take-up in England are more than double that of elsewhere in the UK, with some individual local authorities (e.g. Hampshire) having more users registered than the whole of Scotland. According to Scottish Government figures, rates of take-up of Direct Payments are still far higher in England than in Scotland. Some of the barriers to the takeup of DP included lack of awareness from front-line workers and managers, and the need to invest in advocacy and support organisations to help users manage their payments, as well as concerns expressed about the risks involved for vulnerable users and a resistance to the perceived 'privatisation' of social care.

A closer analysis of areas where there has been a significant uptake of Direct Payments reveals that these areas show a history of strong disability-led user organisations (and a history of quasi-legal DP, for example through third party trusts), and/or a political commitment to the development of markets in social care provision. The twin impetus of strong user demand and a policy move towards mixed markets in social care which has driven the development of DP and related schemes (such as individual budgets) appears to be less prevalent in Scotland, although according to Scottish Government figures there has been a reduction in home care directly provided by local authorities from 82 per cent in 2000 to 44 per cent in 2011, and Scottish users of DP report similar improved outcomes to users elsewhere in the UK.

However, institutional barriers to implementation of Direct Payments in Scotland remained embedded and difficult to tackle, including an ideological resistance to privatisation in social care, a lack of commitment from senior managers, lack of awareness and training on the part of front-line care managers, and perceived budgetary inflexibilities. In order to inform the development of Self Directed Support, the Scottish

Government established three test sites to assess the impact of three interventions (bridging finance, cutting red tape and leadership and training). These lessons had already been learned twenty years earlier in the English context, but the lessons did not transfer to the Scottish context. Nevertheless, according to Scottish Government figures uptake of Self Directed Support in the form of Direct Payments has increased in Scotland from 207 users in 2001 to 4,392 in 2011, and the total value of DPs has increased from £2.1 million in 2001 to £50.2 million in 2011. The sharpest increase nationally has been in recent years, with 29 per cent of DP packages ongoing in March 2011 being in place for less than a year. Under the Self Directed Support (Scotland) Act 2012, service users still need to undergo a community care assessment to see if they have eligible needs. However, take-up of DP in England was reliant on user-led organisations (such as Centres for Independent Living) and user-advocacy organisations such as In Control supporting disabled people to run their own schemes, and offer peer mentoring and support to navigate the complexity of social care. In Scotland there are only two Centres of Independent Living, and they both rely on government funds for their core funding and are thus in a difficult position to provide independent, peer-led support. There are no plans to allow user-led organisations to undertake the assessments for community care services or for self-directed support, nor for them to administer and run Direct Payments schemes directly themselves.

Therefore, despite a rhetoric of 'coproduction', user empowerment and social justice, social work in Scotland has resisted the development of user-directed services until relatively recently: and under Self Directed Support it has retained the option of local authorities managing services on disabled people's behalf, rather than universally rolling out direct user control of resources. In spite of the apparent freedom to diverge from both the norms of policy and their practice, Scottish social services have not developed in a substantially different way to the rest of the UK. Local authorities have the responsibility for providing social care services, which means that, just as in the rest of the UK, there are different service levels, eligibility and access arrangements: thirty-two different local authorities means thirty-two different sets of social care services, including variations in costs for service users. Moreover, council tax freezes have placed constraints on local authorities' ability to meet the growing demand for social care services from an ageing population. In addition, joint working between health and social care for adults has not developed in a seamless fashion, which means that disabled people have been at the mercy of gaps and overlaps in services. Scotland, probably for political rather than policy reasons, has chosen to ring-fence health spending rather than redirect funding to anti-poverty and preventative programmes that would reduce health inequalities, particularly amongst poorer disabled people. As outlined above, self-directed support policy has facilitated the development of user-controlled services, but these do not differ substantially to systems developed in England and Wales. There is substantial marketisation, third sector and not-for-profit sector involvement in the provision of social care services in line with patterns established in the rest of the UK and adopted by Scotland.

So the argument that Scotland has not developed better social policies for disabled people due to it not having control over the full range of spending and welfare policies is not a credible one when the lack of radical policy reform in social care policy to date is examined. The failure to apply policy lessons that lead to improved outcomes for social care users from England effectively, and the failure of Scottish civic society to develop a strong user-led movement that is willing and able to engage constructively in challenging incumbent governments to develop improved social policies, means that Scotland, to date, has not shown much persuasive evidence of a more inclusive approach to social policy for disabled people

Fairness in times of austerity: the challenges and possibilities

With the devolution of further powers under the 2016 Scotland Act, Scotland has a unique opportunity to create a system of welfare that is fair, universal, simple and sustainable. Scotland has long maintained that it is different and fairer to the rest of the UK when comes to its approach to welfare and care. It now has an opportunity to demonstrate that fairness and redesign elements of welfare.

Based on extensive international research, this is what we know about effective disability benefits:

- They are holistic and joined up from the perspective of the user.
- They are designed and run according to a social model of disability, personalised, flexible, and administered by service users themselves.
- They see long-term and social care services as an investment, not a spend.
- They are simple, universal, fair – and with transparent criteria and the right to challenge access decisions, and well-supported advocacy services.

The present complexity of benefits makes no sense, either from a principled or administrative perspective. Payments for disability are to help meet the cost of impairments and illness, and not to compensate for lost work earnings. So why separate out benefits for the over- and under-65s, and industrial injuries from other kinds of impairment? The costs to disabled people are the same regardless of age or reason for injury. Scotland has two main sources of funding for welfare and care. It already has devolved powers over health and social care and it does not have to follow established patterns of spending in either of these areas. With the Scotland Act it has also received new powers over welfare benefits: attendance allowance; disability living allowance/personal independence payments; industrial injuries disablement benefit; severe disablement allowance; and the regulated social fund. This offers substantial opportunities for service redesign. An estimate of these sources of funding based on current expenditure is in Figure 8.6.

There are arguably several radical options that the Scottish government could adopt using a combination of existing and new powers that would make social policy fairer in Scotland than it is in the rest of the UK. It could opt to end the ring-fencing of NHS funding and create joined up health and social care budgets for disabled people, older people, mental health service users and learning disabled adults, and move funding from acute NHS services into community health, and from health into preventative social care services. At the same time it could remove funding for social care from local authorities and instead create a simple nationalised universal social care budget. All of these options are currently under its control.

With its new powers over disability benefits, the Scottish government could combine disability living allowance/personal independence payments, attendance allowance, severe disability allowance and industrial injuries benefits and use the funding, along with the combined SDS/adults social care budget to create one, simple, three-tiered, user controlled benefit (the criteria for the tiers following the social model of disability adapted version of the World Health Organisation's 'Instrumental activities of daily

Social policy in a devolved Scotland 155

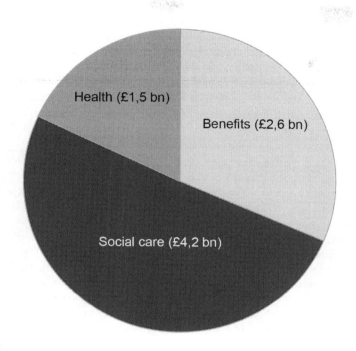

Figure 8.6 Funding sources (£ billion)
Source: Author's own calculations based on current Scottish government data (contains public sector information licensed under the Open Government license v3.0).

living' scale – mild, moderate and severe – which would apply across Scotland). Users could then choose to take this as a weekly direct payment – to spend on services, support, personal care, informal care, aids, etc. – and be assisted by user-run advocacy services both to apply for and manage the payment, or choose to have the payment managed for them by social services departments. This could be combined with an increase in benefits for informal carers so that users can put together the right package of support for them from the state, the community, the market and the family to reflect their own needs using local resources.

Initial set-up costs would be relatively high, but this would translate into significant savings from more cost effective administration of a simpler service, higher levels of independence from more personalised user controlled services, more disabled people and informal carers able to work and pay taxes, and a reduction in the need for directly provided high-level care services.

However, there are substantial barriers to be overcome if such a system of universal, fairer support were to be developed for disabled people in Scotland. First, benefits, not powers, are being devolved under the Scotland Act, with the expectation that no disadvantage would be felt by the rest of the UK. It could be argued that creating a fairer system of benefits and support in Scotland would be unfair on disabled people living in the rest of the UK, although arguably if such a system were successful in Scotland it could be rolled out to the rest of the UK, removing this argument. Second, creating and running the above system would involve significant support from disabled and older people, carers, local authorities, the social work and allied professions, the third sector, and employers. The savings needed to make the system work come from simplifying it and removing some of the statutory workforce needed to run a complex system, so there would be tensions between unions and disability rights organisations. Third, to truly work in a transformative way, Scotland would also have to have full control over taxation systems and employment legislation (e.g. to provide flexible working and leave for carers and disabled people, and to end the benefits trap that makes it unfeasible for disabled people and carers to undertake part-time flexible work). It would make sense if this approach were combined with a 'Citizens Universal Basic Income' (replacing jobseeker's allowance, income support, employment and support allowance, and all workfare benefits).

However, put simply, there is no point having these powers if Scotland is not prepared to risk doing things differently. Social policies that follow this framework are fairer, simpler, more cost effective, and achieve better health and social care outcomes. They also have the potential to reduce the need for expensive acute health services for disabled and older people by preventing degeneration of physical and mental health. This means they can contribute to a reduction in health inequalities, although of course these benefits would take far longer than the lifecycle of one parliament to manifest themselves, and so may prove politically unpopular: no policy maker wants to invest in social policies that cost his or her administration, but which benefit that of one several policy cycles in the future. However, given the significant social policy challenges faced by Scotland it is worth noting that such a framework would have other, more wide reaching social benefits. It has the potential to effectively harness the capacity of the state, families, the market, communities and individuals in providing social care and support. It would also create jobs, and tackle inequalities along the lines of gender, disability, age and ethnicity. The universal nature of such policies means that they would not be punitive or stigmatising – indeed, as the population ages, they would promote social solidarity. Significantly, such policies allow people to combine paid work and care, leading to better social relationships, stronger families and reducing the risk of poverty and social exclusion for disabled people, older people and carers. In other words, you could possibly have Scandinavian levels of social welfare and solidarity since much could be achieved within the existing resource base.

That truly would be a fairer society than Scotland has at present.

Conclusions

In some areas of social policy Scotland can lay claim to being distinctive, embracing policy divergence, and embedding both values and policies of fairness in its approach. Scottish housing policy is rightly claimed to be an international example of a commitment to social rights and to meeting the housing needs of the most vulnerable in society. However, a lack of investment in new social housing stock and the promotion of owner occupation for higher income groups undermines the social cohesion and universality of this provision, and creates wider inequalities between lower and higher income groups in terms of access to material capital and assets. Similarly, by adopting a social justice and inclusion approach to social policy, Scotland has made significant progress in tackling poverty, in particular child poverty, even though it has to date not had control over the key policy levers of taxation and welfare policy that would have enabled it to be even more radical and fair.

However, the two universal 'jewels in the crown' of the welfare state, education and the NHS, demonstrate that other, more powerful policy paradigms have impeded progress towards fairer outcomes for Scottish citizens. In the case of education, the favouring of higher education and the apparently 'fair' policy of not imposing university fees has in fact widened inequalities between the poorest and the elite. Whilst these policies protect Scotland's status in terms of world-class research benefitting the economy, it undermines efforts to facilitate social mobility and the potential for education to be a transformative, equalising force. In order to facilitate fairness and tackle inequalities, resources really should be shifted towards provision of early years education and further, rather than higher, education. However Scotland had the ability to do this even before the 1999 devolution settlement, and certainly between 1999 and the present day, and it has consistently pushed in the opposite direction. A similar narrative emerges when Scottish health policy since devolution is scrutinised. Scotland has chosen to protect and invest in the infrastructure of the NHS and to develop ostensibly 'fair' and 'universal' policies such as no user charges for services. These policies disproportionately benefit higher income and elderly people, and serve to widen, rather than narrow health inequalities. A 'fairer' approach would be not to widen access to preventative health services, but to invest in better access to material, social and cultural resources for the poorest and most vulnerable Scots. Again, Scotland has had the opportunity to do this since the 1999 devolution settlement and has consistently chosen other policy priorities.

In summary, there has been some policy divergence from the rest of the UK, but Scotland has not shown itself willing to make radical and systematic changes to social policy. The new powers it will receive over welfare, particularly disability benefits, do offer the opportunity for a transformative change in social policy that would make Scotland a much fairer society. However, the evidence to date does not indicate that Scotland is willing to make risky and substantial changes to social policy, and where it has embraced policies which seem to be more universal and fair than the rest of the UK, these in fact lead to greater social inequality, although they do promote social solidarity and cohesion.

So Scotland has the potential to be different and fairer in social policy, but the evidence is that it has not yet made significant and radical changes, and there is little indication that further devolution will make a substantial difference to that.

Note

1 Social security, immigration, defence, foreign policy, employment, broadcasting, trade and industry, energy, consumer rights, data protection and constitutional matters.

References

Abel, T. (2008) 'Cultural capital and social inequality in health'. *Journal of Epidemiology and Community Health* 62(7): 1–5.

Alcock, Pete, Christina Beatty, Steven Fothergill, Rob Macmillan and Sue Yeandle (2003) *Work to welfare: How Men Become Detached From the Labour Market*. Cambridge: Cambridge University Press.

Anderson, I. (2009) 'Sustainable solutions to homelessness: the Scottish case'. *European Journal of Homelessness* 1: 163–183.

Audit Scotland (2009) *Overview of the NHS in Scotland's Performance 2008/09*. Available at: www.audit-scotland.gov.uk/docs/health/2009/nr_091210_nhs_overview.pdf.
Birrell, D. (2009) *The Impact of Devolution on Social Policy*. Bristol: Policy Press.
Cairney, Paul (2008) 'Has devolution changed the "British policy style"?'. *British Politics* 3(3): 350–372.
Cairney, Paul (2014) 'The territorialization of interest representation in Scotland: did devolution produce a new form of group-government relations?'. *Territory, Politics and Governance* 2(4); published online 22 September. DOI: 10.1080/21622671.2014.952326.
Cairney, Paul (2015) 'What can governments learn from each other about "prevention" policy?' p.a.cairney@stir.ac.uk, and fellow of the Centre on Constitutional Change. Available at: www.centreonconstitutionalchange.ac.uk/. Full version on the LGIU Scotland website: www.lgiuscotland.org.uk/briefing/what-can-governments-learn-from-eachother-about-prevention-policy/.
Carers UK (2014) *Caring and Family Finances Inquiry Report*. Available at: www.carersuk.org/for-professionals/policy/policy-library/caring-family-finances-inquiry (accessed October 2015).
Croxford, Linda, Cathy Howison, Christina Iannelli, David Raffe and Marina Shapira (2002) *Education and Youth Transitions Across Britain 1984–2002*. Edinburgh: CES, University of Edinburgh.
De Lima, P. (2008) *Poverty and Social Exclusion in Rural Areas*, p. 407. Available at: www.academia.edu/882775/Poverty_and_social_exclusion_in_rural_areas.
De Lima, P. and S. Wright (2009) 'Welcoming migrants? Migrant labour in rural Scotland'. *Social Policy and Society* 8(3): 391–404.
EOC (2006) *Facts About Women and Men in Scotland*. Manchester: Equal Opportunities Commission.
Family Resources Survey (2011/12) (2013) United Kingdom. June. Dept. of Work and Pensions. Available at: www.gov.uk/government/statistics/family-resources-survey-201112 (accessed 8 March 2016).
Ferguson, I. (2008) 'Increasing user choice or privatising risk? The antimonies of personalisation'. *British Journal of Social Work* 37(3): 387–403.
Futureskills Scotland (2009) *Skills in Scotland 2008*. Edinburgh: Scottish Government.
Graham, H. (2009) *Unequal Lives: Health and Socio-economic Inequalities*. Maidenhead: Open University Press.
Grek, Sotiria, Martin Lawn, Bob Lingard, Jenny Ozga, Risto Rinne, Christina Segerholm and Hannu Simola (2009) 'National policy brokering and the construction of the European Education Space in England, Sweden, Finland and Scotland'. *Comparative Education* 45(1): 5–23.
Karlsen, S. and J.Y. Nazroo (2010) 'Religious and ethnic differences in health: evidence from the Health Surveys for England 1999 and 2004'. *Ethnicity and Health* 15(6): 549–568.
Keating, M. (2009) *The Independence of Scotland: Self-government and the Shifting Politics of Union*. Oxford: Oxford University Press.
Keating, M. (2010) *The Government of Scotland: Public Policy Making After Devolution*. Edinburgh: Edinburgh University Press.
King, P. (2010) *Housing Policy Transformed: The Right to Buy and the Desire to Own*. Bristol: Policy Press.
Kintrea, K. (2006) 'Having it all? Housing reform under devolution'. *Housing Studies* 211(2): 187–207.
Knox, W. (1999) *Industrial Nation: Work, Culture and Society in Scotland*. Edinburgh: Edinburgh University Press.
Malpass, P. (2010) 'Housing and the new welfare state'. *Housing Studies* 23(1): 1–19.
McKee, K. (2010) 'Promoting home ownership at the margins: the experience of low-cost homeownership purchasers in regeneration areas'. *People, Place and Policy Online* 2(4): 38–49.
Mitchell, James (2010) 'The narcissism of small differences: Scotland and Westminster'. *Parliamentary Affairs* 63(1): 98–116.
Mitchell, James (2014) *The Scottish Question*. Oxford and New York: Oxford University Press.

Parry, R. (1997) 'The Scottish Parliament and social policy'. *Scottish Affairs* 20 (May): 14–21.
Pawsin, H. and D. Mullins (2010) *After Council Housing: Britain's New Social Landlords*. Basingstoke: Palgrave Macmillan.
Poverty Alliance (2013) *Annual Report, 2013*. Available at: www.povertyalliance.org/userfiles/files/PA_AnnualReport%202013_14.pdf (accessed March 2016).
Poverty Truth Commission (2011) *Nothing About Us Without Us*. Available at: www.faithincommunityscotland.org/poverty-truth-commission/ (accessed October 2015).
Rummery, Kirstein and Craig McAngus (2016) *What Works in Achieving Gender Equality: International Best Practice in Childcare and Long-Term Care*. Bristol: Policy Press.
SCORE (2010) *Midyear Report 2010*. St Andrews: SCORE, Centre for Housing Research.
Scottish Executive (2005) *Building a Health Service Fit for the Future: A National Service Framework for Service Change in the NHS in Scotland*. Edinburgh: Scottish Executive.
Shaw, Mary, Bruna Calobardes, Debbie A.Lawlor, John Lynch, Ben Wheeler and George Davey Smith (2007) *The Handbook of Inequality and Socio-Economic Position*. Bristol: Policy Press.
Shelter (2014) *Homelessness in Scotland: Getting Behind the Statistics*. Available at: http://scotland.shelter.org.uk/__data/assets/pdf_file/0017/1050272/Homelessness_in_Scotland_2014_Getting_behind_the_statistics_FINAL_V2.pdf (accessed October 2015).
Shephard, Mark and Paul Cairney (2005) 'The impact of the Scottish Parliament in amending executive legislation'. *Political Studies* 53(2): 3030–3319.
SHR (Scottish Housing Regulator) (2010) *Registered Social Landlords in Scotland*. Glasgow: SHR.
Sinclair, S. and McKendrick, J.H. (2012) 'From social inclusion to solidarity: anti-poverty strategies under devolution'. In Mooney, G. and Scott, G. (eds) *Social Justice and Social Policy in Scotland*. Bristol: Policy Press.
Wilcox, S. (2007) *UK Housing Review*. Coventry: Chartered Institute of Housing.

9 Gender and equality in Scotland
Mind the gap

Gillian Fyfe and Karen Johnston

Introduction

Devolution in the UK created an asymmetric division of powers between Holyrood and Westminster, with some policies reserved and others devolved. Equal opportunities policy falls within this gap between reserved and devolved powers. It is a policy area that highlights the disparities of responsibilities, obligations, institutional mechanisms, and procedures between Scottish and UK levels of governance. There are variations in terms of the powers and obligations, and the institutions themselves have adopted various practices to deal with equality within their own polity. This has led to variation of the equality agenda and a policy 'gap' between the UK and Scotland (see Fyfe et al. 2009). The policy area also highlights, ironically given it concerns equal opportunities, less than inclusive policy making styles. At the UK and Scottish governance levels there is less variance on the manner in which the policy is formulated, with a tendency towards an expert-bureaucratic approach. It is perhaps explained by the under-representation of women in political institutions and decision making. This chapter therefore explores the politics of equal opportunities policy between Westminster and Holyrood with a focus on gender equality and the representation of women in the policy process.

Scotland: devolution and equality politics

When devolution settlements for Scotland and Wales were being discussed, Westminster fought hard to ensure equal opportunities legislation remained a reserved matter (*Hansard*, 31 March 1998; Beveridge et al. 2000). It seemed reasonable to maintain equal protection in terms of employment and anti-discrimination rights, particularly since much of this regulation is derived from the EU. However, the end result is variation throughout the UK as to powers in terms of equal opportunities, obligations placed upon institutions, and the machinery in place to address equality issues. In terms of the UK, Westminster retains the power to legislate on equal opportunities and a variety of machinery and processes are in place to address equality issues. After the Scottish independence referendum in September 2014 and the UK 2015 General Election there have been demands for further devolution to Scotland ('devo-max') (Scottish Government 2015a). For instance the devolution of quotas for public bodies proposed by the Smith Commission (Smith 2014), in the Scotland Bill 2015–16 (Scotland Office 2015), and the Scottish Government calling for devolution of equality policy to go much further than this.

Nevertheless, devolved institutions have limited impact and powers on equality policy. According to Beveridge et al. (2000: 403) 'tensions may well develop over equalities policies as a result of the mismatch between the processes of the Westminster government and those of the devolved governments'. As such, although Scotland may not have the power to legislate on equal opportunities, equality was an underpinning factor in devolution to Scotland, and the devolution process itself created opportunities for progress on equality.

Equal opportunities is and remains a key principle of the Scottish Parliament (Scottish Office 1998). Thus, although Westminster retains the power to legislate on equal opportunities, exceptions to the reservation are contained in Schedule 5, Part II, L2, of the Scotland Act (1998). This permits:

> The encouragement (other than by prohibition or regulation) of equal opportunities, and in particular of the observance of the equal opportunity requirements.
> Imposing duties on –
>
> a any office-holder in the Scottish Administration, or any Scottish public authority with mixed functions or no reserved functions, to make arrangements with a view to securing that the functions of the office-holder or authority are carried out with due regard to the need to meet the equal opportunity requirements, or
> b any cross-border public authority to make arrangements with a view of securing that its Scottish functions are carried out with due regard to the need to meet the equal opportunity requirements.
>
> 'Equal opportunities' means the prevention, elimination or regulation of discrimination between persons on grounds of sex or marital status, on racial grounds, or on grounds of disability, age, sexual orientation, language or social origin, or of other personal attributes, including beliefs or opinions, such as religious beliefs or political opinions.
>
> 'Equal opportunity requirements' means the requirements of the law for the time being relating to equal opportunities.
>
> 'Scottish functions' means functions which are exercisable in or as regards Scotland and which do not relate to reserved matters.

Thus, there are two aspects to this exception. The first, deemed the 'encouragement exception', allows the Scottish Parliament to 'exhort public authorities and others to adopt equal opportunities policies and to allocate financial and other resources to the encouragement of equal opportunity' (Scottish Executive 2005). The second is referred to as the 'duties exception' and theoretically is applicable to the Scottish Parliament as a Scottish public authority (Bennett et al. 2001). The 'duties exception' allows the Scottish Parliament to impose duties on office holders in the Scottish administration, Scottish public authorities, and cross-border public authorities to ensure their functions are undertaken with due regard to equal opportunities requirements. Taken together the exceptions allow the Scottish Parliament to: 'develop schemes to secure better provision of services to groups who may be the subject of discrimination or to legislate to require certain public authorities and office-holders to have due regard to the equal opportunity requirements' (Scottish Executive 2005). As one interviewee notes: 'the exceptions to the reservation broadly speaking are about things like promotion, education, those kinds of things, encouragement, but stop short of enforcement' (Alexander 2010).

Although useful, these exceptions are not as far-reaching as perhaps envisaged. First, despite the 'duties exception' potentially being applicable to the Scottish Parliament as a Scottish public authority, and unlike statutory duties in place in Wales and Northern Ireland, the Scottish Parliament is not charged with an explicit duty to promote equal opportunities in every aspect of its work. Second, the Scottish Parliament can encourage the observation of equal opportunity requirements, but ultimately the subject of these requirements rests with Westminster at the time of writing this chapter. So while the exceptions are beneficial, Scotland remains limited in the extent to which it can act on equal opportunities. Various interviewees commented on the equal opportunities portion of the Scotland Act 1998. Tim Hopkins (2009) of the Equality Network notes that during the passage of the Scotland Act the Equality Network campaigned for a duty to be placed on the Scottish Parliament and Government to promote equality, akin to that for the Welsh Assembly. However, the response given was that more powers are being devolved to Scotland and therefore the Scottish Parliament will have the ability to promote equal opportunities if it wishes. Ultimately this interviewee felt that as the Scotland Act 1998 was going through the legislative process the reservation of equal opportunities was adjusted, resulting in something of a muddle (Hopkins 2009). Likewise Morag Alexander (2010) notes: 'the exceptions to the reservation were the best we were going to get, so we had to look at how we could make that work'. Despite the exceptions to the reservation in the Scotland Act 1998, currently the situation in terms of the reservation of equal opportunities remains fluid pending the outcome of the Scotland Bill 2015–16 (Scotland Office 2015) process.

Regardless of the Scottish Parliament or Scottish Government's current ability to take action on equality in defined areas, the reservation of equal opportunities has various repercussions for Scotland. Arshad (2002) comments that it could have a negative impact, as campaigners in Scotland may realise Westminster controls progress on equal opportunities and may reduce their activities. Trevor Phillips, then chair of the EHRC, also recognised that the division of powers creates uncertainty over where responsibility lies, and thus issues may fall down the 'devolution gap'.

Although the Scottish Parliament and Government have some powers, albeit 'soft power' in terms of equality opportunities policy which may be bolstered by the Scotland Bill 2015–16, to what extent are minorities, particularly women, represented in the political and policy process, and to what extent do they have a voice in affecting policy outcomes?

Political representation

Hanna Pitkin's (1967) seminal work on political representation encompasses a notion of equality where different groups of citizens are 'present' in political decision making and institutions. Pitkin distinguishes four dimensions of political representation: formalistic; symbolic; descriptive; and substantive representation. Formal representation refers to the institutional rules and procedures for the representation of citizens (Pitkin 1967). In the context of the UK this would refer to legislative institutions such as

Westminster and the Scottish Parliament as well as the rules for the representation of citizens such as voting, legal frameworks, consultation, and committee proceedings. Devolution therefore provides a formulistic framework from which the institutions of the Scottish Parliament and Government can act within the confines of reserved and devolved rules.

Symbolic representation refers to the representation of a group, nation or state through an object to which meaning is attributed (Pitkin 1967; Lombardo and Meier, 2014). This dimension of representation is often studied by feminists as to how women are represented in the media, political and civil institutions with an evocative function and symbolic meanings which prejudice women (Lombardo and Meier 2014). The symbolic representation by the media of the first minister of Scotland, Nicola Sturgeon, during the 2015 General Election campaign exemplifies the negative portrayal of women in politics with derogatory meanings playing on gender stereotypes such as irrationality and sexualisation (see *Independent* 2015).

Descriptive representation refers to the actual physical presence, compositionality and proportionality of citizens represented in political institutions and decision making (Pitkin 1967). In this dimension, it involves the representative such as politician 'standing for' the represented through a resemblance to the represented (ibid.). Here feminist scholars are often concerned with the extent to which women are represented through the presence of the number of female politicians. The lack of female representation in political institutions, globally, often questions the extent to which these institutions could be considered truly democratic. Thus, although women constitute approximately 52 per cent of the world's population (see World Bank 2014), only 18.4 per cent of women are members of legislative institutions (Krook 2010: 162). The Inter-Parliamentary Union report in 2015 showed that only 22.1 per cent of women are represented in parliaments, internationally.

In the UK, after the 2015 General Election, 29 per cent of MPs are now women, representing a high mark in female descriptive representation in Westminster. This is partly accounted for through a number of female Labour Party politicians (43 per cent of Labour MPs) but also the number of female SNP members (36 per cent of SNP MPs) (see House of Commons 2015). In the Scottish Parliament after the 2003 election female representation increased to 39.9 per cent, but there has been a slow decline, with women now constituting 34.8 per cent of Members of the Scottish Parliament (Kenny and Mackay 2012: 75).

Yet, the descriptive representation of women in legislatures does not necessarily translate into the substantive representation of women. Many scholars have examined why the increased proportion of female parliamentarians may not necessarily increase the representation of women in legislative and policy decisions (Childs and Krook 2009). Substantive representation refers to a representative actor, a politician, 'acting for' the represented in a responsive manner (Pitkin 1967). Pitkin (1967) argued that substantive representation is the most important dimension of representation since it encompasses the act and content of representation (Lombardo and Meier 2014). Thus it is when a female politician for example seeks to advance interests and preferences of women (see McBride and Mazur 2010). Mansbridge (1999) argues that representation characteristics such as race, class and gender often act as a proxy for identifying shared experiences with the represented which results in substantive representation when a person is in fact most similar to his or her constituents and acts in their interests. Although there has been much scholarly debate on the descriptive and substantive representation of women (see Mazur and Pollack 2009 and Celis et al. 2007), there remains a lack of representation of women in the public policy process (Miller, 2009).

The European Commission (EC) has attempted to address this lack of gender equality in public policy through the introduction of gender mainstreaming. The EC (1996) defines gender mainstreaming as:

> ... not restricting efforts to promote equality to the implementation of specific measures to help women, but mobilising all general policies and measures specifically for the purpose of achieving equality by actively and openly taking into account at the planning stage their possible effects on the respective situation of men and women (gender perspective). This means systematically examining measures and policies and taking into account such possible effects when defining and implementing them.

In the UK, the Equality Act 2006 codified the concept of gender mainstreaming by adopting a Gender Equality Duty (GED), which represents a statutory commitment to uphold gender mainstreaming. Prior to this there had been positive equality duties for race in the Race Relations (Amendment) Act 2000, disability in the Disability Discrimination Act 2005, and the s75 duty in the Northern Ireland Act 1998, and subsequently the Equality Act 2010 created the public sector equality duty across the eight equality strands.

Mainstreaming means that (gender) equality is considered at every stage of the policy making process, therefore making it more than an 'add-on' at the end of the process (Rees 1998, 2005; Gregory 1999; Williams 2001; Fredman 2001; Donaghy 2004; Edwards 2004; Squires 2004; Witcher 2005; Charlesworth 2005; Stratigaki 2005; Holzleithner 2005; Daly 2005; Hanna 2006; Ben-Galim et al. 2007). Mainstreaming attempts to include equality considerations from the start of the policy process: thereby challenging structures and processes that may perpetuate inequality. Donaghy (2004: 393) defines mainstreaming as a 'strategy that aims to promote an equity perspective throughout the policy-making process, from conception to implementation to review, and all stages in between'. Thus mainstreaming requires that (gender) equality be integrated at all stages and levels of organisations, policies, systems, processes, etc. So concerns about inclusion and recognition that structures, processes, and policies can inadvertently exclude or disadvantage various groups are at the heart of mainstreaming.

The ideation of mainstreaming includes active representation with the interests of minorities articulated into policy. Yet, there are questions as to how interests are represented and included in the policy process. Beveridge et al. (2000) argue that the interests of women in the policy process are incorporated either through an integrationist or agenda setting–participatory approach to gender mainstreaming. According to Beveridge et al. (2000) integrationism primarily involves gender experts and specialists in an expert-bureaucratic model, while the agenda setting–participatory approach involves democratic processes of mobilised interest groups. According to Walby (2005) and Beveridge et al. (2000) the participatory and integrationist approaches represent different ways in which gender mainstreaming is implemented. Thus, those previously excluded from the policy process have an opportunity through gender mainstreaming to improve policy outcomes for women (Walby 2005). Beveridge et al. (2000) argue that to accomplish gender mainstreaming there should be participatory and democratic processes of engaging women's interests. However, according to Walby (2005) citing the Council of Europe (1998), the definition of gender mainstreaming incorporates the notion that it is implemented 'by actors normally involved in policy making' with presumably experts in the area of gender equality and mainstreaming – an integrationist approach. As the research within this chapter will demonstrate, the Scottish policy process tends to over-rely on experts or 'usual suspects' to inform gender equality policies, despite the Scottish Parliament being much more open and accessible than Westminster. This has implications for the way in which policy is formulated and how gender mainstreaming is implemented by the variety of institutions for equality that exist at both UK and Scottish levels.

Institutions of equality

Various equality institutions in Scotland and the UK play a role within the policy process. For instance: Cross Party Groups (CPGs), All Party Parliamentary Groups (APPGs), Committees such as the Equal Opportunities Committee in the Scottish Parliament, and NDPBs or specific organisations or networks funded by Government. However, such a number of institutions can create confusion, and ultimately some can be deemed more influential and effective than others.

Structurally it could be assumed that the Scotland Office would be a conduit from central to devolved Government in Scotland and vice versa, given the role of the Office is often one of co-ordination between UK and Scottish Government (Scotland Office 2012). Despite this some believe the Scotland Office is: 'a waste of time' (O'Donnell 2009) and that the ministers and Office are: 'completely irrelevant' (Kidd 2010). Jim Murphy (2009) also highlights that if both sides are reluctant to engage then the structures in place are of little help. This indicates a somewhat adversarial relationship between the UK Government and current SNP Government, which may contribute to the Scotland Office being undervalued.

Contrastingly the Scotland Office and ministers are viewed by others as playing the positive role of a conduit in ensuring Scottish input on reserved issues and that the Office is eager to play that role (Strachan 2010; Henderson 2009). However, some of these comments stem from those within UK Government departments, GB-wide NDPBs, or the Home Civil Service, which may contrast with opinions of those from solely Scottish organisations. This is bolstered by information received under Freedom of Information indicating that the Secretary of State for Scotland, or Parliamentary Under Secretary of State met with the EHRC (a GB-wide NDPB) at various points during 2007 and 2008 (Scotland Office, UK Government, FOI request, 2009). This shows regular engagement between the Scotland Directorate of the EHRC and the Scotland Office. However this could be because the EHRC is a GB-wide body and like the Scotland Office is answerable to Westminster. It may be that GB-wide NDPBs or organisations find it easier to engage with UK Government departments like the Scotland Office. It could be easy to reach this conclusion given Scotland-specific organisations do not feel the Scotland Office holds any weight in terms of influencing UK Government policy and find it more valuable to lobby the Scottish Government or Parliament.

The competing views of the Scotland Office perhaps point to a distinct policy community or network which engages with the Office, and another which does not. The question is which lobbying route actually provides outcomes in terms of effective and responsive policy? Could or should it be the Scotland Office, given it is a UK Government department and equal opportunities is reserved? Or should groups and individuals be lobbying the Scottish Government and Scottish Parliament? This is something which all those wishing to influence policy have to consider, along with the overall fragmentation of the landscape post devolution and referendum in Scotland.

Cross Party Groups (CPGs) should contain members from across parties who share interests in the subject matter, and can also include individuals from outwith Parliament and must be formed on the grounds of public interest (Scottish Parliament, Standards Committee 1999; Scottish Parliament 2011). While CPGs allow Parliamentarians to mix with those from other parties in a non-adversarial environment (Kidd 2010) the role of CPGs should not be confused with the role of Scottish Parliament Committees, and while CPGs may be acknowledged as a route into the political process; it must be recognised they are not a formal process of consultation. Despite this, CPGs can become dominated by lobbyists, with some being disbanded for this reason (O'Donnell 2009). Numerous CPGs exist and some believe they are often created to boost the self-esteem or ego of the MSP involved (O'Donnell 2009) and that some MSPs tend to: 'collect them like stamps' (Kidd 2010). While CPGs can be useful, and may be more accessible than APPGs, there is a need to maintain a watching brief on the number of groups in existence, and the reasons for their establishment, and to ensure that non-MSP members do not view CPGs as a direct route into Government or Parliament.

Similarly APPGs are informal cross party interest groups, which do not have any official status within Parliament. They are run by and for Members of the House of Commons and House of Lords, although many groups choose to involve individuals and organisations from outside Parliament (House of Commons 2012). Baroness Greengross (2009) admits APPGs can be influential, highlighting one example where she managed to have an issue debated in the House of Lords and another where the Government agreed to a concession.

However, were these successes a result of the work of the APPG or individuals like Baroness Greengross who using her position took the issue to the House of Lords? While undoubtedly these groups can be useful, it may be that they are more influential at Westminster where members of the House of Lords have the ability and time to bring issues to the attention of Parliament, whereas MSPs may not have the same ability, time, or capacity. Yet, the political landscape has further changed following the 2015 General Election, with a major increase in SNP MPs now in the House of Commons. It is therefore foreseeable that Scottish issues will increase on the policy agenda whether via formal structure or groups such as APPGs, but it remains to be seen whether equality issues will likewise rise in prominence.

There are differences between the functions, role, and remit of CPGs and APPGs; and there is a divergence from how those in Scotland view the role of CPGs as opposed to how others view APPGs. CPGs are clearly viewed not as lobbying bodies but information exchanges, therefore there is a difference between Scotland and Westminster as to what all party/cross party groups are for, and what they should and should not be able to do. As such, since Westminster does not have an equal opportunities committee, is the role of APPGs enhanced in this situation, and is this sufficient, or is there a need for an equal opportunities select committee at Westminster, and how does a dedicated committee as it exists in Scotland relate to mainstreaming?

Participation and mainstreaming of equality in the policy process

The concept of mainstreaming has an intriguing interplay and relationship with the Equal Opportunities Committee in the Scottish Parliament. As stated previously, mainstreaming is the idea that equality is considered at every stage of the policy process and attempts to include equality considerations in formulation and all the way through the policy process.

Mainstreaming poses an interesting counterpoint to the Equal Opportunities Committee in the Scottish Parliament, as it could be argued if equality was successfully mainstreamed and considered as a matter of course, then the Committee would become redundant. However, interviewees indicated how mainstreaming remains a relatively new concept and structures such as the Equal Opportunities Committee are still needed to monitor and review progress (O'Donnell 2009; Labour MSP 2010; Kidd 2010). MSPs' insistence on the retention of the Equal Opportunities Committee in the Scottish Parliament could reflect that equality is not yet mainstreamed within the Scottish Parliament or Scottish Government, as per Donaghy's (2004) description of the three elements necessary for successful mainstreaming being political will, resource allocation, and methods of enforcement.

Another interviewee notes that there may remain a perception of a stigma amongst MSPs, that the Equal Opportunities Committee may not provide the same chance to make a name for themselves compared to other committees (Anon D 2010). This statement further emphasises that there may be a policy hierarchy in operation, and equality is still not mainstreamed. If it were it would be a core part of all policy development, and elected members would not view equal opportunities as a narrow area which may do little for their political careers in comparison to being involved in other subject committees.

Various interviewees commented that the Equal Opportunities Committee has demonstrated its ability to promote and enhance the mainstreaming agenda throughout other committees in the Parliament by referring issues back to them for consideration, while maintaining something of an auditing role (Chisholm 2010). While the Equal Opportunities Committee may do this, the onus is then placed on other committees, which again highlights that equality is not mainstreamed. As such there could still be claims of a silo mentality which assumes that the Equal Opportunities Committee is the place where these issues should be discussed, rather than within the core work of other committees.

While visibility may be important, a designated committee or minister can inhibit mainstreaming of equality, as that focal point takes the pressure away from everyone considering equality in their work. A balance must be struck between the need for leadership, a focal point for accountability purposes, and equality being considered by all in Parliament and Government structures as a matter of course.

Baroness Joyce Gould highlights this pivotal issue to such an extent that she would oppose creation of an Equal Opportunities Select Committee at Westminster because: 'equalities goes right across Government ... And if you have a standing committee you could end up being isolated' (Gould 2010). Similarly Jim Murphy (2009) notes the 'potential ghetto-ization' of equality if there were to be an Equal Opportunities Select Committee in the UK Parliament.

These comments relate to Holzleithner (2005), in that covering up something with the label of mainstreaming can be an attempt to legitimise a process that does not further equality. It is clear that mainstreaming equality and the role and work of the Equal Opportunities Committee in the Scottish Parliament have a complex relationship and interplay, and perhaps dependent relationship with each other, and one which is likely to continue until equality is truly embedded into the thinking of the Scottish Government and Parliament.

In addition to Parliamentary and Government structures there are other parts of the machinery which involve consultation and participation in relation to equality, such as the Gender Directors Network, Scottish Women's Convention (SWC), and Engender, and some of these groups are funded to input women's views into Parliament and Government decision making processes.

For instance the SWC is funded by the Scottish Government's Equality Unit to engage with women across Scotland in order to influence and engage with policy making. It carries out a number of activities such as roadshows in order to engage with women across Scotland (Tolmie 2010). The information gathered is then issued to relevant policy and decision makers, and additionally the SWC responds to various UK and Scottish Government consultation papers (SWC 2012). Likewise Engender receives funding from the Scottish Government to carry out work on public participation, and their members form a collective response to Government policy and legislation, providing an informed opinion from grassroots level (Kandirikirira 2010).

The Gender Directors Network brings together the relevant lead officials on equality from the UK, Welsh, Scottish, and Northern Irish Governments. This group meets quarterly and often focuses on co-ordinating responses when there is a need to report on equality internationally. It also helps provide early consideration of issues of policy development and whether these are intended to be UK-wide or whether there will be variations across the UK (Anon B 2009). This appears a useful grouping which allows collective responses where necessary, while also acknowledging the differences in approaches to equality which have emerged in the devolved nations. While this is not so much a consultation process, it is an important mechanism for presenting information collectively and sharing information amongst key civil servants in the different parts of the UK in terms of progress and work on equality and in that sense is a useful form of consultation taking place at official level.

Thus there appears at a devolved level in Scotland an attempt to engage with and indeed contribute funding towards women's civil society organisations or representative groups. However, the extent to which women's interests in the political and policy decision making and institutional process are represented and the progress towards gender mainstreaming remain questionable. This is partly explained by the lack of legislative and enforcement powers, political will and fragmentation of the institutional framework. With regards to political will, the tide may be changing with Nicola Sturgeon as the first female first minister in Scotland. In her maiden speech as first minister, she committed herself to representing the interests of women. She stated that:

> I hope that my election as first minister does indeed help to open the gate to greater opportunity for all women … I hope that it sends a strong, positive message to girls and young women, indeed to all women, across our land – there should be no limit to your ambition for what you can achieve … If you are good enough and if you work hard enough, the sky is the limit and no glass ceiling should ever stop you from achieving your dreams …

Then, referring to her niece, Sturgeon said:

> She doesn't yet know about the gender pay gap, or underrepresentation, or the barriers like high childcare costs that make it so hard for so many women to work and pursue careers. My fervent hope is that she never will, that by the time she is a

young woman she will have no need to know about any of these issues because they will have been consigned to history ... If, during my tenure as first minister, I can play a part in making that so for my niece and for every other little girl in this country, I will be very, very happy indeed.

(BBC 2014)

This statement may be symbolic or may be a genuine commitment to the active representation of women. Nevertheless, there remains a policy problem of effectively implementing gender equality policy, given the gap between reserved and devolved powers.

Mind the gap

Much was made of new ways of working and inclusive and accessible policy making in a post-devolution Scotland. However, in reality the commitment to equality remains questionable for a variety of reasons. These range from: the devolution gap; a London mindset; the fragmentation of equal opportunities; political will; and a potential reliance upon experts and usual suspects. These factors highlight the complexities of an effective policy process for equal opportunities in a devolved Scotland.

Taking the devolution gap first, whereby issues may be lost between Westminster and Holyrood with neither Parliament taking responsibility. Various interviewees concede there is a devolution gap, as the practical implications and consequences for equality and human rights were not considered when the Scotland Act 1998 was drafted (O'Donnell, 2009). Others raise concerns about the division of powers and tensions between Holyrood and Westminster, MSPs frustration about the lack of legislative competency, and the lack of enforcement within the Scotland Act 1998 for equal opportunities, which could all bolster calls for enhanced powers on equal opportunities (Hopkins 2009; Kidd 2010; SNP MSP 2010). Likewise, research carried out by the EHRC Scotland (2009), highlights that while the Scottish Parliament has had a positive influence on tackling inequality, its impact has been limited, due to the complexity of the devolution settlement and the mix of devolved and reserved powers, making equal opportunities one of the most challenging 'grey areas' following devolution.

Does this friction between devolved and reserved powers prevent or inhibit effective policy? If so should there have been calls for further powers for the Scottish Parliament on equal opportunities before now? The lack of calls for further powers to date perhaps indicates the lack of prominence given to this by the current Scottish Government; albeit Scotland's first female first minister has appointed a gender balanced Cabinet, and quotas for public bodies will be devolved to the Scottish Parliament following the Smith Commission (Smith 2014) and the Scotland Bill 2015–16 (Scotland Office 2015).

It can be seen that opinions differ on the existence of a devolution gap. However, what remains is that policy areas such as equal opportunities do rely on a combination of devolved and reserved powers in order to drive progress, and without this the process can become fragmented.

It is contended that a London mindset or policy making which is Whitehall-centric fails to take devolved interests on board at the outset (Hopkins 2009) and can be overly focused on London or Whitehall. To varying degrees politicians, civil servants, and those from equality organisations acknowledge the tendency for policy to be dominated by a Whitehall model of thinking (Murphy 2009; Begg 2009) thereby perhaps indicating a lack of knowledge of devolution (Anon E 2009; Chisholm 2010).

Furthermore various equality organisations in Scotland believe that there is a UK-centric approach, and lack of awareness of the differences in Scotland, and that Scotland is often viewed as an add-on at the end of the policy process (Kandirikirira 2010; Ritch 2009; Hopkins 2009). For instance, documentary evidence reveals the Scottish Affairs Select Committee's lack of understanding of the role of the EHRC in Scotland by questioning the EHRC's neutrality and remit in terms of work and research on potential further devolution or independence (Scottish Affairs Select Committee 2009). Likewise interviewees commented on the adversarial nature of the Committee and its lack of understanding of devolution (Anon G 2009; Anon D 2010). These comments relate to concerns about Westminster being more expert-bureaucratic, influenced by a London mindset, and potentially misunderstanding devolution and how policy and machinery operates in Scotland; thus highlighting the application of a UK-centric approach by the then Scottish Affairs Select Committee. However, with the increased influx of SNP MPs in the 2015 General Election, and the SNP now chairing this Committee, its approach is now likely to change. There are already suggestions as to how the committee may operate and be more accessible in future (Maddox 2015). Nevertheless, devolution is an ongoing process and although those operating in Scotland need to be aware and prepare in the event of enhanced powers or even independence, this does not mean that they are partisan. As the previous Scottish Affairs Select Committee seemed to suggest of the EHRC in Scotland; they are just ensuring that they can be responsive to potential future conditions under which they may be operating.

Could this Whitehall-centric approach to policy making and lack of awareness of devolution account for increased support for the SNP in Scotland in recent years, as the electorate feel Westminster is failing to take into account the needs of Scotland, and the differential impact that policy may have in Scotland? Regardless of whether there is agreement that a devolution gap exists, it is clear that equal opportunities policy requires effective use of devolved and reserved powers and that insufficient understanding of devolution will do little to improve policy in this area.

A variety of phrases are often used to describe the equality landscape in the UK and Scotland, which outline the complexity of equality machinery and policy, especially within a devolved context. Descriptions include: 'a fairly cluttered field' (O'Donnell 2009); 'a crowded and confusing field' (Mitchell 2010); and 'a bit of a hotchpotch' (MP 2009). It is of concern that those involved in the machinery admit the potential for confusion, which raises the question of how the public are expected to engage with and navigate the maze of machinery and successfully influence the outcome of policy and legislation. While there may be claims that the equality landscape is a cluttered field, some point to the establishment of the EHRC as a positive move. Jim Murphy (2009) believes creation of the EHRC was necessary to: 'avoid this plethora of different bodies'. Similarly Morag Alexander (2010) notes that: 'bringing everything together in the Equality and Human Rights Commission has I think given a certain coherence to it'.

Administratively, a single equality commission provides much clarity and acts as a single point of contact. However, those involved in the EHRC in Scotland have a difficult task of ensuring the differences in Scotland in devolved areas such as health or education are understood across the Commission, and any work or projects are adaptable and applicable in Scotland. Therefore although the EHRC may have brought issues together, it can create testing circumstances to work in (Micklem 2009). However, others claim that creation of the EHRC is leading back to centralisation and a lack of autonomy for devolved offices (Anon C 2010).

Gender and equality in Scotland 171

Undoubtedly there is a plethora of equality organisations and bodies across the UK and Scotland, with the potential for much confusion. Therefore perhaps greater co-ordination of activity is needed which also reflects the differences in devolved polities such as Scotland. There is no doubt that it is a difficult task to respect the right and ability of different parts of the UK to forge their own path on equal opportunities, while trying to co-ordinate or make the landscape clearer for the public. Also add to this the discussion around the Smith Commission (2014) and the Scotland Bill 2015–16 on devolution of further powers such as quotas; and the recent independence referendum, and it is clear is that this fragmentation is unlikely to end soon.

Visibility and leadership from individual politicians, Government, and political parties can play a significant role in terms of demonstrating political will and commitment to equality. For instance, strong statements such as those following events like the Glasgow Airport bombing and also the accessibility of Scottish ministers responsible for equality provide visibility on equality from Scottish Government (Anon G 2009). While there are some positive instances of visibility on equality issues by Scottish ministers, there remains disappointment that equality is still not given sufficient prominence. For instance over the course of the first three sessions of the Scottish Parliament, until August 2009, there had only been one ministerial statement under the title of equality and diversity (Scottish Parliament 2009e, 2009f, 2009g). However, there is also a need to consider the purpose of political or ministerial statements, and acknowledge that often statements are in response to events, rather than being proactive (SNP MSP 2010). Additionally, interviewees concede that often ministers make statements on equality outwith Parliament to friendly audiences, as opposed to regularly in Parliament (Kidd 2010; Hopkins 2009; O'Donnell 2009).

Between June and December 2008 Nicola Sturgeon, as cabinet secretary for health and wellbeing, had responsibility for equality and attended a variety of events, including the launch of an ethnic minority project; and the women's aid conference (Scottish Government 2008). Likewise the junior minister at the time, Stewart Maxwell, also attended a variety of equality related events including the EHRC conference, and the STUC women's committee. Furthermore, information received under the Freedom of Information Act (2000) shows a vast amount of engagement between civil servants from the Equality Unit and the relevant ministers Nicola Sturgeon and Stewart Maxwell at the time during 2007/08 (Equality Unit, Scottish Government 2008). These range from written advice to ministers, alerting them of invitations received, advice on legislation, approval of documents, etc. This shows much internal Scottish Government work and engagement on equality (Equality Unit, Scottish Government 2008), but the missing piece of the puzzle seems to be visibility in Parliament. Consequently if political visibility on equality is only outwith Parliament and towards friendly and knowledgeable audiences such as equality conferences, is this just preaching to the converted and behind the scenes, rather than mainstreaming equality into policy?

However, some consider time spent on the chamber floor of the Parliament less significant than influencing policy development and lobbying individual MSPs (SNP MSP 2010). Nevertheless, from an outside perspective, it could easily be argued if equality is not being discussed during sittings of the Parliament the commitment to it is less visible, as there is not an outward projection that equality is significant enough to be discussed by Parliament. It would be reasonable for this to be a commonly held view amongst those outwith the inner circle of policy making, and therefore a possible failure to meet one of the aspects – the political will thought to be necessary for successful implementation of a mainstreaming strategy (Donaghy 2004). Therefore there remains some debate about proactive leadership on equality within Scottish politics and where this visibility, leadership, and consultation should take place.

The capacity of ministers to engage with the equality agenda is another area of concern, given the stretched capacity of the Scottish Government minister responsible for equality (Labour MSP 2010). Taking Nicola Sturgeon's ministerial engagements in 2008, in her capacity as cabinet secretary for health and wellbeing with equality within her remit, these range between 300 and 400 as an estimate, and around 200 to 300 engagements for then junior minister Stewart Maxwell (Scottish Government 2008). In the current Scottish Parliamentary session gender was raised 245 times as questions, motions and answers, representing a small proportion of Parliamentary time for the issue (see www.scottish.parliament.uk/parliamentarybusiness/motions-questions-and-answers.aspx). All Scottish Government ministers have large and diverse remits, which perhaps explains the need for delegation to other ministers as a result. However, this can lead to lack of a focal point for equality within the Scottish Government.

While there may be debate around the visibility and leadership from Scottish ministers on equality, the importance of individual MSPs pushing the equality agenda forward becomes apparent (Kandirikirira 2010; Anon C 2010; Alexander 2010; Labour MSP 2010). This relates to the issue of critical actors (Childs and Krook 2006b; Curtin 2008) and surrogate representation (Tremblay 2006) and is further supported by considering individual MSPs' business in the Scottish Parliament. Across Sessions One to Three, members' business included: International Women's Day; Women's Pay; Gender Pay Gap, Disabled Access; and Wheelchair Users (Scottish Parliament 2008; Scottish Parliament 2009a; 2009b). This shows a number of MSPs were pursuing interests in equality through their individual business in the Scottish Parliament. As such critical actors and surrogate representatives (Childs and Krook 2006; Tremblay 2006; Curtin 2008) can play a role in championing and pushing forward equality issues in Scottish politics.

Likewise, the approach of political parties themselves can also be important and one theme to emerge from those interviewed was that equality is not at the core of the SNP's political beliefs; the focus is undoubtedly on independence (Alexander 2010). As one MSP comments, the SNP's 'raison d'être is independence: so everything else comes second' (Anon A 2010). While independence may be the SNP's ultimate goal, this makes it difficult to have a consistent approach to equality.

Others consider that the SNP inherited a relatively positive situation in terms of equality, and there has been much continuity of policy and so no major differences between how the previous administrations and the current administration would approach equality issues (Chisholm 2010; Anon C 2010). However, Niki Kandirikirira (2010) believes the political will and commitment to equality in Scotland has shifted since the SNP came to power. Likewise another interviewee admits there has: 'been a lessening of commitment; and it really strikes me that the SNP Parliamentarians themselves have been less entrenched in campaigning for equality issues' (Anon I 2009). However, during the independence referendum and the 2015 General Election campaigns the SNP made social justice a core value of their campaign, and recently launched a public 'conversation' on social justice (Scottish Government 2015b). It remains to be seen whether they can and will deliver upon manifesto promises. As such there are mixed opinions as to the approach adopted by the SNP towards equality.

Undoubtedly nationalism is at the core of SNP policy thinking. Also, as the SNP inherited a positive culture on equality, this can make it difficult to measure their impact. Another area of concern is what model of policy making is prevalent in Scotland, and whether it is the expert-bureaucratic model which involves selection from a narrow and defined range of individual or experts to participate, or the participatory-democratic model which focuses on policy makers, inclusive policy making, social partnership, and the involvement of individuals, groups, and stakeholders (Nott 2000; Edwards 2004; Donaghy 2004; Daly 2005).

Various interviewees conceded that policy making is a combination of both approaches (Boyd 2009; Henderson 2009; Gould 2010; Murphy 2009; Anon E 2009; Strachan 2010; Alexander 2010; Chisholm 2010; Smith 2010). However, others believe it is overly expert and bureaucratic led and therefore cannot result in inclusive policy making (Prosser 2009; Anon F 2009; O'Donnell 2009; Ritch 2009; Kandirikirira 2010; Kidd 2010; SNP MSP 2010). Additionally there are concerns over lack of involvement of service users/end users and too much emphasis on experts or equality professionals (Kidd 2010; Kandirikirira 2010; Anon F 2009; Micklem 2009). The SNP-led Scottish Government's policy making style tends to lean towards a reliance on a small group of experts. For example, it established a Fiscal Commission Working Group to advise on macroeconomic policy. The membership consisted of prominent academics such as Professor Joseph Stiglitz and industrialists such as Crawford Beveridge with sympathetic views of Scottish independence.

There were no strong opinions from those interviewed that the policy making process in Scotland is solely participatory-democratic. One can therefore assume that the expert-bureaucratic approach is more prevalent in policy making. However, it is a concern, particularly for equal opportunities policy and the supposed mainstreaming of equality, that there is an over-reliance on experts or professionals, and those whom the policy will impact upon remain the furthest from the decision making, consultation and policy making process.

Likewise, another concern regards those participating in the policy making process, and whether there is reliance on the so-called usual suspects. One interviewee (Anon C 2010) comments that, while consultations attempt to be inclusive, 'my worry would be that the consultations are done with the same old suspects'. This is worrying if potentially more controversial views are being filtered out via an overreliance on such usual suspects. Could consultation of this sort be symbolic or window dressing, as referred to in Arnstein's ladder of citizen participation? (Arnstein 1969) Where consultation is merely superficial, but by consulting this gives an outward facing commitment that engagement has taken place, even though this may be unlikely to influence the end result, and only the comments of friendly rather than dissenting voices are heard?

However, on the positive side it was felt that policy making and consultation in Scotland is more inclusive than at Westminster, and gives the public a better level of interaction with elected politicians and ministers (Anon E 2009; SNP MSP 2010). Malcolm Chisholm (2010) believes Westminster is more expert-bureaucratic and more influenced by special advisors, and considers the strength of the approach in Scotland to be engaging external stakeholders in policy development.

It would appear that a substantial cross section of those interviewed believe Scotland has a more inclusive and participatory approach to policy making than Westminster due to issues of scale, visibility and accessibility (Henderson 2009; Smith 2010; Cairney and McGarvey 2013). This is encouraging; however, this approach also has to be coupled with Government and Parliamentary machinery that is well equipped to deal with equality matters and the parts of which interact well with one another; and the existence of necessary political will and commitment to the agenda. That is not to negate the fact that progress has been made, and that the structures in Scotland appear to be more accessible than at Westminster, but this has to be sustained across all of Government and Parliamentary work and prevent an overreliance on usual suspects or experts.

Conclusion

This chapter highlights the impact of devolution in Scotland in terms of the equality agenda. It focusses on issues of political representation; institutions of equality; participation and mainstreaming of equality in the policy process; and raises questions about the lack of political will and commitment to equality in Scotland.

Many believe that Scotland has a more inclusive and participatory approach to policy making than Westminster, and that devolution offered new innovative approaches and ways of working which could enhance the equality agenda. However, it appears that the commitment to equality is not as strong as it could be, with questions over the political will and commitment to equality, along with a somewhat cluttered sphere of governance in terms of the split between devolved and reserved powers. The result is significant gaps in the formulation and implementation of gender equality policy. This begs the questions: How could this be improved, and is further devolution of equality policy to Scotland the solution?

The Smith Commission (2014) for Further Devolution of Powers to the Scottish Parliament established after the referendum on Scottish independence touched on equalities in its final report. It stated that:

> The Equality Act 2010 will remain reserved. The powers of the Scottish Parliament will include, but not be limited to, the introduction of gender quotas in respect of public bodies in Scotland. The Scottish Parliament can legislate in relation to socio-economic rights in devolved areas.
>
> (Smith 2014)

It is interesting and pertinent that the Smith Commission highlighted equality, when previous commissions such as the Calman Commission (Commission on Scottish Devolution 2009) chose to avoid discussion of the subject. The UK Government subsequently published the Heads of Agreement in January 2015 for further devolution in Scotland via the forthcoming Scotland Bill (Cabinet Office 2015). This included a clause to:

> devolve to the Scottish Parliament the power to legislate on equalities in respect of public bodies in Scotland, which will include but not be limited to the introduction of gender quotas and the consideration of socio-economic inequality when making strategic decisions.
>
> (Cabinet Office 2015)

At the time of writing the Scotland Bill 2015–16 continues to make its passage through Westminster, and it will be interesting to see the outcome of the legislative process and what this means for equality in Scotland going forward. It will be particularly interesting given that the Scottish Government when publishing its draft clauses for the Bill in June 2015 proposed that the Scottish Parliament have full devolved responsibility for equal opportunities and equality legislation (Scotland Office 2015). This is a strong statement from the Scottish Government, which follows on from First Minister Sturgeon's decision to appoint a gender balanced Cabinet, the surge in support for the SNP and the independence campaign from women, and the Scottish Government's pledge to increase diversity in boardrooms via their commitment to 50:50 by 2020 (Office of the First Minister of Scotland 2015). Nevertheless, some may argue that the Scottish Government is failing to use its current powers to effectively advance the equality agenda. For instance, there could be greater use and enthusiasm for the exceptions to the reservation of equal opportunities (Alexander 2010). In addition, the sudden call for devolution of equal opportunities and equality legislation could be deemed opportunistic or perhaps symbolic, when data highlighted above show a somewhat questionable political will and commitment to the equality agenda in recent years.

Nevertheless, this remains an interesting time for equality in Scotland, with all eyes on the outcome of the Scotland Bill 2015–16, and then ultimately what Scottish ministers choose to do with any further powers on equality that are devolved as a result of this process; and many will hope that further devolution seeks to ensure that Scotland becomes a more equal society.

Sources for Further Reading and Study

Books and journal articles

Chappell, L. (2002) 'The 'Femocrat' Strategy. Expanding the Repertoire of Feminist Activities'. *Parliamentary Affairs* 55: 85–98.
Hafner-Burton, E.M. and Pollack, H.A. (2009) 'Mainstreaming Gender in the European Union: Getting the Incentives Right'. *Comparative European Politics* 7(1): 114–138.
Kantola, J. (2010) *Gender and the European Union*. Basingstoke: Palgrave Macmillan.
Lovenduski, J. (2005) *Feminising Politcs*. Cambridge: Polity Press.

Reports and websites

Council of Europe (1998) *Gender Mainstreaming. Conceptual Frameworks, Methodolgy and Presentation of Good Practice*. Strasbourg: Council of Europe, EG-S-MS (98) 2.
European Commission (2008) *The Life of Women and Men in Europe: A Statistical Portrait*. Luxembourg: EUROSTAT.
European Women's Lobby. Available at: www.womenlobby.org/site/abstract/asp?doc.id=2040andv.11d (accessed 12 December 2010).

References

Alexander, Morag (2010) Commissioner, Equality and Human Rights Commission Scotland. Interviewed by Fyfe.
Anon A. (2010) Interviewed by Fyfe.
Anon B. (2009) Interviewed by Fyfe.
Anon C. (2010) Interviewed by Fyfe.
Anon D. (2010) Interviewed by Fyfe.

Anon E. (2009) Interviewed by Fyfe.
Anon F. (2009) Interviewed by Fyfe.
Anon G. (2009) Interviewed by Fyfe.
Anon I. (2010) Interviewed by Fyfe.
Arnstein, S.R. (1969) 'A Ladder of Citizen Participation'. *Journal of the American Planning Association* 35(4): 216–224.
Arshad, R. (2002) 'Daring to Be Different: A New Vision of Equality', Chapter 12 in Hassan, G. and Warhurst, C., *Tomorrow's Scotland*. London: Lawrence & Wishart.
BBC (2014) 'New Scottish First Minister Nicola Sturgeon Makes Gender Equality Pledge'. Available at: www.bbc.co.uk/news/uk-scotland-scotland-politics-30105262 (accessed 7 June 2015).
Begg, A. (2009) MP, Chair of All Party Parliamentary Group on Equalities. Interviewed by Fyfe.
Ben-Galim, D., M. Campbell, and J. Lew (2007) 'Equality and Diversity: A New Approach to Gender Equality Policy in the UK'. *International Journal of Law in Context* 3(1): 19–33.
Bennett, C., D. Booth, S. Yeandle and CRESR, Sheffield Hallam University, in collaboration with Reeves, D., University of Strathclyde (2001) *Mainstreaming Equality in the Committees of the Scottish Parliament*. Available at: www.scottish.parliament.uk/business/committees/historic/equal/resports-03/eo03-mer.pdf (accessed 10 August 2007).
Beveridge, F., S. Nott and K. Stephen (2000) 'Mainstreaming and the Engendering of Policy-making: A Means to an End?' *Journal of European Public Policy* 7(3): 385–405.
Boyd, S. (2009) Assistant Secretary, Scottish Trades Union Congress. Interviewed by Fyfe.
Cabinet Office (2015) *Scotland in the United Kingdom: An Enduring Settlement*. Available at: www.gov.uk/government/uploads/system/uploads/attachment_data/file/397079/Scotland_EnduringSettlement_acc.pdf (accessed 27 July 2015).
Cairney, P. and N. McGarvey (2013) *Scottish Politics*. Basingstoke: Palgrave Macmillan.
Celis, K., S. Childs, J. Kantola and M. Krook (2007) 'Rethinking Women's Substantive Representation'. European Consortium for Political Research, Joint Sessions of Workshops, Helsinki, Finland, 7–12 May.
Charlesworth, H. (2005) 'Not Waving But Drowning: Gender Mainstreaming and Human Rights in the United Nations'. *Harvard Human Rights Journal* 18: 1–18.
Childs, S. and M. Krook (2009) 'Analysis of Women's Substantive Representation: From Critical Mass to Critical Actors'. *Government and Opposition* 44(2): 125–145.
Childs, S. and M.L. Krook (2006b) 'Should Feminists Give Up on a Critical Mass? A Contingent "Yes"'. *Politics and Gender* 2(4): 522–530.
Chisholm, M. (2010) Interviewed by Fyfe.
Commission on Scottish Devolution (2009) Available at: www.commissiononscottishdevolution.org.uk/uploads/2009-06-12-csd-final-report-2009fbookmarked.pdf (accessed 1 December 2012).
Council of Europe (1998) *Gender Mainstreaming: Conceptual Framework, Methodology and Presentation of Good Practices*. Strasbourg: Council of Europe, EG-S-MS (98) 2.
Curtin, J.C. (2008) 'Women, Political Leadership and Substantive Representation: The Case of New Zealand, 2009'. *Parliamentary Affairs* 61(3): 490–504.
Daly, M. (2005) 'Gender Mainstreaming in Theory and Practice'. *Social Politics* 12(3): 433–450.
Donaghy, T.B. (2004) 'Applications of Mainstreaming in Australia and Northern Ireland'. *International Political Science Review* 4: 393–410.
EC (European Commission) (1996) 'Incorporating Equal Opportunities for Women and Men into All Community Policies and Activities'. COM (1996) 67 final.
Edwards, J. (2004) 'Mainstreaming Equality in Wales: The Case of the National Assembly Building'. *Policy and Politics* 32(1): 33–48.
EHRC Scotland (2009) 'An Uncertain Mix: Equality and Scottish Devolution'. Available at: www.equalityhumanrights.com/scotland/research-in-scotland (accessed 14 October 2012).
Equality Unit, Scottish Government (2008) FOI request.
Fredman, S. (2001) 'Equality: A New Generation?', *Industrial Law Journal* 30(2): 145–168.

Fyfe, G., K. Johnston, K. Miller and D. McTavish (2009) 'Muddling Through in a Devolved Polity: Implementation of Equal Opportunities Policy in Scotland'. *Policy Studies* 20(2): 203–219.
Gould, J. (2010) Interviewed by Fyfe.
Greengross, S. (2009) Equality and Human Rights Commission, Commissioner. Interviewed by Fyfe.
Gregory, J. (1999) 'Revisiting the Sex Equality Laws'. In Walby, S., *New Agendas for Women*. London: Macmillan Press.
Hanna, C. (2006) 'Empowering Women Ten Years After the Beijing Conference'. *Georgetown Journal of International Affairs* 7(2): 173–182.
Henderson, A. (2009) Assistant Secretary, Scottish Trades Union Congress. Interviewed by Fyfe.
Holzleithner, E. (2005) 'Mainstreaming Equality: Dis/Entangling Grounds of Discrimination'. *Transnational Law and Contemporary Problems* 14(3): 927–958.
Hopkins, T. (2009) Interviewed by Fyfe.
House of Commons (2015) Available at: http://commonslibraryblog.com/2015/05/09/general-election-2015-women-mps-and-candidates/ (accessed 5 June 2015).
House of Commons, (2012, 'Guide to the Rules on All-Party Groups'. Available at: www.parliament.uk/documents/pcfs/all-party-groups/guide-to-the-rules-on-apgs.pdf (accessed 3 December 2012).
Inter-Parliamentary Union (2015) Available at: www.ipu.org/wmn-e/world.htm (accessed 5 June 2015).
Kandirikirira, N. (2010) Executive Director, Engender. Interviewed by Fyfe.
Kenny, M. and F. Mackay (2012) 'More of the Same? Women and Scottish Local Government Elections 2012'. Available at: http://genderpoliticsatedinburgh.wordpress.com/2012/04/18/more-of-the-same-women-and-the-scottish-local-government-elections-2012-5-2/ (accessed 8 January 2015).
Kidd, B. (2010) MSP. Interviewed by Fyfe.
Krook, M.L. (2010) 'Why are Fewer Women than Men Elected? Gender and the Dynamics of Candidate Selection'. *Political Studies Review* 8(2), pp. 115–168.
Labour MSP (2010) Interviewed by Fyfe.
Lombardo, E. and P. Meier (2014) *The Symbolic Representation of Gender: A Discursive Approach*. Farnham: Ashgate.
Maddox, D. (2015) 'Wishart Eyes to End Scottish Affairs Committee Ban'. *Scotsman*. Available at: www.scotsman.com/news/politics/top-stories/wishart-eyes-end-to-scottish-affairs-committee-ban-1-3801641 (accessed 27 July 2015).
Mansbridge, J. (1999) 'Should Blacks Represent Blacks and Women Represent Women? A Contingent "Yes"'. *Journal of Politics* 61(3): 628–657.
Mazur, A.G. and M.A. Pollack (eds) (2009) 'Gender and Public Policy in Europe'. Special Issue of *Comparative European Politics* 9(1).
McBride, D. and A.G. Mazur (2010) *The Politics of State Feminism*. Philadelphia, PA: Temple University Press.
Micklem, R. (2009) Equality and Human Rights Commission, Scotland. Interviewed by Fyfe.
Miller, K. (2009) 'Public Policy Dilemma: Gender Equality Mainstreaming in UK Policy Formulation'. *Public Money and Management* 29(1): 43–50.
Mitchell, M. (2010) MSP and Convenor of Equal Opportunities Committee of Scottish Parliament. Interviewed by Fyfe.
MP (2009) Interviewed by Fyfe.
Murphy, J. (2009) MP and Secretary of State for Scotland. Interviewed by Fyfe.
Nott, S. (2000) 'Accentuating the Positive: Alternative Strategies for Promoting Gender Equality'. In Beveridge, F., Nott, S. and Stephen, K., *Making Women Count: Integrating Gender into Law and Policy Making*. Dartmouth: Ashgate.
O'Donnell, H. (2009) MSP. Interviewed by Fyfe.
Office of the First Minister of Scotland (2015) '50:50 by 2020: Working for Diversity in the Boardroom'. Available at: https://firstminister.gov.scot/5050-by-2020-working-for-diversity-in-the-boardroom/ (accessed 30 July 2015).

Pitkin, H.F. (1967) *The Concept of Representation*. Berkeley and Los Angeles: University of California Press.

Prosser, M. (2009) Deputy Chair, Equality and Human Rights Commission. Interviewed by Fyfe.

Rees, T. (1998) *Mainstreaming Equality in the European Union Education, Training and Labour Market Policies*. London: Routledge.

Rees, T. (2005) 'Reflections on the Uneven Development of Gender Mainstreaming in Europe'. *International Feminist Journal of Politics* 7(4): 555–574.

Ritch, E. (2009) Project Manager, Close the Gap. Interviewed by Fyfe.

Scotland Act (1998) Available at: www.legislation.gov.uk/ukpga/1998/46/pdfs/ukpga_19980046_en.pdf.

Scotland Office (2015) *The Scotland Bill 2015–2016*. Available at: http://services.parliament.uk/bills/2015-16/scotland.html (accessed 19 July 2015).

Scotland Office (2012) 'Business Plan 2012–2013'. Available at: www.scotlandoffice.gov.uk/scotlandoffice/files/Businesspercent20planpercent202012-13.pdf (accessed 2 December 2012).

Scotland Office, UK Government (2009) FOI request.

Scottish Affairs Select Committee (2009) *Work of the Equality and Human Rights Commission, Scotland, Third Report of Session 2008–2009*. Available at: www.publications.parliament.uk/pa/cm200809/cmselect/cmscotaf/176/176.pdf (accessed 30 September 2012).

Scottish Executive (2005) 'Mainstreaming Equality and Equal Opportunities Information for Bill Teams'. Available at: www.scotland.gov.uk/Resource/Doc/70242/0023294.pdf (accessed 28 May 2007).

Scottish Government (2015a) *Further Devolution Beyond the Smith Commission*. Available at: www.gov.scot/Resource/0047/00479761.pdf (accessed 27 July 2015).

Scottish Government (2015b) *Creating a Fairer Scotland: What Matters to You?* Available at: www.gov.scot/Resource/0047/00479666.pdf (accessed 27 July 2015).

Scottish Government (2008) *Proactive Release of Engagements*. Available at: www.scotland.gov.uk/Resource/Doc/918/0089216.pdf (accessed 20 December 2012).

Scottish Office (1998a) *Shaping Scotland's Parliament, Report of the Consultative Steering Group on the Scottish Parliament*. Available at: www.scotland.gov.uk/library/documents-w5/rcsg-24.htm (accessed 22 July 2007).

Scottish Parliament (2009a) 'Factsheet, Members Business by Subject and Party, Session 2'. Available at: www.scottish.parliament.uk/business/research/factsheets/documents/MembersBusinessbySubjectandPartySession2.pdf (accessed 27 August 2009).

Scottish Parliament (2009b) 'Factsheet, Members Business by Subject and Party, Session 3'. Available at: www.scottish.parliament.uk/business/research/factsheets/documents/MembersBusinessbySubjectandPartyS3.pdf (accessed 27 August 2009).

Scottish Parliament (2009e) 'Scottish Parliament Factsheet, Ministerial Statements: Session 1'. Available at: www.scottish.parliament.uk/business/research/factsheets/documents/MinisterialStatemets-Session1.pdf (accessed 27 August 2009).

Scottish Parliament (2009f) 'Scottish Parliament Factsheet Ministerial Statements: Session 2'. Available at: www.scottish.parliament.uk/business/research/factsheets/documents/MinisterialStatementssession.2.pdf (accessed 27 August 2009.

Scottish Parliament (2009g) 'Scottish Parliament Factsheet, Ministerial Statements: Session 3'. Available at: www.scottish.parliament.uk/business/research/facsheets/documents/MinisterialStatementsSession3.pdf (accessed 27 August 2009).

Scottish Parliament (2011) *Code of Conduct for Members of the Scottish Parliament, 5th edition*. April.

Scottish Parliament, Standards Committee (1999) *2nd report 1999, Regulation of Cross Party Groups*. Available at: http://archive.scottish.parliament.uk/business/committees/historic/standards/reports-99/str02-c.htm (accessed 30 October 2012).

Smith, E. (2010) Interviewed by Fyfe.

Smith, R. (Baron Smith of Kelvin) (2014) *Report of the Smith Commission for Further Devolution of Powers to the Scottish Parliament*. Available at: www.smith-commission.scot/wp-content/uploads/2014/11/The_Smith_Commission_Report-1.pdf (accessed 19 July 2015).
SNP MSP. (2010) Interviewed by Fyfe.
Squires, J. (2004) 'Equality and Diversity: A New Framework for Britain?' Womens Studies Seminar. Available at: www.bath.ac.uk/esm/wsc/archive.htm (accessed 8 February 2007).
Strachan, Y. (2010) Deputy Director for Third Sector, Equality and Communities, Scottish Government. Interviewed by Fyfe.
Stratigaki, M. (2005) 'Gender Mainstreaming vs Positive Action: An Ongoing Conflict in EU Gender Equality Policy'. *European Journal of Women's Studies* 12(2): 165–186.
SWC (2012) www.scottishwomensconvention.org/ (accessed 5 November 2012).
The Independent (2015) 'Nicola Sturgeon Accuses *The Sun* of Sexism over Miley Cyrus Poster'. 16 March.
Tolmie, A. (2010) Chair, Scottish Women's Convention. Interviewed by Fyfe.
Tremblay, M. (2006) 'The Substantive Representation of Women and PR: Some Reflections on the Role of Surrogate Representation and Critical Mass'. *Politics and Gender* 2(4): 502–511.
Walby, S. (2005) 'Introduction: Comparative Gender Mainstreaming in a Global Era'. *International Feminist Journal of Politics* 7, December, pp. 453–470.
Williams, C. (2001) 'Can Mainstreaming Deliver? The Equal Opportunities Agenda and the National Assembly for Wales'. *Contemporary Wales* 14: 57–79.
Witcher, S. (2005) 'Mainstreaming Equality: The Implications for Disabled People'. *Social Policy and Society* 4(11): 55–64.
World Bank (2014) http://data.worldbank.org/indicator/SP.POP.TOTL.FE.ZS/countries (accessed 5 June 2015).
www.scottish.parliament.uk/S4_PublicPetitionsCommittee/Generalpercent20Documents/code_final.pdf-pdf (accessed 3 December 2012).

10 Scotland and the world

Michael Keating

The rise of paradiplomacy

There was a time when it was possible to distinguish clearly between domestic and external policy, the latter being to do with peace and war and the high politics of international relations. So, in federal and devolved states, large slices of domestic policy could be transferred to the lower level, but foreign affairs was kept for the centre. It is this principle that underlies the Scotland Act of 1998, in which foreign relations is one area clearly reserved to Westminster and Whitehall. The transformation of government over recent decades, however, means that international relations are no longer confined to traditional diplomacy or monopolized by ministries of foreign affairs, but have a strong economic component going beyond the setting of tariffs to encompass questions of national competitiveness, technology and knowledge exchange. Other new issues on the international agenda include environmental policy, education, drug- and people-trafficking and culture, as well as moral issues such as slavery or human rights. The old distinction between domestic and foreign policy thus breaks down.

At the same time, government has rescaled as functions have migrated to new levels, both above and below the state (Keating 2013). At one time, it was thought that sub-state devolution and transnational integration or 'globalization' were in contradiction, the one pointing to ever-larger units, the other to fragmentation. It is now broadly accepted that they are complementary processes, challenging the old monopolies of the nation-state from above and below and opening up new spaces for politics and policy. As markets have internationalized, regions and cities have consequently entered into competition to attract investment by making themselves into attractive locations. Environmental issues know no borders, whether of states or sub-state entities. Devolution across European states has highlighted the resulting dilemmas as some of the very same policies that have been devolved are also subject to transnational effects and transnational institutions, such as UNESCO (United Nations Education and Cultural Organization) for education or the OECD (Organization for Economic Cooperation and Development) for economic policy and (again) education. The European Union poses the question in a particularly stark form, since it issues laws binding on both state and devolved governments, although officially it is only the states (and, through the European Parliament) citizens that are represented in its decision-making bodies. This has sparked demands for sub-state governments to have external competences corresponding to their internal powers, a principle enshrined in Belgium as *in foro interno, in foro externo*.

Specifically, devolved and federated governments have been drawn into external action in the fields of economic development; education; the environment; culture; migration; and ethical issues. Some have gone further and used external action to promote nation building or press the case for independence, an activity sometimes described as protodiplomacy. Relations with the European Union pose particular issues and deserve separate treatment. There is now a substantial literature on paradiplomacy, the external activity of non-sovereign territorial governments (Duchacek et al. 1988; Aldecoa and Keating 1999; Criekmans 2010).

Scotland has been part of this movement since before devolution, but in recent years the issue has assumed an increasing importance. Some of the resulting initiatives have been controversial and sparked accusations of seeking independence by stealth, but there has been a notable element of continuity between successive Labour/Liberal Democrat and SNP administrations. Indeed, some of the issues about representing Scotland abroad go back to before devolution (Archer and Main 1980).

Economic development

The strongest motive for paradiplomacy around the world has been economic. From the 1960s, Western European states developed ever more elaborate regional policies aimed at evening out growth and integrating declining or underdeveloped territories into national economies. Instruments included infrastructure investment and 'diversionary policies' such as grants and permits, in order to steer private investments to preferred locations. In Scotland, this strategy peaked in 1974 when the whole country was designated as eligible for development aid at one level or another. Regional policy was responsible for attracting such investments as the Ravenscraig steel mill, the motor plants at Linwood and Bathgate, the Invergordon aluminium smelter and the paper mill at Fort William (all since closed).

Diversionary policy has since become more difficult if not impossible. Mobile investors prevented from locating in one part of a country can move out altogether, perhaps to Eastern Europe or to Asia. Investment subsidies became unaffordable after the economic crisis of the 1970s and have been progressively outlawed under European Union competition policy. The EU Commission now produces a map of where they are permissible. At the same time, theories of economic development have moved away from emphasizing the importance of national markets to recognize the twin logic of global and European forces in determining the location of production, and of specific conditions within cities and regions themselves. There has been a resulting competition among sub-state territories for inward investment, high technology and market opportunities. Many economists dispute the extent to which regions (as opposed to firms) do really compete in the market place but the idea has taken hold and politicians in devolved institutions make great play out of the idea of competition.

Scotland is no exception. It is telling that, while the Scotland Act of 1978 kept all economic development powers in the hands of the UK Government (albeit with a role for the Scottish Office), the 1998 Act devolves key matters like the distribution of regional aid, Scottish Enterprise and Highlands and Islands Enterprise. Scotland is thus pitched more directly into international competition. This, of course, also puts it into competition with other parts of the United Kingdom and this is bound to cause some tensions. The issue of whether Scotland could mount its own inward investment effort erupted in the 1980s when UK departments complained about the activities abroad of the Scottish

Development Agency (SDA). The result on that occasion was a compromise, under which Invest in Scotland was set up as a joint initiative of the SDA and the Scottish Office, the latter being a government department and thus under central control.

External economic promotion also includes export promotion, partnerships and technology development. Small firms are particularly dependent on government help here since they do not have the international presence that larger corporations enjoy. Since devolution the external effort has been beefed up in the form of Scottish Development International (SDI), which looks after inward investment and trade promotion. SDI currently has forty-two offices world-wide, located in economically strategic cities rather than national capitals; so the Norway office is in Stavanger, the oil centre, while the US offices are in New York, Boston, Houston, Chicago and Silicon Valley.

Yet, if economic development has been largely devolved, there is still a broader UK context. If the nations and regions of the UK compete for development and, in particular, inward investment, there is a danger of beggar-my-neighbour behaviour as each seeks to gain at the expense of the others. To prevent this happening at a European level, there are strict limits on the assistance that can be given to firms (called 'state aids' in EU language). At the UK level, there is a Memorandum of Understanding governing financial assistance and an International Business Development Forum including UK Trade and Investment and the devolved administrations. This regulates, but does not entirely prevent, competition for attracting investment.

A key aspect of economic development is research and knowledge exchange. This is a matter that is increasingly globalized in the form of collaboration and large research programmes but also localized, as research is seen as a vital contribution to the new models of development based on innovation. As Scotland has one of the world's largest academic research outputs relative to its size but is a small nation, these international connections are critical. Higher education itself is increasingly internationalized and has become big business. Overseas students are an important source of fee revenue for universities, while graduate students make a significant contribution to the research effort.

Education and culture

For stateless nations with a distinct language and culture, such as Quebec, Catalonia and the Basque Country, external recognition is crucial and is one of the main motives for paradiplomacy. For Quebec, this means co-operating with French-speaking countries. In the other two, it is a matter of ensuring external recognition for their languages and securing their presence in cultural centres and university departments of Spanish. Scotland does not have a comparable language question but it does share with these cases the aspiration to project its culture and distinct personality. Much of this is of intrinsic value, to enhance Scottish cultural production and enrich it by exposure to others. So there is support for Scottish artists to travel and for foreign artists to come to Scotland. There is also a commercial motive, as culture is an important economic sector and source of investment and export earnings.

There is also a broader notion of cultural diplomacy, activities designed to create a positive image of a country and promote international understanding. For some, this is a form of 'soft power', providing influence for the nation by shaping the way it is perceived and its contribution to world order. Sub-state governments have been active in this field and the Scottish Government has jointly sponsored a Centre for Cultural Relations at the University of Edinburgh in order to advance this line of activity.

Cultural promotion always poses the question of what the identity, culture and values of the nation are and indeed whether one can or should attach particular values to a nation. Scotland, compared with many non-independent jurisdictions, has the advantage of name-recognition throughout the world. Yet there are competing visions of the nation, archaic and modern, closed and open. Small nations are not unique here but they are perhaps particularly vulnerable to being stereotyped, romanticized and reduced to folklore, given their weak international presence in the world of hard power. This is a recurring theme in Scotland. Walter Scott was the inventor not just of a vision of Scotland but of literary romanticism across Europe, although his work is now recognized as a sophisticated effort to deal with modernity and the union without giving up on the idea of Scotland. In the early twentieth century Scotland laboured under the 'kailyard' image, itself challenged by the literary renaissance of the 1930s. The late twentieth century was marked by something of an artistic renaissance, covering literature, poetry, theatre, music and the visual arts. Arthur Hernan's (2001) book *How the Scots Invented the Modern World* recounted the history and influence of the Scottish Enlightenment. Yet in 1995 the film *Braveheart* brought back the most clichéd images of a primitive people resisting colonization by an advanced but brutal neighbour. Scots were credited with influencing the American Declaration of Independence, which some have even claimed was based on the Declaration of Arbroath. Yet neo-confederate groups in the southern United States have claimed Scottish inspiration and adopted Scottish symbology.

Post-devolution Scotland has also grappled with what Tom Nairn (1977) famously called the 'tartan monster' at odds with the idea of projecting Scotland as a modern, dynamic society. Tartan Day in North America symbolizes the issue. Invented in the 1980s by Canadians and Americans of Scots descent, it was adopted by the US Congress under the sponsorship of Senator Trent Lott and proclaimed by President George W. Bush in 2008. Scottish politicians felt obliged to attend, although First Minister Jack McConnell caused some comment when he turned up in a pinstripe kilt. The event later saw a rare appearance of a kilted First Minister Alex Salmond. There were other unwelcome associations. Its chief Senate sponsor, Trent Lott, was removed from his position as minority leader after regretting that the segregationist Strom Thurmond had failed in his 1948 bid for the presidency. Since then, Scotland has been more effective in promoting a more pluralist and dynamic image and the tartanry has been contained with a Scotland Week devoted to promoting the record of the nation across a range of achievements.

These activities feed into a still wider concept, that of public diplomacy, activities aimed at the citizens or civil society of other countries as a means of enhancing influence and spreading good ideas. Flanders has put a lot of emphasis on promoting itself as model of economic competitiveness, implicitly contrasting itself with its poor relation, Wallonia. The Basque Government has sought to change the image of its country, often marked by political violence, in the direction of economic dynamism and democratic engagement. In Scotland there is an emphasis on Scotland's progressive credentials and contribution to democracy and liberalism.

Education and culture are also fields that are wholly devolved in Scotland but also subject to international regulation and benchmarking. UNESCO represents states, but stateless nations with their own language, culture and education systems, such as Quebec and Catalonia, have put great stress on seeking a presence there. This is less of an issue in Scotland. In education, the PISA system of student assessment, run by

OECD, has become an important instrument for international benchmarking and Scotland is entered as a separate country from the other nations of the United Kingdom. In 2015, the OECD was called in to provide an assessment of the introduction of the Curriculum for Excellence.

Global citizenship

Small nations, whether independent or not, will often position themselves as good global citizens, able to lead by example where larger states are constrained by their geopolitical interests or powerful lobbies. So Norway has made a speciality out of promoting peace initiatives while the Basque Country prides itself on meeting the UN target of 0.7 per cent of GDP for overseas development assistance. Cities and states in the USA have taken action on climate change in the face of reluctance on the part of the Congress. Other small nations have pressed issues of human rights.

The Scottish Government (2015) does emphasize these issues in its strategy. It has made great play of its legislated targets on renewable energy (although these have been criticized within Scotland for being rather symbolic). It has supported international action on climate change and sought a presence in climate-change conferences. It has set up a modest international development budget of £9 million; half to goes Malawi, an African country with which Scotland has historic ties. There is a commitment to promoting human rights. The Scottish Parliament has also played a role in global citizenship, including an initiative to aid the development of parliamentarism in the western Balkans.

In some ways, it is easier for sub-state governments to play the role of good global citizens as they do not face the direct consequences of making enemies that often push nation-states into realpolitik. So there is a tradition of cities, regions and stateless nations across Europe and North America giving moral leadership. Yet they do face many of the same dilemmas as do states. The Scottish Government has been criticized for supporting action on climate change while also supporting an expansion of air travel in the interest of economic competitiveness. In 2012 there was criticism of Alex Salmond when neither he nor other Scottish ministers met the Dalai Lama when he was in Scotland, the suggestion being that the SNP government were afraid of upsetting China, with consequent dangers to trade and investment.

Protodiplomacy

Paradiplomacy, including the activities examined above, is essentially about the extension of domestic competences into the international sphere, as a result of the rescaling of activities (Keating 2013) and the merging of internal and external politics. Protodiplomacy is more directly political, aimed at nation-building (or region-building) through external action aimed at consolidating the political identity of the territory and securing greater autonomy or even independence. Governments of places like Quebec, Catalonia and Flanders have sought to gain recognition as more than just regions of their respective states but as nations in fact or in the making, able to take their place on the world stage. During the 1992 Olympic Games in Barcelona, the Catalan Government placed adverts in the international press asking, 'Where is Barcelona?', the correct answer, for them, being Catalonia not Spain.

When sub-state governments start to promote independence and paradiplomacy moves into protodiplomacy, relations with their respective states not surprisingly become more tense. The Catalan Government, seeking to stage a referendum on independence, has in recent years mounted a big effort to convince international opinion of its case. It has set up an organization called Diplocat, described as a public diplomacy council and including representatives of civil society as well as government, to explain Catalonia to the world and garner sympathy. While it does not have the explicit mission of supporting independence, it does present the cause of self-determination around the world. Similarly, in the run-up to the Quebec referendum of 1995, the government worked to convince world opinion of the legitimacy of its case. During the long referendum campaign in Scotland, Scottish ministers were present around the world, especially in North America and Europe, stating their case, although there was a much less intensive external campaign than in the Quebec or Catalan cases.

It would be fair to say that neither in the Catalan nor in the Scottish case was there much of a response from foreign governments. While insisting that the referendum was a matter for the Scottish people, foreign leaders including Barack Obama made clear their preference for keeping the United Kingdom together. There was a big argument about the European Union, with the No side suggesting that an independent Scotland would find it hard if not impossible to secure membership. The Scottish Government made a big effort to present its pro-European credentials and to demonstrate how membership could be secured with minimal disruption. This may at least have led other member states to reserve their position, neither agreeing nor disagreeing with the Scottish Government. The president of the European Commission, Jose Manuel Barroso, did make some outspoken remarks but these were widely judged to have been excessive and unhelpful. In European circles in Brussels, there was more of an understanding of Scotland as a nation as a result of this argument, although national capitals tended to follow the lead of the UK Government in issues to do with recognition of Scotland.

There is a certain natural sympathy among nationalist parties seeking independence from larger states but this does not always translate into concrete action or mutual help. There is usually one movement that is in advance of the others and unwilling to adapt to the pace of the slowest. In the 1990s, the leader was Quebec while in recent years it has been Scotland. Scottish nationalist leaders are aware that, were Scotland to vote for independence, it would need friends among existing states, including Canada for help in the Commonwealth and NATO, while it would need Spain, whatever its reservations about setting a precedent for Catalonia, at least to be accommodating within the European Union. So the SNP, and the Scottish Government under its control, have had rather ambiguous relations with other nationalist movements. Many SNP politicians have good relations with their counterparts elsewhere and there is general good will towards the cause of self-determination, but in government nationalists have been cautious. In 2013, the Parti Québécois premier of Quebec, Pauline Marois, got a rather cool reception in Edinburgh, with no photo-op with the First Minister, to the surprise and consternation of her supporters back home. Catalan nationalists were held at a distance during the referendum period and there has been no open support for their demand on the 'right to decide'. Nationalists from Quebec and Catalonia, by contrast, have shown immense interest in the Scottish case and were present in force on the day of the referendum. SNP leaders are also aware that, while the Catalan and Quebec independence movements are rooted in liberal and democratic principles, that is not true of all secessionist parties, some of whom are on the extreme right and prone to xenophobia.

Migration

Immigration, citizenship and control of borders are among the key competences of the modern nation-state, often linked to sovereignty. Yet migration is also a matter that concerns sub-state governments. Quebec is allowed to select its own immigrants within the overall Canadian limit, allowing them to give preference to French-speakers and match their own labour market requirements. It also has its own integration programmes. Spain does not grant a similar provision to its own internal nations but the Catalan government does seek to integrate incomers through the Catalan language.

This has become an issue in Scotland as successive Labour/Liberal Democrat and SNP administrations have taken a more pro-immigration stance than their counterparts in London. They have framed migration as a demographic issue, linked to Scotland's population, which was declining up to the start of the twenty-first century, and to the economic potential of skilled migrants. For a while, they were able to secure a provision allowing foreign graduates of Scottish universities to work for a period after graduation, a provision that was extended more broadly in the UK before being abolished – its reinstatement remains a demand of the Scottish Government. The Scottish Government has also opposed restrictions on the free movement of labour within the EU, as demanded by Eurosceptics. As this became a key issue in the debate about the renegotiation of the UK's membership of the EU, a divide opened up between the parties at Holyrood and those in Westminster. The refugee crisis from 2015 also provoked different reactions in Scotland and England, with the Scottish Government and Parliament adopting a more liberal stance than that of the Westminster administration.

Geographical priorities

In the early days of devolution, sub-state governments around the world were keen to establish links with Scotland and many understandings and agreements were reached. By 2003 the Scottish Executive had signed co-operation agreements with Catalonia, Tuscany, North-Rhine Westphalia and Bavaria, and there were proposals for links with a French region and one in a new EU member state, as well as regular co-operation with Flanders. Since then, there has been an effort to focus efforts and limit the scope of partnerships. For economic matters, the focus is on North America and, increasingly, on Asia, notably China and India. Development assistance is focused on Africa, notably Malawi.

The arrival of the SNP in office did not fundamentally change the strategy, with the emphasis remaining on economic promotion, but there has been a certain shift towards protodiplomacy. The new Government did not see Scotland as a European region but as a nation-state in the making and downplayed links with German *Länder* in favour of comparing themselves with small independent states. Until the financial crisis of 2008, the favourite example was from the 'arc of prosperity' of small, independent northern European nations. Links with Flanders were retained, since this is both a region with comparable issues and a putative nation, with wide autonomist ambitions. In the United States, tartanry was downplayed in favour of promoting Scotland as a serious modern nation, focused on Scotland Week.

Mechanisms

Paradiplomacy works through various types of mechanism. There are direct links with governments abroad, be these sovereign or devolved; there are independent offices; there is a presence embedded with the diplomatic representation of the state itself; and there are links in civil society independent of government. Specialized and general-purpose organizations of regions and stateless nations provide another outlet. Most of Scotland's international partnerships have been with devolved or federal units, although there has been an effort to include small independent states, especially its Nordic neighbours. It is easy to sign partnership agreements, much more difficult to sustain them in the face of competing priorities, which is one reason for the decision to restrict their number.

Scotland has established a network of international offices to represent its interests. The offices of Scottish Development International are located in the economically strategic places. Elsewhere, as in Washington and in Ottawa, there are Scottish Affairs offices in the British embassies, giving its representatives shelter and diplomatic status. These are essentially responsible for looking after Scottish interests in devolved matters. Scotland is also a presence within the British Council, which promotes culture overseas and has the duty to present all the home nations.

All of this is governed by a Memorandum of Understanding and a Concordat on the role of devolved governments in international affairs, which has specific provisions for Scotland, Northern Ireland and Wales (HM Government 2013). The Scottish one covers exchange of information; formulation of United Kingdom policy and conduct of international negotiations; implementation of international obligations; co-operation over legal proceedings; representation overseas; secondments and training co-operation; visits; public diplomacy; the British Council and BBC World Service; trade and investment promotion; and diplomatic and consular relations.

Scotland is active in most of the inter-regional associations in Europe, including the Assembly of European Regions, and the Conference of Peripheral Maritime regions. It is also involved in networks of industrial regions (RETI), for environmental policy (ENCORE) and for other policy fields, their importance at any time depending on the quality of their leadership and the effort their members are prepared to invest. These governmental networks are complemented by parliamentary links, including membership of the Commonwealth Parliamentary Association and the Conference Europe of Regional Legislative Assemblies (CALRE) and links with the National Conference of State Legislatures (USA). The European Regions Research and Innovation Network (ERRIN) is a network of EU regions and their Brussels-based representative offices which facilitates knowledge exchange, joint action and project partnerships in the area of research and innovation. The European Association of Development Agencies (Eurada) includes Scottish Enterprise among its members.

Some sub-state governments put a lot of emphasis on the role of their diaspora around the world; the Basque government has been particularly active on this. There is a strong Irish diaspora, especially in North America, although the role of the Irish Government in promoting it is quite recent. It is generally considered that the sense of identity among people of Scottish descent living abroad is weaker and less organized, but since devolution the Scottish Government has begun to see them as an asset. The Global Scot network is an association of business leaders with connections to Scotland, founded by Scottish Enterprise and aimed at promoting trade and investment. Global

Friends of Scotland targets individuals and communities. Homecoming festivities have been organized in 2009 and 2014, in order to attract members of the diaspora to visit and so strengthen networks, although not surprisingly the 2014 events got caught up in political arguments around the referendum.

Scotland in Europe

The European Union poses a specific set of challenges, since it is not quite domestic policy, not quite foreign policy either but rather a supranational order with its own decision-making powers, sharing sovereignty with its member states. Scottish attitudes to European integration have changed over time. When the United Kingdom joined the then European Economic Community in 1973, most of its MPs were opposed since they were Labour and the Labour Party was officially against. When the Labour Government put the issue to a referendum in 1975 (after claiming that it had got better terms), Scotland voted Yes but by a smaller margin than England or Wales. The SNP was at that time opposed to European integration although, like Labour, it contained a pro-European minority. Its electoral successes in northeast Scotland in 1974 had owed at least something to disquiet about Europe and particularly the Common Fisheries Policy. Jim Sillars and his short-lived breakaway Scottish Labour Party was an isolated voice in making a link between Scottish self-government and Europe. In 1975 he favoured withdrawal from the EEC but said that, if the UK were to vote to stay in, Scotland would need its own voice there.

It was in the late 1980s that matters began to change. Labour was converted to supporting Europe by Commission President Jacques Delors' concept of 'social Europe', which looked attractive in the context of Thatcher's Britain. The SNP were converted by Sillars, now a leading SNP figure and by-election victor, adopting the slogan 'Independence-in-Europe'. This allowed the SNP to present itself as a modern, internationalist party, while the European framework would resolve many of the difficult economic questions, including market access, that an independent Scotland would have to face. It was less clear exactly what kind of Europe the SNP favoured but they leaned towards one that was more intergovernmental than supranational and were able to claim thus that membership did not undermine Scottish sovereignty and so frustrate independence. Scottish civil society also has a pro-European tilt, including business, trade unions and the voluntary sector, producing a different tone to the debate from that found in England.

Opinion polls over the years have been less clear. There is consistently less Euroscepticism than in England but not a great deal of Europhilia (Jeffery et al. 2015). Occasionally, the gap between those wanting to stay in and those wanting to come out has been small enough to suggest that Scotland's slightly less Eurosceptic sentiment could, in a referendum on withdrawal, lead it to vote to stay in while England voted to stay out. For most of the time, however, the most that can be said is that the passive consensus on Europe has persisted longer in Scotland and that Euroscepticism is not an issue on which parties can build much advantage. Table 10.1 gives a snapshot of opinion about the EU in 2014, while Table 10.2 indicates that were a referendum to have been held in that year, there might indeed have been a Scotland–England split. Interestingly, analysis of successive Scottish Social Attitudes Surveys from the decade of the 2000s showed that the pro-European tilt in Scotland was not down to nationalist voters but that all party supporters were less Eurosceptic than in England, but most notably Labour voters (Keating 2009).

Table 10.1 Attitudes to EU, 2014

	Good thing	Bad thing	Neither	Don't know
England	34	34	19	13
Wales	35	32	20	13
Scotland	43	27	17	13

Source: Future of England Survey (Jeffery et al. 2014).

Table 10.2 Voting intention in EU referendum, 2014

	Remain	Leave	Don't know/not vote
England	37	40	22
Wales	39	35	26
Scotland	48	32	18

Source: Future of England Survey (Jeffery et al. 2014).

The political class in Scotland, however, has been overwhelmingly pro-Europe and successive governments have sought to position the nation within it. The SNP has pursued the independence-in-Europe agenda, with increasing emphasis on the European element. The Labour/Liberal Democrat coalition, for its part, sought to play the game of Europe of the Regions, a movement to give sub-state governments a greater role in EU affairs that gained momentum in the 1990s.

The original impetus for the Europe of the Regions was the recognition that, in countries with devolved or federal systems, Europe was taking up powers from state governments in two ways. Some matters that were devolved in domestic constitutions were being handed up to Europe; and since it was member states that were represented in the decision-making Council of Ministers, they were able to re-enter these domains themselves. In the Treaty on European Union (Maastricht Treaty) of 1992, three concessions were made. First, under certain conditions member states could be represented in the Council of Ministers by regional ministers; although these still need to represent the state as a whole, not themselves. Second, a consultative Committee of the Regions was established with the same status as the existing Economic and Social Committee to represent sub-state governments. Third, the principle of subsidiarity was re-affirmed and could be read as to extend below the member state level although this was not an implication that the United Kingdom officially accepted. Ironically, at the crucial Edinburgh summit it was the UK Government that pressed for subsidiarity (to protect member state interests) while in the street below 20,000 demonstrators called for it to be extended down to Scotland.

Although some people believed that the Committee of the Regions (CoR) could become a kind of third chamber (with the Council of Ministers and the European Parliament) in a European federation, it never really lived up to its promise. Its role is purely consultative and, while this has been extended to cover a wide range of issues, it has little power. Matters are not helped by its procedures, which involve complex resolutions rather than focused inquiries. It represents all sub-state governments, from stateless nations, to powerful federal entities, to municipal governments, who often have little in common. During the 2000s, especially in the negotiations around the unsuccessful European Constitutional Treaty and the subsequent Lisbon Treaty, a group of larger and more powerful devolved governments, the Regions with Legislative Powers (RegLeg) emerged within CoR to argue for special recognition but made little headway in the face of opposition from other members. Under the Labour/Liberal Democrat coalition, Scotland played a prominent role in these initiatives. First Minister Henry McLeish defied the misgivings of the UK Government and signed the Declaration of Flanders of 2001, sponsored by a group calling themselves 'constitutional regions'. His successor Jack McConnell, was also active in European regional networks, including the CoR. After the Lisbon Treaty, the momentum of the Europe of the Regions movement slackened and little further has been achieved (Elias 2008). The SNP Government between 2007 and the referendum of 2014 did continue to participate in events but its main focus was on independence and using Europe as a vehicle to achieve it.

The United Kingdom has made use of the mechanism allowing devolved governments access to the Council of Ministers but this is by invitation of the UK Government and not, as in the federal countries of Germany and Belgium, by right. It applies only when the Council is considering devolved matters, including agriculture and fisheries, environment and education (although this last is not a major concern of the EU). The crucial matter is not just attendance at the plenary meetings of the Council of Ministers but participation in the preparatory meetings of officials in drawing up the UK negotiating position. Participation has rarely been denied but the SNP has tried to insist on a stronger provision, guaranteeing their right to attend. On the other hand, the Scottish Government would not have the capacity to attend all relevant meetings. There is another drawback, in that Scottish ministers must speak to an agreed UK line and not for Scotland separately. Any differences must be resolved in advance in the Joint Ministerial Committee (Europe), the only one of the JMCs that has functioned continuously since the start of devolution; here the UK Government has the last word. Scotland's strongest arguments have been over participation in the Council on fisheries matters, since this is unique case of Scotland having a larger stake than England in the issue, given the respective sizes of their fishing fleets.

Generally, Scotland has worked smoothly with the UK Government, under successive administrations at both levels, but there have been points of friction. There have been persistent complaints that the Scottish minister has not been able to take the lead on fisheries matters, even when a UK minister has not been available. The Smith Commission report on further devolution recommended that this be the practice in future, but since it only applies when the UK minister is not able to make it, the concession is very minor. Scotland has also been excluded from more informal meetings of ministers, including meetings on culture and bilateral and trilateral meetings on agriculture and fisheries.

Scotland's and other devolved territories' influence through these channels can be most effective to the degree that Europe proceeds under the 'community method', that is the traditional mode of policy making involving the Commission, the Council of Ministers (using qualified majority voting) and, in recent years, the Parliament. There has, however, been a tendency to move away from these to other kinds of intergovernmental policy making, largely monopolized by states. The European Council, the summit meeting of heads of government, is now part of the regular mechanism, meeting several times a year. There is no provision for participation by devolved governments on the lines of that provided in the Council of Ministers, although there are meetings of the JMC (Europe) in advance. Other policies have been taken forward through the Open Method of Coordination, under which states work together in a less binding way, and without the need for the Commission to take the leading role it has in other matters. It was developed to deal with the Lisbon Strategy for competitiveness, which has since been succeeded by Europe 2020. It can be difficult for devolved territories to get into these processes (McPhail 2006) but the Scottish Government has both provided an input into the UK National Reform Programme required under Europe 2020 and adopted is own one, which is sent directly to the Commission and gets a response.

A matter of increasing importance is the representation of Scotland and other devolved territories in constitutional negotiations in Europe. In the Review of Competences undertaken by the UK Government during the Parliament of 2010–15 with a view to renegotiation of the UK's relations with Europe, the devolved territories were consultees rather than participants. In 2013/14 the UK had to decide whether to opt in to the treaty provisions on Justice and Home Affairs, opt out entirely, or opt out and then selectively opt back in. Much of this field is devolved in Scotland but the Scottish Government complained about lack of consultation at official or political level, and even a lack of information. At the UK General Election of 2015, the Conservatives were returned with a majority, allowing them to proceed with an in–out referendum on membership of the EU, after renegotiating the terms of membership. Once again, the devolved governments were consultees rather than participants although the Scottish Government has indicated that its priorities are quite different from those of the UK Government, for example over the free movement of workers.

Further difficulties arise over Conservative proposals to repeal the Human Rights Act, so curtailing the application of the European Convention on Human Rights (ECHR), and replacing it with a British Bill of Rights. The ECHR, which is governed not by the European Union but by the Council of Europe, was incorporated into the law in Scotland twice. The Scotland Act of 1998 provides that it apply directly in devolved matters, so that the courts can strike down legislation of the Scottish Parliament (and pre-devolution legislation in devolved fields) where it is incompatible with the Convention. In reserved matters (and in England) the courts can only make a declaration of incompatibility inviting Westminster to use a fast-track procedure to amend the offending law. Conservative proposals to repeal the Human Rights Act would not in themselves affect the direct application of the ECHR in devolved matters but it would create different rights regimes in different parts of the United Kingdom and, in Scotland, for devolved and non-devolved matters. The more radical proposals by some Conservatives to opt out of the ECHR altogether would pose the question of whether Scotland (and the other devolved territories) could opt to remain in when the signatory state was no longer there. None of these issues seems to have been considered in the initial proposals on repealing the Human Rights Act, which were conceived entirely in London. It is not clear at the time of writing how proposals from the majority Conservative Government elected in 2015 will work in Scotland, but the issue could generate serious differences.

The key to influence in European matters often lies less in formal participation in ministerial meetings than in networking around the European institutions in Brussels and with other governments. Scotland's representation in Brussels was an issue even before devolution, when there was no Scottish Government to be represented. Instead, the Scottish Office promoted Scotland Europa, founded in 1992 as a body representing Scottish civil society and economic interests but officially at arm's length from government. Following devolution, Scotland Europa was maintained but supplemented by the Scottish Government EU Office, located in the same building. The office is linked to the UK Permanent Representation as part of the 'UKREP family' and its officials have UK diplomatic status, allowing for an exchange of information and wide access to diplomatic networks. The key to influence is frequently getting information in time and being able to intervene when policy proposals are in their early stages. The complex process of EU policy making, involving the Commission, national governments, interest groups and the Parliament, provides multiple points of access and gives a premium to those who have something to contribute to the European project, rather than just lobbying for their own interests. Knowing the right people is crucial, as is having fellow-nationals in key positions, something at which the UK has not been very good in recent years as the number of EU officials of British origin has diminished. The Scottish Government has therefore sought to enhance its own networks.

In the other direction, there are offices in Edinburgh of the European Commission and the European Parliament. These provide advice for business and citizens on linking into the European institutions, as well as a more political role in informing the public about Europe and its benefits.

Conclusion: conflict and co-operation

Paradiplomacy, as the external expression of internal devolution, is not necessarily conflictual and for the most part Scotland's international and European strategies have been complementary to those of the United Kingdom. Indeed, the Foreign and Commonwealth Office has been more accommodating of the devolved territories than have some domestic departments. Protodiplomacy is another matter, as it can entail competing claims to sovereignty and representation. Often it is not the substance of the issue that makes the difference but the way in which it is framed, as a practical humdrum matter or as a question of principle. Relationships between London and Edinburgh on external affairs are necessarily tenser when the SNP is in office in Scotland than it was when both levels were dominated by Labour, but the politicization of the issue may depend on the political circumstances of the time. There was also more competition with the UK Government, as when the Frst Minister and the Secretary of State visited China in successive months, essentially on the same mission. The referendum campaign was a time of some tension, although the confrontation was not as open or dramatic as it was at the same time between the governments of Spain and Catalonia.

With independence off the agenda, at least for the time being, after the referendum, there is a renewed emphasis on what Scotland can do to project itself within the limits of extended devolution. Paradiplomacy features prominently here. The SNP have repeatedly asked for 'direct' representation in European matters, although it is not clear exactly what this means. Only member states are directly represented in the sense of casting votes in the Council of Ministers, participating in the European Council and nominating commissioners. The demand seems, rather, to be for more presence, attending the Council of Ministers by right (albeit as part of a single UK delegation) and being more fully involved in European 'comitology', the complex network of bodies through which policy is made. Much of this is available already to Scotland, but requires time and resources, which are in short supply. There is also talk of a Scottish input into UK foreign policy and diplomatic presence, even in non-devolved matters where there is a distinct Scottish interest. This takes the issue beyond paradiplomacy understood as the doctrine of *in foro intero, in foro externo*, to a form of plurinational diplomacy (Aldecoa and Keating, 1999), in which the external presence of the United Kingdom is itself plurinational. In 1905 it was external commercial policy that pushed Norway, which already had maximum internal home rule, into independence. In Scotland's case, it could be the demand for more say on external policy, especially in relation to Europe, that pushes the devolution settlement to its limit.

The UK devolution settlement has not yet reached its limit and, perhaps surprisingly, external engagement on the part of sub-state governments is still regarded by some observers as an oxymoron, but it is becoming part of the mainstream of the new multilevel politics of complex and plurinational states.

Sources for further reading and study

Aldecoa, F. and M. Keating (eds) (1999) *Paradiplomacy in Action: The External Activities of Subnational Governments*. London: Frank Cass.
Keating, M. (2010) *The Government of Scotland: Public Policy Making after Devolution* (2nd edn). Edinburgh: Edinburgh University Press.
Scottish Government (2015) 'Scotland's International Strategy'. Available at: www.gov.scot/Topics/International/strategy.

References

Aldecoa, F. and M. Keating (eds) (1999) *Paradiplomacy in Action. The External Activities of Subnational Governments*. London: Frank Cass.
Archer, C. and J. Main (1980) *Scotland's Voice in International Affairs*. London: Hurst.
Criekmans, D. (ed.) (2010) *Regional Sub-state Diplomacy Today*. The Hague: Martinus Nijhoff.
Delphine, A., M. Boyle and R. Kitchin (2009) *The Scottish Diaspora and Diaspora Strategy: Insights and Lessons from Ireland*. Edinburgh: Scottish Government.
Duchacek, I., D. Latouche and G. Stevenson (1988) *Perforated Sovereignties and International Relations*. New York: Greenwood.
Elias, A. (2008) 'Introduction: Whatever Happened to the Europe of the Regions? Revisiting the Regional Dimension of European Politics'. *Regional and Federal Studies* 18(5): 483–492.
Hernan, Arthur (2001) *How the Scots Invented the Modern World*. New York: Crown Publishing.
HM Government (2013) *Memorandum of Understanding and Supplementary Agreements between the United Kingdom Government, the Scottish Ministers, the Welsh Ministers, and the Northern Ireland Executive Committee*. Presented to Parliament by Command of Her Majesty and presented to the Scottish Parliament and the Northern Ireland Assembly and laid before the National Assembly for Wales. London: HMSO.
Jeffery, C., A. Henderson, R. Scully, D. Wincott and R. Wyn Jones (2015) 'Does the EU divide England and Scotland?' Centre on Constitutional Change. Available at: www.centreonconstitutionalchange.ac.uk/blog/does-eu-divide-england-and-scotland.
Jeffery, C., R. Wyn Jones, A. Henderson, R. Scully and G. Lodge (2014) *Taking England Seriously: The New English Politics*. The Future of England Survey 2014. Edinburgh: University of Edinburgh Centre on Constitutional Change. Available at: www.centreonconstitutionalchange.ac.uk/sites/default/files/news/Taking%20England%20Seriously_The%20New%20English%20Politics.pdf.
Jones, B. and M. Keating (eds) (1995) *The European Union and the Regions*. Oxford: Oxford University Press.
Keating, M. (2013) *Rescaling the European State: The Making of Territory and the Rise of the Meso*. Oxford: Oxford University Press.

Keating, M. (2009) *The Independence of Scotland*. Oxford: Oxford University Press.
MacPhail, E. (2006) 'Sub-national Authorities and the Open Method of Coordination: A New Opportunity or the Same Old Community?' *Journal of Contemporary European Research* 2(1): 58–75.
Nairn, T. (1977) *The Break-Up of Britain: Crisis and Neo-Nationalism*. London: New Left Review Books.
Scottish Government (2015) 'Scotland's International Strategy'. Available at: www.gov.scot/Topics/International/strategy.
Wright, A. (2005) *Who Governs Scotland?* London: Routledge.

11 A small country in a bigger country or a small country in a big world?

Richard Kerley

Introduction

Some twenty years ago I published a book (Kerley 1994: x) which in the contents pages alerted readers that:

> The terms used in this book refer to: Scotland, England, England and Wales. Great Britain is the term used for all three countries and the phrase the United Kingdom includes Northern Ireland.

The emphasis on such precise social/geographical labelling was not the personal statement of an affronted citizen of one of the three smaller entities within the United Kingdom. It was a simple statement intended to introduce clarity into empirical data often interchangeably used in discussing local government statistics related to the constituent countries of the United Kingdom.

The prevalent tendency amongst both the ostensibly informed and the uninformed is very often to subsume Scotland, Wales and Northern Ireland into the wider more casually used generic term 'England'.

The extent to which a range of already quite extensive and distinct differences between the four component jurisdictions of the UK are lost in the greater whole of the largest of four countries is captured in the Ludovic Kennedy (1995) book *In Bed with an Elephant: A Journey through Scotland's Past and Present*. This phrase continues to echo down to us over the years (Devine 2013).

It is almost a daily occurrence to find instances in print and broadcast media of confusion of simple terminology: competences, responsibilities and accountabilities as between the constituent parts of the UK. That confusion is to be found in the UK itself, and similar confusion is apparent in other countries that observe the UK from a distance.

In a recent well informed and policy relevant instance, a distinguished academic geneticist (Fabre 2015) suggested proposals for enhancing participation and governance in the NHS:

> A clinically strong and democratically legitimate NHS England board, along with equivalent boards for *the other UK regions* …
>
> (my emphasis)

It is not at all unusual to find a lack of recognition that the four NHS systems of the UK are distinct (and increasingly more distinctive entities) with the service in Scotland separately legislated for in the National Health Service (Scotland) Act 1947. This, and similar mistakes are easily and often made, and can serve to confuse and hinder effective policy making. Such instances of both the relatively trivial (songs at sporting matches) and the more substantial (lack of awareness of policy difference) can reinforce views in different parts of the UK about the relationship between the constituent parts of the UK and lead to poor understanding of distinctive policy choices and political/administrative processes.

There remains a very clear sense amongst a large number of those resident in Scotland that the 'No' decision of 2014 was not the definitive end of the debate over the consitutional status of Scotland (Ipsos MORI 2015). The 2014/15 process of preparing for legislation to enhance powers for the Scottish Parliament (Smith Commission 2015); the recent debate on 'English Votes for English Laws'; proposed changes in Wales; and some uncertainty in Northern Ireland all suggest that the entity status of all parts of the UK and the relationships between those parts are emergent, dynamic and not fixed.

To discuss Scotland in any kind of international context is to simultaneously talk about at least three, four, or even more forms of polity. A country with a distinct domestic legislature and also a *shared* legislature with the UK, potentially an entity within a confederation, or federation of some kind and potentially an independent state that *might* still share some institutions as well as long established values with the remainder of the UK. To be more precise, the changes now under legislative discussion will further change the nature of the relationship of the Scottish Parliament and Government to the UK Parliament and Government and the quadripartite relationship between the three devolved jurisdictions and the UK Parliament.

The intention of this chapter is to discuss and illustrate some of the features, aspects, and implications of these proximate options and those that might further emerge. This is all in the context of a multi-layered state that is the current United Kingdom; the position that Scotland currently has within that multi-layered state; and the position it may have in the future, either within, or in some relationship to what will potentially be a different UK.

So it is also important to stress that given the very live and lively discussion that continues at both Westminster and Holyrood and in the popular media – print, broadcast, and virtual – this chapter will try and walk a fine line between discussing Scotland as an entity within a quasi-federal or quasi-confederal system and as an independent state. This may be in some parts frustrating – though it is hoped not too confusing – for the reader, but it is unavoidable in our current circumstances.

This will be illustrated by reference to some of the difference and similarity between the constituent parts of the UK; and the difference and similarity with other comparator countries globally which are often described as independent states.

The state of our nations

A starting point for this exercise is to compare and discuss just some of the different powers, competences and everyday assumptions that characterise the different components of the UK and the complex institutional relationships between them. As other contributors to this collection discuss, the relationships and institutional structures that characterise England, Wales, Scotland and Northern Ireland are complex; not as long and as settled as some occasionally like to think; and continue to evolve. That evolution seems generally to lead in the direction of a more federalised or confederalised governance system in ways we often overlook, ignore, or in the heat of campaigning and debate simply discount.

The general tenor of some of the arguments in favour of independence for Scotland that preceded – and have continued to follow the 2104 referendum – were that in many ways the UK was a declining state economically. Certainly the arguments advanced by the Scottish National Party majority Scottish Government[1] constantly reiterated that the economic position of Scotland was better than that of the UK – although that claim is contestable (Philips and Tetlow 2014). Interpretations can be dependent on years and time periods chosen, assumptions made on future policy trajectories, whether Scotland converges or diverges with policy priorities in the rest of the UK – inevitably involving degrees of speculation.

> We raise more tax and our public finances have been stronger than those of the UK as a whole over the past 32 years.
> (Scottish Government 2013: 23)

Collateral arguments were advanced by various campaigners that the entity referred to as the UK was not merely declining, but showed characteristics that signalled an imperfect, institutionally flawed entity with serious democratic weaknesses. These included the absence of a codified constitution, an unelected Upper House and a flawed Westminster voting system. The Scottish Government was not directly associated with such strongly stated claims, but this line of rhetoric was a commonplace element of referendum claims from some campaigners.

The institutional incoherence that appears to characterise a political jurisdiction such as the UK that is still malleable and emergent in form even after some 300 or more years, is even to be found in the language used by protagonists of change for Scotland. The somewhat confused usage of words is interesting for both variety and what it says about the uncertainty of Scottish national status:

> the eyes of the world will be on Scotland as our ancient nation emerges – again – as an independent country. ... 194th member of the United Nations.
> (Scottish Government 2013: 3)

> [the referendum] ... shows the world that Scotland is ready to be a nation.
> (Scottish Government 2013: 3)

> Of course Scotland should control its own broadcasting, of course Scotland should be an independent nation.
> (Linda Fabiani MSP, quoted in Peterkin 2015)

These words and phrases used illustrate the point about a confusion of terms that are all relevant to any construction or comparison of country, nation, state or 'polity', a term coined by Ferguson and Mansbach (1996).

Now, clearly protagonists for a cause use words and phrases in whatever manner they can stretch, adapt and assemble to best make their case. However, there is more here than simply the use of words as tools of persuasion rather than classification.

It would be hard to find disagreement amongst informed opinion in the UK in describing Scotland as a *country* with a clear and undisputed border (over several centuries) to the contiguous *country* of England. The word *nation* is more historically debatable in meaning and weight, although it is very clear that for the overwhelming majority of independence supporters and SNP members the emphasis is on 'civic nationalism' rather than the more romantic and occasionally darker tones associated with ethnic nationalism.

A passage from the White Paper cited above also refers to the United Nations, and a predecessor institution, the League of Nations. Both of these are, on consideration, curious titles for international assemblies of *states* to adopt. Membership of both is, and was, actually conditional on the formal jurisdictional entity being a recognised state, as Articles 3 and 4 of the UN charter confirm:

> The original Members of the United Nations shall be the *states* ... membership in the United Nations is open to all other peace-loving *states* which accept the obligations contained in the present Charter and, in the judgement of the Organization, are able and willing to carry out these obligations.
>
> (my emphasis)

For reasons that are complex and mixed, the use of the word *state* did not figure much in discussions of possible independence, and seems uncomfortable to some, perhaps partly because of a historic sense of forced emergence through disruption and some bloody periods of European history (Spruyt 1991).

It might be that the very word 'state' is seen as somehow less warm and less intuitively welcoming than the words country and nation are. We can see such usage in condemnatory phrases such as 'police state', a phrase that emerged concurrently with the planned changes to create one single Scottish police force (Police and Fire Reform [Scotland] Act 2012):

> If Scotland does gain its independence in September we will merely become the newest member of the confederation of independent police states.
>
> (McKenna 2014)

> Centralising, illiberal, catastrophic: the SNP's one-party state.
>
> (Tomkins 2015)

The second article cited has, at the time of my writing, and on the eve of the SNP Autumn 2015 conference, caused an extensive exchange of views on Twitter, with many asserting: 'but we're not a state'.

In addition to such sometimes confusing usage, we should recall that the question eventually put in the Referendum vote of September 2014, that had been subject to voter testing exercises and assessment by the Electoral Commission (2013) was as follows:

Should Scotland be an independent country? – Yes/No.

In contrast to this, the publication in mid-2014 of a 'Draft Scottish Independence Bill' (Scottish Government 2014) was the first most significant mention of a Scottish *state*.

In various clauses of a putative Scottish constitution, words such as State; Head of State; State Accountability were all used as might be expected in a formal foundational document.

The historical and contemporary realities of distinct 'polities' within a state

There is a generally accepted proposition that Scotland is a *country*; there is a *nation* called Scotland (often used interchangably with the word Scots); however, Scotland is not a *state*. As argued above, had there been a vote in favour of independence in 2014, and had all gone smoothly after that, it would have *become* a state, although the mechanisms for that might have actually been more complex than implied by the Scottish Government, as discussed by Murkens et al. (2002) a decade previously.

On the other hand, Scotland is distinct and separate from the other constituents of the UK in some frequently referred to respects.[2] And, indeed all the four constituent elements of the UK are constitutionally distinct from each other (formally: two countries, a principality and a province), and since the devolution project of the late 1990s they have been ever more distinct. The core of Scotland/UK distinctions go back to the eighteenth century and centre on the assumption in the policy consequences of the Acts of Union of a separate 'national' church; a separate education system; and a distinct and separate legal system.

The distinctiveness of the legal system is an important feature of differences between the constituent parts of the UK. As Collier (2001) describes one key difference:

> For the purposes of the English *conflict of laws*, every country in the world which is not part of *England and Wales* is a foreign country and its laws foreign. This means that not only totally foreign independent countries such as France or Russia ... are foreign countries but also *British Colonies* such as the *Falkland Islands*. Moreover, the other parts of the United Kingdom – Scotland and Northern Ireland – are foreign countries for present purposes, as are the other *British Islands*, the *Isle of Man, Jersey* and *Guernsey*.

This apparently clear separation of the three extant legal systems within the United Kingdom is apparently not reflected in one part of the Scotland Act 1998, or the documents developed by and discussed in the work of the Smith Commission.

Schedule 5 of the Act (Reserved Matters) and the Smith Report retains *Extradition* as a power reserved to Westminster. In context, this clearly applies to extradition out of, and into, the United Kingdom as a whole, rather than between the three legal jurisdictions of the UK. Between the constituent countries of the UK there are reciprocal cross border police powers provided for by other legislation.

In such matters, pragmatic working relationships between different countries also can cross the boundaries of different states. As Spencer (p. 1) observes:

> [*Extradition is supported by*] 'the backing of warrants'. Here, the authorities of the jurisdiction where the person is wanted issue their normal warrant of arrest, which is sent directly to the authorities of the jurisdiction where he is, who endorse it if it appears to be in order, and give it to their policemen to execute it as if it were their own. ... This is the system that has operated as long as anyone can remember between the different parts of the UK. This entity at one time included the whole

of Ireland; and surprisingly perhaps, the backing of warrants survived the war of independence and the emergence of the Republic of Ireland as an independent state.

(Spencer, n.d. my emphasis)

The separate status of the Scottish legal system agreed in 1707 is one of the factors that underpins the practice by Westminster governments of all parties to generally legislate separately for domestic policy changes that are often similar in form and much substance between Scotland and England & Wales (c.f. the Local Government Act, 1978 and the Local Government [Scotland] Act, 1978). Interestingly the most recent legislation referring to cross-border arrests is found in the Criminal Justice and Public Order Act (1994) where matters related to England & Wales, Scotland and Northern Ireland are covered in one Act. Again this illustrates the pragmatic acceptance of commonality of purpose being served by a common policy and legislative approach, an arrangement always available if chosen by successive governments over more than 300 years.

This unchallenged agreement on the acceptability of the UK-wide Parliament legislating for the separate legal/administrative systems of England & Wales and Scotland was also reflected in that part of the 1998 Act (Clause 28 [7]) that came to be referred to as the 'Sewell Convention' described in a House of Commons Library Note (2005) in this way:

> The Sewell Convention is just that: a convention. It is not enshrined in the Scotland Act 1998. However it was embodied in a Memorandum of Understanding between the UK government and the devolved executives which was drawn up in 1999.

The extent to which there is a long-term broad acceptance in both UK and Scottish parliaments of some commonality on administrative and policy related legislation is not so readily found in criminal law matters, although there is common legislation on some matters such as misuse of drugs. So, for example, two long established aspects of Scottish criminal law have been the requirement of corroboration of a criminal act, and the three verdicts available in a criminal trial: guilty, not guilty, not proven.[3] Although corroboration – in the sense of two witnesses – has been under some challenge recently, it has long distinguished Scots criminal law from that of England & Wales. The not proven verdict also distinguishes the two systems.

In almost all respects the legal system in Scotland has a character and procedures distinct from the legal system in England & Wales, albeit with some linkages at the highest levels of appeal. Perhaps the most stark instance of this separation was the occasion when the Scottish Justice Secretary determined to release the one man convicted of the Lockerbie plane sabotage, Abdel Baset al-Megrahi. The decision was reported in the US media and linked White House reaction to the views of families and friends:

> although the White House on Thursday said Scotland should not have released him ... President Barack Obama called the release a mistake.
>
> (NBC News 2009)

Other reports suggested that at least some sections of the US government tried to persuade UK government officials to intervene in the parole decision, an intervention power simply not available to any UK government minister.

In education – which has also been historically very distinct in the different parts of the UK – consistently separate characteristics and separate legislation to achieve different systems has been a long standing feature. So for example, in three parts of the United Kingdom, the commencement of compulsory schooling is at five years, in Northern Ireland at four. In France, including overseas departments, a state where the maintenance of widespread and large numbers of local governments is seen as a sign of healthy democracy, the age of compulsory schooling universally starts at five.

The features of Scottish education that most distinguish it from education elsewhere in the UK are: transfer to secondary school at 12; fewer years of secondary attendance, even for the most academically successful students; and a wider subject spread and usually four years study for a first degree. Interestingly, these features generally remain completely unremarked upon by public, academic, or elite commentary. The one most prominent instance of this even being raised was a slightly overstated press report headlined:

Gordon Brown: Scots want 'UK-wide school system'.

(Maddox 2014)

The other long acclaimed distinctive feature of post-1707 Scotland was the distinct status of the Church of Scotland, which remains socially, politically and intellectually influential, albeit now in a similar manner to other faiths observed in Scotland.

The re-emergence and strengthening of a Scottish 'administrative state' (Mitchell 2003) commenced in the late nineteenth century and continued to be strengthened throughout the first ninety-nine years of the twentieth until the vesting of the Scottish Parliament in 1999. One of Scotland's leading historians (Devine, 2013) argues with an historical perspective that for the better part of 200 years, Westminster treated Scotland with 'benign neglect' allowing Scottish politicians to informally determine matters then formally agreed by the Imperial Parliament.

This general acceptance of Scottish difference, regardless of the form of entity that was assumed to be different, was followed by governments led or dominated by all of the major parties that exercised governance in the UK over that time. This was reflected in different legislation (Education Act 1944 and Education (Scotland) Act 1945) intended to achieve the same broad purpose. This was the case even if the scope of the legislation was seen to cover broadly very similar affected bodies that were perceived to operate on a UK-wide basis (Higher and Further Education Act 1992, and Higher and Further Education (Scotland) Act 1992). These acts enable the designation of polytechnics (England and Wales) and Central Institutions (Scotland) as universities by the same progression process.

There were always exceptions, characterised in two bimodal forms of legislation that covered different parts of the UK in one bill: the broadly accepted – e.g. the Criminal Justice Act, referred to above – and the highly controversial and politically charged. So, for example, the Local Government, Planning and Land Act (1980) which introduced compulsory competitive tendering covered both England/Wales, Wales and Scotland in one Bill because of the entrenched parliamentary and extra parliamentary objection anticipated during the implementation of this Act.

There are still further distinctions that can be seen between the constituent jurisdictions of the UK, regardless of whether the policy domain is long entrenched or even whether the specific intervention is fairly recent in initiation. Bowel screening is an example.

In England, biennial bowel screening is offered to both men and women of 60–74; there is also an invitation to a bowel scope test at 55. In Wales and Northern Ireland, bowel screening is offered biennially to men and women aged 60–74. In Scotland, bowel screening is offered biennially at age 50–74, and bowel scoping is currently being piloted (Cancer Research UK, 2015).

The state of other nations – how does Scotland compare?

Given the nature of the continuing discussion that underpins all governmental, political and policy matters in Scotland, there is value in comparing some aspects of this to the position in other countries. In this section we look at, comparisons, constitutions, legislative institutions and what we can reasonably describe as 'the quirks of comparative democracies'.

A continuing theme of some of those campaigning for independence for Scotland has been to anticipate a putative new state with formalised, and what are assumed will be more democratic institutions and processes. This is usually contrasted with a historical entity with multiple confusions about identity and sovereignty and some remaining pre-democratic institutions, the most often cited being the Upper House at Westminster:

> the House of Lords is wholly unelected.
> (Scottish Government 2014: 11)

Implicit in this discourse, both during and after the referendum was the social and political benchmarking of both the UK and Scotland against other countries, particularly the continental Scandinavian countries. At an earlier period, the then first minister would himself refer to the 'arc of prosperity' stretching from Ireland, through Iceland and into Norway and thence to the other three Scandinavian neighbours. In the period after 2008 the emphasis on this arc in ministerial speeches was downplayed and subsequently dropped (McSmith 2008) in favour of narrower comparators:

> Nations that are similar to Scotland – such as Norway, Finland, Denmark and Sweden – sit at the top of world wealth and wellbeing tables.
> (Scottish Government 2014: 43)

Notwithstanding this change of comparators, the observation that Scotland has over time done less well than elsewhere remained a buttress for change arguments:

> Similar countries to Scotland have seen higher levels of economic growth over the past generation. That is because they have the bonus of being independent and are able to make the right choices for their nation and economy.
> (Ibid.: 23)

Such a claim of greater economic success in states elsewhere is in some respects correct; and indeed there are comparisons on many dimensions that can show others performing more successfully than either the UK or the four constituent countries of the UK, whether it be in GDP, health outcomes or happiness.

As always in such exercises whether developed for campaigning purposes or as part of a more formal analysis, it depends on the features we compare and how we treat data. Gallup (2013) published their most recent listing of self-reported *median* household income (before tax and social security reductions) for a number of countries and the top five included the four continental Scandinavian countries and Luxembourg. The UK was ranked nineteenth. The Credit Suisse (2015) report on Global Wealth estimate of *median wealth per adult* indicated the UK was behind Norway and Iceland; however Sweden, Denmark and Finland were significantly further down the table. To set alongside any intra-state comparisons of income and wealth it is worth noting that almost all analysis describes the UK as one of the more unequal states in the developed world. Though the fine detail of positioning is debatable and contested, the UK and the four constituent polities all have a more unequal income distribution than the often cited four continental Scandinavian countries (Wilkinson and Pickett 2010; Atkinson 2015).

More broadly it is worth considering a comparison exercise between some of the institutional architecture observed in those countries often referred to so favourably, as clearly such architecture is linked to their various forms of success.

The general presumption, both implicit and explicit, in discussing the institutional architecture of a putative independent Scotland is that the creation of a formal written constitution is an essential, characteristic of a separate state, whether long established (e.g. the USA) or recently emergent (e.g. South Sudan – where there is an interim constitution dating to 2011). Indeed there are very few states in the United Nations that do not have formally codified constitutions often – though not always – expressed in one written document. Those that have uncodified constitutions form a short list, usually headed by the UK, and also including New Zealand, Saudi Arabia and Israel.

However, Canada, often seen as a natural reference point for Scotland (Nova Scotia, early political leaders, clan branches, etc.), sits at a mid-point with a formalised Constitution Act (1982), and various prior and consequent related legislation, but this is recognised as not being the totality of their constitutional architecture:

> The Constitution is more than a written text. It embraces the entire global system of rules and principles which govern the exercise of constitutional authority. A superficial reading of selected provisions of the written constitutional enactment, without more, may be misleading.
> (Supreme Court of Canada 1998 [*Reference Re. Secession of Quebec* 1998])

Possession of a codified constitution is certainly not in itself sufficient to ensure a well maintained state in which to live. It is commonplace to observe that in many countries with codified constitutions the stated intent of the various clauses is routinely ignored or violated by governments. In Syria, the state is described as the guarantor and protector of personal freedom and dignity. Elsewhere, the founding of divided judicial decisions on often contested interpretations of the 'black letter' or 'constructionist' view of the constitution does not always make for stable social policy or even maximise public safety. In the USA, abortion rights are currently based on Supreme Court judgements founded on the right to privacy provisions rather than specific legislation; and the Article 2 right to bear arms is linked to the maintenance of a 'sound militia' a somewhat outdated concept.

Even if we ignore these and other instances of constitutional disjunction, the overstated faith in reliance on a codified constitution can be found in many more everyday settings that are echoed in the constitution suggested for an independent Scotland.

Let us consider the case of local government, an institution whose importance to society is based both on the services provided and by its position as one of the small number of institutions usually elected by universal suffrage – hence the use of the term government, not administration.

The discussions and conclusions of the Convention of Scottish Local Authorities sponsored Commission on Local Democracy[4] Report (2014) were informed by evidence from other countries outside the UK. The overall drive of the report was related to greater community engagement, subsidiarity and greater responsibility for communities and local governments (see also Chapter 6).

Drawing on the evidence submitted by many people and organisations from elsewhere in the UK and overseas, the report observed:

> Local democracy in Scotland today is almost unique amongst western democracies because it has no status or protection in law and its institutions are wholly subject to the will of Parliament ... major changes to local democratic institutions can, and have proceeded without the kinds of checks and balances ... legally required to secure the assent of local communities in most other countries.
>
> (p. 31)

A comparison between the UK, Scotland and the four Scandinavian comparators is interesting for what it illustrates about the substance that can be found, or not found, for such claims of constitutional protection.

Review of these comparative items of codification suggests that in contrast to the CoSLA statement cited above, constitutional protection for local government is not as ironclad as is sometimes claimed.

It appears reasonably clear from each of those states that if the respective governments wish to make change to sub-state institutions they can do. The principal difference might only be that such change can be affected in the different jurisdictions of the UK more rapidly than is the case in those states with codified constitutions where there may be various delay mechanisms.

The test of this protection can be seen in the changing position of local government in the countries referred to above – and others.

As a CCRE report (2009) states:

> There has been an across the board trend towards a reduction in the number of municipalities across Europe for several decades ... Sweden ... reducing to less than an eight of the number ... Denmark to a fifth, Finland to a somewhat lesser degree.
>
> (Hermennier 2009: 5)

Such reduction in the numbers of local government units in different countries shows both that some policy drivers are widespread in governments internationally, and not really hindered by constitutional codification.

In Sweden, the state with the most ostensibly entrenched constitutional arrangements and protections, Erlingsson and Ödalen (2013) observe:

> In a comparative perspective Swedish local government is often taken to enjoy a strong constitutional status, a rather high degree of policy-making autonomy and financial independence ...
>
> (p. 29)

Table 11.1 Constitutional and statutory position of local government: some international comparators

State/country	Statutory position of local government	Comment
England; Wales; Scotland; Northern Ireland (No codified constitution)	Created by legislation; institutions can be amended by Act (e.g. Local Governance (Scotland) Act 2004).	Can be reorganised (even abolished) by Act of Parliament in any of the four jurisdictions.
Scotland (putative constitution)	There is to continue to be local government in Scotland (17.1). Local government is to be administered by local councils which have autonomy over the carrying out of their functions (17.2) (Scottish Government, 2014).	Silent on institutional shape and form, and change effected by usual legislative process.
Denmark (Constitution)	The right of municipalities to manage their own affairs independently, under State supervision, shall be laid down by statute (Art. 82). May be subject to reorganisation by legislation.	Can be reorganised by legislation; there is general provision for discretionary entrenchment on passage of legislation. Legislation can require delay and possible referendum.
Sweden (Constitution)	Swedish democracy ... shall be realised through a representative and parliamentary polity and through local self government. Public power shall be exercised under the law (Ch. 1, Art. 1). Sweden has municipalities and county councils. The decision-making power in these local authorities is exercised by elected assemblies (Ch. 1, Art. 7). The principle governing changes in the division of the Realm into local government districts, and the principles governing the organisation and working procedures of the local authorities and local taxation, are determined in law. Provisions relating to the competence of local authorities in other respects, and to their responsibilities, are likewise laid down in law (Ch. 8, Art. 5).	Can be changed by the usual legislative procedures.
Norway (legally established but not in Constitution)	Municipalities are referred to in the constitution but only in reference to other matters rather than any specific clauses about local government.	Can be changed by the usual legislative procedures.

State/country	Statutory position of local government	Comment
Finland (Constitution)	The exercise of public powers shall be based on an Act (Section 3). Finland is divided into municipalities, whose administration shall be based on the self-government of their residents. Provisions on the general principles governing municipal administration are laid down by an Act. The municipalities have the right to levy municipal tax. Provisions ... are laid down by an Act (Section 121).	Can be changed by the usual legislative procedures.

Source: Author, based on reference to relevant government websites. Accessed on various occasions.

> There is a consensus among scholars who have scrutinised the legislation, that local self-government actually does not enjoy protection in the constitution ... The mentioning of 'local government' in the constitution's first paragraph is not judicially binding.
>
> (p. 29)

In reviewing the extent and practice of constitutional codification, the entrenchment of powers and the defence of existing institutions from whimsical change, it seems that the difference in practice is not as great in practice as it is sometimes perceived from here.

The exceptionalism of comparative democracies

Outcomes

Much discussion that characterised the lengthy debate about the 2014 referendum was based on comparisons with reference to desirable outcomes better achieved in other states and jurisdictions.

The stronger published work has tended to both compare *and* contrast,[5] as for example, Keating and Harvey (2014: 17) who in their first chapter remind us:

> Big states have frequently been aggressive and expansionist; some small states have sought to expand their borders; and some small states have been peaceful and content within their own frontiers. Good and bad can be found in all categories.

To strengthen their thoroughly comparative focus, they largely concentrate on economic and social welfare factors in looking at the Scandinavian countries, the Baltic countries and Ireland – pre- and post-economic crisis.

However, in general terms the tenor of claims, even in substantial forms of publication, often implies that comparator countries demonstrated a totality of effectively integrated, sounder and more democratic institutions and processes. With these advantages of ostensibly more robust and contemporary forms of democracy, better outcomes are often claimed to have been achieved by these states. To cite the Scottish Government White Paper again:

> it is small independent European nations that have the best record of generating more wealth for all and of sharing it more fairly across society.
> (Scottish Government 2013: 56)

> Countries of comparable size to Scotland take lead roles in international organisations. Sweden, New Zealand, Switzerland and Finland have all made significant global contributions to security, peace and reconciliation initiatives.
> (Scottish Government 2013: 224)

Independent contributors to the referendum debate tend to make enthused comparisons of the positive features of other countries and cultures. So, in Riddoch (2013), the arguments the author makes for a variety of 'better elsewhere' is put much more strongly than the counter arguments. It is argued that a far greater respect for local democracy in particular, and the wider institutions of democracy are simply better provided for in Scandinavian countries; economic opportunities are better elsewhere; housing is better organised, financed and provided elsewhere – notably Germany; and health outcomes generally much better because of the way in which such contributory elements aid better health and wellbeing. Riddoch does, however, acknowledge (in an early edition of the book) that:

> This book suggests a change of constitutional control will not be enough to transform Scotland.

If we look for some contra-indicators of progress in comparator states to Scotland we are unlikely to find them in publications intended to be exhortatory and campaigning in their purpose. So, for example, what is not mentioned in either of the publications cited immediately above is that suicide rates are almost twice as high in Iceland and Finland as they are in the UK, and *all* the Scandinavian countries show suicide rates higher than the UK as a whole. Indeed suicide rates in Northern Ireland, Scotland and Wales are higher than the UK figure (WHO 2012; Samaritans 2015). It is notable that the more nuanced Wilkinson and Pickett (2010: 175) does discuss and suggest causes of this apparent anomaly in overall health and social wellbeing data.

It is not simply in policy decisions and outcomes that the curiosities or exceptionalism of comparator polities is often not discussed. The legislative and administrative architecture and processes of other states and jurisdictions are not usually analysed in any detail. One instance of this is the form and composition of different legislatures, particularly in those states which are bicameral and therefore have the often awkward and continuing balance between lower and upper house.

The geography of history

At a macro-institutional level we can actually observe that just as some similarities are cited between smaller more equal states, so there are similarities between both small and large post-imperial states. Consider some examples:

Denmark, always cited as a successful, happy and with a high level of equality is formally styled The Kingdom of Denmark, with two semi-autonomous entities in the Faroes and Greenland.

The Netherlands too, is formally styled The Kingdom of the Netherlands, which comprises Holland and three territories in the Caribbean. Additionally, there are four 'special municipalities' in the former Dutch Antilles whose residents can vote in Dutch national elections and European elections.

President de Gaulle frequently claimed that 'the Mediterranean divides France as the Seine divides Paris'. Algeria was physically far closer than are the 'overseas collectivities' in the Pacific and Indian Oceans and the group of islands off Newfoundland, all of which elect members to both houses of the French Parliament.

When this array of international post-imperial legacies is considered, it suggests that the similar array of semi-incoherent entities that comprise the UK and geographies associated closely with it (Gibraltar, Channel Islands, Isle of Man) is not so unusual after all. The legacy of empire is perhaps inherently untidy and some states find it hard to tidy it.

Unicameralism and scrutiny

The intentions of the Scottish Government in the event of independence have always appeared to be the development of a sovereign, all encompassing parliament upon the foundations of what is already a unicameral domestic parliament. Similarly, in Wales and Northern Ireland the devolved bodies have been unicameral. In contrast, the Parliament of Northern Ireland – 1921–1972 – had both a House of Commons and Senate (Government of Ireland Act 1920).

It appears that there are several reasons for this wish to maintain unicameralism. A considerable number of the comparator countries whose experience has been drawn on in building momentum for the independence case are now unicameral. Second, the characterisation of the House of Lords – wholly unelected – is seen as a significant feature of an unhealthy democracy in the current UK. Perhaps also there is tacit recognition that a government majority in its pomp is happier without a revising chamber. Part of that tension between two houses in any legislature is reflected in various states, where membership of the second chamber is achieved by means that are often not publicised or recognised globally to the extent lower house elections are.

In Ireland for example, the upper house has a combination of prime ministerial appointment, election from elite universities and vocational panel elections – all of which are sometimes manipulated by the governing parties. In France, the upper house is elected by, and solely from amongst, a population of regional and local elected officials, so privileging an entrenched rural conservative majority. In Germany, the upper house members are representatives appointed by *Länder* governments, and their votes there are cast in a block. There are other examples sufficiently widespread globally to suggest that the upper/lower house tension is not an issue found to be problematic solely in one or two jurisdictions.

However, as in other unicameral parliaments, in order to achieve effective legislative and executive scrutiny, committees have been seen as an alternative to a revising chamber. There has over time been much (declaratory) weight placed on the centrality of committees to the processes of the Scottish Parliament. In earlier years a variation of the phrase 'committees are at the heart of the Parliament' was frequently heard. This drew upon the emphasis – and the words – the Scottish Constitutional Convention (1995) gave to powerful initiating and scrutinising committees in its preparatory work aimed at achieving a parliament. Such phrases are less frequently heard now and even some majority MSPs are beginning to question the current culture of apparent committee acquiescence in the majority parliament. One recently commented, as part of a discussion on the role of committees:

> changing the system in itself is [not] the answer.
> Rather my feeling is that the answer is in the attitude of the Members of the Scottish Parliament ...
> I do think there needs to be a realisation amongst backbench members in the same party as the Government that part of their role is to scrutinise legislation and policy and hold the Government to account.
> (Robertson 2015)

The future?

This phrase is used in preference to the word 'conclusion' even though any future direction or outcome is simply impossible to predict or project.

At a political level there does appear to be an emergent, though still not openly discussed, view amongst some members of the SNP about the extent to which there were flaws in the last independence prospectus. In the Westminster Parliament – where legislation affecting the status of all parts of the UK is decided – the current prospect is of further institutional and constitutional change, but of a confused and emergent nature.

What this chapter has discussed is the degree and extent to which the complexity of the current and emergent constitutional/institutional status of the four parts of the United Kingdom and therefore of the United Kingdom will continue to influence future outcomes for both the UK and Scotland.

It is exceptionally hard to classify the form which constitutional, institutional and political architecture actually gives to the United Kingdom as a whole. It was, right from inception, not a unitary state, in the way France is and has been described as a 'union state' (Mclean and McMillan 2005). Equally it is not a federal state, in the classic sense that the United States is categorised. It is not the 'not the snappiest slogan for a political campaign' (Open Democracy 2013) but we appear to be in what I suggest we might describe as a state, the UK, that is in practice one of Assymetrical Juridical Quasi Federalism.

It is clear that the twists and turns of the continuing discussion and campaigning about the position of Scotland; the other jurisdictions of the UK; and the UK itself will continue. It also seems apparent now that a new or transformed state cannot simply emerge from, or with, a 'tabula rasa', or 'White Paper', as Locke (1996), translates that phrase. We must look forward to more White Papers.

Notes

1 The publication 'Scotland's Future: Your Guide to an Independent Scotland' (2013) was often referred to as a White Paper (as the covers were) and integrated aspects relevant to the

referendum vote and what a prospective SNP majority government would campaign upon in elections for the legislature of an independent country.
2 There are similar, indeed perhaps even greater complex aspects of the position on Northern Ireland and the various closer island entities associated with the UK.
3 The terms used are not those formally applied in Scottish courts; commonly used language may provide greater clarity. I am aware that through this I run the risk of enraging lawyers as well as supporters of independence.
4 *Declaration of Interest*: The author was a member of and academic adviser to the Commission and fully endorses the overall direction of the report.
5 It may be coincidence that the experience of marking student academic work over many years suggests that weaker students often ignore the dual aspect of compare *and* contrast questions.

Sources for further study and reading

Much of the current and live material is often best accessed through a wide range and variety of institutional and quasi-campaigning websites; two examples are:

The Centre on Consitutional Change: www.centreonconstitutionalchange.ac.uk/centre.
Open Democracy: www.opendemocracy.net/uk.

Bogdanor (see references) is prolific and in various outputs.
Keating and Harvey (see references) is a fascinating and detailed comparison of Scotland with other countries often cited as comparators.

References

Atkinson, A. (2015) *Inequality – What Can Be Done?* Cambridge, MA: Harvard University Press.
Bogdanor, V. (2009) *The New British Constitution*. London: Bloomsbury.
Breitenbach, E. (2013) 'Review of "Blossom"'. *Scotsman*, 21 September.
Cancer Research UK (2015) 'Cancer Research'. Available at: www.cancerresearchuk.org/our-research (accessed 5 October 2015).
Collier, J.G. (2001) *Conflict of Laws*. Cambridge: Cambridge University Press.
Commission on Local Democracy – Report (2014) Edinburgh: Convention of Scottish Local Authorities.
Constitutional Convention (1995) *Scotland's Parliament: Scotland's Right*. Edinburgh: Convention of Scottish Local Authorities.
Credit Suisse (2014) *The Success of Small Countries*. Zurich: Credit Suisse.
Credit Suisse (2015) *Global Wealth Data Book*. Zurich: Credit Suisse.
Devine, T. (2013) 'In Bed With an Elephant: Why Has the Union Survived for Over Three Centuries?' Lecture at the University of Edinburgh. Available at: www.youtube.com/watch?v=asMPMceNWpY (accessed 29 September 2015).
Electoral Commission (2013) News Release on Question and Campaign Spending. 30 January.
Erlingsson, G. and J. Ödalen (2013) 'How Should Local Government Be Organised? Reflections from a Swedish Perspective'. *Local Government Studies* 39(1): 22–46.
Fabre, John. (2015) 'A New Partnership: Clinicians and Politicians Must Work Together to Decentralise and Depoliticise the NHS'. *Fabian Review*, Autumn: 8.
Ferguson, Y. and R. Mansbach (1996) *Polities: Authority, Identities, and Change*. Charlotte: University of South Carolina Press.

Gallup (2013) 'Median Global Income About $10,000'. Available at: www.gallup.com/poll/166211/worldwide-median-household-income-000.aspx (accessed 1 October 2015).
Hermennier, H. (2009) 'The Quest for "Perfect Territorial Organisation" in Europe'. In seminar report. Brussels: Council of Municipalities and Regions (CCRE).
HM Government. (1920) Government of Ireland Act, London: House of Commons.
HM Government. (1994) Criminal Justice and Public Order Act. London: HMSO.
HM Government. (1944) Education Act. London: HMSO.
HM Government. (1945) Education (Scotland) Act. Edinburgh: HMSO.
HM Government. (1992) Higher and Further Education Act. London: HMSO.
HM Government. (1992) Higher and Further Education (Scotland) Act. Edinburgh: HMSO.
HM Government. (1978) Local Government Act. London: HMSO.
HM Government. (1978) Local Government (Scotland) Act. Edinburgh: HMSO.
HM Government. (1947). National Health Service (Scotland) Act. HMSO: Edinburgh.
HM Government. (1998) Scotland Act. HMSO: Edinburgh.
House of Commons Library (2005) 'The Sewel Convention'. SN/PC/2084.
Ipsos MORI (2015) 'SNP Increase Lead in the Run Up to 2016 Holyrood Election'. 2 September. Available at: www.ipsos-mori.com/researchpublications/researcharchive/3622/SNP-increase-lead-in-the-run-up-to-2016-Holyrood-election.aspx (accessed 4 September 2015).
Keating, M. and M. Harvey (2014) *Small Nations in a Big World – What Scotland Can Learn*. Edinburgh: Luath Press.
Kennedy, L. (1995) *In Bed With an Elephant: A Journey Through Scotland's Past and Present*. London: Bantam.
Kerley, R. (1994) *Managing in Local Government*. Basingstoke: Macmillan.
Locke, J. (1996) [1689] *Essay Concerning Human Understanding*. Abridged by Kenneth Winkler. Indianapolis, IN: Hackett.
Maddox, D. (2014) 'Gordon Brown: Scots Want "UK-wide School System"'. *Scotsman*, 17 June. Available at: www.scotsman.com/news/education/gordon-brown-scots-want-uk-wide-school-system-1-3445973#ixzz3pUV5r8jN (accessed 10 October 2015).
Massie, A. (2015) 'J.K. Rowling and Her Heroic Attack on the Wicked Cybernats'. *CapX*. Available at: www.capx.co/jk-rowling-and-her-heroic-attack-on-the-wicked-cybernats/ (accessed 19 October 2015).
McKenna, K. (2014) 'Welcome to Scotland, the SNP's Police State'. *The Guardian*, 19 January.
McLean, I. and A. McMillan (2005) *State of the Union*. Oxford: Oxford University Press.
McSmith, A. (2008) 'Warm Words for Icelandic Boom Return to Haunt Salmond'. *Independent*, 15 October.
Mitchell, J. (2003) *Governing Scotland: The Invention of Administrative Devolution*. London: Penguin.
Murkens, J.E., P. Jones, and M. Keating (2002) *Scottish Independence – A Practical Guide*. Edinburgh: Edinburgh University Press.
NBC News (2009) 'Lockerbie Kin: Release of Terrorist Is "Sickening"'. Available at: www.nbcnews.com/id/32494106/ns/us_news-life/t/lockerbie-kin-release-terrorist-sickening/#.VikOPpWFOUm (accessed 14 October 2015).
Open Democracy (J. Osmond) (2013) 'Wales Is Leading Debate on Federal UK'. Available at: www.opendemocracy.net/ourkingdom/john-osmond/wales-is-leading-debate-on-federal-uk (accessed 6 October 2015).
Peterkin, T. (2015) 'Anger at SNP Call to 'Control Broadcasting''. *Scotland on Sunday*, 18 October.
Philips, D. and G. Tetlow (2014) 'Taxation, Government Spending and the Public Finances of Scotland: Updating the Medium Term Outlook'. IFS Briefing Note 148. London.
Riddoch, L. (2013) *Blossom: What Scotland Needs to Flourish*. Edinburgh: Luath Press.
Robertson, A. (2015) 'SNP MSP John Mason Claims Some Party Colleagues "Too Wedded to the Party Line"'. *Holyrood Magazine*. Edinburgh. Available at: www.holyrood.com/articles/inside-p

olitics/snp-msp-john-mason-claims-some-party-colleagues-too-wedded-party-line (accessed 10 October 2015).
Samaritans (2015) *Suicide Statistics Report*. London: Samaritans.
Scottish Government (2012) Police and Fire Reform (Scotland) Act. Edinburgh: Scottish Government.
Scottish Government (2013) *Scotland's Future – Your Guide to an Independent Scotland*. Edinburgh: Scottish Government.
Scottish Government (2014) Scotland Independence Bill – Draft. Edinburgh: Scottish Government.
Smith Commission (2015) www.smith-commission.scot/ (accessed 3 October 2015).
Spencer, J.R. (n.d.) 'The European Arrest Warrant'. Mimeo.
Spruyt, H. (1994) *The Sovereign State and Its Competitors: An Analysis of Systems Change*. Princeton, NJ: Princeton University Press.
Supreme Court of Canada (1998) *Reference Re Secession of Quebec*. Available at: www.scc-csc.gc.ca/home-accueil/index-eng.aspx (accessed 29 September 2015).
Tomkins, A. (2015) 'Centralising, Illiberal, Catastrophic: The SNP's One-Party State'. *Spectator*, 14 October.
WHO – World Health Organisation (2012) *Suicide Rates – Data by Country*. Available at: http://apps.who.int/gho/data/node.main.MHSUICIDE?lang=en. (accessed 7 October 2015).
Wilkinson, R. and K. Pickett (2010) *The Spirit Level – Why Equality Is Better for Everyone*. London: Penguin.

12 The future of Scottish government and public policy
A distinctive Scottish style?

Paul Cairney

Introduction

The Scottish Government has developed a reputation for a particular 'policy style', which refers broadly to the way in which it makes and implements policy, and specifically to a comparison with the 'British policy style'. In this sense, the Scottish Government makes policy following *relatively extensive* consultation and negotiation with 'pressure participants' (Jordan et al. 2004) such as interest groups, local government organisations and unions. Further, when focused on implementation, it signals a *relative ability or willingness* to devolve the delivery of policy to other organisations in a meaningful way. It produces a national strategy, invites local bodies to produce policies consistent with it, and measures performance using broad, long term outcomes. In particular, it now encourages local authorities to cooperate with a range of other bodies in the public sector (including health, enterprise, police, fire and transport), private and 'third' sector (voluntary or charitable organisations) via 'Community Planning Partnerships' (CPPs), to produce a 'strategic vision' for each local area.

For some commentators, including the last two Scottish Government permanent secretaries, this approach marks a major departure from UK government policymaking (Elvidge 2011; Housden 2014). In turn, this departure may reflect great expectations for a new culture of politics and policymaking in Scotland, following devolution-inspired political reforms based on a rejection of 'old Westminster' (Cairney and McGarvey 2013). Certainty, the post-devolution Scottish Government has become the hub for a meaningful level of policymaking in concert with interest groups: a 'territorial policy community' (Keating et al. 2009). Further, these developments in policymaking culture have the potential to make a major impact on Scottish politics and policy.

However, it is difficult to appreciate the significance of these developments with a limited focus on Scottish distinctiveness. The UK comparison, and the idea of 'new Scottish politics', can be useful *initial* points of reference, but a sole focus on the Scottish style in relation to the UK can distract us from more important discussions, such as the extent to which:

- all governments face the same policymaking constraints, and tend to respond in similar ways;
- a 'Scottish style' takes place in a complex multi-level policymaking system, of which the Scottish Government is one of many important actors; and
- key organisations such as the Scottish Parliament are peripheral to the policymaking process.

In other words, we need to know what to expect of *any system* to be able to identify distinctly Scottish elements, and we should not assume that the 'Scottish policy style' produces relatively good outcomes simply because political reforms in Scotland produced alleged advantages over UK policymaking (Cairney et al. 2015).

Consequently, in this chapter I examine critically the idea of a distinctly Scottish style of policymaking, in four main ways. First, I outline academic descriptions of the 'Scottish policy style', as a broad way to describe the ways in which the Scottish Government makes and implements policy in a new 'territorial policy community', and the 'Scottish approach to policymaking' (SATP), as the specific way in which the Scottish Government describes its approach. Second, I compare two main explanations for the development of a new policymaking culture in Scotland: does it reflect the impact of political reforms and/or more practical reasons, such as the size and scale of the Scottish Government and its responsibilities? Third, drawing on policy theory, I examine the extent to which this approach is distinctly Scottish or consistent with the expectations that we would have for any government. Fourth, I consider the potential unintended consequences of this kind of policymaking, focusing on the wider Scottish political system, new issues of accountability, and the Scottish Government's relationship with the Scottish Parliament and 'the people'. In the concluding discussion, I use these points to consider the likely effect of future constitutional changes such as further devolution in 2015.

Territorial policy communities and the Scottish policy style

Keating et al. (2009: 54) use the term 'territorial policy communities' to describe the development of new policy networks in Scotland, caused by the devolution of new responsibilities to the Scottish Government, which prompted significant levels of UK interest group devolution, the proliferation of new Scottish groups, and the involvement of other 'pressure participants' such as businesses, unions and public bodies. These new arrangements were characterised initially by:

- a *period of adjustment*, in which ministers and civil servants adapted to their new policymaking role and groups sought new opportunities or felt obliged to lobby Scottish political institutions;
- *'cognitive change'*, in which policy problems became defined increasingly from a territorial perspective; and
- a *new group–government dynamic*, in which groups formed new relationships with their allies (and competitors).

Participants increasingly followed a devolved policy agenda. These arrangements replaced those associated with the pre-1999 Scottish Office which, as a UK government department, was responsible primarily for policy implementation: the tendency of groups to form coalitions to oppose or modify UK Conservative government policies at the margins. Now, participants respond to Scottish Government demands for new policy ideas, and often compete as well as cooperate with each other to draw attention to and define policy problems. Interview evidence suggests that some groups addressed that task more quickly than others (Keating 2005; 2010; Keating et al. 2009; Cairney and McGarvey 2013: 159). Some groups improved on links that were already partly established (in areas such as health and education), some reinforced the links that they developed with the Labour government from 1997 (including 'third sector' groups in areas such as social policy), some maintained dual UK and Scottish links, to reflect limited devolution in their areas (such as unions focusing primarily on employment policy), and others took time to get over their opposition to devolution and find a clear role (including businesses and business groups).

Still, in general, participants report a positive image of devolution and an improvement in meaningful access to policymakers and policy discussion. They refer to two aspects of a 'Scottish policy style' identified in the academic literature:

1 *Consultation.* The Scottish Government's reputation for pursuing a consultative and cooperative style with pressure participants (Keating 2005; 2010; Cairney 2009a; 2011b; 2013; Cairney and McGarvey 2013).
2 *Implementation.* Its pursuit of a distinctive 'governance' style, or a relative ability or willingness to devolve the delivery of policy to public bodies, including local authorities, in a meaningful way (Cairney 2009b).

They are generally positive about Scottish policymaking, describing low barriers to access, their ability to engage with the Scottish Government frequently, and the sense of a close network or the 'usual story of everybody knowing everybody else' (Keating et al. 2009: 57; see also Tisdall and Hill 2011: 33–35).

Many contrast these arrangements with their perception of the UK policy process as less consultative, more top-down, less reliant on professional groups or policy networks, and with more willingness to encourage groups to compete with each other. The Scottish and UK governments may also exhibit different 'governance' styles, in which the former relies more on traditional forms of public service delivery (placing its trust in bodies such as local authorities), and the latter has traditionally sought to manage a larger and more fragmented public sector landscape by relying more on 'new public management' methods such as quasi-markets and competition between service providers, and short term policy targets and relatively punitive forms of performance management (Cairney 2009b: 360–361).

Greer and Jarman (2008: 172–173) make this argument most strongly in a comparison of Scottish and British styles, in education, local government, and health, from 1999 to 2007 (when Labour was in office in the UK, and led a coalition government in Scotland). The UK government encouraged a range of different schools, relatively independent of local authority control, to compete with each other, using mechanisms such as pupil testing to help build up league tables of school performance. It introduced tuition fees and encouraged universities to compete with each other to recruit students. It set specific and rigid targets for local authorities and used an audit and inspection regime to make sure that they were met. Further, in health policy, it set targets on aims such as reducing waiting times for treatment (backed by strong punishments to chief executives for non-compliance) and encouraged relatively independent 'foundation' hospitals to compete with each other for business (2008: 173–178). In contrast, the Scottish Government oversaw a 'comprehensive' schooling system, relatively subject to local authority control, with less competition based on pupil testing. It rejected the introduction of tuition fees to Scottish students. It set targets for local authorities but used fewer punitive measures to ensure delivery, and it set health policy targets but without competition within health service markets or a punitive regime (2008: 178–183).

Notably, these developments took place before the election of an SNP-led government which, from 2007, criticised its predecessors in the Scottish Government for being obsessed with short term targets and performance management. The wording used by former first minister Alex Salmond to signal a new Scottish governance style – 'The days of top-down diktats are over' – was largely rhetorical, but it signalled an intention to redefine the relationship between central and local government (Cairney 2011a: 130; Cairney and McGarvey 2013: 142; Cairney 2014: 9).

The 'Scottish approach to policymaking'

These developments, before and after the election of an SNP Government in 2007, can be linked strongly to the ways in which the Scottish Government has described its own policy style. An early version of the 'Scottish approach' developed before 2007. The Scottish Government's former permanent secretary Sir John Elvidge (2011: 31–35) describes a 'Scottish model of government', linked to the potential to exploit its relatively small size, and central position in a dense network of public sector and third sector bodies, to pursue a form of 'holistic' government, in which ministers – and their equivalents in the civil service – had briefs which spanned traditional departmental divides and came together regularly to coordinate national strategies (see also Parry 2001; Parry and Jones 2000).

Elvidge (2011: 31) describes 'the concept of a government as a single organisation' and 'the idea of "joined up government" taken to its logical conclusions'. He links this agenda to his belief that 'traditional policy and operational solutions' based on 'the target driven approach which characterised the conduct of the UK Government' would not produce the major changes in policy and policymaking required to address major problems such as health and educational inequalities and low economic growth. Instead, they required 'more integrated approaches, such as the approach to the early years of children's lives ... which looked across the full range of government functions [and] offered the scope for some significant and unexpected fresh policy perspectives' (2011: 32).

Elvidge (2011: 32) suggests that this approach took off under the SNP-led Scottish Government, elected in May 2007, partly because his ideas on joined up government complemented the SNP's:

> manifesto commitments to: i) an outcome based approach to the framing of the objectives of government and to enabling the electorate to hold the Government to account for performance; ii) a reduced size of Cabinet, which was an expression of a commitment to an approach to Ministerial responsibilities that emphasised the collective pursuit of shared objectives over a focus on individual portfolios with disaggregated objectives.

By 2007, the 'Scottish approach' combined the pursuit of joined up government with the SNP's 'outcomes based approach to delivering the objectives of government', a 'single statement of purpose, elaborated into a supporting structure of a small number of broad objectives and a larger, but still limited, number of measurable national outcomes' (2011: 34).

The Scottish Government introduced a government-wide policy framework, the *National Performance Framework* (NPF), based on a single 'ten year vision' and a shift towards measuring success in terms of often-long term outcomes (Scottish Government

2007: 2014). The NPF has a stated 'core purpose – to create a more successful country, with opportunities for all of Scotland to flourish, through increasing sustainable economic growth'. It seeks to turn this broad purpose into specific policies and measures of success in two main ways. First, it articulates in more depth its national approach via a 'purpose framework' – linked to targets gauging its economic growth, productivity, labour market participation, population, income inequality, regional inequality and (emissions based) sustainability – and five 'strategic objectives':

1   Wealthier and Fairer – Enabling businesses and people to increase their wealth and more people to share fairly in that wealth.
2   Healthier – Helping people to sustain and improve their health, especially in disadvantaged communities, ensuring better, local and faster access to health care.
3   Safer and Stronger – Helping communities to flourish, becoming stronger, safer places to live, offering improved opportunities and a better quality of life.
4   Smarter – Expanding opportunities to succeed from nurture through to lifelong learning ensuring higher and more widely shared achievements.
5   Greener – Improving Scotland's natural and built environment and the sustainable use and enjoyment of it.

These objectives are mapped onto sixteen 'National Outcomes' and fifty 'National Indicators'. It then works in partnership with the public sector to align organisational objectives with the NPF. In some cases, this involves public sector reform and/or some attempts at centralisation: it obliged non-departmental public bodies (NDPBs, or 'quangos') to align their objectives with the NPF, after reducing their number, and it created a single police force and single fire service.

In the case of local authorities, its approach was different. It required them to produce 'Single Outcomes Agreements' (SOAs), in partnership with their stakeholders (and public sector partners), but with local government discretion to determine the balance between a range of priorities as long as their outcomes were consistent with the NPF's vision (Keating 2010: 123–124; Matthews 2014). The Scottish Government reinforced this sense of discretion by signing a Concordat with the Convention of Scottish Local Authorities (COSLA) which contained a package of Scottish Government aims, but also its agreement to halve the amount of 'hypothecated' budgets and reject a tendency to 'micromanage' local government – albeit within the context of a system in which the Scottish Government controls almost all of local authorities' total budgets (Scottish Government and COSLA 2007; Cairney 2011a; Cairney and McGarvey 2013: 139–140; Housden, 2014: 68).

Since 2013, the Scottish Government has sought to reinforce the 'Scottish approach' with reference to three broad principles (Scottish Government and ESRC 2013: 4):

1   *Improvement*. The pursuit of improvement in public services, to help it deliver on its holistic government agenda, in partnership with stakeholders. For example, it has overseen the development of the 'Early Years Collaborative', in which the Scottish Government identifies promising policy interventions and asks practitioners to experiment with their own projects in their local areas (Housden 2014: 68). This approach is designed partly to address the idea that local policymakers are more likely to adopt interventions if they are developed locally and/or tailored to local circumstances.

2 *Assets*. A focus on the 'assets of individuals and communities, rather than only focusing on perceived deficits' (Scottish Government and ESRC 2013: 4). Housden (2014: 67–68) suggests that, 'we look always to build on and strengthen the assets and resilience of individuals, families and communities. Community grant schemes and devolved budgets can build assets and stimulate local action and decision-making. Recovery programmes for those seeking to exit drug use look to draw on the resources and potential of those in recovery themselves to assist others on the journey.'

3 *Co-production*. The 'co-production' of public services 'by both service providers and the citizens and communities who receive and engage with those services' (Scottish Government and ESRC 2013: 4). Housden (2014: 67) suggests that, 'we put a real premium on the idea of co-production, with services designed and delivered with service users and organisations. This ranges from self-directed care for elderly people and those managing chronic conditions or disabilities, to the networks of support for children with learning difficulties with parents and voluntary organisations at their heart.'

Overall, the 'Scottish approach' began as a broad idea about how to govern by consensus in a new era of devolved politics, but developed into a way to pursue: holistic government, an outcomes-based measure of policy success, greater local authority discretion in the delivery of national objectives, and several governance principles built primarily on localism and the further inclusion of service users in the design of public policy. According to Elvidge (2011) and Housden (2014), this approach contrasts markedly with UK policymaking and, in particular, the UK Labour Government's approach from 1997 (as described by Greer and Jarman, above).

Why is there a Scottish policy style?

It is easier to identify the sense, among participants, that they are part of a new policymaking culture in Scotland, than to describe it in detail and explain its origin. There are two main potential explanations. The first is that Scottish policymaking now reflects the 'new Scottish politics' agenda, which refers to an extensive series of political reforms made possible during the establishment of new Scottish institutions in 1999. The phrase 'new politics' should be understood with reference to 'old Westminster'. These phrases represented important reference points for the 'architects of devolution', or the reformers keen to present devolution as a way to transfer policymaking responsibilities *and reform political practices* (Cairney and McGarvey 2013: 12). These aims can be associated with two foundational documents. The Scottish Constitutional Convention's (1995) influential document, *Scotland's Parliament: Scotland's Right*, made a general case for political reform:

> the coming of a Scottish Parliament will usher in a way of politics that is radically different from the rituals of Westminster: more participative, more creative, less needlessly confrontational.

To all intents and purposes, it drew on an understanding of politics associated more broadly with Lijphart's (1999) distinction between Westminster-style 'majoritarian' democracies and 'consensus' democracies associated with countries such as

Switzerland. In a majoritarian democracy the plurality voting system exaggerates governing majorities by (generally) granting a majority of seats in the legislature to a party which commands only a plurality of the vote. Lijphart (1999: 2–3) associates majoritarian democracies with an 'exclusive, competitive and adversarial' mentality in which parties compete within Parliament, interest groups are more likely to compete with each other than cooperate, and governments are more likely to impose policy from the top down than seek consensus. In a consensus democracy, the proportional electoral system generally produces no overall majority and power is dispersed across parties, encouraging the formation of coalitions based on common aims and a spirit of 'inclusiveness, bargaining and compromise'. This spirit extends to group–government relations, with groups more likely to cooperate with each other and governments more willing to encourage corporatist alliances (see also Cairney and McGarvey 2013: 157; compare with Jordan and Cairney 2013; Cairney and Widfeldt 2015).

Then, the report of the Consultative Steering Group (CSG) (1998), which designed the operation of the Scottish Parliament with regard to four key principles – 'power sharing', 'accountability', 'equal opportunities' and 'openness and participation' – reinforced the idea that Scottish Government policymaking would take place in a new political context. For example, the Scottish Parliament would represent a key hub for new forms of participation – including a new petitions process – and monitor the quality of draft legislation with regard to the Scottish Government's consultation process.

Yet, we should not expect too much from the agenda set by each document. For example, the SCC effectively describes its *hopes* for a new political culture to develop from political reform, but without the introduction of specific measures – beyond a new and more proportional electoral system – to deliver that aim. Further, in many ways, the CSG describes a fairly traditional Westminster system of government, in which popular participation is often peripheral to the policy process and parliamentary engagement is generally restricted to the scrutiny of government policy (Cairney and Johnston 2014).

In that context, the second explanation may seem more convincing: the Scottish policymaking culture generally reflects a pragmatic response to the size and scale of the Scottish Government and its responsibilities. The Scottish Government can do things differently because the public sector landscape is smaller, which allows its government to develop closer relationships with key actors, and develop relatively high levels of trust in other bodies to deliver public services (Cairney 2013). Further, the small research capacity of the Scottish Government prompts civil servants to rely more on external experts and the organisations with experience of policy implementation. Indeed, the Scottish Government's relative willingness to trust policy delivery to those organisations may reflect its reliance on them to make policy work. In that sense, a move from UK to Scottish government added a new 'territorial' dimension to 'universal' drivers in policymaking.

Policymaking in Scotland: which aspects are territorial, and which are 'universal'?

Most policy theories identify key processes that are common to political systems. They are abstract enough to be considered 'universal', or applicable to any time period or political system. The most relevant concept is 'bounded rationality' (Simon 1976: xxviii), which contrasts with the ideal-type, 'comprehensive rationality', in which a policymaker has a perfect ability to translate her values and aims into policy following a comprehensive study of all choices and their effects. Instead, policymakers have limited resources: the time to devote to research, the information to inform decisions, the knowledge to understand the policy context, and the ability to pay attention to issues.

Policymakers cannot process issues comprehensively. By necessity, they have to make decisions in the face of *uncertainty* and *ambiguity* (Kingdon 1984; Zahariadis 2007: 66; Cairney 2012: 234). Uncertainty relates to the amount of information they have to inform policy and policymaking: policymakers use short cuts to gather information and understand complex issues, such as by relying on particular sources and types of information. Ambiguity relates to the way in which they understand policy problems: policymakers use emotional or 'gut level' shortcuts to understand issues, and pressure participants compete to draw attention to certain problems and determine the main way in which policymakers understand them (Schneider et al. 2014; Dearing and Rogers 1996: 1; Baumgartner and Jones 1993; 2009).

A common response to the limits of bounded rationality, in many if not most political systems, involves policymakers developing the routines that we might be tempted to attribute specifically to Scottish policymaking: they consult and form relationships with pressure participants. The establishment of 'policy networks' or 'sub-systems' is widespread, because the same logic of policymaking exists across a wide range of countries. The size and scope of most states is so large that their responsibilities are potentially unmanageable: policymakers only have the cognitive ability to pay attention to, and manage, a small proportion of their responsibilities. Consequently, governments break their component parts down into more manageable policy sectors and sub-sectors, with power spread across government and shared with pressure participants.

Ministers and senior civil servants devolve the bulk of decision-making to less senior officials who consult with participants such as interest groups, professional bodies, unions, businesses, public bodies and service providers. In a sense, they share power or responsibility for policy because they are able to exchange or combine their resources: civil servants offer access to policymaking, while participants offer resources such as information, advice, expertise, and the ability to generate wider support for, or smooth the implementation of, policies. This exchange encourages group 'ownership' of policy and maximises governmental knowledge of possible problems.

'Policy community' often describes well this relationship between civil servants and certain groups (Jordan and Cairney 2013). A sense of 'membership' of that community is often based on the willingness of its members to follow and enforce the same 'rules of the game'. When civil servants and groups form relationships, they recognise the benefits – such as institutional stability and policy continuity – of maintaining regular dialogue based on past agreements, which can produce the sense that they 'insulate' their decision-making routine from the wider political process. For example, inclusion within the community might depend on gaining the personal trust of policymakers, built on providing reliable information or acting in a reasonable way when you don't secure the policies you favour. Or group–government relationships might become based on a 'common culture' in which there is strong agreement on the nature of, and best solutions to, policy problems. In other words, policymakers develop networks to generate information and reduce uncertainty, and they interact with participants to agree on the nature of the policy problem, to reduce ambiguity.

We can derive two main conclusions from this basic insight. First, since this process is common to political systems, we need to identify more than the Scottish

Government's reputation for consultation before we conclude that Scottish policy-making is distinctive (Cairney 2008: 358). Indeed, Richardson (1982) originally used the term 'policy style' to challenge us to rely on more than policymaking reputations. His edited volume, on styles in Western Europe, identified policymaking similarities in ostensibly different political systems: a tendency to build on past policies and engage in regular consultation, even in the UK. This argument has been reinforced regularly in the literature which focuses on the UK or compares its policymaking with other countries (see, for example, Jordan and Cairney 2013; Kriesi et al. 2006: 357–358; Adam and Kriesi 2007: 140; Cairney 2011b; Cairney 2012: 88–91; Cairney and Widfeldt 2015).

Second, a focus on 'communities' helps us examine a different image of policy-making in systems such as Scotland: as being relatively closed or insulated. If policy-making is built on factors such as resources and trust, built up through regular discussion, then time-strapped Scottish policymakers may often rely on the 'usual suspects' rather than a wide and inclusive process to gather information and advice (Cairney and McGarvey 2013: 163). Not all groups have the resources to engage on a day-to-day basis, or to develop long term links with policymakers. Many groups can participate in set-piece events, designed to gather as many responses as possible in a short period of time, but not the more regular interaction in which policymakers and participants generate agreement on which problems to solve first, how to understand them, and how to turn a broad policy aim into detailed objectives.

This limitation takes on greater significance when we consider that policymaking takes place in a multi-level system. The idea of a 'Scottish policy style' is often misleading when so many policies affecting Scotland take place at other levels of government. This complication provides a major dilemma for interest groups seeking influence but recognising the need to maintain multiple channels of access. For example, some groups only have the resources to lobby the Scottish Government, and rely on their networks with other groups to lobby UK and EU bodies. Other groups are regional branches of UK organisations and can focus on Scotland in the knowledge that their colleagues maintain other important links.

Much depends on the policy issue or area and the extent to which policy responsibilities can be contained primarily in one level of government (Cairney and McGarvey 2013: 164–167). For example, major banks, businesses, and unions maintain Scottish links but focus their attention largely on issues – such as macroeconomic policy, export regulations, and employment laws – reserved to the UK Government and/or influenced by EU bodies. Groups seeking influence over environmental or agricultural policy recognise that they are heavily 'Europeanised'. This leaves key examples of devolved areas, such as education, health, local government, and housing, in which groups are most likely to direct their attention primarily to the Scottish Government.

Yet, even in such cases, there is a tendency for devolved issues to contain many aspects of UK and EU responsibility. For example, public health is largely devolved, but responsibility for alcohol and tobacco control spans the three levels (Cairney et al. 2012; Asare et al. 2009). Further, the Scottish Government's legislation to introduce a minimum unit price on alcohol (Holden and Hawkins 2012) has been challenged by the alcohol industry in the courts, providing a good example of an imbalance of resources – to support or challenge policies – among participants.

The multi-level nature of policymaking has also taken on new significance following the Scottish Government agenda to produce broad strategies, in consultation with participants, then delegate a meaningful level of responsibility for policy decisions to local public bodies, such as local authorities, which are expected to develop their own policymaking arrangements and policy strategies with stakeholders. Participants now face the need to maintain multiple channels of access with many local public bodies, to monitor and further influence the progress of policy. This new requirement produces new imbalances of influence and may undermine the sense of a uniformly 'Scottish' style of consultation and delivery when power is devolved locally.

Overall, while the Scottish Government oversees an open and consultative system, this process is situated within a complicated set of multi-level arrangements, in which groups may only be effective if they have the resources to engage in many arenas. The 'Scottish policy style' may be distinctive, but it still produces winners and losers, favouring some groups and excluding others.

The new Scottish political system: the role of the Scottish Parliament and 'the people'

These arguments, about the potential for insulated decision-making, and the complications of multi-level policymaking, also have a particular relevance to the 'new politics' inspired idea of 'power sharing' between the Scottish Government, Parliament, and 'the people. In practice, the 'Scottish style' operates within a Westminster-style political system in which the Scottish Parliament is often peripheral to the policy process and meaningful levels of wider public participation are hard to find. There may be specific examples of public participation in policy design, but they are generally managed by the Scottish Government, not the Scottish Parliament (with the exception of some high profile petitions). Further, developments I described in relation to Scottish governance have the potential to further undermine the role of Parliament.

This issue is best demonstrated with a focus on accountability. Like all members of the 'Westminster family', the Scottish Parliament is part of an apparently simple accountability process: power is concentrated in the hands of ministers, who are accountable to the public through Parliament (Cairney and Johnston 2014). With this model, power and responsibility go hand in hand since, if you know who is in charge, you know who to reward or punish in the next election. Until then, you know who to hold to account through parliamentary processes. In Westminster systems, this 'parliamentary tradition' – of the transmission of electoral opinion and consent to the executive via a representative institution – has persisted over time as the foundation of the British state (Judge 1993: 5). In a system 'with a dominant executive and without legal checks provided by a constitutional court', ministerial accountability to Parliament is the main way in which the government legitimises its actions (Woodhouse 1994: 3). The 'presumption of the ultimate authority of Parliament', delegated to ministers, allows a government to portray its policies as 'authoritative' and 'binding' (Judge 1990: 29–30; 1993: 2; Norton 1990: 178).

As in Westminster, this simple picture of ministerial accountability is increasingly misleading. Ministers are not accountable to Parliament in this way because they are not in control of the policy process. Instead, they can only pay attention a fraction of the issues for which they are responsible, and delegate the remainder to policy communities. This informs our understanding of the 'Scottish policy style' in relation to consultation: these relatively open, consensual, and sometimes superficial processes take place in one arena, conducted by the Scottish Government and overseen by the

Scottish Parliament. However, the more day-to-day consultation and negotiation, associated with policy communities, takes place out of the parliamentary spotlight, often with minimal scrutiny.

Further, parliamentary scrutiny does not operate well alongside the Scottish Government's *governance* style. The Scottish Government inherited a large and complicated public sector landscape, consisting of government agencies, quangos, local authorities, health boards, and service delivery organisations in the third and private sector. While it has an extensive regulatory and audit function to address this proliferation of bodies and arrangements (Cairney and McGarvey 2013), there is little clarity about what is responsible to who in any meaningful sense. There is no simple diagram to visualise the public sector accountability landscape. Instead, as in the UK, we can identify Scottish Government attempts to develop a strategy to balance potentially contradictory aims:

1 To maintain Westminster-style democratic accountability, which requires a strong sense of central government and ministerial control.
2 To further the role of institutional accountability, through performance management measures applied to the chief executives of public bodies, such as elected local authorities and unelected agencies and quangos.
3 To advance the idea of shared 'ownership' of policy choices, partly through consultation, and partly through delegation and the encouragement of 'community planning partnerships' to bring together local authorities, public bodies, and stakeholders in local areas.
4 To develop user based notions of accountability, when public bodies and users 'co-produce' and share responsibility for the outcomes.

This is a difficult balancing act, to recognise the realities of 'complex government' over which ministers have limited control (Cairney 2015), but take responsibility for how they address this problem. The pursuit of institutional accountability could help clarify the responsibility of public bodies, or it could produce a fragmented public landscape in which no one seems to take responsibility. A move away from hierarchy and central targets, to focus more on 'co-production' of services with users could promote user-based accountability and/or diminish a sense of democratic accountability (Gains and Stoker 2009). A focus on community partnerships could diminish the sense that we can hold any of the individual actors to account.

Many of these issues could be addressed by a Scottish Parliament focused on holding ministers to account and developing direct relationships with public bodies. Yet, the evidence to date suggests that Scottish Parliament committees have limited resources to scrutinise policy and question ministers effectively. They rarely engage in meaningful or direct contact with civil servants, they struggle to gather information on the work of public bodies, and, local authorities generally argue that they are accountable to their electorates, not Parliament (Cairney 2011a: 56). Consequently, no parliament can hope to monitor the entirety of the policy process over which it has official control. For example, to focus on the areas of most visible ministerial action is to pay attention to a tiny fraction of public sector activity. To go beyond this focus requires resources that no parliament possesses.

At the heart of this issue is a puzzle that all governments face: how do you strike a balance between central government control and local government discretion (Cairney et al. 2015)? In the case of the Scottish Parliament, the question relates to a balance between traditional Westminster-style democratic accountability, and new forms of institutional, local and individual accountability. In broader terms, the trade-off is between 'loaded' terms, such as 'local flexibility' versus a 'postcode lottery' in the delivery of services within the same political system. It should prompt us to consider what 'Scottish policy' or a 'Scottish style' means when important decisions are made at local levels. It should also prompt us to reflect on the extent to which our focus on high-stakes Scottish Parliament elections, based on the Scottish Government's record and its delivery of specific policies, accords with this chapter's focus on new governance relationships, based on a national strategy, broad and long term measures of outcomes, and local discretion.

Concluding discussion: what is the future of Scottish policymaking?

The academic phrase 'Scottish policy style' sums up the ways in which the Scottish Government makes and implements policy. Most academic accounts, and particularly those based on interviews with participants, describe a relatively high willingness to pursue consensus through consultation and place their trust in public bodies, such as local authorities, to deliver policy. To many participants, this setup compares favourably with that of the UK government, which they describe as less consultative and based on mechanisms, such as punitive performance management and market-based measures, which demonstrate a relatively low level of trust in delivery bodies. The Scottish Government tells a similar story of devolved policymaking in which there is a 'Scottish approach' that is more inclusive, strategic, joined up, and better equipped to solve policy problems than its UK government equivalent.

It is important to question how accurate this story is. For example, it is tempting to relate it to the idea of 'new Scottish politics' and conclude that a tendency towards consensus reflects political reforms which reinforced a Scottish tradition of inclusive and participative politics. Yet, other explanations often seem more convincing: the logic, generated from a wealth of policy studies, that the 'Scottish' style actually operates, in similar forms, in many political systems; and, a sense that a distinctively Scottish policymaking culture relates more to the size and capacity of Scottish Government and its public sector.

It is also important to consider different interpretations, or less positive aspects, of these arrangements. For example, there are alternative stories about the limited extent to which the Scottish Government 'lets go' and encourages local discretion, focusing on a budget system with little local input and a tendency to centralise or reform many of the parts of the public sector (in other words, the bodies which tend to be local government's key partners). Further, as in any political system, there are clear winners and losers, not only in relation to policy decisions, but also the ability of pressure participants to engage in multi-level politics. Some groups only have the ability to engage with the Scottish Government, and struggle to respond to a new governance agenda in which local authorities are expected to produce their own policy strategies in concert with stakeholders.

Perhaps most importantly, these arrangements have a clear impact on the Scottish Parliament and its role as the embodiment of democratic accountability. They reduce the ability of the Scottish Parliament to monitor Scottish Government policy in detail, while new forms of accountability – institutional, community, service user – perhaps compensate for a diminished parliamentary role.

In other words, there are good reasons to maintain and reinforce the use of policy communities and local policymaking arrangements, but they make it increasingly difficult to know who is responsible for policy outcomes and, therefore, who or what to hold to account. In the Scottish political system, the Scottish Government processes the vast majority of policy, but delegates a large part of that responsibility to other organisations, the Scottish Parliament is generally peripheral to that day-to-day policy process, and the public has limited opportunities for direct influence.

This is important background which should inform debates on constitutional change, such as the further devolution afforded by the Scotland Act 2015 (or indeed the prospect of Scottish independence in the future): are they accompanied by measures to ensure a meaningful degree of accountability or, for example, will the Scottish Parliament have to scrutinise more ministerial activity with the same paltry resources? As things stand, people already struggle to know who to hold to account in a relatively simple system in which there is a quite-clear list of devolved powers and tax/welfare powers stay with the UK. When more powers become shared between the UK and Scottish governments, the idea of Scottish ministerial accountability to the Scottish Parliament may become even more misleading or limited.

Such developments may prompt discussions about three types of reform. The first relates to a greater need to develop local participatory capacity, to take on the functions performed less by national organisations. For example, the ERS Scotland's (2014) suggestion is that more local devolution could produce a more active local population. Even so, we still need to know more about how and why people organise. For example, local communities may organise in an *ad hoc* way to address major issues in their area as they arise; to engage in a small part of the policy process at a particular time. They do not have the resources to engage in a more meaningful way, compared to a Parliament and collection of established groups which maintain a constant presence and develop knowledge of the details of policies over time.

The second relates to governance reforms which focus primarily on the relationship between elected local authorities, a wide range of unelected public bodies, and service users. There is some potential to establish a form of legitimacy through local elections but, as things stand, local authorities are expected to work in partnership with unelected bodies – not hold them to account. There is also some scope to develop a form of user-driven public service accountability, but separate from the electoral process and with an uncertain focus on how that process fits into the wider picture.

The third relates to parliamentary reform. The Scottish Parliament has begun to respond significantly to governance trends and a shift to outcomes-focused policymaking (largely via inquiries and procedural reforms by its Finance Committee). However, in many ways, its main role is to scrutinise draft Scottish Government legislation as it is introduced and its committees devote two to three months per year to the scrutiny of the annual budget bill. In general, this scrutiny has a very narrow focus, with a limited emphasis on pre- or post-legislative scrutiny, and its value is unclear. It has the potential to change its role. It can shift its activities towards a focus on Scottish Government policy in broader terms, through the work of inquiries in general and its finance and audit functions in particular. However, its role will remain limited as long as it has a small permanent staff. The devolution of greater responsibilities to the Scottish Government, without a proportionate increase in Scottish Parliament research capacity, could simultaneously *enhance and undermine* the Scottish Parliament's powers.

Sources for further study

Journal articles

Cairney, P., S. Russell, and E. St Denny (2015) 'The "Scottish Approach" to Policy and Policymaking: What Issues Are Territorial and What Are Universal?' *Policy and Politics*, Early view (open access) available at: https://paulcairney.files.wordpress.com/2013/08/cairney-russell-st-denny-2015-pp-scottish-approach.pdf.

Housden, P. (2014) 'This Is Us: A Perspective on Public Services in Scotland'. *Public Policy and Administration* 29(1): 64–74.

Blog posts and websites

Paul Cairney (2015) 'Politics and Policymaking in Scotland'. Available at: https://paulcairney.wordpress.com/polu9sp/.

Zoe Ferguson (2015) 'What Is "the Scottish Approach"?' Available at: www.alliance4usefulevidence.org/what-is-the-scottish-approach/.

Peter Housden (2014) 'This Is Us'. Available at: https://quarterly.blog.gov.uk/2014/04/16/this-is-us/.

Centre on Constitutional Change. Available at: www.centreonconstitutionalchange.ac.uk/.

References

Adam, S. and H. Kriesi (2007) 'The Network Approach'. In Sabatier, P. (ed.) *Theories of the Policy Process* (2nd edn). Boulder, CO: Westview Press.

Asare, B., P. Cairney and D. Studlar (2009) 'Federalism and Multilevel Governance in Tobacco Control Policy: The European Union, United Kingdom, and Devolved Institutions'. *Journal of Public Policy* 29(1): 79–102.

Baumgartner, F. and B. Jones (1993; 2009) *Agendas and Instability in American Politics* (1st and 2nd edns). Chicago, IL: Chicago University Press.

Cairney, P. (2008) 'Has Devolution Changed the British Policy Style?'. *British Politics* 3(3): 350–372.

Cairney, P. (2009a) 'The "British Policy Style" and Mental Health: Beyond the Headlines'. *Journal of Social Policy* 38(4): 1–18.

Cairney, P. (2009b) 'Implementation and the Governance Problem: A Pressure Participant Perspective'. *Public Policy and Administration* 24(4): 355–377.

Cairney, P. (2011a) *The Scottish Political System Since Devolution: From New Politics to the New Scottish Government*. Exeter: Imprint Academic.

Cairney, P. (2011b) 'The New British Policy Style: From a British to a Scottish Political Tradition?' *Political Studies Review* 9(2): 208–220.

Cairney, P. (2012) *Understanding Public Policy: Theories and Issues*. Basingstoke: Palgrave.

Cairney, P. (2013) 'Territorial Policy Communities and the Scottish Policy Style: The Case of Compulsory Education'. *Scottish Affairs* 82(Winter): 10–34.

Cairney, P. (2014) 'The Territorialisation of Interest Representation in Scotland: Did Devolution Produce a New Form of Group–Government Relations?' *Territory, Politics, Governance*, advance access, available at: http://dx.doi.org/10.1080/21622671.2014.952326.

Cairney, P. (2015) 'What Is Complex Government?'. *Public Money and Management* 35(1): 3–6.

Cairney, P. and J. Johnston (2014) 'What Is the Role of the Scottish Parliament?' *Scottish Parliamentary Review* 1(2): 91–130.

Cairney, P. and N. McGarvey (2013) *Scottish Politics* (2nd edn). Basingstoke: Palgrave.

Cairney, P., S. Russell, and E. St Denny (2015) 'The "Scottish Approach" to Policy and Policymaking: What Issues Are Territorial and What Are Universal?' *Policy and Politics*, Early view (open access).

Cairney, P., D. Studlar and H. Mamudu (2012) *Global Tobacco Control: Power, Policy, Governance and Transfer*. Basingstoke: Palgrave.

Cairney, P. and A. Widfeldt (2015) 'Is Scotland a Westminster style Majoritarian Democracy or a Scandinavian-style Consensus Democracy?'. *Regional and Federal Studies* 25(1): 1–18.

Consultative Steering Group (1998) *Shaping Scotland's Parliament: Report of the Consultative Steering Group on the Scottish Parliament*. Edinburgh: Scottish Office.

Dearing, J.W. and E.M. Rogers (1996) *Agenda Setting*. London: Sage.

Elvidge, J. (2011) *Northern Exposure: Lessons from the First Twelve Years of Devolved Government in Scotland*. London: Institute of Governance. Available at: www.instituteforgovernment.org.uk/publications/44/.

ERS (Electoral Reform Society) Scotland (2013) *Democracy Max*. Edinburgh: ERS. Available at: www.electoral-reform.org.uk/images/dynamicImages/erss_roundtable_book_a5_v3_web(1).pdf.

Gains, F. and G. Stoker (2009) 'Delivering "Public Value": Implications for Accountability and Legitimacy'. *Parliamentary Affairs* 62(3): 438–455.

Greer, S. and H. Jarman (2008) 'Devolution and Policy Styles'. In Trench, A. (ed.) *The State of the Nations 2008*, Exeter: Imprint Academic, pp. 167–197.

Holden, C. and B. Hawkins (2012) '"Whisky gloss": The Alcohol Industry, Devolution and Policy Communities in Scotland'. *Public Policy and Administration* 28(3): 253–273.

Housden, P. (2014) 'This Is Us: A Perspective on Public Services in Scotland'. *Public Policy and Administration* 29(1): 64–74.

Jordan, G. and P. Cairney (2013) 'What Is the "Dominant Model" of British Policy Making?' *British Politics* 8(3): 233–259.

Jordan, G., D. Halpin and W. Maloney (2004) 'Defining Interests: Disambiguation and the Need for New Distinctions'. *British Journal of Politics and International Relations* 6: 195–212.

Judge, D. (1990) 'Parliament and Interest Representation'. In Rush, M. (ed.) *Parliament and Pressure Politics*. Oxford: Clarendon Press.

Judge, D. (1993) *The Parliamentary State*. London: Sage.

Keating, M. (2005; 2010) *The Government of Scotland* (1st and 2nd edns). Edinburgh: Edinburgh University Press.

Keating, M., P. Cairney and E. Hepburn (2009) 'Territorial Policy Communities and Devolution in the United Kingdom'. *Cambridge Journal of Regions, Economy and Society* 2(1): 51–66.

Kingdon, J. (1984) *Agendas, Alternatives and Public Policies*. New York: HarperCollins.

Kriesi, H., S. Adam and M. Jochum (2006) 'Comparative Analysis of Policy Networks in Western Europe'. *Journal of European Public Policy* 13(3): 341–361.

Lijphart, A. (1999) *Patterns of Democracy*. New Haven, CT: Yale University Press.

Matthews, P. (2014) 'Being Strategic in Partnership – Interpreting Local Knowledge of Modern Local Government'. *Local Government Studies* (ahead of print) available at: www.tandfonline.com/doi/abs/10.1080/03003930.2013.859141#.Uv433cZFCUk.

Norton, P. (1990) 'Public Legislation'. In Rush, M. (ed.) *Parliament and Pressure Politics*. Oxford: Clarendon Press.

Parry, R. (2001) 'The Role of Central Units in the Scottish Government'. *Public Money and Management* 21(2): 39–44.

Parry, R. and A. Jones (2000) 'The Transition from the Scottish Office to the Scottish Government'. *Public Policy and Administration* 15(2): 53–66.

Richardson, J.J. (ed.) (1982) *Policy Styles in Western Europe*. London: Allen & Unwin.

Schneider, A., H. Ingram and P. deLeon (2014) 'Democratic Policy Design: Social Construction of Target Populations'. In Sabatier, P. and Weible, C. (eds) *Theories of the Policy Process* (3rd edn). Boulder, CO: Westview Press.

Scottish Constitutional Convention (1995) *Scotland's Parliament: Scotland's Right*. Edinburgh: Convention of Scottish Local Authorities.

Scottish Government (2007; 2014) 'Performance'. Edinburgh: Scottish Government. Available at: www.scotland.gov.uk/About/Performance.

Scottish Government and COSLA (2007) 'Concordat Between the Scottish Government and COSLA'. Edinburgh: Scottish Government.
Scottish Government and ESRC (2013) 'What Works Scotland (WWS)'. Available at: www.esrc.ac.uk/_images/WWS%20Call%20spec%20FINAL%2006%20Jan%202014_tcm8-29575.pdf.
Simon, H. (1976) *Administrative Behavior* (3rd edn). London: Macmillan.
Tisdall, K. and Hill, M. (2011) 'Policy Change under Devolution: The Prism of Children's Policy'. *Social Policy and Society* 10(1): 29–40.
Woodhouse, D. (1994) *Ministers and Parliament: Accountability in Theory and Practice.* Oxford: Clarendon Press.
Zahariadis, N. (2007) 'The Multiple Streams Framework'. In Sabatier, P. (ed.) *Theories of the Policy Process* (2nd edn). Boulder, CO: Westview Press.

13 Scotland and British constitutional reform
'Oops, I did it again!' Blair, Cameron and the Britney Spears model of constitutional reform

Matt Qvortrup

Introduction

'Oops, I Did It Again', the 2000 hit by pop princess Britney Spears, could be a leitmotif of constitutional reforms undertaken by successive UK governments since the 1970s. This theme has also characterised proposed changes to Scotland's relationship with the rest of the United Kingdom. This chapter will look at some UK constitutional changes generally and view Scotland in this context.

There is a tendency among constitutional lawyers to see the lawgivers as idealists; politicians seek the best possible outcomes; that they carefully weigh up the consequences of their actions and act accordingly. As far as constitutional reforms in Britain go this approach seems rather misplaced. British constitutional reform with very few exceptions has followed the *Britney Spears Model of Constitutional Reform* (BSMCR) of haphazard changes, which with the benefit of hindsight, were imprudent and ill thought through.

Some may see the British Constitution as inspired by high-minded principle, philosophical deliberation and a concern for good governance. In reality, so it will be argued in this chapter, the process of constitutional reform has followed a pattern of opportunism and hastily enacted changes, many of which had unintended and unforeseen consequences; and many of which backfired.

In short, it is not best described by the eloquence of Burke, nor by the genius of Bagehot but by Britney, who provides the best model of how constitutional reform in Britain has come about.

The process of British constitutional change and reform will be analysed through the Britney Model. After an overview of the alternative approach, the Ackerman-inspired model of *Constitutional Moments* and its application in Britain, the chapter will consider how constitutional changes have been proposed as a result of partisan considerations. The chapter will focus on three distinct periods: the abandonment of the principle of parliamentary sovereignty in the 1970s, New Labour's constitutional reforms in the 1997 Parliament, and finally the contemporary issues pertaining to Scottish independence.

Ackerman and constitutional moments: the idealised view

In other democratic countries, the Constitution is a fundamental law. All democratic countries bar New Zealand, Israel and the United Kingdom have written, single document constitutions. These are documents that cannot normally be challenged through ordinary legislative procedures. The Germans' *Grundgesetz* is – literally – 'The

Basic Law'. This *Gesetz* can only be changed if there is a political consensus about the higher principles. Thus, the fundamental federalism reform of 2006 was only enacted when the two largest parties, the CDU/CSU and the Social Democrats, found themselves in a grand coalition for the first time since 1969 (on this see: Qvortrup 2016).

But back to Britain. At the end of the 1990s there were some signs that British politics was entering a new phase of constitutional reform. The – arguably – out-dated constitutional settlement with an unelected House of Lords (complete with hereditary peers – a system Bismarck had abolished in 1870!) still prevailed. Further, parts of Britain were governed by a party that received only limited support (e.g. especially in Scotland where Conservatives had negligible support despite forming UK governments throughout the 1980s and most of the 1990s) and human rights legislation was not incorporated into British law.

New Labour, Tony Blair's newly christened centre-left party, set out to change Britain's institutional set-up. As Peter Mandelson and Roger Liddle suggested in *The Blair Revolution*:

> A government setting out to modernise Britain cannot be conservative about Britain's institutions. We cannot face the challenges of the twenty-first century with a hangover of habits, attitudes and privileges that reflect views of parliamentary representation as it was in the nineteenth. We need to institute a modern view of the relationship between the citizen and the state.
>
> (Mandelson and Liddle 1996: 112)

Britain was ripe for reform. Like in 1832, 1867 and 1911 a new chapter was about to be written. Political scientist Andrew Gamble even spoke of 'the most far-reaching programme of constitutional reform since 1832' (Gamble 2003: 18).

In the more theoretical jurisprudential literature on constitutional reform it is customary to talk about Constitutional Moments, a phrase coined by the American lawyer and legal theorist Bruce Ackerman. In a much-cited article, he wrote:

> Although constitutional politics is the highest kind of politics, it should be permitted to dominate the nation's life only during rare periods of heightened political consciousness. During long periods between these *constitutional moments*, a second form of activity – I shall call it normal politics – prevails. Here factions manipulate the constitutional forms of political life to pursue their own narrow ends.
>
> (Ackerman 1984: 1022, italics added)

With hindsight, nothing that happened in British constitutional politics in the period 1997–2015 – with the possible exception of the peace agreement in Northern Ireland – deserves the epithet 'constitutional moment'. Rather, politicians have tended to especially use constitutional issues 'to pursue their own narrow ends'. David Cameron's brief speech after the result of the Scottish independence referendum was a case in point.

A day in September

It was 7 a.m. precisely on the 15th of September when Prime Minister David Cameron stepped out of the black door of No. 10 Downing Street. The PM looked relieved, and declared:

The question of English votes for English laws – the so-called West Lothian Question – requires a massive answer. Just as Scotland will vote separately in the Scottish Parliament on issues of tax, spending and welfare, so too England, as well as Wales and Northern Ireland, should be able to vote on these issues ... We will set up a Cabinet Committee right away.

(Cameron quoted in Seldon and Snowdon 2015: 421)

A few hours before – around 5 a.m. – he had received a phone call from the Labour politician Alistair Darling, the former chancellor of the exchequer and latterly leader of the Better Together campaign. Darling was not amused. He warned Cameron against stirring up hostility. Nick Clegg, the deputy prime minister and leader of the Liberal Democrats, was not best pleased either. In a conversation with the latter the day before, Cameron had told his coalition partner, 'I have to lead into the English issue' (Cameron quoted in Seldon and Snowdon 2015: 420). Clegg responded, 'I've got a problem with my English flank and I have to deal with it now ... You can say whatever you like but we don't agree on this – you are not speaking on behalf of the coalition' (Clegg quoted in Seldon and Snowdon 2015: 420).

The exchange between the three leading politicians on a fundamental constitutional issue is in many ways indicative of the way reform of the most fundamental institutions of state are proposed and resolved in the United Kingdom. A system that in this case would allow only English MPs to vote on 'English laws' would be unique in countries with devolved assemblies. In other countries with similar arrangements, such as Spain, Denmark and Canada, all MPs can vote on all matters. Such constitutional niceties, to speak nothing of the possible consequences of changing them (i.e. effectively creating two classes of Members of Parliament) do not seem to have weighed heavily on the prime minister's mind. His concern was purely political, he had to 'lead into the English issue'; for political purposes he had to calm his backbenchers. Nick Clegg's objection too had all the hallmarks of political calculation. The deputy PM was concerned not about the constitutional principles but about his 'English flank'.

Once again, an important political issue of constitutional importance was being discussed *not* at a constitutional convention and *not* as a part of a process of consensus. There was no 'constitutional moment' on the 15th of September 2014.

In the end the proposal for EVEL ('English Votes for English Laws') came to something very close to naught. In this particular instance an opportunist attempt to change the constitution for party political gain was avoided.

Oops, Cameron (nearly) did it again! The prime minister was back to where he used to be; someone who was rather uninterested in constitutional reform. The man who had told the Conservative Party Conference in 2013 that he was against 'pointless constitutional tinkering' was back to being his usual self. Rather like Britney Spears, his apparent passion and enthusiasm was only skin-deep. To quote the pop princess, 'It might seem like a crush/But it doesn't mean that I'm serious'.

BSMCR in the 1970s. Creation of a precedent: British membership of Europe

Although nominally a conservative, David Cameron did not seem to heed the wise words of the David Hume, who was known as 'the sceptical Tory'. The Scottish philosopher famously wrote:

> To tamper, therefore, in this affair (i.e. with new constitutions), or try experiments merely upon the credit of supposed argument and philosophy, can never be the part of a wise magistrate, who will bear a reverence to what carries the marks of age; and though he may attempt some improvements for the public good, yet will he adjust his innovations, as much as possible, to the ancient fabric, and preserve entire the chief pillars and supports of the constitution.
>
> (Hume 1987: 24)

But Cameron was not the first one to fall into the trap of that constitutional opportunism, which is the source of the Britney Spears Model of Constitutional Reform. The same approach can be identified in the 1970s – and, arguably even earlier in British constitutional history.

There are strong parallels found in the way governments in Britain in the 1960s and 1970s have dealt with constitutional reform. The Wilson governments (1964–1970, 1974–1976) provide a starting point.

It is the fundamental – perhaps *the* only – principle of the British Constitution that 'whatever the Queen in Parliament decides is law' (Bogdanor 2009: xii). This basic principle is also summed up in the axiom of 'Parliamentary Sovereignty' – as expressed by the Victorian lawyer and constitutionalist A.V. Dicey, namely what 'Parliament doth, no authority on earth can undo' (Dicey 1983 [1915]: 5).

In the light of this background it was not surprising that the role of the people in the British Constitution traditionally has been rather limited. In his book *Thoughts on the Constitution*, L.S. Amery, a former Conservative cabinet minister and a fellow of All Souls College, observed, 'our system is one of democracy, but democracy by consent and not by delegation, of the people, for the people, with, but not by, the people' (Amery 1947: 21).

Harold Wilson – although from the other side of politics – agreed with Amery. At Prime Minister's Question Time on the 14th of July 1966, John Lee, a Labour backbencher, asked Wilson if he would 'introduce legislation to provide for the use of the referendum as part of British constitutional practice' (*House of Commons Debates, vol. 731*, 14 July 1966, col. 1718). Wilson promptly responded with a monosyllabic 'No' (ibid.).

Unsatisfied with the answer, Mr Lee once again asked:

> Is my right hon. Friend aware that in the happily very unlikely event of this country being in a position to enter the Common Market, no machinery exists to enable the British people to end what Hugh Gaitskell called a thousand years of British history?
>
> (Ibid.)

Once again, Wilson was clear:

> The tradition for a considerable part of that thousand years is that decisions of great moment of this kind have to be taken by the elected Government of the day, responsible to this House. The constitutional position is that whatever this House decides in such a matter, or any other matter, is the right decision.
>
> (Ibid.)

At this stage British membership of the European Economic Community (the EU's predecessor) was, as John Lee had put it a 'very unlikely event'. The French had blocked British entry. But this changed after the death of President Charles de Gaulle. Once *Le Général* was gone, more positive mood music issued from Paris.

British membership was now a distinct possibility, indeed a likely one. By the end of 1969, it seemed a matter of time before Britain would become a member of what was often referred to as 'the Common Market'. And once again, this prompted questions from those opposed to joining.

The Labour backbencher Keith Campbell was one. He argued, very credibly, that the referendum was needed as the prevailing system of representative government failed in the case of the EEC issue. Those voters who did not share the major parties' desire to join the 'Common Market' had no way of expressing their reservations; no party that represented their position. A few months before the election Campbell proposed a ten-minute rule Bill. This would:

> allow the electors of Great Britain and Northern Ireland the right to decide by way of referendum whether Great Britain should enter the European Economic Community. I submit that legislation of this kind is necessary because without it the people of Britain, who have never been consulted on this important issue, will never be consulted. The three major political parties have all declared themselves to be in favour of this country joining the Common Market. It therefore follows that this question will never be an election issue and the people will have absolutely no chance of ever being able to express their views on it through the ballot box at a General Election.
>
> (*House of Commons Debates*, vol. 793, 10 December 1969, col. 442)

Such theoretically sound arguments of political theory did not cut any ice with the political leaders of any of the parties. Far from it! The very idea of holding a referendum was still anathema to the politicians of all the major parties. And constitutionally this was understandable. After all, a referendum would be a direct challenge to the fundamental principle of parliamentary sovereignty.

During the 1970 election, the incumbent prime minister Harold Wilson was still adamant in his opposition to any referendum on constitutional grounds – and so were the other party leaders, the Conservative Edward 'Ted' Heath and the Liberal leader Jeremy Thorpe. Indeed, in the television *BBC Election Forum*, the latter even declared that, 'One of the principles of democracy – and people may not like it, they may not like democracy – is that you elect members of Parliament to use their own judgement' (Thorpe quoted in Butler and Kitzinger 1976: 11). The referendum, the Liberal leader said in a throw-back to Edmund Burke's 'Speech to the Electors of Bristol', was undemocratic. Burke had said, 'Your representative owes you, not his industry only, but his judgment; and he betrays, instead of serving you, if he sacrifices it to your opinion' (Burke 1854 [1774]: 447).

Burke's twentieth-century compatriots were of the same opinion, it seemed. Wilson remained aggressively opposed to the referendum under any circumstances. Asked if he would contemplate a plebiscite on membership of the EEC, he was blunt and unequivocal; 'the answer to that is "No" … The answer is I shall not change my mind on that' (Wilson quoted in Goodhart 1971: 17).

Once Wilson had lost the election (the Conservatives won with a majority of thirty-one seats), many other pressures began to build up for the Labour Party leader. His party was evenly split on the merits of membership of the EEC and many of the backbenchers – and the then powerful unions – made it very clear to him that they were less than enthused by the prospect of joining the Common Market.

Yet, Wilson's position suddenly changed and his very public and unambiguous denunciation of the referendum was reversed. Political calculation set in. And his principled constitutional considerations evaporated.

It should be noted, in fairness, that Wilson's conversion to the referendum cause did not happen overnight. His change of heart must be understood in the context of both political and economic changes and challenges at the time.

There is often a danger of focusing too narrowly on superficial similarities between political epochs. Sometimes such comparisons are exaggerated to a degree that basic factors are overlooked in pursuit of that elusive general pattern which academic scholars cherish. It is easy to draw parallels between the travails of Harold Wilson in the 1970s and those of Conservative prime ministers like John Major twenty years later and David Cameron forty years after.

But in simply looking for a pattern, by simply assuming that history somehow repeats itself, we fail to acknowledge the way in which idiosyncratic developments played a role. And, above all, by narrowly focusing on signs of recurrent patterns, we fail to acknowledge how different the situation was in the early 1970s.

The negotiations over EEC membership did not happen in isolation. There were many interrelated factors that prompted the Labour Party to seek alternative policies to force what was considered to be a weak government to resign or call an election. Harold Wilson was a politician who – to put it kindly – was not overly burdened by doctrine, principle or commitment to cast iron values. And the political developments offered him opportunities aplenty.

The Heath Government was going through a rough patch. In January 1972 thirteen innocent civilians had been shot dead in Northern Ireland in what became known as 'Bloody Sunday', the prime minister was locked in a struggle with coal miners, and unemployment rose to 900,000. All these factors added to the pressure on, and the unpopularity of, the government.

There was a considerable chance – or risk – that Heath would be forced to resign. The reason was not least the disquiet about the European Communities Bill, which only slowly was moving through its various parliamentary stages. Many Tory MPs were defying the party whip and made it clear that they were willing to vote the government down even if this would result in a general election.

In this climate it was not surprising that Labour sought to find ways of defeating the government. Tony Benn, a left-wing member of the Shadow Cabinet and MP for Bristol (curiously in Burke's old constituency!), had been an early advocate of referendums and a critic of the theory of pure representative democracy espoused by his distant predecessor.[1] Benn had already proposed a referendum at a Special Party Conference in July 1971, though this came to naught.

With his idealistic commitment to more direct democracy and his political desire to see the government defeated, Benn once again proposed that a referendum be held on EEC membership.[2] At a Shadow Cabinet meeting on 15 March 1972, Wilson spoke against the idea and Benn's proposal was defeated.

But then something changed. The following day French president Georges Pompidou announced that instead of letting the French legislature vote on the EEC accession treaty (which would allow Britain to join), he would use the provision for an advisory referendum contained in the French constitution and ask the people. Moreover, a week later Ted Heath, struggling to find a way out of the impasse in Northern Ireland, introduced direct rule in the six counties. William Whitelaw, the secretary of state for Northern Ireland, proposed that regular referendums be held to determine whether the citizens in Northern Ireland wanted to join the Republic of Ireland.[3] All of a sudden referendums had become legitimised almost by default.

If the French, and even the UK government itself, accepted that a plebiscite could be held to determine the complex question of Northern Ireland, surely the issue of EEC membership too should be submitted to the voters. Undeterred by his defeat in the Shadow Cabinet, Tony Benn – now wearing his hat as party chairman[4] – once again proposed a referendum but this time he proposed it to the National Executive Committee. The NEC backed it and only two weeks after the Labour Shadow Cabinet had rejected the very idea of a referendum, it now endorsed it when it met on the 29th of March. Wilson himself was now in favour of a referendum. Two weeks is a long time in politics!

But some Conservatives – most notably Enoch Powell – were determined to stop the transfer of powers to Brussels. While Powell's commitment to referendums was at best opportunist, he tabled an amendment to the European Communities Bill calling for a referendum. There was now a real chance that the Heath government could be defeated – provided, that the Labour Party stayed united. But it didn't. Not all members of the shadow cabinet were as relaxed about constitutional principle as Harold Wilson. His deputy Roy Jenkins[5] resigned and fired a parting shot against the idea of a referendum, 'By this means [a referendum]', said Jenkins, 'we would have forged a powerful continuing weapon against progressive legislation than anything we have known in this country since the curbing of the absolute powers of the House of Lords' (Jenkins quoted in Butler and Kitzinger 1976: 19). That the Lords was an unelected body of aristocrats, and not the 'people' themselves, seemed of minor importance to the future Baron Jenkins of Hillhead.

The revolt against Wilson's volte-face saved the Heath government. While 209 Labour MPs supported the Shadow Cabinet's new position and voted for the amendment, 63 abstained – among them Roy Jenkins. The European Communities Bill was adopted by 284 votes to 235 on the 18th of April 1972.

It was on the basis of this decision that in 1975 a referendum was held on membership of the EEC, a vote that resulted in a clear endorsement of continued membership of the Common Market (to use the common expression of the era).

Now how, it, it might be asked, was this decision an example of the BSMCR? Apart from being pragmatic (or opportunist) how can it be claimed that this decision was an example of the 'Oops, I did it again!' pattern of constitutional reform?

To understand this it is necessary to look at the next constitutional issue on the agenda for the Parliament elected in October 1974: devolution.

BSMCR in the 1970s. A precedent created – and devolution

The tale of the 1975 referendum – and the abandonment of the principle of parliamentary sovereignty – would perhaps suggest that everything in those days happened as a result of knee-jerk reaction and with a view to solving short-term political problems.

It is hard to deny that partisan considerations – rather than objective policy goals – were the driving force behind constitutional reform proposals in the time of Wilson. Yet, earlier in his premiership Wilson was willing to contemplate careful deliberation rather than merely making up constitutional politics on the hoof. The issue was what Wilson perceived to be the threat from the SNP.

It happened more or less by chance – and it was never the intention that the voters should be involved. The SNP – hitherto a fringe political party of nationalist romantics – had been founded in 1934. And although the party had won a by-election in Motherwell in 1945, Robert Douglas McIntyre's time as an MP lasted only three months as he lost his seat in the general election in the same year. Yet, when the SNP's Winnie Ewing won a by-election in the previously safe Labour seat of Hamilton in 1967, Prime Minister Wilson became concerned. He established the Kilbrandon Commission. A majority of the Commission's members suggested that Scotland and Wales be given devolved parliaments.

So far, it would seem, a measured and sensible approach to a challenging constitutional issue – and not, at first sight, a knee-jerk reaction of the sort so characteristic of later constitutional policies.

After the 1975 referendum the devolution issue moved up the agenda. Support for the proposals was – at best – skin deep. It was difficult to find much enthusiasm in the governing party for a Scottish Parliament. As a commentator later put it, 'Scottish Labour was intensely unhappy having been forced to adopt devolution in 1974. They had effectively been ordered by Wilson to support a Scottish Assembly which many in the party believed was an over-reaction to the Hamilton by-election' (MacWhirter 2014: 193).

Anxious to defeat the proposals for devolution – but equally concerned not to bring down the Callaghan government (James Callaghan took over as prime minister after Wilson stepped down in 1976) – Scottish backbench MPs, including Robin Cook, suggested that a referendum should be held.

This is where the BSMCR comes in. Wilson's decision to abandon the principle of parliamentary sovereignty backfired retrospectively. By having opened the door to popular involvement with the referendum on EEC membership, his successor had little choice but to accept the principle of a referendum on the other fundamental constitutional issue of the day. Thus, Labour's volte-face on the referendum on EEC membership, a tactical manoeuvre to defeat the Heath Government, had implications down the line. Due to a short-term calculation, a major policy, namely devolution, was defeated. It was in short, 'Oops'.

BSMCR and New Labour

As noted above, the Labour Party under the leadership of Tony Blair (he was elected leader in 1994) immediately embarked on a process of constitutional reform. In the words of two observers, 'constitutional reform played a significant role in the 1997 Labour manifesto' (Finn and Seldon 2013: 22).

Even without access to the original minutes and Cabinet papers, it is clear from the available sources that the motivation for the reforms was (short and long term) party political advantage; and so it will be argued the result was unintended consequences, which could have been avoided.

Three major reforms took place on Tony Blair's watch: the (partial) reform of the House of Lords, devolution for Scotland and Wales and the enactment of the Human Rights Act.

As in the 1970s, the constitutional reforms should be seen in context. The victory of John Major's Tories in the 1992 election raised doubts as to whether Labour could ever win an election outright again. It was – many felt – necessary to court the Liberal Democrats. As Andrew Rawnsley has chronicled, it was this electoral concern which prompted Blair to seek cooperation with Paddy Ashdown (Rawnsley 2001: 1). Not all Labour politicians were convinced that constitutional reform was necessary – but they were whipped into line.[6]

The degree to which Blair was driven by party political opportunism was vividly illustrated by Ashdown in the latter's *Diaries*, according to which the two men concluded their discussion by agreeing that a set of proposed reforms would lead to the – for them – desirable outcome that 'the Tories would break up' (Ashdown 2001: 353).

Devolution was a major plank of the New Labour programme. Not, it seems, because the party, let alone Blair himself, was committed to this but out for the aforementioned expediency. The manifesto in 1997 openly admitted that the proposal for a Scottish Parliament (and a Welsh Assembly) was, in part, intended to stem the tide of nationalism. To wit, 'the Union will be strengthened and the threat of separatism will be removed' (Labour Party Manifesto, quoted in Dale 2000: 376).

It is well known that the choice of electoral system (a partially proportional, additional member system – see Chapter 2) was designed to prevent the SNP from winning a majority (Finn and Seldon 2013: 25).

But rather than engaging in a constitutional debate involving all parties – as would have been the norm in most other democratic countries (Elster 1995) – the devolution legislation was steamrolled through Parliament without much in the way of consultation. In other European countries – with the possible exception of Hungary[7] – constitutional reforms are intended to be manifestations of a 'constitutional moment'. Not so under New Labour (or their Conservative–Liberal Democrat successors).

The Blair government was not inconvenienced by international research in this policy area, which suggested that support for independence had not died away in Spain after devolution, and subsequently varying degrees of autonomy were granted to Galicia, Catalonia and the Basque Country (Muro and Quiroga 2005). It was essential to push through the changes for political purposes to outflank the nationalists, or as some leading Labour figures put it, to 'kill the nationalists stone dead' – and to do so fast. The result of the haste in 1997 came in 2007, when the SNP won a majority of the seats in the Scottish Parliament. *Oops, they did it again!*

The House of Lords reform was another example of the BSMCR in practice. The Labour Party manifesto in 1997 contained a rather tame and unambitious commitment, which read:

> The House of Lords must be reformed. As an initial, self-contained reform, not dependent on further reform in the future, the right of hereditary peers to sit and vote in the House of Lords will be ended by statute. This will be the first stage in a process of reform to make the House of Lords more democratic and representative. The legislative powers of the House of Lords will remain unaltered.
> (Labour Party Manifesto, quoted in Dale 2000: 376)

Even this goal was not achieved. After a backroom deal Lord Cranborne (the Conservative leader in the Lords) was able to save ninety-two of the hereditary peers. In short, the 'right of hereditary peers' was *not* ended by statute! But the compromise with the 7th Marquis of Salisbury had the unintended consequence that the peers became more emboldened and started to challenge and in some cases even veto legislation. As Cowley and Stuart reported shortly after:

> The pre-reform House of Lords – conscious that its legitimacy was limited by the presence of so many hereditary peers – frequently practices [sic] a self-denying ordinance pulling back from many confrontations with the Government. But with

the hereditaries largely gone, those peers that remain see themselves as more legitimate and have become more assertive than before. If the government hoped it had created a poodle of an upper chamber, then it was much mistaken. The full consequences of reform became clear during the second Blair term ... the 2001–5 Parliament saw the government defeated on 245 separate occasions.

(Cowley and Stuart 2005: 38)

It seems appropriate to conclude *'Oops, they did it again!'*

The Human Rights Act 1998 was another case of miscalculation. In this case, the concern was not party political advantage vis-à-vis the Tories that motivated New Labour. Not directly at least. The case for reform was in part motivated by the concern that it was impossible for an individual without significant funds to challenge the legality of government encroachment upon civil liberties.

But the incorporation of the European Convention of Human Rights into British law was also motivated by a concern for the position of the Liberal Democrats (Finn and Seldon 2013: 31). Not knowing whether they would win an outright majority in 1997, New Labour's pre-election commitment to the Human Rights Act was a political down payment for Liberal Democrat support in the event of a hung Parliament (Rawnsley 2001: 1).

As chronicled elsewhere (Qvortrup 2013: 55–67), the reform did not go to plan. The judiciary acted in a way Blair and his colleagues had not expected. Large parts of the Government's so-called anti-terror legislation was ruled incompatible with the Human Rights Act, for example in the Belmarsh Case of 2004, where the Law Lords ruled that indefinite detention of foreign terrorist suspects without trial was unlawful' (Finn and Seldon 2013: 31).

One can have forgiven Tony Blair if he had quietly murmured *'Oops, I did it again!'*

Conservative–Liberal Democrat coalition and constitutional change

The Conservative–Liberal Democrat government of 2010 to 2015 had less of a constitutional reform programme – although Nick Clegg declared that the coalition would preside over the 'biggest shake-up of our democracy since 1832' (cited in Bogdanor 2010: xii). To be sure, the Fixed Term Parliament Act and the (unsuccessful) referendum on the Alternative Vote were important constitutional pieces of legislation.

However, it was the unexpected SNP victory in the Scottish Parliament elections of the 6th of May 2011 (on the same day as the AV referendum) which prompted the Cameron-led coalition into constitutional action – though with some hesitation.

Having initially resisted a referendum on independence, the prime minister changed his mind and accepted that a referendum could be held after all. The assumption in Downing Street was 'that holding a winning a referendum would seize the initiative north of the Border, and put a lid on the nationalist clamour' (Seldon and Snowdon 2015: 126).

The reason for this assessment was – it seems – a misreading of the signals from Bute House (the Scottish first minister's official residence). Cameron believed that he could wrong-foot Alex Salmond, and for this reason the PM conceded a referendum and signed the Agreement between the United Kingdom Government and the Scottish Government on a Referendum on Independence for Scotland (the 'Edinburgh Agreement') on the 15th of October 2012.

During 2013 and the first part of 2014, the polls hardly moved at all. Cameron seemed vindicated in his assessment that a Scottish referendum would be lost by the Scottish Nationalists. However, in the spring of 2014, the Yes Campaign gained momentum. Cameron's biographers reported on his mood: Cameron was 'deeply shaken'. 'Shit we might lose this', was his reported reaction (Seldon and Snowdon 2015: 414).

To stave off what Cameron regarded as a disaster the PM, alongside Nick Clegg and Labour leader Ed Miliband, flew to Scotland, where all three signed the 'Vow', which promised more power to the Scottish Parliament in the event of a No vote. New powers were promised by St Andrew's Day (30 November). This, and a timely intervention by former prime minister Gordon Brown, apparently stemmed the tide of Yes in Scotland. 'Better Together' won by a 10 per cent margin.

The promised constitutional changes did not materialise – at least not in the form envisaged by many of those who decided to vote 'No'. In a Parliamentary debate on the First Reform Act of 1832, the Whig politician and historian Thomas Babington Macaulay (1800–1859) spoke of 'the danger of disappointing the expectations of the nation' (*House of Commons Debates, vol. 2*, 2nd March 1831, col. 1220). It is possible that the 'expectations' of the Scots were 'disappointed' when the promised constitutional promises, arguably, were not delivered; it is possible that it was this 'disappointment' that led to the thundering success of the Scottish National Party in the 2015 UK general election. Not since the Victorian age has a nationalist party achieved the success of the SNP.

David Cameron's assessment that a win in the referendum 'would seize the initiative north of the Border', and even more the belief that such a result would 'put a lid on the nationalist clamour', turned out to be unfounded. 'Oops,' Cameron 'did it again!'

Conclusion

> You see my problem is this
> I'm dreaming away
> Wishing that heroes, they truly exist.

Thus sang Britney in her 2000 hit. Constitutionalists, activists and academics with an interest in political institutions may be 'dreaming away' and wishing that constitutional 'heroes, they truly exist' – like they did in the case of the American Founding Fathers in 1787 and earlier still, in the form of the mythical Solon the Wise of Athens (638–558 BC).

In Britain, alas, constitutional 'heroes' do not exist. There was no constitutional moment after 1997 – or at any other time earlier in British constitutional history. The United Kingdom, regrettably, has suffered the indignity of not having political institutions designed with a view to the common good. Constitutional politics has been even more partisan than what Ackerman called 'normal' politics; it has been characterised by short-term gain and with scant regard for the implications of reform. As a result, 'Oops, I did it again!' has been *the* leitmotif, and *the* recurrent pattern of constitutional change in Britain. However, there can also be positive outcomes and indeed unintended consequences. Given Scotland's political position in the UK – and its position in the British Constitution – it could be argued that the 'flexible pragmatism' (or political opportunism) approach which as this chapter shows has driven much constitutional change and reform will not address recent (or perhaps likely future) developments in the Scottish political firmament. This can be illustrated by four issues:

- First, although the Scottish Parliament will achieve increased powers in the Scotland Act 2015, the UK political arrangement is far from a federal one given the dominance of Westminster; existing asymmetric devolution across the UK may make the devolved arrangements within a unitary constitution unstable – especially given the influence which Westminster will continue to retain over resourcing in an era of fiscal restraint.
- Second, is the concept of English Votes for English Laws (EVEL) easy (or possible) to implement in a 'sovereign national, unitary UK Parliament' without causing tensions between Scottish and other MPs?
- Third, Scottish MPs since the May 2015 general election are overwhelmingly SNP, so are potentially a disturbance factor in terms of Scotland's constitutional position within the UK – though a similarly successful election result for the Bloc Québécois in Canada (enabling the BQ to become the opposition in the federal parliament), was not repeated in subsequent federal elections and led to a period of quiescence if not stability in Quebec's constitutional relationship within Canada (Lachapelle 2003).
- Fourth, should there be political pressure for another referendum in Scotland, this can only be legally held if the UK Parliament permits the Scottish Parliament to do so since constitutional matters are reserved and not devolved. This of course gives scope for political opportunism and strategy playing between political parties at Holyrood, and at Westminster, and between Scottish and UK Governments.

Constitutional changes may backfire! To quote Britney Spears' other hit, 'Toxic' (from 2003), a thing like constitutional reform 'Should wear a warning / It's dangerous'!

Notes

1 Inspired by the student revolts in Paris in 1968 and the general interest in direct participation spurred by the student movement, he sent a letter to his constituents in 1970 in which he advocated a referendum. He wrote, 'If people are not to participate in this decision [on whether to join the EEC], no one will ever be taken seriously again' (Benn quoted in Butler and Kitzinger 1976: 12).
2 The following account is based on Butler and Kitzinger (1976: 18–19).
3 The referendum held a year later on 8 March 1973 was boycotted by the Nationalist and Republican minority in Northern Ireland.
4 The formal title was *Chairman of the Annual Conference of the Labour Representation Committee*. Benn held this position in 1971–1972. See (Butler and Butler 1994: 144–145).
5 Roy Jenkins later became president of the European Commission (1977–1981).
6 See for example Scottish Labour MP Ian Davidson's remark, 'What's all this constitutional reform shite?' quoted in Mullin (2010: 336).
7 In 2013 Prime Minister Viktor Orbán's right wing Fidesz government enacted a new constitution without consulting the opposition (Landau 2013).

Suggestions for Further Study and Reading:

Generally on constitutional changes

Ackerman, B.A. (1984) 'The Storrs Lectures: Discovering the Constitution'. *Yale Law Journal* 93(6): 1013–1072.
Elster, J. (1995) 'Forces and Mechanisms in the Constitution-Making Process'. *Duke Law Journal* 45: 364–396.
Ginsburg, Tom, Elkins, Zachary and Blount, Justin (2009) 'Does the Process of Constitution-Making Matter?' *Annual Review of Law and Social Sciences* 5(5): 201–223.

On the British constitution

Bogdanor, V.B. (2009) *The New British Constitution*. Oxford: Hart.
Dicey, A.V. (1983 [1915]) *An Introduction to the Study of the Law of the Constitution*. Indianapolis, IN: Liberty Fund.
King, A. (2009) *The British Constitution*. Oxford: Oxford University Press.
Qvortrup, M. (2015) *The British Constitution: Continuity and Change* (2nd edn). Oxford: Hart.

Blog

LSE British Politics and Society Blog: http://blogs.lse.ac.uk/politicsandpolicy/

Website

The Constitution Society: www.consoc.org.uk

References

Ackerman, B.A. (1984) 'The Storrs Lectures: Discovering the Constitution'. *Yale Law Journal* 93 (6): 1013–1072.
Amery, L.S. (1947) *Thoughts on the Constitution*. Oxford: Oxford University Press.
Ashdown, P. (2001) *The Ashdown Diaries, Vol. 1, 1988–1999*. London: Allen Lane.
Bogdanor, V. (2009) *The New British Constitution*. Oxford: Hart.
Bogdanor, V. (2010) *The Coalition and the Constitution*. Oxford: Hart.
Burke, E. (1854 [1774]) 'Speech to the Electors of Bristol'. In *The Works of the Right Honourable Edmund Burke*, 6 vols, London: Henry G. Bohn, p. 447.
Butler, D. and G. Butler (1994) *British Political Facts 1900–1994*. London: Macmillan.
Butler, D. and U. Kitzinger (1976) *The 1975 Referendum*. London: Macmillan.
Cowley, P. and M. Stuart (2005) 'Parliament'. In Seldon, A. and Kavanagh, D. (eds) *The Blair Effect 2001–5*. Cambridge: Cambridge University Press, pp. 20–42.
Dale, I. (2000) *Labour Party General Election Manifestos 1900–1997*. London: Routledge.
Dicey, A.V. (1983) [1915] *An Introduction to the Study of the Law of the Constitution*. Indianapolis, IN: Liberty Fund.
Elster, J. (1995) 'Forces and Mechanisms in the Constitution-Making Process'. *Duke Law Journal* 45: 364–396.
Finn, M. and A. Seldon (2013) 'Constitutional Reform Since 1997: The Historians' Perspective'. In Qvortrup, M. (ed.) *The British Constitution: Continuity and Change*. Oxford: Hart, pp. 17–37.
Gamble, A. (2003) 'Remaking the Constitution'. In Dunleavy, P., Heffernan, R., Cowley, P. and Hay, C., *Developments in British Politics 8*. Basingstoke: Palgrave Macmillan.
Goodhart, P. (1971) *Referendum*. London: Tom Stacey.
House Magazine (2010) 'Quote of the Week'. 1 February.
Hume, David (1987 [1754]) 'The Idea of a Perfect Commonwealth'. In Hume, David (1982) *Essays: Moral, Political and Literary*. Indianapolis, IN: Liberty Fund.
Lachapelle, G. (2003) 'Nation, State and Society in Quebec'. Conference: Quebec in the New Century: New Dynamics, New Opportunities, October (Vol. 31).
Landau, D. (2013) 'Abusive Constitutionalism'. *UC Davis Law Review* 47(Fall): 189–260.
Macwhirter, I. (2014) *Road to Referendum: The Essential Guide to the Scottish Referendum*. Glasgow: Cargo.
Mandelson, P. and R. Liddle (1996) *The Blair Revolution: Can New Labour Deliver?* London: Faber & Faber.
Mullin, C. (2010) *Decline and Fall: Diaries 2005–2010*. London: Profile.

Muro, Diego and Alejandro Quiroga (2005) 'Spanish Nationalism: Ethnic or Civic?'. *Ethnicities* 5(1): 9–29.
Qvortrup, M. (2013) '"Let Me Take You to a Foreign Land": The Political and Legal Constitution'. In Qvortrup, M. (ed.) *The British Constitution: Continuity and Change*. Oxford: Hart, pp. 17–37.
Qvortrup, M. (2016) *Angela Merkel*. London: Duckworth.
Rawnsley, A. (2001) *Servants of the People: The Inside Story of New Labour* (2nd edn). London: Penguin.
Seldon, A. and P. Snowdon (2015) *Cameron at No. 10: The Inside Story 2010–2015*. London: William Collins.

14 The media and politics in Scotland

David Hutchison

Politics and the mass media

Whatever view one takes of politics as practised in the West, and there are commentators who are less then impressed by its supposedly democratic credentials, there is general agreement on the importance of the mass media in providing opportunities for civic debate. We may not inhabit the kind of idealised public realm described by Jürgen Habermas (Habermas, 1989), but nor do we find ourselves living in authoritarian or totalitarian regimes. Most of us believe that without the media we would have difficulty in discussing political issues in any meaningful way. Our reliance on the media increases with distance. It is relatively easy to come to conclusions about how well our local council discharges its responsibilities, since the evidence may literally be on our own doorsteps, and normal social interaction provides us with much relevant information. But our ability to formulate judgements on what is happening, for example, in Myanmar, is almost entirely dependent on what we read in newspapers and hear and see on radio and television. When it comes to events in Scotland and the UK we have access to information from a variety of sources but are also reliant on the media for both facts and alternative perspectives.

The research evidence about the relationship between the media and political behaviour is less than conclusive. Although politicians have always believed there is considerable effect: Sir Robert Walpole, prime minister of Britain in the early eighteenth century, reputedly spent £50,000 of government money securing favourable press coverage (Harris 1978: 5). And all of his successors have sought to influence editors and proprietors. In more recent times, the Labour leaders, Tony Blair and Gordon Brown, endeavoured to curry favour with the head of Newscorp, Rupert Murdoch. The same gentleman was on occasion invited to Christmas lunch by Conservative prime minister Margaret Thatcher.

For politicians broadcasting is equally, if not more, important. In the UK broadcasters are enjoined by the state to be balanced and fair in their reporting, and cannot engage in the kind of open partisanship to be seen in the press, which is why surveys tell us that the public trust broadcast journalists rather more than they trust print ones (though now apparently trust Wikipedia's anonymous contributors more than they trust either (Yougov, 2014)). During the Scottish referendum campaign both the major Scottish broadcasters staged debates between Alex Salmond and the leader of the Better Together campaign, Alistair Darling, which were watched by audiences as large as those gained by major sporting events (*The Guardian* 2014).

It therefore follows that politicians will use their appearances on the airwaves to maximise advantage and to outsmart rivals and potentially truculent interviewers. A political leader nowadays who is not 'good on television' is deemed to be at substantial disadvantage, no matter their other attributes.

In a useful review of the academic research on the impact of the media on political behaviour, Raymond Kuhn considers the various models which have been developed, ranging from the propaganda model, which assumes a very strong impact, through the partisan reinforcement model, which argues that the media simply bolster people's existing views, to the model in which the citizen actively seeks and reviews the information presented (Kuhn 2007: 256–257). A number of studies of voter behaviour in recent UK general elections suggest that the media do not have a very strong impact but may affect the decisions of uncommitted voters as campaigns progress (see for example Newton and Brynin 2001). It seems a reasonable assumption that as party affiliations decline, and other organisations such as trade unions diminish in influence, the average voter is, at the very least, likely to turn to the media seeking information. That surely explains the large audiences for the referendum debates and for general election debates on television.

Even if academic research were to demonstrate that the media had no impact whatsoever on voter behaviour – an unlikely outcome – politicians will continue to assume the opposite, and will seek to cajole newspapers and pressurise broadcasters. The BBC's political editor, Nick Robinson, revealed that he had been in the company of the Conservative leader David Cameron during the 2015 general election on an occasion when, irritated by a particular report, Cameron threatened that he would close down the BBC (*The Guardian* 2015: 32). Robinson said that he was unsure whether this was intended as a joke but there was no doubt in the minds of those BBC reporters who heard the remark that they were being pressurised. It is the responsibility of reporters to resist all such pressure, but with the renewal of the BBC's Charter looming (it is the government of the day which draws up the Charter) the prime minister's remark was a potential constraint on their work. Robinson also contended that during the Scottish referendum Alex Salmond had sought to push BBC coverage in a direction favourable to the Yes side. Robinson himself attracted the ire of some on that side for his allegedly biased reporting (*Daily Telegraph* 2014).

One fruitful approach to the analysis of political journalism is to consider it not in terms of open partisanship but in terms of 'agenda setting' and 'framing'. Different issues can be highlighted, and others downplayed: for example, during an election the media might emphasise economic matters rather than social ones, domestic affairs rather than foreign affairs. And, to take another example, armed intervention in a foreign country could be 'framed' as a humanitarian act or as an aggressive one. Highly relevant here is the fact that these processes take place over time, so that when elections are actually called 'agendas' have been set and 'framing' has taken place. The Labour leader Neil Kinnock was often presented as a 'Welsh windbag' in the tabloid press and that impression became difficult to shift; likewise, after the ejection of the UK from the European exchange rate mechanism in 1992, the then prime minister, John Major, found himself constantly presented in the press as incompetent. It is worth considering whether the defeat of the Labour party under Kinnock in 1992 and the Conservatives under Major in 1997 owed something to the 'framing' of these two leaders.

On the other hand, it could be argued that the recent success of the SNP in securing 45 per cent of the votes in the independence referendum and 50 per cent of votes in the subsequent 2015 UK general election demonstrates the political weakness of newspapers: only one title, the *Sunday Herald*, unequivocally supported a Yes vote, while all the others, Scottish based and Scotticised versions of English titles, opposed independence and most of them did not support the SNP in May 2015. Brian McNair commented on the result of the 2007 Holyrood election that there 'appeared to be little obvious relationship to media coverage of the contest. There had been overwhelming pro-Union bias in the Scottish press for years leading up to the poll but still the SNP won the election' (McNair 2008: 240).

Partisanship in the press has been on the rise for a considerable time. In 1998 the distinguished journalist, Peter Riddell, commented on what he saw as the increase in newspaper partisanship in the UK, particularly with regard to Britain's membership of the European Union (Riddell 1998: 15–16). Riddell took the view that this is a worrying development and, if the effect is to obscure the actual facts in particular cases, it is hard to disagree. However, readers, even those sympathetic to the partisanship in question, cannot but notice what is going on, and it is a reasonable assumption that, even if they enthuse about the vigour of the opinions expressed in print, when they turn to broadcasting they will expect a more dispassionate account of the issues. But the problem with dispassionate accounts and their need to be balanced and impartial is that they can rob political discussion of engaged polemic, for which there is clearly a place. If only our newspapers all adhered to the dictum of the distinguished editor of *The Guardian*, C.P. Scott, who declared that 'comment is free but facts are sacred'. Alas, that is a mantra ignored by many – though not all – newspapers in Scotland and in the rest of Britain.

The media in Scotland

Successive commentators have emphasised the importance of the media to Scottish life. Kellas in his classic study of the political system north of the border, while opining that the 'quality of Scottish broadcasting is not equal to that of the best network productions', conceded that 'Scotland has a volume of broadcasting about politics in its area, both at election and non-election times, which is unmatched by any other part of Britain' (Kellas 1989: 209–210), and that the media as a whole provide 'ample support ... for the operation of an autonomous Scottish political system'. Schlesinger, writing on the eve of devolution, argued that 'Scotland's media are a crucial element of the country's civil society. Their role in the development of the new Scottish political culture once the parliament is established will be substantial' (Schlesinger 1998: 61). Lynch, writing a few years later, also emphasised the distinctiveness of the Scottish media and commented on the way in which the terms 'Scottish' 'Scots' and 'Scotland' were used in press and broadcasting as badges of identity (Lynch 2001: 156–157), while McGarvey and Cairney in 2008 argued that the media 'played a key role in the fuelling of expectations for new politics during the campaign for home rule' (McGarvey and Cairney 2008: 39), but then noted that some newspapers became very critical of the Holyrood Parliament in its early years.

The Scottish reader can choose among home-grown titles and those which, with or without Scottish editions, are London newspapers circulating throughout the British Isles (see Table 14.1 for current circulations). Each major city boasts at least one daily, and sometimes a Sunday newspaper also. In the capital are the *Scotsman,* and *Scotland on Sunday*, in Glasgow the *Herald, Sunday Herald, Daily Record* and *Sunday Mail*,

Table 14.1 Daily newspaper ciculations in Scotland

Scottish titles	
Courier	46,991
Daily Record	193,093
Herald	37,044
Press and Journal	60,292
Scotsman	26,283
English titles	
Daily Express	44,895
Daily Mail	89,526
Daily Mirror	15,093
Daily Star	38,625
Daily Telegraph	15,805
Financial Times	2,126
Guardian	9,078
Independent/The i	2,431/17,106
Sun	226,195
Times	18,124

Source: Audit Bureau of Circulations/allmediascotland. The figures for the English titles and the *Daily Record* are for the year ending February 2015; the figures for the other Scottish titles are for the period July to December 2014.

while in Dundee are the *Courier* and the *Sunday Post*; in Aberdeen the *Press and Journal*. Each of these cities also has an evening paper. There are indigenous titles to be found in Wales too, but not on the Scottish scale, so dominant are the Fleet Street titles in the principality (the Northern Irish situation is more comparable to the Scottish one). The reasons for the survival of the Scottish press are several. In the first place, the railway system in the late nineteenth and early twentieth century was not fast enough to allow London titles to penetrate the Scottish market properly in the way that they were able to penetrate the English and Welsh ones, and to wipe out much regional competition in the process. Furthermore, Scottish titles, even when they have aspired to cover the entire country, have always had a strong regional orientation which has enabled them to build local loyalty. On the other hand, there have been times in the past when an English title with a strong Scottish edition offered very fierce competition to indigenous titles; the most obvious example before the 1990s was the *Scottish Daily Express* which in the 1950s was the dominant paper in Scotland, happy to outspend its rivals in order to sustain that position (Reid 2006: 83ff).

In recent times newspapers throughout the Western world have faced serious circulation declines driven by the increasing power of the electronic and digital media and the apparent indifference of many younger people to the print medium (Brock 2013: 234). Indeed there are moments when circulation figures suggest that thirty years from now physical newspapers may even have disappeared. Scottish titles have not been exempt and they have also faced a serious loss of market share within Scotland, as English titles, with or without Scottish editions, have improved their relative position. In the mid-1970s Scottish dailies took 64 per cent of sales and Sundays took 66 per cent

(Hutchison 2008: 66). The Scottish Sundays continue to outsell their English rivals by a slim margin but the dailies' share of the market is now 43 per cent. Clearly better resourced English titles can offer a wider range of material than their Scottish competitors, and if they also provide a fair amount of Scottish news, sport and comment, they are an attractive buy, particularly if they engage in competitive pricing, as some have done.

It remains puzzling, however, that the once mighty *Daily Record* has been so vulnerable to the onslaught of the Scottish edition of the *Sun*; the *Record* sold three quarters of a million copies in the 1980s, a startling figure. What is even more surprising is that the general loss of market share has accelerated since devolution, rather than been halted. In fairness, it should be noted that both the *Courier* and the *Press and Journal* have been much more resilient, probably because of the skill with which they blend local, Scottish and UK material (with a smattering of international news). All Scottish based titles have an online presence but none have been any better than newspapers elsewhere at turning 'visitors' into revenue streams adequate to offset the precipitate loss of circulation and advertising revenue. In this challenging context, when staff numbers have been falling, it was remarkable that at the end of 2014 the *National* was launched by the Herald Group as an overtly pro-independence title; whether it will attract sufficient readers and advertising revenue remains to be seen.

Scottish papers have a variety of proprietors. The Dundee company D.C. Thomson owns the papers in that city and in Aberdeen. That company, while notorious in left wing circles for its historic antipathy to trade unions, has been the most successful of all Scottish media organisations in moving out from its home base to penetrate markets beyond Scotland. This it has done largely through the production of comics and magazines for young people, which were responsible for the creation of such iconic characters as Desperate Dan, Dennis the Menace, Lord Snooty and the Bash Street Kids (Rosie 1978). The Johnston Press owns the Edinburgh titles, and can still be regarded as a Scottish company, although from its original Falkirk base it has expanded its presence in the local paper market throughout the UK – and in the process saddled itself with substantial borrowings. The *Herald* group is owned by Newsquest, a subsidiary of the American Gannett Corporation, publisher of *USA Today*, which, like the Johnston Press, has extensive holdings in the local market UK-wide. The London based Trinity Mirror Company owns the *Daily Record* and its sister Sunday title, the *Sunday Mail*. It too has large regional holdings, and also owns the London based titles of Mirror Group Newspapers.

Local papers, it should be stressed, remain an important part of the media mix north of the border. Their circulations vary widely, from the relatively small – the *Annandale Observer* sells 5,038 copies weekly – to the much larger – the *Ayrshire Post* sells 17,016 (ABC, Dec. 13–14). Unlike daily and Sunday titles, locals, most of which are published once a week only, tend to avoid open partisanship. Politicians at all levels of government have a reasonable chance of seeing their activities fairly covered, not least through their own weekly columns, and are unlikely to find themselves attacked in editorials; letters pages are rather different and are often characterised by vigorous debate about issues from the parochial to the international. Overt partisanship in such papers would be a serious disservice to democracy since the vast majority of them are monopolists in their circulation areas.

If the indigenous Scottish press is weaker than it has been in the past, broadcasting is in better shape. Scottish viewers and listeners have access to a range of UK-wide services and also to several designed in whole or in part for Scotland. ITV, which was once a federation of strong regional broadcasters, such as Granada and Yorkshire, is now a national service with some regional opt-outs. North of the border it is available via Scottish Television (STV) which, until Ulster was purchased by ITV in late 2015, was one of two independent commercial broadcasters not owned directly by ITV plc. However most of STV's output is provided by ITV, and its own opt-out programming consists mainly of news, current affairs and sport. STV's strong record in popular drama petered out after the crime series *Taggart*, which had begun in 1983, ceased to be commissioned by ITV in 2011. This means the company makes relatively minor contributions to the UK network. Channel 4 does not have a strong record on commissioning production beyond England, although the UK telecoms regulator Ofcom announced at the beginning of 2014 that it was proposing that from 2020 the 'out of England' quota would be 9 per cent by volume and spend, a major increase on the current 3 per cent (Ofcom 2014).

The BBC's two main channels, BBC1 and BBC2, have the suffix 'Scotland' added north of the border. In practice this means that there is a significant amount of opt-out programming, mainly, though not exclusively, on BBC1. This takes the form of news, current affairs, documentaries, sport and some light entertainment and drama. It is the aspiration that drama and situation comedy should be purchased by the network but this is not inevitable (Cook 2008: 130; Mowatt 2008: passim). There has been a recurring argument about the amount of programming commissioned directly by the Corporation's national networks from Scotland (an argument very much replicated in other parts of the UK). Following the establishment by the SNP minority government of its Broadcasting Commission in 2007, the BBC's then director general undertook to work towards a target of network production coming from Scotland equivalent to the country's share of UK population, which is just over 8 per cent (BBC 2007). There has been progress towards that figure but also some controversy about the 'warehousing' of existing network programmes in Glasgow rather than the commissioning of original productions. *Question Time*, for example, the weekly discussion programme, is now headquartered in Glasgow but can hardly be regarded as a Scottish production.

BBC Alba is a Gaelic medium television service jointly financed by the BBC and the Scottish Government. It broadcasts up to seven hours per day and its establishment in 2008 was a victory for a long running campaign by Gaeldom. It continues to attract audience numbers well in excess the number of Scots who speak the language, not least because of its sports coverage and judicious use of subtitles (BBC Alba 2014). Its programme, *Eòrpa* (originated by BBC Scotland in 1993) can claim to be the only long running UK current affairs production entirely focused on Europe.

A wide range of other specialist channels is available terrestrially and via satellite, cable and the internet. Channel 5 has no significant Scottish input.

In radio Scottish listeners have access to all of the BBC's national UK services and two stand-alone services, BBC Radio Scotland (there are similar channels in Wales and Northern Ireland) and Radio nan Gaidheal, a Gaelic channel. In addition, the country is covered by a range of commercial stations (mostly owned now by the Bauer Media Group of Germany), and some small community stations. BBC Scotland makes some programmes for the network services Radio 3 and Radio 4.

Broadcasting is therefore in a much healthier condition in Scotland than the press but it too faces challenges. The extraordinary decision by the Westminster coalition government in the middle of a licence fee period, and without recourse to the House of

Commons, to impose cuts and to compel the Corporation to fund activities it had not previously funded has had an impact on staff numbers throughout the UK (BBC 2011). The election of a Conservative government in 2015 meant that the Corporation faced further financial constraints for the foreseeable future, whatever the result of the Charter review process initiated after the election. Commercial broadcasters in radio and television have had difficult moments in recent years as advertising revenue has fluctuated in a challenging economic environment. But STV, having had a turbulent time in the past when the company over-expanded, now seems solidly based and able to offer the BBC competition in at least some areas of programming, including news and current affairs.

Newspapers and broadcasters, in particular the BBC, have sought to develop strong online presences. It was noted earlier that the press has struggled to secure adequate financial returns in cyberspace, even although many titles have now introduced partial paywalls. It has to be acknowledged that in the BBC they face a formidable competitor which is financed by the licence fee, does not charge for access and has one of the largest corps of journalists in the world. What the Corporation cannot offer, however, is the kind of partisan comment to be found in the press, although many of its correspondents do provide commentary which goes well beyond basic reporting.

Online operations by mainstream media organisations function alongside internet-only operations such as the *Scottish Review*, which began life in 1995 as a print magazine and moved online in 2008, and other sites such as *Wings over Scotland* and *Newsnet Scotland* which have always been based online. While the latter two are committed to the independence movement, the former takes a more sceptical approach to all politicians and public bodies and has pursued a number of important stories: for example, after a long period of official obfuscation, it succeeded in obtaining information about the rather large salaries paid by Scottish health boards to senior managers and clinicians, a task which it might have been expected would have been carried out by one of our newspapers, or a broadcaster. Beyond the sites just discussed is the world of Facebook and Twitter which enables all who wish to offer their views to those willing to pay attention to do so. Politicians have not been slow to seek to use these means of communication but they have also found themselves subject to criticism and sometimes intemperate abuse.

The legal and constitutional frameworks within which the traditional media operate in Scotland are distinct (McInnes 2010). For example, north of the border, journalists are obliged to take account of a tougher regime on contempt of court than prevails in England, which means that prejudicial reporting about an arrested person before or during a trial will almost certainly lead to proceedings against those responsible. English laws on defamation, although they have been recently revised, have historically made it easier for people who consider themselves to have been libelled to secure very substantial damages, largely because of the fact that most cases in England were being heard in front of juries who had developed an enthusiasm for awarding large sums to aggrieved plaintiffs. In Scotland such cases have usually been heard by judges who do not have the same enthusiasm for punitive awards. It is possible for a plaintiff to seek a jury trial north of the border and that is exactly what happened in the case of Tommy Sheridan, the left wing politician, who in 2006 sued the Scottish edition of the *News of the World* which had printed allegations about his extra-marital sexual activities. He won his case and the jury, by a majority, awarded him £200,000 but the paper appealed, and the money was not handed over. However, the following year Sheridan himself was tried for perjury, found guilty and jailed. The ramifications of the case continued into 2015 when Bob Bird, the former editor of the by now defunct *News of the World*, who had been charged with attempting to pervert the course of justice in relation to the original trial, was told that the case against him had been dropped, and Andy Coulson, the former UK editor of the paper who had already served a jail sentence in England in connection with his paper's hacking activities, had the charge of perjury against him abandoned in the High Court in Edinburgh.

This saga raises a number of important issues for the reporting of politics, or rather the reporting of the private activities of politicians. Is it legitimate to print allegations about the behaviour of politicians when there is no connection with their public activities and no laws have been broken? A case can easily be made that, for example, allegations about child abuse should be brought into the public realm, but if a politician visits a so-called 'swingers' club' or has a string of extra-marital affairs or is a closet homosexual (less likely nowadays but still a possibility), can it not be argued that none of this should concern the rest of us? Or is it now the general view that everything a politician does can legitimately be reported?

The methods employed by some newspapers to obtain information about the private lives of prominent individuals became a matter of great public concern in the UK as a whole in 2011 when the phone hacking activities of these titles were exposed by another paper, *The Guardian*, with a little help from the *New York Times*. The establishment by the then government of the Leveson Inquiry led to the demise of the *News of the World* (to be replaced shortly afterwards by the *Sun on Sunday*) and proposals for a new system of press regulation to replace the discredited Press Complaints Commission. However, at the time of writing the parliamentary proposal that any new regulatory organisation should be given official approval via a royal charter seems to be a non-starter and the new voluntary body established and financed by most British newspapers, the Independent Press Standards Organisation (IPSO), is up and running; it has significant Scottish representation.

In the post-Leveson period many observers were rather startled to discover that press regulation was a devolved matter. This is surprising because decisions on mergers and acquisitions are not devolved, and as far as broadcasting is concerned, the BBC is responsible to Westminster, while Ofcom operates on a UK-wide basis. However, Scotland does have its own Freedom of Information legislation and Information Commissioner; several journalists, such as Paul Hutcheon of the *Sunday Herald*, have made assiduous use of that office in pursuing stories. In the wake of Leveson the Scottish Government set up an Expert Group which in its report in 2013 proposed that 'all publishers of news-related material' should come under the jurisdiction of a new regulatory body (Scottish Government 2013). Nothing has come of this proposal.

As has just been noted, most media regulation is carried out on a pan-UK basis. There are significant anomalies. Policy on film production is deemed to be part of cultural policy and so is devolved. Creative Scotland, which is responsible to Holyrood, makes modest grants to film projects and both it and the Scottish Government have been involved in discussions about whether and how to build a large film studio in the country. Many films are produced or co-produced by the BBC and film has a natural affinity with television drama. However, the BBC answers to Westminster and STV to Ofcom. Both broadcasters attend Holyrood committees to discuss their activities but political oversight lies elsewhere.

However, Holyrood has taken an interest in non-devolved media areas. In 2010, for example, one of its committees mounted an inquiry into the health of the local press. That resulted in the abandonment of a proposal whereby local authorities would have moved much of their informational advertising online, and in the process deprived local titles of an important source of revenue (Scottish Government 2010). It can be argued that sooner or later the future viability of the Scottish daily and Sunday press will also have to be seriously discussed by the Scottish Parliament; subvention from public funds on the Scandinavian model might have to be considered if we are to retain a vibrant indigenous press.

The most significant intervention by Holyrood was the setting up by the SNP minority government elected in 2007 of the Scottish Broadcasting Commission, which was mentioned earlier. That body reported in 2008 and recommended that a new digital channel should be established (Scottish Government 2008). Subsequently it was suggested by an Expert Group appointed by the Scottish Government that the BBC licence fee should be top-sliced in order to provide the £70 million per year necessary to fund the channel. This proposal was never likely to be implemented, and when in 2010 the Conservative/Liberal coalition imposed the cuts on the BBC, also referred to earlier, the proposal died. If the Holyrood parties – all of which declared their support for the proposed channel – had been willing to vote some funding towards the venture, the outcome might have been very different. However, even in difficult economic times, pressure for the establishment of such a channel and/or the development of a genuinely federal BBC seems unlikely to diminish. The Smith Commission's post-referendum proposals:

> There will be a formal consultative role for the Scottish Government and the Scottish Parliament in the process of reviewing the BBC's Charter. The BBC will lay its annual report and accounts before the Scottish Parliament and submit reports to, and appear before, committees of the Scottish Parliament in relation to matters relating to Scotland in the same way as it does in the UK Parliament.
>
> The power to approve OFCOM appointments to the board of the MG Alba will rest solely with Scottish Ministers.
>
> (Smith Commission 2014: 17)

seem far too modest to offer the prospect of a permanent settlement, as became clear in the summer of 2015 when discussions began on the renewal of the Corporation's Charter and the first minister argued that the BBC should be reorganised on a federal basis and that additional services should be provided in Scotland (First Minister 2015).

Reporting post-devolution

The establishment of a Scottish Parliament in 1999 led to a major shift in the focus of Scottish political journalism. Although the Scottish Office had had a strong presence in Edinburgh, the centre of power had been the Westminster Parliament. Now there was another forum, one where the bread and butter issues which affected voters' everyday lives were discussed, and policies developed. Education, the health service, and a range of other matters were now the responsibility of Holyrood. Inevitably the Scottish media turned much of their attention to Edinburgh. For some observers this produced a dangerous imbalance. Brian Wilson, former government minister, and himself a journalist, commented that:

by far the most urgent and pernicious trend surrounding Scottish coverage of Westminster lies in the determination of large sections of the Scottish media for a variety of reasons, to marginalise it while building up Holyrood as the more relevant institution.

(Wilson, 2008: 247)

There is no question that the visibility of Westminster has declined, with the result, for example, that the average Scottish viewer of current affairs television is likely to be familiar with a range of MSPs but scarcely know the names of Scottish MPs unless they are in government or leading figures in one of the other parties. Many Scottish backbenchers at Westminster have simply become invisible.

It is not the case, however, that the relationship between Holyrood and the media, particularly the press, has always been harmonious. Michael Keating comments: 'relations between the press and the Scottish parliament got off to an extremely bad start' (Keating 2010: 104), while McGarvey and Cairney argue that:

the media played a key role in the fuelling of expectations for new politics during the campaign for home rule. This may explain why many sections of the print media are now so quick to criticise the new political institutions in Scotland.

(McGarvey and Cairney 2008: 39)

Expectations were probably too high and in the early years the governing Labour/Liberal coalition lost two first ministers in a row, first through the untimely death of Donald Dewar and then through embarrassment over an expenses issue, which led to Henry McLeish's resignation. Under Jack McConnell a period of more stable government ensued. The SNP's election in 2007, initially as a minority government, led to a paradox: SNP ministers received rather more favourable treatment in the press than some of their predecessors had done, and the party was widely endorsed in editorials in the 2011 election as the one best able to run Scotland, but the overwhelming majority of papers remained opposed to independence.

The referendum debate and the 2015 UK election

What follows draws on more extensive analysis published elsewhere (Hutchison 2015; 2016).

The Scottish government published its White Paper on 26 November 2014. For the purpose of this analysis the early evening and late evening news and current affairs programmes of the BBC, ITV and Channel 4 at UK level, and the output of BBC Scotland and STV transmitted to the domestic audience only, were examined, a total of ten programmes. Coverage in the press the next day was also considered.

The first observation to be made is that the television output reflected the general approach of public service broadcasting in the UK, whether financed by licence fee or advertising, that is to say it is obliged to report events factually and to treat matters of current controversy in an even handed way. All of the programmes led with the White Paper and gave it substantial coverage. *Channel 4 News* (also provided by ITN, the news service of ITV) was the only one not to do so; it led with a 13-minute item on another UK political story before moving on to the White Paper. In the presentation of the contents of the document there was again a similarity. A correspondent, not the programme anchor, outlined what was in it, while clips from the launch event were used as illustration. By way of balance, there was brief comment from the leader of the Better Together campaign, Alistair Darling. Anchors then either interviewed fellow specialist journalists or introduced filmed packages. Not all of these reports were from Scotland. STV's early evening bulletin ran interviews with London taxi drivers and Channel 4 had one of its reporters in Spain discussing the relationship between the Scottish and forthcoming Catalan referendums. Experts/pundits, many of them familiar certainly to Scottish domestic viewers, appeared across the output.

There were extended interviews on all of the programmes with Alex Salmond and with Alistair Darling or the Scottish Secretary Alistair Carmichael. The agenda for the Salmond interviews tended to focus on the issues of access to the pound sterling for an independent Scotland and its entry to the EU. Defence and the SNP's determination to remove nuclear weapons from Scotland while remaining a member of NATO, also featured, as did the White Paper's proposal to improve childcare. And that led to some sharp questioning as to why, since childcare is a devolved matter, the improvement could not be implemented immediately: the first minister's response was that it was only within a Scottish budget that such a plan could be afforded. He emphasised that the British government's debt had been built up under the chancellorships of the current incumbent, George Osborne, and the leader of the Better Together campaign, Alistair Darling. The interview which veered away from this general trend was conducted by Gordon Brewer on *Newsnight Scotland*. Brewer tackled the currency issue but put it to the first minister that, once committed to the pound, there would be no escape for Scotland; Brewer also raised the impact on the standing of the UK in the world if Scotland became independent. This was the sole interview in which there was real friction. Several British broadcast interviewers have a reputation for being aggressive towards politicians, but what was striking about the Salmond interviews considered here is that they were not particularly abrasive: the first minister laid out his case and was rarely interrupted. The only exception was the Brewer interview where Salmond reacted rather testily when Brewer referred to a poll of a large number of senior pupils in Aberdeenshire which showed a substantial majority against independence.

The interviews with Alistair Darling focused on the issues referred to already, and the former chancellor dismissed the White Paper as a 'work of fiction'; he emphasised the difficulties in implementing a currency union and the financial implications of an ageing population.

The main difference between the coverage south and north of the border was that the latter was far more extensive, sometimes wearyingly so. Both sets of programmes reflected what was taken to be the general view – or 'frame' – that the White Paper had not answered some of the central questions, but journalists carefully hedged their bets on the likely outcome of the vote.

Some commentators were highly critical of the BBC's general performance during the referendum. Professor John Robertson of the University of the West of Scotland, for example, argued that there was systematic bias against the Yes side and produced analysis of several strands of programming to back his thesis (OpenDemocracy 2014). The Corporation vigorously contested Robertson's conclusions, while Blair Jenkins, head of the Yes campaign, on a number of occasions stated that, while there had been some reports which his side regarded as unfair, he did not see evidence of systematic bias. But there is no doubt that there is a legacy of bitterness among supporters of independence which is directed against the BBC.

All Scottish newspapers and the Scottish editions of English titles the next day led on their front pages with the White Paper. However, the English editions of the latter preferred to lead on allegations made at the trial of former employees of the celebrity cook Nigella Lawson that she was a cocaine user, or on a migration story.

The Scottish broadsheets' extensive coverage set out the basic content of the document. Columnists in the *Herald* and the *Scotsman* argued the cases for and against independence. The *Herald* declared in an editorial that the White Paper 'goes some way to filling the vision vacuum' although 'big questions remain unanswered', while the *Scotsman*'s leader argued that there was now a challenge to the Better Together campaign to clarify its position on several issues. With an eye on part of its regional audience, the *Press and Journal*'s front page headline highlighted the White Paper's pledge that, post-independence, more power would be devolved from Edinburgh to the Scottish islands. The paper's editorial, like that in the *Herald*, argued that key questions 'remain in the air'. The *Courier*, like the *Scotsman*, in its leader urged readers to study the White Paper which it described as a 'curate's egg'. The most overtly hostile coverage was in the *Daily Record*. The front page headline asked 'Did he [the first minister] FORGET ABOUT THE PRICE TAG?' The White Paper's contents were reported inside but that was followed by a piece headlined 'DARLING PULPS ALEX'S FICTION'. In its critical editorial the *Record* declared 'On key issues ... the answers rang hollow'.

The tone of editorials and columnists in these Scottish titles varied but two recurring themes emerged, that a number of key questions remained to be answered by the Yes side and that the Better Together campaign needed to articulate a more convincing case for the union than it had yet offered.

The Scottish edition of the *Sun* took a similar editorial line. The paper provided more extensive coverage than the *Record*'s, and gave space to both Salmond and Darling to argue their cases. The London edition of the paper, however, carried one report which was hostile to independence, and no editorial.

'THE GREAT PRETENDER' was the front page headline in the Scottish edition of the *Daily Mail* and the same page featured a cartoon of Alex Salmond in *Braveheart* guise. The accompanying report was unambiguous in its hostility to independence, a hostility replicated throughout the paper's coverage, although it would have been possible to discern what the basic ideas in the White Paper were. The rather long editorial was very critical of the 'menu without prices' and ended by describing the break up of the UK as 'Scotland's nightmare – a desolate prospect that this dodgiest of dossiers fails to camouflage'. The London edition ran an equally hostile editorial and a two-page report in similar vein.

The *Telegraph* was also hostile to the SNP's vision, and in its north of the border edition its Scottish editor, Alan Cochrane, one of the commentators most opposed to independence and the SNP, poured scorn on what he regarded as an empty document. The editorial carried by both editions asked why, when the ties with England would remain so close, there was any point in independence at all. *The Times* in both its editions carried a cartoon showing Salmond as Mickey Mouse in front of a hillside with the inscription 'Holyrood'. The paper's leading article argued that the White Paper 'asks all the right questions but fails to give many satisfactory answers'.

Both of these London broadsheets provided the basic facts, though in more extensive form in their Scottish editions. The *Guardian* does not have a Scottish edition. Its coverage included a report, an editorial which referred to 'many unanswered questions', and a couple of columnists whose pieces seemed sympathetic to the Scottish desire for more power over the country's affairs. The *Financial Times* in its editorial said that 'while the *Financial Times* strongly favours the continuation of the union, we accept that there is an arguable – if flawed – case for independence'. The editorial – unsurprisingly – went on to focus on the difficulties on the currency front.

As can be seen from the foregoing, the themes which arose north and south of the border in editorials and commentary pieces were fairly similar.

What is very striking is that at that juncture no paper was offering support to the independence movement; columnists certainly did so in the *Herald* and the *Scotsman*, space was offered to Salmond and Nicola Sturgeon, but there was no support in editorial columns in the papers examined here. However, what was clear at that point was that the tone of editorials in a non-daily title, the *Sunday Herald*, was more sympathetic than what was found elsewhere, so it was not a total surprise when that paper later in the campaign became the sole title to support the Yes side. It has to be acknowledged too that those on the Yes side who believed that the No camp, with the connivance of some media outlets, was running a 'Project Fear' could find evidence for that belief in some of the press coverage reviewed here.

There were many discussion programmes on the airwaves in the run-up to the vote but arguably the most important were two television debates between Darling and Salmond. The first took place on 5 August and lasted for two hours (less commercials). It was transmitted north of the border though it was available online in the rest of the UK. The debate was moderated by STV's political editor and – perhaps rather surprisingly – the audience was allowed to cheer and boo the answers as the protagonists questioned each other and responded to questions from the floor. There had been low expectations for Darling's performance, but as he pushed Salmond repeatedly on the currency issue, it became clear that he was doing rather better than had been anticipated. Salmond for his part put Darling in a corner on the question of the promised new powers for the Scottish Parliament but the first minister did not acquit himself as well as expected. Newspaper coverage the next day reflected that impression. Overall the tone of reporting across the press veered from triumphalist to puzzled. The refusal of all of the UK political parties to enter into a currency deal seemed to have become the major item on the agenda. That was also reflected in subsequent broadcasting coverage.

The second debate on 25 August was staged by the BBC and it was transmitted throughout the UK. It lasted for an hour and half with no breaks for comments from journalists (which had been a feature of the previous encounter). As with the STV debate, it was moderated by a journalist who sought questions and comment from a lively audience. The protagonists made opening and closing statements and cross-examined each other. The issues covered included the currency, social policy, oil reserves and possible new powers for Holyrood, a similar agenda to the STV one. The general impression was that Salmond had the edge, and this was reflected in newspaper coverage the following day. The general view across the press was that Salmond had won the debate, although there was much emphasis on the amount of shouting in which the protagonists had indulged, and much editorial comment to the effect that the Yes side had still not won the argument for independence.

There was clearly a marked contrast overall between press coverage of the referendum and the way in which many papers had offered the SNP support when it sought re-election to Holyrood in 2011. But support for the SNP handling Scotland's domestic affairs, usually on the grounds that it had done a competent job as a minority government and deserved to be given another chance, has never led on to support for independence (although in April 2015 the Scottish edition of the *Sun* backed the SNP in the Westminster election, while its London-based stablemate urged support for the Conservatives). The lack of press support was a serious problem for the Yes side. It had to hope that the more balanced broadcast coverage would work against this general hostility and the virulence of some of the papers opposed to independence. On the other hand, the public may have tired of the unpleasantness of some of the coverage, even in papers they regularly purchased, particularly as they contrasted it with the ways in which a number of the more polished performers on the Yes side handled themselves in television discussions and debates. Could it even be the case that this unremitting hostility was self-defeating, for after a time voters might have resented such coverage, particularly coverage by English newspapers in their Scottish editions, which might ultimately have seemed not just anti-SNP or anti-independence but anti-Scottish? And if that was in fact what happened, how many percentage points was it worth to the Yes side?

A similar question might be asked about the 2015 general election campaign. David Cameron argued with increasing frequency that the choice facing Britain was a government led by him or a Labour government under a weak leader in hock to the SNP. That approach was noisily amplified by several newspapers, for example:

> NICOLA: MY PLAN TO RUN BRITAIN!
> Nicola Sturgeon is to make a breathtaking bid to seize control of the UK – despite her lifelong dream of tearing it apart.
> (*Scottish Mail on Sunday*, 19 April)

Such stories and other equally hostile coverage may well have persuaded wavering Labour voters in England to cast in their lot with the Conservatives, but might it also have led to some highly irritated Scottish voters defecting from their original parties of choice to the SNP? That party entered the election with overt editorial support from the *Sunday Herald*, the recently established *National* and in what some observers regard as a cynical ploy, the Scottish edition of the *Sun* (as noted above, the parent title in London supported the Tories). The victory for the SNP as it secured just over 50 per cent of the popular vote, and almost all Scottish Westminster seats, might suggest that newspapers when they are openly partisan have very little impact on voters' behaviour. To this observer it highlights the importance of broadcast political coverage on the British model and perhaps also serves to remind us too of the importance of the world beyond the media (including the new media of cyberspace), in which citizens interact with their families, friends, acquaintances and the wider culture as they make up their minds which group of politicians they wish to support.

Concluding remarks

Scottish citizens have access to a wide range of newspapers and broadcast channels. Some of the papers make a genuine effort to inform their readers about the terms of political debates, while others are fiercely partisan; when partisanship spills over from editorial and commentary columns into news reporting that is a disservice to democracy. The fact that there is a long tradition of unbridled bias in some British press reporting does not make it any less objectionable. Broadcasting north and south of the border endeavours to pursue the ideals of balance and fairness in its reporting. For that reason alone it is vital that both the BBC and ITV/STV remain able to finance high quality journalism which reports what is happening and also seeks to question those in authority. It is not only the broadcasters who have a responsibility here, so do the politicians. And north of the border that responsibility must fall very heavily on the shoulders of SNP leaders whose remarkable electoral triumphs could encourage the temptation – which assails all political leaders – to pressurise and even bully broadcasters to offer favourable coverage of their policies and activities. For a party, the achievement of whose ultimate ambition must lead to the dissolution of an organisation the very name of which proclaims the existence of the United Kingdom, that temptation could be dangerously strong.

Sources for further reading and study

Among the books mentioned in the References, the sections on the media in the volumes by Keating, Kellas, Lynch and McGarvey and Cairney are well worth reading, but note the publication dates of each. Kuhn's book offers a good general discussion of the relationship between the media and politics, while the volume edited by Blain and Hutchison contains a number of relevant essays on the Scottish situation. *Scotland's Referendum and the Media* (EUP 2016) edited by the same two academics, specifically addresses how that event was reported in Scotland, the rest of the UK and the wider world. For up to date information on newspaper sales figures the Audit Bureau of Circulation's website should be looked at, and for broadcasting policy developments the Ofcom website. Information on BBC governance issues can be obtained via the Corporation's website. The magazine *Scottish Affairs* provides an ongoing forum for discussion of Scottish politics, including the media aspect.

References

BBC Alba (2014) www.bbc.co.uk/alba/about/ (accessed 21 June 2015).
BBC (2007) http://news.bbc.co.uk/1/hi/scotland/7004263.stm (accessed 25 June 2015).
BBC (2008a) http://news.bbc.co.uk/1/hi/entertainment/7532858.stm (accessed 25 June 2015).
BBC (2008) http://news.bbc.co.uk/1/hi/entertainment/7373131.stm. (accessed 23 June 2015).
BBC (2011) www.bbc.co.uk/news/entertainment-arts-15165926 (accessed 22 June 2015).
Brock, George (2013) *Out of Print*. London: Kogan Page.
Cook, John (2008) 'Three Ring Circus: Television Drama About, By and For Scotland'. In Blain, N. and Hutchison, D. (eds) *The Media in Scotland*. Edinburgh: Edinburgh University Press, pp. 107–122.
Daily Telegraph (2014) www.telegraph.co.uk/news/uknews/scottish-independence/11095752/Scottish-independence-Nationalists-demand-Nick-Robinson-sacking-in-vocal-anti-BBC-protest.html (accessed 21 June 2015).
First Minister (2015) https://firstminister.gov.scot/a-bold-and-ambitious-bbc (accessed 21 June 2015).
The Guardian (2014) www.theguardian.com/media/2014/aug/26/scottish-independence-tv-debate-bbc2-salmond-darling (accessed 21 June 2015).
The Guardian (2015) www.theguardian.com/media/2015/jun/21/nick-robinson-cameron-threatened-close-down-bbc-election-bus (accessed 25 June 2015).
Habermas, Jürgen (1989) *The Structural Transformation of the Public Sphere*. Cambridge: Polity Press.
Harris, Michael (1978) '1620–1780'. In Boyce, G., Curran, J. and Wingate, P. (eds) *Newspaper History from the Seventeenth Century to the Present Day*. London: Constable, pp. 19–40.

Hutchison, David (2008) 'The History of the Press'. In Blain, N. and Hutchison, D. (eds) *The Media in Scotland*. Edinburgh: Edinburgh University Press, pp. 55–70.

Hutchison, David (2015) 'The Media and the Referendum: Uncharted Waters, Perilous Seas?'. In Müller, K.P. (ed.) *Scotland 2014 and Beyond: Coming of Age and Loss of Innocence?* Frankfurt am Main, Germany: Peter Lang, pp. 117–135.

Hutchison, David (2016) 'Broadcasting and the Press: Some Key Moments'. In Blain, N. and Hutchison, D. (eds) *Scotland's Referendum and the Media*. Edinburgh: Edinburgh University Press,.

Keating, Michael (2010) *The Government of Scotland: Public Policy Making after Devolution* (2nd edn). Edinburgh: Edinburgh University Press.

Kellas, James (1989) *The Scottish Political System* (4th edn). Cambridge: Cambridge University Press.

Kuhn, Raymond (2007) *Politics and the Media in Britain*. Basingstoke: Palgrave Macmillan.

Lynch, Peter (2001) *Scotttish Government and Politics*. Edinburgh: Edinburgh University Press.

McGarvey, P. and N. Cairney (2008) *Scottish Politics: An Introduction*. Basingstoke: Palgrave Macmillan.

McInnes, Rosalind (2010) *Scots Law for Journalists*. Edinburgh: W. Green/Thomson Reuters.

McNair, Brian (2008) 'The Scottish Media and Politics'. In Blain, N. and Hutchison, D. (eds) *Scotland's Referendum and the Media*. Edinburgh: Edinburgh University Press, pp. 226–242.

Mowatt, Ian (2008) 'Broadcast Comedy'. In Blain, N. and Hutchison, D. (eds) *Scotland's Referendum and the Media*. Edinburgh: Edinburgh University Press, pp. 137–150.

Newton, K. and M. Brynin (2001) 'The National Press and Party Voting in the UK'. *Political Studies* 49: 265–284.

Ofcom (2014) http://stakeholders.ofcom.org.uk/consultations/renewal-c4-licence-out-of-england-quota/ (accessed 23 June 2015).

OpenDemocracy (2014) www.opendemocracy.net/ourkingdom/john-robertson/bbc-bias-and-scots-referendum-new-report.

Riddell, Peter (1998) 'Members and Millbank: The Media and Parliament'. In Seaton, Jean (ed.) *Politics and the Media: Harlots and Prerogatives at the Turn of the Millennium*. Oxford: Blackwell, pp. 8–18.

Reid, Harry (2006) *Deadline: The Story of the Scottish Press*. Edinburgh: St Andrew Press.

Rosie, George (1978) 'The Scots Comics'. In Hutchison, David (ed.) *Headlines: The Media in Scotland*. Edinburgh: EUSPB, pp. 22–29.

Schlesinger, Philip (1998) 'Scottish Devolution and the Media'. In Seaton, Jean (ed.) *Politics and the Media: Harlots and Prerogatives at the Turn of the Millennium*. Oxford: Blackwell, pp. 55–74.

Scottish Government (2008) www.scottishbroadcastingcommission.gov.uk/about/Final-Report.html (accessed 21 June 2015).

Scottish Government (2010), http://archive.scottish.parliament.uk/s3/committees/ellc/reports-10/edr10-07.htm (last accessed 21 June (2015).

Scottish Government (2013) www.gov.scot/Publications/2013/03/5750/downloads#res416412 (accessed 21 June 2015).

Smith Commission (2014) www.smith-commission.scot/wp-content/uploads/2014/11/The_Smith_Commission_Report-1.pdf (accessed 21 June 2015).

Wilson, Brian (2008) 'The View from Westminister'. In Blain, N. and Hutchison, D. (eds) *Scotland's Referendum and the Media*. Edinburgh: Edinburgh University Press, pp. 243–247.

Yougov (2014) https://yougov.co.uk/news/2014/08/09/more-british-people-trust-wikipedia-trust-news/ (accessed 21 June 2015).

Politics in Scotland

Conclusion

Duncan McTavish

Politics in Scotland at the present time and in the short-medium term can best be explained around three dimensions. The first is the political position of Scotland in the UK, specifically around the fact that the UK–Scotland relationship is not federally structured. Several chapters (e.g. Chapters 11 and 13) have pointed out that there is no planned federal (or any other) design which underpins or provides rationale for Britain's constitutional governance. The speed and process by which major constitutional developments have taken place (barely eighteen months from independence referendum, to 'vow', to legislation (Scotland Act) is much more easily explained by reaction to events and political opportunism than by close attention to constitutional principles or notions of good governance. This approach to constitutional change in Britain is far from unusual, as Chapters 1, 4, 11 and 13 testify.

Within this political context, it is unlikely that the post-referendum passage of the Scotland Act with further devolved powers to the Scottish Parliament will provide any sort of conclusion to Scotland–UK relationships, given the very asymmetric nature of devolution throughout the British state. As Chapter 11 points out, 'we must look forward to more White Papers'. The extent to which Scottish politics and policy diverge from those of Westminster will clearly be of interest. It may not be possible to create entirely different social policies given the partial devolution, for example, of welfare powers co-existing alongside reserved powers as well as reserved UK-level eligibility criteria (as with universal credit and in-work benefits). So the path adopted by some federal governments to opt out of federal programmes instead using federal moneys to design sub-state policies and programmes (regional or provincial) – as for example has been done in Quebec – may not be possible.

Some have gone so far as to suggest that the arrangements set out in the Scotland Act amount to a hybrid 'hotch potch' devolving some tax raising and welfare powers (including the ability to 'top up' UK determined benefit levels), but without fuller fiscal and macro-economic powers, many distinctive policies can only be implemented at the expense of other policies, a form of zero sum game (Sime 2015). Others indicate that by using powers devolved since 1999 (in health and some areas of local authority implementation of social policy), new powers may be used to achieve distinctly Scottish policy approaches; for example by using newly devolved powers on attendance allowance or carers allowance alongside existing health competencies, distinctive approaches to aspects of social care could be possible. Indeed, Chapter 8 indicates that existing devolved powers could conceivably be used to craft radically different Scottish policies, though the political feasibility of this may be another matter.

The dynamic or indeed political (in)stability of the devolved settlement raises many interesting issues. Chapter 13 gives instances of how the flexible, opportunistic and politically inspired approaches to constitutional change may be pragmatic and positive in outcome. But the chapter also indicates current political circumstances that may create instabilities, ranging from the dominance of SNP representation of Scottish seats at Westminster to the 'English votes for English laws' mechanism introduced at Westminster. The parameters of political opportunity strategies for parties are starting to form with the Conservatives, while supporting the retention of business, corporate, national insurance and so on as reserved revenue sources, strongly supporting a devolved fiscal regime which forces more Scottish spending to align with Scottish tax receipts: presumably the Conservatives' attempt is to position themselves as a relatively low tax-and-spend party much in line with the UK party while taunting the SNP (from the 'right') to say how they will fund their anti-austerity message (see Parry 2015). Conversely, Scottish Labour has moved to indicate it will be redistributive and use tax powers at top rate level to make up for income losses suffered by claimants through UK Government reductions in working tax credits, thereby taunting the nationalists (from the 'left') and attempting to recapture some left of centre territory from the SNP. As for the SNP, its position as a nationalist party is interesting. At first blush the politics of the referendum can be seen as a binary divide and a political alignment between nationalism and unionism, as Chapter 2 indicated (though nationalism and unionism are historically nuanced – see Chapter 1). In other devolved environments with strong pro-independence parties we can see strong polarisation with politics defined around the national/territorial debate. For example in Catalonia the polarisation of electoral competition for and against independence has squeezed parties with a less strong view on territorial politics (especially the Socialist party) (see Leon 2015). Yet to view Scottish politics through this prism may be misleading and/or premature. As Chapters 2 and 4 point out, much SNP success has to do with valence politics; SNP voting numbers have often stretched beyond those supporting independence, and the overwhelming victory of the SNP at the 2015 UK general election continued this trend.

The second – related – dimension is about the roles and positions taken by key institutional players around the Scottish national dimension to politics. To make sense of this requires analysis beyond the structures and institutions. Institutional positions (e.g. of Westminster and Holyrood governments, political parties) on 'the elephant in the room', that is independence and another referendum on such, will no doubt present a constant backdrop but the hidden wiring will be significant. For example the SNP's tactical view that there is unlikely to be a call for a referendum in the short term unless 'material circumstances' alter may signal not simply a tactical retreat but also an alternative perspective to the binary nationalism versus unionism debate – a polarised or binary perspective which was rather inevitable in the 2014 referendum campaign where voters were offered a yes or no response. But varieties of nationalism (and unionism) do have historical precedence, as Chapter 1 indicates. Future patterns are likely to be determined by the actions and perspectives on intergovernmental relations displayed by the UK Government. Benign neglect as a strategy appears to have smoothed tensions in Canada, where the previous federal government under Stephen Harper stayed out of policy areas where provinces had jurisdiction, though the resourcing and policy ties remaining in the UK's devolved setting even after enhanced devolution, make such a strategy more difficult here: 'benign neglect' may be more easily presented as ignoring devolved polities' needs. The reverse of a relatively hands off approach, a pan-British initiative to bind the union together, seems unlikely, the only recent attempt at this being Gordon Brown's call for pooling risks and resources at UK level within current political arrangements; and arguably such initiatives are unlikely anyway given the UK Government's desire for a smaller-scale state. A move towards hard budget constraints – which as Chapter 5 shows has at least partially been delivered with increased devolution – is unlikely to provide for stable intergovernmental relations with a pro-independence majority at Holyrood, rather it is more likely to lead to calls for greater fiscal powers.

Just beneath the surface of these macro political arrangements, there are developments of great significance to any analysis of how politics – and policy – in Scotland will play out and whether this will be done through a desire to pursue Scottish interests (however these are articulated) and/or have distinctly Scottish approaches. Chapter 10 indicates the increasing involvement of Scotland in paradiplomacy and protodiplomacy. This will continue and the form it takes could well be as significant as the more obvious arguments and debates about devolution or independence. For example, more involvement in European 'comitology' (the network of bodies and organisations through which policy is made) or the desire for greater involvement in UK foreign policy may through interdepartmental and intergovernmental relationships have effects which determine where and how far devolved institutions can be stretched with regard to Westminster's sovereignty. In areas of social policy and gender equality, Chapters 8 and 9 show that distinctly Scottish approaches are in evidence but that optimising these stated policies of fairness (in social policy) and greater equality (in gender representation) does not always occur.

The third dimension around which Scottish politics can be studied is the extent and nature of 'new politics'. As a number of chapters have indicated, this was part of the discussion and campaigning of much of political and civic Scotland in the years preceding the devolved Parliament's creation. Part of this new approach to politics was a partly proportional electoral system, and since the first Scottish Parliamentary elections it has produced a variety of results: coalition governments; single party but no overall majority government; single party overall majority government. Other aspects of 'new politics' (more open, participative, deliberative, less executive-dominated) should be viewed with some circumspection, since in reality the Scottish Parliament is part of the 'Westminster family' of parliaments (Mitchell 2010); one can see many examples of Westminster approaches, ranging from executive dominance to adversarial politics. The Scottish Parliament has in fact been defined by two narratives, the first often termed 'new politics' giving a more participatory and inclusive tone to politics, the second along more traditional thinking about accountability of government (Cairney and Johnston 2013). A key area of interest will be the extent to which 'maximalist' approaches to the first of these narratives, new politics, (as outlined in Chapter 3) – including a range of social and political outcomes (see Chapters 8 and 9) – gain traction in Scotland: the referendum campaign stimulated political involvement from parts of civic Scotland not previously politically engaged, and this seems to have carried over with Scotland displaying considerably higher levels of turnout than the rest of the UK at the 2015 election. In fact, over time the dual narrative can be seen in much of Holyrood's activities. As Chapter 12 points out, much service delivery is more decentralised than elsewhere in Britain, and key interests can more easily access government, though as Chapter 6 indicates too there is a long-standing pattern of local government being seen as an implementation tool of central government policy and service delivery rather than an instrument to promote subsidiarity.

Accountability of the Scottish Government to the Scottish Parliament will be interesting to observe. While the general public seems relatively well disposed to Scottish Government and Parliament compared to other parts of UK (McCrone 2009) the role of the Scottish Parliament in holding government accountable is worth considering. The Scottish Parliament was designed as a unicameral institution and its electoral system established partly to ensure no single party could gain an overall majority. Unicameral arrangements clearly impose a greater burden on the legislature in terms of legislative and scrutiny processes; and without appropriate policy and research capacity the institution will not be able to carry out these functions as fully as possible. Add to this: the multi functional nature of parliamentary committees, where at Holyrood the committees have legislative and scrutiny responsibilities (unlike Westminster where separate committees exist for each function); the size of the Scottish Parliament (small), the committees approaching twenty in number and when government ministers are excluded this leaves about eighty MSPs available for committee service, and one can appreciate the challenges of Parliamentary scrutiny. The Parliament has undertaken an enquiry of its committee system prior to the 2016 election to examine inter alia number and size of committees, impact of new devolved powers, party balance, selection of convenors and members, resources required, etc. (for a good account of this see Lynch 2015).

Taken as a whole this book has addressed the essence of politics in Scotland at the present time. Its coverage ranges from an outline of the historical nuancing of the unionist–nationalist narrative in Scottish politics, to an account of recent British constitutional change and the case of Scotland, an analysis of political parties and voting behaviour as well as 'new politics', and an examination of the machinery of government and funding arrangements of the devolved Parliament. There are also evaluations and critical analyses of aspects of Scotland's developing international political interactions and other policy areas too. The key role played by the media in Scotland is also outlined, in the context of media–political relations in a political democracy. Finally the key areas and dimensions of analysis to enable us to capture and understand political developments in Scotland over the coming period are indicated.

References

Cairney, P. and J. Johnston (2013) 'What Is the Role of the Scottish Parliament?' *Scottish Parliamentary Review* 1(2): 91–130.

Leon, S. (2015) 'The Curse of Polarised Politics in Catalonia'. Available at: www.centreonconstitutionalchange.ac.uk/blog/curse-polarised-politics-catalonia (accessed 14 November 2015).

Lynch, P. (2015) 'How Effectively Does the Scottish Parliament Scrutinise the Scottish Government?' Available at: www.democraticauditscotland.com/how-effectively-does-the-scottish-parliament-srutinise-the-scottish-government (accessed 30 October 2015).

McCrone, D. (2009) 'Conundrums and Contradictions: What Scotland Wants'. In Jeffery, C. and Mitchell, J. (eds) *The Scottish Parliament 1999–2009: The First Decade*. Edinburgh: Hansard Society with Luath Press, pp. 93–104.

Mitchell, J. (2010) 'The Narcissism of Small Differences: Scotland and Westminster'. *Parliamentary Affairs* 63: 98–116.

Parry, R. (2015) 'The Scotland Bill: The Conservatives as the Devo Max Party'. Available at: http://centreonconstitutionalchange.ac.uk/blog/scotland-bill-the-conservatives-as-devomax-party (accessed 11 November 2015).

Sime, M. (2015) 'It Is Time To Kill the Scotland Bill Because It Will Never Last Anyway'. *The Herald*, 17 October.

Index

Aaronovitch, D. 74
Abel, T. 150
Aberdeen Press and Journal 245, 246, 247, 254
accountability of government 35, 43, 45–46, 48, 84, 86, 95, 97, 98, 214; accountability deficit 2; democracy, quality of 51; fiscal accountability 97, 101; local accountability 112, 119; ministerial accountability 222–23; to Scottish Parliament 262
Ackerman, Bruce 230
Act of Union (1707): civil service, government machinery and 126; social policy 140, 144
Adam, S. and Kriesi, H. 221
Aikman, C. 14
Alcock, P. et al. 148
Aldecoa, F. and Keating, M. 181, 193
Alexander, Morag 162, 170, 172, 173, 175
Alexander, Wendy 53, 91, 105n1, 130
Alexander group discussions on Scotland's future 91
All Party Parliamentary Groups (APPGs) on equality 165, 166
Alternative Member System (AMS) 24; referendum on 238
American Founding Fathers 239
Amery, L.S. 232
Anderson, I. 142
Annandale Observer 247
anti-austerity message 143, 260
anti-Conservative perspective 43
anti-discrimination rights 160
anti-poverty strategies 146–47
Archer, C. and Main, J. 181
Arnstein, S.R. 173
Arshad, R. 162
Asare, B. et al. 222
Ashcroft, Brian 105n1
Ashdown, Paddy 236, 237
Assembly of European Regions 187
asymmetric devolution: constitutional reform 240; unionism and nationalism, historical perspective 9, 18
Atkinson, A. 203

attendance allowances 259
Aucoin, Peter 138
Ayrshire Post 247

Balls, Ed 95
Barnett formula: local government 114–15; political parties 80; Scottish Labour Devolution Commission and 98; soft budget restraint and 96; unionism and nationalism, historical perspective 18
Barroso, José Manuel 185
Basque Country: diplomacy, international affairs and 182, 183, 184, 187; political parties 81
Bauer Media Group 248
Baumgartner, F. and Jones, B. 220
Bavaria 186
BBC 244, 248–49, 250, 251, 252, 253, 255, 256, 257
BBC Alba 248
In Bed with an Elephant: A Journey through Scotland's Past and Present (Kennedy, L.) 195
Begg, A. 169
Ben-Galim, D. et al. 164
Bengtsson, H. et al. 52
Benn, Tony 234, 235
Bennett, C. et al. 161
Bennie, L. et al. 28
Beveridge, Crawford 173
Beveridge, F. et al. 160, 161, 164
Beveridge Report (1942) 141
Biagini, E.F. 7
Billig, Michael 37
Bird, Bob 249
Birrell, D. 151
Blair, Colonel P.J. 11
Blair, Tony (and government of) 17, 28, 31, 38, 128, 230, 236–38, 243
The Blair Revolution (Mandelson, P. and Little, R.) 230
Bloc Québécois 240
block grant, need for 92, 105–6n7

264 Index

Blond, Phillip 20n21
'Bloody Sunday' in Northern Ireland, effects of 234
Bogdanor, Vernon 210, 232, 238
Borchert, H. and Zeiss, J. 74
Borders Railway 135
bounded rationality, concept of 219–20
Boyd, S. 173
Bradbury, J. et al. 53
Brewer, Gordon 253
British Council 187
British Motor Corporation, Bathgate 61
Britishness: shared history of 6; voting behaviour and 37–8
Britney Spears Model of Constitutional Reform (BSMCR) 229; British membership of Europe and 231–35; devolution, SNP perceived threat and (1970s) 235–36; New Labour and 236–38; precedent creation (1970s) 231–35
broadcast media 243–44, 247–49
Broadcasting Commission 248
Brock, George 246
Brooks, D. 7
Brown, A. 42, 51
Brown, A. et al. 28
Brown, Gordon 60, 66, 95, 201, 239, 243, 261
Brown, Keith 130
Brown, S.J. 7
Buchanan Smith, Alick 61
Bühlmann, M. et al. 45, 46
Bühlmann, Marc 45
Bulpitt, J. 81
Burke, Edmund 233
Burness, C. 8
Bush, President George W. 183
Butler, D. and Kitzinger, U. 233, 235
Butler, D. et al 15

Cabinet Office and Scottish Executive, concordat between 127
Cairney, P. and Johnston, J. 219, 222, 261
Cairney, P. and McGarvey, N. 173, 213, 214, 215, 216, 217, 218, 219, 221, 223
Cairney, P. and Widfeldt, A. 219, 221
Cairney, P. et al. 214, 222, 223
Cairney, Paul ix, 51, 52, 114, 140, 141, 151, 213–28
Callaghan, James 236
Calman Commission (2009): funding government 91, 92, 94, 97–98, 99, 104; gender, equality and 174
Cameron, David (and government of) 53, 95, 230–31, 234, 239, 244, 256
Cameron, Ewen ix, 6–23, 60
Campbell, D.F.J. et al. 47, 50
Campbell, Keith 233

Canada: constitutional arrangements in 231; constitutional relationships within 240; Quebec and 80–81; reference point for Scotland 203
Capello, Fabio 133
Carers UK 149
Carman, C. and Johns, R. 35
Carman, C. et al. 84
Carmichael, Alistair 253
Carney, Mark 133
Carrell, S. 73
cartel parties: development of 77–78; shift towards 85
Catalonia 82, 182, 183, 184–85, 186; Convergencia i Unio (CiU) in 81; Olympic Games (1992) in Barcelona 184; Socialist Party of Catalonia (PSC) 82
catch-all parties: development of 77; shift towards 85
Celis, K. et al. 164
Centre for Cultural Relations, University of Edinburgh 182
Channel 4 News 252
Channel 5 TV 248
Charlesworth, H. 164
Childs, S. and Krook, M. 163, 172
China 184, 186
Chisholm, Malcolm 167, 169, 172, 173
Church of Scotland, status of 201
Churchill, Winston S. 19n4
Citizens Universal Basic Income 156
civil service, government machinery and 2, 123–39; Act of Union (1707) 126; Borders Railway 135; Cabinet Office and Scottish Executive, concordat between 127; Civil Service Code 128; *Civil Service Impartiality in the Scottish Referendum*, investigation into 132; consolidated administration and networks without reorganisation 135–37; constitutional project, civil service support for 131; Constitutional Reform and Governance Act (2010) 126, 128; Council of Economic Advisers 134; Creative Scotland 136; derivative nature of devolved system 123, 126–27; devolved areas and decisions, overlaps with 131; devolved system: Barnett consequentials and 135; civil service role in 127–28; public sector workers in 124–25; start of 123, 129; director-general for strategy and external affairs, appointment of 133; Edinburgh Agreement (2012) 131; evolution of governmental institutions, pace of 123; Fiscal Commission Working Group 134; foreign managers, introduction of 132–33; further reading, sources for 138–39; Futures Project (2006) 127; *Government Expenditure and Revenue in Scotland*

('GERS') 127; Historic Environment Scotland 136; Home Civil Service 124, 126–27, 134, 135, 138, 165; independence referendum, civil service and 131–32; inherited legacy 126–27; Institute of Government 127; landscape of government 123; Local Government in Scotland Act (2003) 136; machinery of government 124–25; National Objectives, 'Single Outcome Agreements' and 136; National Statistics 127; nationalists in government, relating to 128–30; NHS in Scotland 135, 136–37; *Northern Exposure* (Elvidge, J.) 137–38; permanent secretaries 132–34; personality of SNP ministers in relations with officials 129–30; Plaid Cymru 128; planning in policy areas, legal and political advice in 134; Police Scotland 136; practices set (by 2007) 129; public administration, conservatism in 126; public employment 124–25; Public Services Reform (Scotland) Act (2010) 136; 'quango-culls,' 'simplification' and 135; reassessment of government model 137–38; reinforcement of government machine, analytical work on independence and 134–35; Scotland Act (2012) 129; Scotland Analyses series of papers (UK Government, 2013) 134–35; Scotland Performs rubric 129; *Scotland's Future: Your Guide to an Independent Scotland* (SNP, 2013) 132; Scottish Executive 129; Scottish Fire and Rescue service 136; Scottish Government, introduction of terminology of 129; Scottish National Party (SNP) 123; consolidation amongst elites post-2007, need for 124; preservation of UK administrative styles by 124; regime change management and 128–30; relations with officials, personalities of ministers in 129–30; Scottish Public Pensions Agency 135; Scottish Rate of Income Tax (SRIT) 135, 137; Smith Commission 135; machinery of government and 137; social security administration 135; special advisers 130; Strategic Board 127–28; tartanised versions of joined-up government 127–28; UK administrative styles, preservation of 124, 126–27; Welfare Reform Act (UK, 2012) 135; Welsh Assembly Government 129; Workforce 2015 on senior staff paybill 127

Clarke, H.D. and Stewart, M.C. 36
Clarke, H.D. et al. 37
Clegg, Nick 231, 238, 239
Cochrane, Alan 254
Collier, J.G. 199
Commission on Local Democracy Report (2014) 120, 204
Committee of the Regions (CoR) 189–90
Common Fisheries Policy 188
Commonwealth Parliamentary Association and the Conference Europe of Regional Legislative Assemblies (CALRE) 187
Community Care and Health (Scotland) Act (2003) 152
Community Charge ('Poll Tax'), reaction to 15
Community Empowerment Scotland Act (2015) 109, 116
Community Planning Partnerships (CPPs) 213
Community Safety Partnerships 142
Concordat with Convention of Scottish Local Authorities (COSLA) 217
Conference of Peripheral Maritime Regions 187
Conservative-Liberal Democrat coalition and constitutional change 238–39
Conservative party in Scotland: change and opportunity structures for 62–64; Declaration of Perth 61; decline of 14–16, 26–7, 28; perspectives on 15–16; devolution and 81–82; membership of 69; Scottish Policy Forum 69; supporting foundations of 59, 60–61; Unionist Party (until 1965) 60
Constance, Angela 130
constitutional reform 4–5, 229–41; Alternative Vote, referendum on 238; American Founding Fathers 239; asymmetric devolution 240; Bloc Québécois 240; 'Bloody Sunday' in Northern Ireland, effects of 234; Britney Spears Model of Constitutional Reform (BSMCR) 229; British membership of Europe and 231–35; devolution, SNP perceived threat and (1970s) 235–36; New Labour and 236–38; precedent creation (1970s) 231–35; Canada: constitutional arrangements in 231; constitutional relationships within 240; Conservative–Liberal Democrat coalition and constitutional change 238–39; constitutional matters, reserved nature of 240; constitutional moments, Ackerman and model of 229–30, 231; constitutional politics in UK, partisan nature of 239; constitutional reform: New Labour and 229, 236–38; Wilson government (1964–69) and 232; dangers in 239–40; Denmark, constitutional arrangements in 231; devolution legislation, steamrollering of 237; *Diaries* (Ashdown, P.) 237; Edinburgh Agreement (2012) 238; English votes for English laws 230–31, 240; European Convention of Human Rights (ECHR) 238; European Economic Community (EEC), issue of 232–35; First Reform Act (1832) 7, 239; Fixed Term

Parliament Act (2011) 238; flexible pragmatism, constitutional change and 239–40; House of Lords reform 237–38; Human Rights Act (1998) 236, 238; independence, contemporary issues pertaining to 229, 239–40; Kilbrandon Commission 236; parliamentary democracy, members' judgement and principle of 233; parliamentary sovereignty, abandonment of principle of 229, 231–35, 236; political opportunism 229, 232, 237, 239, 240; referendum on EEC membership, proposal for 234–35; referendums, anathema of 233; reform of constitutional arrangements, UK attitudes to 231; Scottish National Party (SNP): foundations of 236; majority in Scottish Parliament 237; thundering success in 2015 UK General Election 239; Solon the Wise of Athens 239; Spain: autonomy for regions in 237; constitutional arrangements in 231; *Thoughts on the Constitution* (Amery, L.S.) 232; transfer of powers to Brussels 235; 'Vow' on powers for Scottish Parliament 239; West Lothian Question 231

Constitutional Reform and Governance Act (2010) 126, 128

Consultative Steering Group (CSG): democracy, quality of 42, 47, 48, 50, 51; future for government and public policy 219

Convention of Scottish Local Authorities (COSLA) 204

Cook, John 248

Cook, Robin 236

Corbyn, Jeremy 19n16, 40

corporation tax, comparisons between 2004 considerations and 2014 recommendations on 94

Coulson, Andy 250

Council of Economic Advisers 134

Council of Ministers 190

Council of Municipalities and Regions (CCRE) Report (2009) 204

council tax, 'freeze' on 108, 116

Coyle, Diane 105n1

Craig, F.W.S. 9

Creative Scotland: civil service, government machinery and 136; media and politics 250

Crewe, I. 64

Crewe, I. et al. 36

Criekmans, D. 181

Criminal Justice and Public Order Act (1994) 200, 201

Cross Party Groups (CPGs) on equality 165, 166

Crossman, Richard 12, 19n15

Crowther-Hunt, Lord 86

Crowther-Kilbrandon Commission 12

Croxford, L. et al. 144

Curriculum for Excellence: diplomacy, international affairs and 184; social policy 144

Curtice, John 35

Curtin, J.C. 172

Dahl, R.A. and Tufte, E. 43, 46

Dahl, Robert A. 44

Daily Express 246

Daily Mail 246, 247, 254

Daily Mirror 246

Daily Record 245, 246, 247, 254

Daily Star 246

Daily Telegraph 244, 246, 247, 254

Dalai Lama 184

Dale, I. 237

Dalton, Russell J. 36

Daly, M. 164, 173

Dalyell, Tam 19n17

Darling, Alistair 67, 231, 243, 253, 254, 255

Davidson, Ruth 53, 64, 81

Davidson, Sarah 133

D.C. Thomson 247

De Gaulle, Charles 208, 233

De Lima, P. 148

De Lima, P. and Wright, S. 148

Deacon, Susan 67

dealignment thesis 36

Dearing, J.W. and Rogers, E.M. 220

decentralisation (devolution), referendum on (1979) 42

Declaration of Flanders (2001) 190

Declaration of Perth (1968) 12

Delivering for Health (White Paper, 2005) 151

Delors, Jacques 188

democracy, quality of 3, 42–56, 262; accountability, issue of 51; adversarial relationships 52; anti-Conservative perspective 43; closed-list PR system 49; committee systems 51; Consultative Steering Group (CSG) 42, 47, 48, 50, 51; decentralisation (devolution), referendum on (1979) 42; democracy, referendum debate and questions of 53–54; Democracy Barometer 45; democracy in Scotland, aspiration of enhancement of 42–43, 51; democratic quality 43–47; democratic quality rankings 47; devolution, blueprint for 47–50; economic inequality 46–47, 55; equality, issue of 44, 46, 55; female membership of Scottish Parliament 52–53; Freedom House dataset 46; Global Democracy Ranking 1; 'inputs' and 'outputs,' disagreements on focus 43–45; The Logic of Democracy (McGann, A.) 44; maximalist conceptualisation of democratic quality 43, 45, 46, 47, 48, 50, 52, 54, 55; minimalist conceptualisation of democratic quality 43–44, 45, 46, 47, 48, 50, 51, 52, 53, 55; minority governments 52; mixed-member proportional (MMP) system 48–49, 49–50, 52–53; new politics, aspiration for 42–43, 51; *Patterns of Democracy* (Lijphart, A.) 44–45; Plaid Cymru 53; political participation, voter turnout and 54–55; Polity IV dataset 46; *Polyarchy* (Dahl, R.) 44; proportional electoral system 51, 55; proportional representation (PR) system in Germany 48; Radical Independence Campaign 54; reconceptualisation of democracy, Munck's perspective on 44–45; record since devolution 50–53; referendum (2014) 53–55; *Scotland's Future: Your Guide to an Independent Scotland* (SNP, 2013) 53–54; Scottish Constitutional Commission 48; Scottish Constitutional Convention 42, 48–49, 50; House of Commons election system, criticism of 49; key principles of 48; Scottish Parliament electoral system, criteria for 49; Scottish National Party (SNP), rise of 42; single transferable vote (STV) system 49–50; smaller is better perspective 46–47; social equality, aim for enhancement of 54; socioeconomic inequality 44, 46, 55; unicameral legislature 44, 46, 50, 55; voter turnout 54–55; Westminster system, democratic deficiencies in 54; Women for Independence 54; women's representation, issue of 50, 52–53

Denmark, constitutional arrangements in 231
Denver, D. et al. 72
descriptive representation 163
Devine, T.M. 6, 59, 63, 64, 195, 201
devolution: Barnett consequentials and 135; blueprint for 47–50; civil service role in 127–28; devolution gap, London mindset and 169–74; devolved and federated governments, external actions and 181; devolved and reserved powers, friction between 169–70; devolved areas and decisions, overlaps with 131; devolved powers, uses of 259; devolved settlement, dynamic of 260; independence demands and 17–18; interest group devolution 214; legislation on, steamrollering of 237; partial devolution 259; political parties, future under 80–84; positive image of 215; public sector workers in 124–25; start of 123, 129; subsidiarity and 108–10; Unionists as party of 10–11

Dewar, Donald 31, 60, 127, 133, 140, 252
d'Hondt, Victor 40n1
Diamond, L. and Morlino, L. 45
Diamond, L. and Tsalik, S. 46

Diaries (Ashdown, P.) 237
Dicey, A.V. 232
Dickson, A.D.R. 16
Diplocat 185
diplomacy, international affairs and 4, 180–93, 261; Asia 186; Assembly of European Regions 187; Basque Country 182, 183, 184, 187; Bavaria 186; British Council 187; Catalonia 182, 183, 184–85, 186; Centre for Cultural Relations, University of Edinburgh 182; China 184, 186; Committee of the Regions (CoR) 189–90; Common Fisheries Policy 188; Commonwealth Parliamentary Association and the Conference Europe of Regional Legislative Assemblies (CALRE) 187; 'community method' of policy making 190–91; Conference of Peripheral Maritime Regions 187; conflict 192–93; cooperation 192–93; Council of Ministers 190; cultural diplomacy 182–84; cultural promotion 183; Curriculum for Excellence 184; Declaration of Flanders (2001) 190; devolved and federated governments, external actions and 181; Diplocat 185; diversionary policy 181; economic development 181–82; education 182–84; environmental issues 180; environmental policy (ENCORE) 187; Europe of the Regions 189; European Association of Development Agencies (Eurada) 187; European Commission (EC) 181; European Convention on Human Rights (ECHR) 191; European Regions Research and Innovation Network (ERRIN) 187; European Union (EU) 180, 185; attitudes towards 189; referendum on leaving, voting intentions in (2014) 189; relations with 181; Europhilia 188; Euroscepticism 188; Flanders 183, 186; functions of government, rescaling of 180; further reading, sources for 193; geographical priorities 186; German Länder 186; global citizenship 184; Global Friends of Scotland 188; Global Scot network 187–88; globalization, transnational integration and 180; government, transformation of 180; Highlands and Islands Enterprise 181; *How the Scots Invented the Modern World* (Hernan, A.) 183; India 186; international affairs, role of devolved governments in 187; International Business Development Forum 182; Invest in Scotland 182; Joint Ministerial Committee (Europe) 190; Lisbon Treaty (2007) 189–90; Malawi 184, 186; markets, internationalisation of 180; mechanisms of paradiplomacy 187–88; migration 186; National Conference of State Legislatures (USA). 187; networks of industrial regions (RETI) 187;

North America 186; North Atlantic Treaty Organisation (NATO) 185; North-Rhine Westphalia 186; Olympic Games (1992) in Barcelona 184; Open Method of Coordination 190–91; Organization for Economic Cooperation and Development (OECD) 180, 184; paradiplomacy: involvement of Scotland in 261; mechanisms of 187–88; rise of 180–81; Parti Québécois 185; PISA system of student assessment 183–84; plurinational diplomacy 193; protodiplomacy 184–85, 261; public diplomacy 183; Quebec 182, 183, 185, 186; regional policy 181; Regions with Legislative Powers (RegLeg) 189–90; Review of Competences 191; Scotland Act (1978) 181; Scotland Act (1998) 180, 191; Scotland Europa 191–92; Scotland in Europe 188–92; Scottish Development Agency (SDA) 181–82; Scottish Development International (SDI) 182, 187; Scottish Enterprise 181; Scottish Social Attitudes Surveys 188; Scottish Week in US 186; stateless nations 182, 183; 'tartan monster' problem 183; Treaty on European Union (Maastricht Treaty, 1992) 189; Tuscany 186; UN Education and Cultural Organization (UNESCO) 180, 183–84; Wallonia 183
Direct Payments in lieu of standard community care services 152–53; institutional barriers to implementation of 152–53
disability benefits, effectiveness of 154
Disability Discrimination Act (2005) 164
disabled people, social policies for 152–54
Donaghy, T.B. 164, 167, 172, 173
Douglas-Home, Alec 12
Duchacek, I. et al. 181
Dugdale, Kezia 53, 69
Duncan, Joseph 19n2
Duncan, Sir Andrew 60
Duncanson, Hilary 55
Dundee Courier 245, 246, 247, 254

economic development 181–82
economic inequality 46–47, 55
economic performance 16
Eden, Anthony 20n21
Edinburgh Agreement (2012): civil service, government machinery and 131; constitutional reform 238
education: diplomacy, international affairs and 182–84; early years and further education, barriers to investment in 145; education policy 143–45, 157; future for government and public policy 215; in Scotland, distinctive nature of 201; Scottish interest in 14
Edwards, J. 164, 173

EHRC (Equality and Human Rights Commission) 162, 165, 169, 170, 171
Eichhorn, J. 84
elected politicians, representativeness of 73–76
Electoral Commission 69
electoral politics, fundamental changes in (1979–96) 27–8
Elias, A. 190
Elster, J. 237
Elvidge, Sir John 124, 127, 129, 135, 138, 213, 216, 218
employment 147–49; access to 148; employment rights 160; rates of (16–63) in four countries of UK (2002–2014) 148
Engender 168
English, J. 65
English votes for English laws (EVEL): constitutional reform 230–31, 240; status and relationships within UK and internationally 196; unionism and nationalism, historical perspective 17–18
environmental issues 180
environmental policy (ENCORE) 187
equal opportunities: duties exception 161–62; encouragement exception 161–62; principle of Scottish Parliament 161; retained power on 160
Equal Opportunities Committee in Scottish Parliament 165, 167
Equal Opportunities Select Committee at Westminster 167
equalisation, principle of 105n3
equality, issue of 44, 46, 55
Equality Act (2010) 164, 174
equality agenda, ministerial engagement with 171–72
Equality Network 162
equality *see* gender, equality and
Erk, J. and Veenendaal, W. 46
Erlingsson, G. and Ödalen, J. 204
Europe of the Regions 189
European and External Relations Committee 84
European Association of Development Agencies (Eurada) 187
European 'comitology' 261
European Commission (EC): diplomacy, international affairs and 181; gender, equality and 164
European comparison on local government 113–14
European Convention on Human Rights (ECHR): constitutional reform 238; diplomacy, international affairs and 191
European Economic Community (EEC) 232–35
European Regions Research and Innovation Network (ERRIN) 187

European Union (EU) 180, 185; attitudes towards 189; referendum on leaving, voting intentions in (2014) 189; relations with 181
Europhilia 188
Euroscepticism 186, 188
Evans, Leslie 124, 130, 133
Ewing, Winifred 11, 26
expert-bureaucratic model of policymaking 173

Fabiani, Linda 197
Fabre, John 195
fairness in social policy 140, 141, 143–44, 145, 151–52, 156–57; in austerity 154–56
federal structure: Crossman's argument for 12–13; problem of including small units within 9
Ferguson, I. 152
Ferguson, W. 7
Ferguson, Y. and Mansbach, R. 197
Financial Times 246, 254–55
Finlay, R.J. 10
Finn, M. and Seldon, A. 238
First-Past-The-Post (FPTP) electoral system 24–5, 27, 28, 30
fiscal autonomy 95, 102–3, 106n10, 109, 116
Fiscal Commission Working Group: civil service, government machinery and 134; gender, equality and 173
Fixed Term Parliament Act (2011) 238
Flanders 183, 186
flexible pragmatism, constitutional change and 239–40
foreign managers, introduction of 132–33
Forsyth, Michael 63
Foster, J. 60
franchise, extensions of 7, 10
Francis, Matthew 20n21
Fraser, I. 63
Fraser, Murdo 81
Fredman, S. 164
Freedom House dataset 46
Freedom of Information Act (2000) 171
Fresh Talent Initiative 84
funding government, Scotland Act (2015) and 2, 91–106; Alexander group discussions on Scotland's future 91; Barnett formula: Scottish Labour Devolution Commission and 98; soft budget restraint and 96; block grant, need for 92, 105–6n7; borrowing, comparisons between 2004 considerations and 2014 recommendations on 93; Calman Commission (2009) 91, 92, 94, 97–98, 99, 104; corporation tax, comparisons between 2004 considerations and 2014 recommendations on 94; equalisation, principle of 105n3; fiscal autonomy 95, 102–3, 106n10, 109, 116; ; hard budget constraint (HBC): Barnett formula, continuation of 94, 95–97; Calman Commission and Scotland Act (2012) 94, 97–98; constraints suggested, hardness of 94–104; desirable effects on sub-central government 95; Holtham Commission (2010) on Wales extended to Scotland 95, 99–100; independence and 104–5; Scotland Bill (2015) and Act (2016) 95, 103–4; Scottish Conservatives (2014) 95, 101–2, 106n9; Scottish Green Party (2014) 95, 103; Scottish Labour Devolution Commission (2014) 94, 98–99; Scottish Labour's lack of appreciation of 94, 98–99; Scottish Liberal Democrats (2014) 95, 100–101; Smith Commission and adoption of 92; SNP and continuing Scottish Government (2014) 95, 102–3; income tax, comparisons between 2004 considerations and 2014 recommendations on 93; macroeconomic stabilization, comparisons between 2004 considerations and 2014 recommendations on 93; marginal tax rule 94; minor taxes, comparisons between 2004 considerations and 2014 recommendations on 93; oil tax revenues, comparisons between 2004 considerations and 2014 recommendations on 93; political parties in Scotland, hard budget constraint (HBC) and 94–104; Scotland Act (1998) 92, 103–4; Scotland Act (2012) 92, 94, 97–98; Scotland Act (2016) 91; Scotland Bill (2015) 91; Scottish Executive, lack of hard budget constraint on 91; Smith Commission, enhanced devolution and 91–94; soft budget constraint (SBC) 95, 96, 104; value added tax, comparisons between 2004 considerations and 2014 recommendations on 93
future for government and public policy 4, 213–26, 261; adjustment period 214; ambiguity, decision-making in conditions of 220; bounded rationality, concept of 219–20; British policy style 213; central government control and local government discretion, balance between 224–224, 225; civil service, policy community and 220; cognitive change 214; communities, focus on 221, 225; Community Planning Partnerships (CPPs) 213; complex government, realities of 223; comprehensive rationality, concept of 219–20; Concordat with Convention of Scottish Local Authorities (COSLA) 217; constitutional change, debates on 225; consultation 215, 219, 221–23, 224; Consultative Steering Group (CSG) 219; contradictory aims, strategies to balance 223; devolution, positive image of 215;

education 215; ; future for Scottish policymaking 224–25; government as single organisation, concept of 216; group-government dynamic 214–15, 220–21; health 215; implementation 215; interest group devolution 214; joined up government 216; local government 215; multi-level nature of policymaking 221–22; National Performance Framework (NPF) 216–17; strategic objectives 217; non-departmental public bodies (NDPBs) 217; parliamentary scrutiny, governance style and 223, 225; participatory capacities, development of 225; policy communities 214–18, 220, 221, 225; policy responsibilities, containment of 221; policy style 213–14; policymaking: constraints on 213; process of 213, 215, 220–21, 221–22; territorial and universal aspects of 219–22; political system, Scottish Parliament and people, roles of 222–24; politics and policymaking, culture of 213–14; reasons for Scottish policy style 218–19; *Scotland's Parliament: Scotland's Right* (Constitutional Convention, 1995) 218–19; Scottish Constitutional Convention 218, 219; Scottish policy style 213–14; arrangements of, character of 214; assets, principle of focus on 218; co-production, principle of 218; improvement, principle of 217; principles of 217–18; Single Outcomes Agreements (SOAs) 217; territorial policy communities, Scottish policy style and 214–18; top-down UK policy process 215; uncertainty, decision-making in conditions of 220
Futures Project (2006) 127
Fyfe, G. et al. 160
Fyfe, Gillian ix, 160–79

Gains, F. and Stoker, G. 223
Galbraith, Sam 67
Gamble, Andrew 230
Gannett Corporation 247
Geddes, Sir Eric 60
gender, equality and 3, 160–75; All Party Parliamentary Groups (APPGs) on equality 165, 166; anti-discrimination rights 160; Calman Commission (2009) 174; Cross Party Groups (CPGs) on equality 165, 166; descriptive representation 163; devolution gap, London mindset and 169–74; devolved and reserved powers, friction between 169–70; Disability Discrimination Act (2005) 164; EHRC (Equality and Human Rights Commission) 162, 165, 169, 170, 171; employment rights 160; Engender 168; equal opportunities: duties exception 161–62; encouragement exception 161–62; principle of Scottish Parliament 161; retained power on 160; Equal Opportunities Committee in Scottish Parliament 165, 167; Equal Opportunities Select Committee at Westminster 167; Equality Act (2010) 164, 174; equality agenda, ministerial engagement with 171–72; equality landscape (UK) 170–71; Equality Network 162; equality policy, limited impact and powers on 161; equality politics, devolution and 160–62; European Commission (EC) 164; expert-bureaucratic model of policymaking 173; external stakeholders, engagement with 173; female descriptive representation in Westminster 163; Fiscal Commission Working Group 173; Freedom of Information Act (2000) 171; Gender Directors Network 168; Gender Equality Duty (GED) 164; gender mainstreaming 164–65, 166–69; gender pay gap 168–69; General Election (2015) 163, 172; Home Civil Service 165; institutions of equality 165–66; Inter-Parliamentary Union Report (2015) 163; mainstreaming: counterpoint to Equal Opportunities Committee in Scottish Parliament 167; ideation of 164–65; inhibition of 167; successful implementation of strategy for 171–72; non-departmental public bodies (NDPBs) 165; participation and mainstreaming equality in policy process 166–69; participatory-democratic model of policymaking 173; policy process, participation and mainstreaming equality in 166–69; policymaking: models of 173; Scottish approach to (as opposed to Westminster) 173–74; UK-centric approach to 170; political parties' approach on 172; political representation 162–65; powers, asymmetric division of 160; Race Relations (Amendment) Act (2000) 164; Scotland Act (1998) 161–62, 169; Scotland Bill (2015–16) 160, 162, 169, 171, 174–75; Scottish Affairs Select Committee 170; Scottish Government Equality Unit 168, 171; Scottish Office, competing perspectives of 165–66; Scottish Parliament, members' business on 172; Scottish Women's Convention (SWC) 168; Smith Commission 160, 169, 171, 174; STUC women's committee 171; substantive representation 163–64; symbolic representation 163; visibility, need for leadership and 171; women's civil society organisations, funding for 168–69
general elections: General Election (2015) 160, 163, 166, 172, 191; seats won (1945–1970) 27; seats won (1974–2015) 27

Germany: Basic Law *(Grundgesetz)* in 229–30; federalism in 80; German Länder 186; proportional representation (PR) system 48
Gibb, A. 14, 15
Gilmour, Sir John 19n6
Gladstone, William 7, 8, 18
Glendinning, M. 11
global citizenship 184
Global Democracy Ranking 1
Global Friends of Scotland 188
Global Scot network 187–88
Global Wealth 203
Goldie, Annabel 53
Goodhart, P. 233
'Goschen formula' for funding 18
Gould, Baroness Joyce 167, 173
Government Expenditure and Revenue in Scotland ('GERS') 127
Graham, H. 149
Green, J. and Hobolt, S.B. 36
Greengross, Baroness S. 166
Greer, S. and Jarman, H. 215, 218
Gregory, J. 164
Grek, S. et al. 144
Groves, J. 74
Guardian 243, 244, 245, 246, 250, 254
Gunlicks, A.B. 74

Habermas, Jürgen 243
Hallwood, Paul ix, 91–107
Hanna, C. 164
hard budget constraint (HBC): Barnett formula, continuation of 94, 95–97; Calman Commission and Scotland Act (2012) 94, 97–98; constraints suggested, hardness of 94–104; desirable effects on sub-central government 95; Holtham Commission (2010) on Wales extended to Scotland 95, 99–100; independence and 104–5; Scotland Bill (2015) and Act (2016) 95, 103–4; Scottish Conservatives (2014) 95, 101–2, 106n9; Scottish Green Party (2014) 95, 103; Scottish Labour Devolution Commission (2014) 94, 98–99; Scottish Labour's lack of appreciation of 94, 98–99; Scottish Liberal Democrats (2014) 95, 100–101; Smith Commission and adoption of 92; SNP and continuing Scottish Government (2014) 95, 102–3
Harper, Stephen 260
Harris, Michael 243
Harvey, M. and Lynch, P. 32
Harvie, C. 10
Harvie, P. and Chapman, M. 95, 103
Hassan, G. and Shaw, E. 26, 27, 31, 65
Hassan, Gerry 15

Heald, D. 92
health: framework for health policy, ideological basis for 151; future for government and public policy 215; Health and Social Care Partnerships 114; Health and Sport Committee Report (2015) 151; social care and 149–54; integration of 114; *see also* NHS
Heath, A. et al. 36
Heath, Edward (and government of) 12, 61, 233, 234–35, 236
Henderson, A. 165, 173
Herald 245, 246, 247, 254, 255
Hermennier, H. 204
Hernan, Arthur 183
Highlands and Islands Development Board 12
Highlands and Islands Enterprise 181
Historic Environment Scotland 136
Högström, John 46
Holden, C. and Hawkins, B. 222
Holzleithner, E. 164, 167
Home Civil Service: civil service, government machinery and 124, 126–27, 134, 135, 138, 165; gender, equality and 165
Home Rule bills (1886, 1893, 1912) 18
Homelessness Task Force 142
Hood, C. and Dixon, R. 127
Hopkin, J. and Bradbury, J. 66
Hopkins, Tim 162, 169, 171
Hoppen, K.T. 7
Housden, Sir Peter 124, 132, 133, 213, 217, 218
House, Sir Stephen 136
House of Lords reform 237–38
Housing Act (Scotland, 2001) 142
Housing (Homeless Persons) Act (1977) 142
housing policy 141–43, 157; inequalities and 142–43
Housing (Scotland) Act (2003) 142
Housing (Scotland) Act (2010) 142
How the Scots Invented the Modern World (Hernan, A.) 183
Human Rights Act (1998) 236, 238
Hume, David 231–32
Hutcheon, Paul 250
Hutchison, David ix, 243–58
Hutchison, I.C.G. 7, 8, 10

ideology: Conservative policies, ideologically-driven 14–15, 16; framework for health policy, ideological basis for 151; ideological divide 11
Ilbert, Courtenay Peregrine 19n4
income tax, comparisons between 2004 considerations and 2014 recommendations on 93
Independent 246
Independent Press Standards Organisation (IPSO) 250

India 186
Inter-Parliamentary Union Report (2015) 163
interdepartmental relationships 261
intergovernmental relations 260–61
international affairs, role of devolved governments in 187
International Business Development Forum 182
Inverforth, Lord 60
Invest in Scotland 182
Irish Home Rule 8
ITV 247, 248, 252, 256

Jackson, A. 9, 18
Jaensch, D. 13
Jeffery, C. 83, 84
Jeffery, C. and Hough, D. 34
Jeffery, C. et al. 188, 189
Jenkins, Blair 253
Jenkins, Roy 235
Johns, R. et al. 33, 34, 37, 38
Johnston, Karen ix–x, 160–79
Johnston Press 247
Joint Ministerial Committee (Europe) 190
Jordan, G. and Cairney, P. 219, 220, 221
Jordan, G. et al. 213
Judge, D. 222

Kandirikirira, Niki 168, 170, 172, 173
Kane, N. 9
Karlsen, S. and Nazroo, J.Y. 149
Katz, R. and Mair, P. 77
Katz, R.S. and Cross, W. 78
Keating, M. and Cairney, P. 73
Keating, M. and Harvey, M. 206
Keating, M. et al. 213, 214, 215
Keating, Michael x, 83, 140, 143, 151, 180–94, 214, 215, 217, 252
Keen, R. 69, 70
Kellas, James 35, 245
Kemp, Arnold 63
Kendle, J. 9
Kendrick, S. and McCrone, D. 16
Kennedy, J. 9
Kennedy, Ludovic 195
Kenny, M. and Mackay, F. 163
Kenny, M. et al. 72
Kerley, Richard x, 195–212
Kerslake, Sir Bob 132
Kidd, B. 165, 166, 167, 169, 171, 173
Kidd, C. 11, 19n16
Kilbrandon Commission: constitutional reform 236; political parties 60, 86n1; *see also* Crowther-Kilbrandon Commission
Kingdon, J. 220
Kinnock, Neil 244
Kintrea, K. 143

Kirchheimer, O. 77
Knox, W. 148
Kriesi, H. et al. 221
Krook, M.L. 163
Kuhn, Raymond 244

labour market, segregation of 148–49
Labour party in Scotland 59–60; change and opportunity structures for 64–67; decline of 28–9, 39; devolution and 82–83; domination in Scotland (1997–2015) 28–9; free personal care, introduction of 67; higher education fees and 66; membership of 69; supporting foundations of 59–60
Lachapelle, G. 240
Lamont, Johann 53
Landau, D. 240n7
Lawson, Nigella 254
Lee, C.H. 16
Lee, John 232–33
legal system in Scotland: distinctiveness of 199; separate status of 200
Leon, S. 260
Leveson Inquiry 250
Liberal Democrat party in Scotland: devolution and 83; membership of 70
Liberal/SDP Alliance 14
Liberalism, dominant position of 7–9
life expectancy, rise in (and effects of) 149–50
Lijphart, Arend 44, 45, 46, 48, 49, 51, 218, 219
Liñeira, Robert 35
Linwood 61
Lisbon Treaty (2007) 189–90
Lithgow, Sir James 60
Little, Roger 230
Lloyd, Elizabeth 130
local government 2, 108–22, 261; Barnett formula 114–15; Commission on Strengthening Local Democracy (2014) 120; Community Empowerment Scotland Act (2015) 109, 116; community planning system 118; 'concordat' with, SNP initiative of 115–16; constitutional protection for, lack of 111; corporate bureaucracies, remoteness of 109; council tax, 'freeze' on 108, 116; devolution, subsidiarity and 108–10; European comparison with Scotland 113–14; fiscal constraint, new reform agenda and 115–16; ; future for government and public policy 215; health and social care, integration of 114; Health and Social Care Partnerships 114; local democratic governance in Scotland, erosion of 108–9; localism: participation and, promotion of 120; tensions between capacity and 116–17; options for future 119–21; Police Scotland

114; political parties 65; public service reform, key focal points for 115; rationalisation and (de)localisation of local government 109; remoteness of corporate bureaucracies 109; 'representative' and 'participative' democracy, tensions between 116, 118; review of, key requirements of 119–20; review of (1992–3) and further revolution (1996) 112–14; revolution in (1974) 110–12; scale, assumption of need for 110–11, 113; scale and standardisation, tensions between 116–17; Scottish Departmental Expenditure Limit (DEL) 116; Scottish Fire and Rescue Service 114; Scottish Parliament and 109–10, 114–15; 'sectoral' and 'whole system' focus, tensions between 116, 118–19; service focus, tension between outcomes and 116, 117; Smith Commission 108; specialisation and integration, tensions between 116, 117; strategic planning 112; structural reform, difficulties of 119; subordinate status of 111; subsidiarity 108, 109, 113, 119–20, 121; decentralisation and, empowerment and 121; devolution and 108–10; 'service delivery' perspective and, tensions between 116, 117; technocratic concerns 110, 113; tensions today in 114–16; Wheatley Commission (1969) 110–12, 113; assumptions underpinning recommendations 110; rationalistic design, frustrated localism and 111; recommendations of 111; revolutionary effect of 110–11; services and service delivery, emphasis on 112
Local Government, Planning and Land Act (1980) 201
Local Government in Scotland Act (2003) 136
Local Government (Scotland) Act (1978) 200
Locke, John 209
The Logic of Democracy (McGann, A.) 44
Lombardo, E. and Meier, P. 163
Lott, Trent 183
Lundberg, Thomas x, 42–58
Lynch, Peter 51, 68, 245, 262
Lythe, C. and Majmudar, M. 16

McAngus, Craig x–xi, 24–42
McAskill, Kenny 130
Macaulay, Thomas Babington 239
McBride, D. and Mazur, A.G. 163
McConnell, Jack 31, 38, 127, 129, 183, 190, 252
McCrone, David. 31, 262
McCrone, G. 18
McDermott, J. 19n16
MacDonald, Ronald x, 91–107
McEwan, N. 84

McGann, Anthony J. 44, 53
McGarvey, P. and Cairney, N. 245, 252
McInnes, Rosalind 249
McInstry, L. 74
McIntyre, Robert Douglas 236
McKee, K. 143
McKenna, K. 198
MacKintosh, John P. 19n17, 60
MacLay, Lord 60
McLean, I. and McMillan, A. 209
McLeish, Henry 67, 82, 127, 190, 252
Macmillan, Harold 12
McMillan, J. and Fox, R. 52
McNair, Brian 245
Macpherson, Sir Nicholas 134
McSmith, A. 202
McTavish, Duncan xi, 1–5, 59–90, 259–62
MacWhirter, I. 236
Maddox, D. 170, 201
mainstreaming: counterpoint to Equal Opportunities Committee in Scottish Parliament 167; ideation of 164–65; inhibition of 167; successful implementation of strategy for 171–72
Mair, Colin x, 108–22
Mair, P. 68, 73
Major, John 234, 236, 244
Malawi 184, 186
Malpas, P. 143
Mandelson, Peter 230
Mansbridge, J. 163
marginal tax rule 94
markets, internationalisation of 180
Marr, Andrew 17
Mas, Artur 81
mass parties 76
Matheson, Michael 130
Matthew, H.C.G. et al. 10
Matthews, P. 217
Maurois, Pauline 185
maximalist conceptualisation of democratic quality 43, 45, 46, 47, 48, 50, 52, 54, 55
Maxwell, J. 64
Maxwell, Stewart 171, 172
Mazur, A.G. and Pollock, M.A. 164
media and politics 4, 243–57, 262; *Aberdeen Press and Journal* 245, 246, 247, 254; agenda setting 244; *Annandale Observer* 247; *Ayrshire Post* 247; Bauer Media Group 248; BBC 244, 248–49, 250, 251, 252, 253, 255, 256, 257; BBC Alba 248; bias in British press, tradition of 256–57; broadcast media 243–44, 247–49; Broadcasting Commission 248; *Channel 4 News* 252; Channel 5 TV 248; Creative Scotland 250; *Daily Express* 246; *Daily Mail* 246, 247, 254; *Daily Mirror* 246; *Daily Record*

245, 246, 247, 254; *Daily Star* 246; *Daily Telegraph* 244, 246, 247, 254; D.C. Thomson 247; *Dundee Courier* 245, 246, 247, 254; *Financial Times* 246, 254–55; ; Gannett Corporation 247; *Guardian* 243, 244, 245, 246, 250, 254; *Herald* 245, 246, 247, 254, 255; Holyrood and media, relationship between 251–52; *Independent* 246; Independent Press Standards Organisation (IPSO) 250; ITV 247, 248, 252, 256; Johnston Press 247; legal and constitutional frameworks 249–50; Leveson Inquiry 250; local papers 247; media, reliance on 243; media and political behaviour, research evidence about relationship of 243, 244; media in Scotland 245–51; Mirror Group Newspapers 247; *National* 247, 256; *New York Times* 250; *News of the World* 249–50; Newscorp 243; *Newsnet Scotland* 249; *Newsnight Scotland* (BBC TV) 253; newspapers 249; circulations in Scotland 246; declines in circulations of 246–47; hacking scandal 250; political weakness of 244–45; Newsquest 247; non-devolved media areas 250–51; OFCOM 250, 251; online media 249; partisanship 244, 245; politics and mass media 243–45; Press Complaints Commission 250; press support for 'Yes' in referendum 255–56; *Question Time* (BBC TV) 248; Radio Scotland (BBC) 248; referendum coverage, north and south of border 253–55; referendum debate and 2015 UK election 252–56; referendum debates 255; audiences for 244; reporting post-devolution 251–52; *Scotland on Sunday* 245; *Scotland's Referendum and the Media* (EUP, 2016) 257; *Scotsman* 245, 246, 254, 255; *Scottish Affairs* 257; Scottish Broadcasting Commission 251; *Scottish Daily Express* 246; *Scottish Mail on Sunday* 256; Scottish Office, presence in Edinburgh 251–52; *Scottish Review* 249; Scottish Television (STV) 248; Smith Commission 251; *Sun* 246, 247, 254, 255–56; *Sun on Sunday* 250; *Sunday Herald* 245, 250, 255, 256; *Sunday Mail* 245, 247; *Sunday Post* 245; survival of Scottish press 246; *Times* 246, 254; Trinity Mirror Company 247; *USA Today* 247; *Wings over Scotland* 249
al-Megrahi, Abdel Baset 200
Merkel, Wolfgang 45
Micklem, R. 170, 173
Midwinter, A. 112, 114
migration: diplomacy, international affairs and 186; migrant labour, demand for 148
Miliband, Ed 239
Millar, David 42

Miller, K. 164
Miller, Raymond 46
minimalist conceptualisation of democratic quality 43–44, 45, 46, 47, 48, 50, 51, 52, 53, 55
ministerial accountability 222–23
Mirrlees, James 134
Mirror Group Newspapers 247
Mitchell, J. and Johns, R. 35
Mitchell, J. and van der Zwet, A. 29
Mitchell, J. et al. 31, 61–62, 68, 70, 71
Mitchell, James 8, 16, 27, 28, 36, 51, 140, 201, 261
mixed-member proportional (MMP) system 48–49, 49–50, 52–53; voting behaviour and 24, 31
Moreno, Luis 40n4
Morlino, Leonardo 43
Mowatt, Ian 248
Müller, Lisa 45
Mullin, C. 240n6
Munck, Gerardo 44, 45, 46
Murdoch, Rupert 243
Murkens, J.E. et al. 199
Muro, D. and Quiroga, A. 237
Murphy, Jim 165, 167, 169, 170, 173

Nairn, Tom 183
National 247, 256
National Conference of State Legislatures (USA) 187
National Conversation 84
National Health Service (Scotland) Act (1947) 196
national identity: claims to 140; voting behaviour (1999–2014) and 37
National Objectives, 'Single Outcome Agreements'; and 136
National Performance Framework (NPF) 216–17; strategic objectives 217
National Statistics 127
nationalism: nationalists in government, relating to 128–30; unionist surveys of 12; *see also* unionism and nationalism, historical perspective; Scottish National Party (SNP)
Neil, Mike 130
networks of industrial regions (RETI) 187
New Labour, landslide victory for (1997) 28
new politics, aspiration for 42–43, 51
New York Times 250
News of the World 249–50
Newscorp 243
Newsnet Scotland 249
Newsnight Scotland (BBC TV) 253
newspapers 249; circulations in Scotland 246; declines in circulations of 246–47; hacking scandal 250; political weakness of 244–45
Newsquest 247

Newton, K. 46
Newton, K. and Brynin, M. 244
NHS (National Health Service): in Scotland, government machinery and 135, 136–37; Scottish interest in 14; social policy and 142–43, 147, 151, 154, 157
Nicholson, Linda 20n22
Nicolson, Stuart 42
Noel, A. 81
non-departmental public bodies (NDPBs): future for government and public policy 217; gender, equality and 165
North America 186
North Atlantic Treaty Organisation (NATO) 80, 185, 253
North-Rhine Westphalia 186
Northern Exposure (Elvidge, J.) 137–38
Norton, P. 222
Nott, S. 173

Oates, W.E. 105n5
Obama, Barack 185
Oborne, P. 74
O'Donnell, H. 165, 166, 167, 169, 170, 171, 173
O'Donnell, Sir Gus 133
OFCOM 250, 251
oil reserves, discovery of 13
oil tax revenues, comparisons between 2004 considerations and 2014 recommendations on 93
Olympic Games (1992) in Barcelona 184
online media 249
Open Method of Coordination 190–91
opportunity structures, change and 62–68
Orange Protestantism: unionism and nationalism, historical perspective 10; voting behaviour 26
Organization for Economic Cooperation and Development (OECD) 180, 184
Osborne, George 253
Osowska, Francesca 134
Ott, Dana 46
Our National Health Report (2000) 150–51

Panebianco, A. 68
paradiplomacy: involvement of Scotland in 261; mechanisms of 187–88; rise of 180–81
Parry, R. and Jones, A. 216
Parry, Richard xi, 123–39, 216, 260
Parti Québécois 185
Patterns of Democracy (Lijphart, A.) 44–45
Paun, A. and Munro, R. 127
Pawsin, H. and Mullins, D. 142
Peacock, Professor Alan 86
Pemberton, H. and Wickham-Jones, M. 69
Pentland, G. 12
Perkin, H. 74

Peterkin, T. 197
Philips, D. and Tetlow, G. 197
Philips, J. 64
Phillips, Trevor 162
Pickett, K. and Bambra, C. 150
PISA system of student assessment 183–84
Pitkin, Hanna F. 162, 163
Plaid Cymru: civil service, government machinery and 128; democracy, quality of 53
plurality in elections 24–5
plurinational diplomacy 193
Police Scotland: civil service, government machinery and 136; local government 114
policy communities 214–18, 220, 221, 225
policymaking: 'community method' of 190–91; constraints on 213; expert-bureaucratic model of 173; models of 173; multi-level nature of 221–22; policy process, participation and mainstreaming equality in 166–69; policy responsibilities, containment of 221; policy spaces, opening up of 140–41; policy style 213–14; process of 213, 215, 220–21, 221–22; Scottish approach to (as opposed to Westminster) 173–74; territorial and universal aspects of 219–22; UK-centric approach to 170
political parties 3, 59–87; active memberships 85; Barnett formula 80; Basque Country 81; British Motor Corporation, Bathgate 61; Canada, Quebec and 80–81; cartel parties: development of 77–78; shift towards 85; Catalonia 82; Convergencia i Unio (CiU) in 81; Socialist Party of Catalonia (PSC) 82; catch-all parties: development of 77; shift towards 85; Conservative party in Scotland: change and opportunity structures for 62–64; Declaration of Perth 61; devolution and 81–82; membership of 69; Scottish Policy Forum 69; supporting foundations of 59, 60–61; Unionist Party (until 1965) 60; devolution and future for 80–84; elected politicians, representativeness of 73–76; Electoral Commission 69; European and External Relations Committee 84; female elected representatives, case for 72–73; Fresh Talent Initiative 84; gender and party membership 71, 85; Germany, federalism in 80; immediate trends, appreciation of 85; Kilbrandon Commission 60, 86n1; Labour party in Scotland 59–60; change and opportunity structures for 64–67; devolution and 82–83; free personal care, introduction of 67; higher education fees and 66; membership of 69; supporting foundations of 59–60; leaders and party members 78–80; Liberal Democrat party in Scotland: devolution and 83; membership of 70;

Linwood 61; local government 65; long-term trends, appreciation of 85; mass parties 76; membership levels 68–70; motivations of members 70–71; National Conversation 84; opportunity structures, change and 62–68; party members: characteristics of 71; leaders and 78–80; party representation (Scotland, 1999) 66; party representation (UK, 1979–96) 62; party type 76–80; Political Parties, Elections and Referendums Act (2002) 69; post-referendum and post-2015 election environment, political thought in 86; professional politicians, rise of 73–76; profiles of 68–76; Ravenscraig 61; representation of members' views 72–73, 85; Royal Bank of Scotland (RBS) 63; Scotland Act (2016) 81–82; Scottish Assembly (1972) 60; Scottish Constitutional Convention 63; Scottish Greens 70, 72, 73, 75, 85; Scottish National Party (SNP): change and opportunity structures for 67–68; Choosing Scotland's Future conversation 79–80; devolution and 83–84; National Executive Committee (NEC) 68, 72, 79–80; professionalization of 68; supporting foundations of 61–62; Scottish Office Development Department 61; Scottish Trades Union Congress (STUC) 60, 64; Smith Commission 80; social housing, growth of 64–65; Spain, Socialist Workers Party (PSOE) in 82; supporting foundations of main parties 59–62; terrain of politics in Scotland 86
Polity IV dataset 46
Polyarchy (Dahl, R.) 44
Pompidou, Georges 234
Pottinger, W.G. 20n26
poverty, absolute and relative 146–47
Poverty Alliance 149
Powell, Bingham 44, 45
Powell, Enoch 235
Press Complaints Commission 250
Pringle, Kevin 130
Prosser, M. 173
protodiplomacy 184–85, 261
public administration, conservatism in 126
public diplomacy 183
public employment 124–25
public service reform, key focal points for 115
Public Services Reform (Scotland) Act (2010) 136

quadripartite relationship between devolved jurisdictions and UK Parliament 196
'quango-culls,' 'simplification' and 135
Quebec 182, 183, 185, 186
Question Time (BBC TV) 248

Qvortrup, Matt xi, 229–42

Race Relations (Amendment) Act (2000) 164
Radical Independence Campaign 54
Radio Scotland (BBC) 248
Rafferty, John 127
Ramsay, A. 70
Ravenscraig 61
Rawnsley, Andrew 236, 238
Redmond, John 1
Rees, T. 164
referendum (1979) 27
referendum (1997) 30–31
referendum (2014) 53–55
Reform Acts (1832) 7, 239
Regions with Legislative Powers (RegLeg) 189–90
Registered Social Landlords 141–42
Reid, Harry 246
Reif, K. and Schmitt, H. 34
reserved powers 3, 169–70, 174, 259
Review of Competences 191
Reynolds, A. et al. 49
Richardson, J.J. 221
Riddell, Peter 74, 245
Riddoch, L. 207
Rifkind, Malcolm 61, 63
Ringen, Stein 43, 45
Ritch, E. 173
Roberts, Andrew 43, 45
Robertson, A. 209
Robertson, George 42
Robertson, Professor John 253
Robinson, Nick 244
Robison, Shona 130
Rose, R. 68
Rosie, George 247
Ross, Willie 12
Royal Bank of Scotland (RBS) 63
Rummery, K. and McAngus, C. 145, 147
Rummery, Kirstein xi, 140–59
rural to the urban, shift in representation from 9
Russell, Mike 130
Russell, Sir Muir 127, 132
Rycroft, Philip 134

Salmond, Alex 38, 53, 54, 68, 183, 184, 238–39; civil service, machinery of government and 129, 130, 134; media and 243, 244, 254, 255; social policy in devolved Scotland 140, 143
Sanders, Bernie 19n16
Sartori, Giovanni 49
Saward, M. 74
scale in local government: assumption of need for 110–11, 113; standardisation and, tensions between 116–17

Scarrow, S.E. and Gezgor, B. 71
Schakel, Arjan H. 34
Schlesinger, Philip 245
Schneider, A. et al. 220
Scotland Act (1978) 181
Scotland Act (1998): diplomacy, international affairs and 180, 191; funding government, Scotland Act (2016) and 92, 103–4; gender, equality and 161–62, 169; social policy 140; status and relationships within UK and internationally 199–200; unionism and nationalism, historical perspective 17; voting behaviour 30
Scotland Act (2012): civil service, government machinery and 129; funding government, Scotland Act (2015) and 92, 94, 97–98
Scotland Act (2016): political parties 81–82; social policy 141
Scotland Act (2016) 259; arrangements set out in, hybrid 'hotch potch' nature of 259; funding government, Scotland Act (2015) and 91; social policy 154, 156
Scotland Analyses series of papers (UK Government, 2013) 134–35
Scotland Bill (2015): funding government, Scotland Act (2016) and 91; gender, equality and 160, 162, 169, 171, 174–75
Scotland Europa 191–92
Scotland in Europe 188–92
Scotland on Sunday 245
Scotland Performs rubric 129
Scotland's Future: Your Guide to an Independent Scotland (SNP, 2013): civil service, government machinery and 132; democracy, quality of 53–54; status and relationships within UK and internationally 197–98, 210n1
Scotland's Parliament: Scotland's Right (Constitutional Convention, 1995) 218–19
Scotland's Referendum and the Media (EUP, 2016) 257
Scotsman 245, 246, 254, 255
Scott, James 19n7
Scott, Sir Walter 183
Scott, Tavish 52
Scottish Affairs 257
Scottish Affairs Select Committee 170
Scottish Assembly: political parties and 60; proposals for (1972) 27
Scottish Broadcasting Commission 251
Scottish 'Claim of Right' 17
Scottish Constitutional Commission 48
Scottish Constitutional Convention 42, 48–49, 50; future for government and public policy 218, 219; House of Commons election system, criticism of 49; key principles of 48; political parties 63; Scottish Parliament electoral system, criteria for 49; unionism and nationalism, historical perspective 17
Scottish Daily Express 246
Scottish Departmental Expenditure Limit (DEL) 116
Scottish Development Agency (SDA) 181–82
Scottish Development International (SDI) 182, 187
Scottish distinctiveness, Unionist tradition of recognition of 12
Scottish Election Study 38–9
'Scottish Enlightenment' in education 144
Scottish Enterprise 181
Scottish Executive: civil service, government machinery and 129; lack of hard budget constraint on 91
Scottish Fire and Rescue Service 114; civil service, government machinery and 136
Scottish Government, introduction of terminology of 129
Scottish Government Equality Unit 168, 171
Scottish Greens 70, 72, 73, 75, 85
Scottish Home Rule Association 8–9
Scottish Mail on Sunday 256
Scottish National Party (SNP) 123; change and opportunity structures for 67–68; Choosing Scotland's Future conversation 79–80; consolidation amongst elites post-2007, need for 124; devolution and 83–84; electoral success 37–9; foundations of 236; as governing party in Scotland 31–2; majority in Scottish Parliament 237; National Executive Committee (NEC) 68, 72, 79–80; organisation building 13; preservation of UK administrative styles by 124; professionalization of 68; regime change management and 128–30; relations with officials, personalities of ministers in 129–30; rise of 11–12, 26–7, 32–3, 42; supporting foundations of 61–62; thundering success in 2015 UK General Election 239; valence politics and 36–7, 38, 40, 260
Scottish Office: competing perspectives of 165–66; Development Department 61; presence in Edinburgh 251–52; social policy 140
Scottish Parliament: accountability of government to 262; committee system, enquiry into 262; disappointment at achievements of 31; election results (1999–2011) 32; elections seen as distinct but with UK influences 35; elections to 30–33; variety of results 261; electoral system 32; first election to (1999) 31; Holyrood and media, relationship between 251–52; local government and 109–10, 114–15; members' business on gender and equality 172; multi-level

voting effects 34–5; pledge of, Blair's honouring of 17; share of constituency vote in elections to (1999–2015) 33; share of regional vote in elections to (1999–2015) 34; social policy 140–41; split voting for 33; UK Parliament and, relationship between 196; 'Vow' on powers for 239

Scottish policy style 213–14; arrangements of, character of 214; assets, principle of focus on 218; co-production, principle of 218; improvement, principle of 217; principles of 217–18

Scottish Public Pensions Agency 135

Scottish Rate of Income Tax (SRIT) 135, 137

Scottish Review 249

Scottish Social Attitudes Surveys 188

Scottish Television (STV) 248

Scottish Trades Union Congress (STUC) 60, 64; democracy, quality of 51; women's committee 171

Scottish Week in US 186

Scottish Women's Convention (SWC) 168

Scottishness, voting behaviour and 38

Scully, Roger 34

SDP-Liberal Alliance 28, 29

Seawright, D. and Curtice, J. 16

Seldon, A. and Snowdon, P. 238–39

Self Directed Support (Scotland) Act (2012) 153

Sewell Convention 200

Seyed, P. and Whiteley, P. 70

Shaw, M. et al. 149

Shelter 142

Shephard, M. and Cairney, P. 141

Sheridan, Tommy 249

Shugart, M.S. and Wattenberg, M.P. 49

Sillars, Jim 188

Sime, M. 259

Simon, H. 219

Sinclair, S. and McKendrick, J.H. 147

Sinclair, Sir Archibald 10, 19n7

Single Outcomes Agreements (SOAs) 217

Single Transferable Vote (STV) system 30, 49–50

Skelton, N. 14

Smith, John 17, 60

Smith Commission: civil service, government machinery and 135; enhanced devolution and 91–94; gender, equality and 160, 169, 171, 174; local government 108; machinery of government and 137; media and politics 251; political parties 80; status and relationships within UK and internationally 196, 199–200

Smith of Kelvin, Baron Robert 92, 93, 94, 108, 137

Snow, C.P. 245

social care, distinctive approaches to aspects of 259

social equality, aim for enhancement of 54

social exclusion 147, 149, 156

social/geographical labelling 195

social housing, growth of 64–65

social inclusion 147

social justice 140, 141, 143–45, 153, 157

social mobility through education, outcomes of 144–45

social policy 3, 140–57, 259; Act of Union (1707) 140, 144; anti-poverty strategies 146–47; benefits, complexity of 154; Beveridge Report (1942) 141; Citizens Universal Basic Income 156; Community Care and Health (Scotland) Act (2003) 152; Community Safety Partnerships 142; Curriculum for Excellence 144; Delivering for Health (White Paper, 2005) 151; Direct Payments in lieu of standard community care services 152–53; institutional barriers to implementation of 152–53; disability benefits, effectiveness of 154; disabled people, social policies for 152–54; doing things differently, need to face risk in 156, 157; early years and further education, barriers to investment in 145; education policy 143–45, 157; employment 147–49; access to 148; rates of (16–63) in four countries of UK (2002–2014) 148; fair support for disabled people, suggestions for implementation of 155–56; fairness 140, 141, 143–44, 145, 151–52, 156–57; in austerity 154–56; funding sources 155; gendered dimension of 'work' 149; health and social care 149–54; Health and Sport Committee Report (2015) 151; Homelessness Task Force 142; household income, equality of (Scotland *vs.* UK) 146; Housing Act (Scotland, 2001) 142; housing associations 142; housing budget 143; Housing (Homeless Persons) Act (1977) 142; housing policy 141–43, 157; inequalities and 142–43; Housing (Scotland) Act (2003) 142; Housing (Scotland) Act (2010) 142; ideological framework for health policy 151; labour market, segregation of 148–49; life expectancy, rise in (and effects of) 149–50; managerialism in social work services 152; migrant labour, demand for 148; mortality rates for major diseases in Glasgow 150; national identity, claims to 140; NHS (National Health Service) 142–43, 147, 151, 154, 157; Our National Health Report (2000) 150–51; partnership, co-production and 141; path dependency 141; policy spaces, opening up of 140–41; poverty, absolute and relative 146–47;

premature deaths, rate of 150; Registered Social Landlords 141–42; relative poverty, after housing coats, Scotland and UK 146; Scotland Act (1998) 140; Scotland Act (2016) 141, 154, 156; 'Scottish Enlightenment' in education 144; Scottish Office 140; Scottish Parliament 140–41; Self Directed Support (Scotland) Act (2012) 153; social exclusion 147, 149, 156; social inclusion 147; social justice 140, 141, 143–45, 153, 157; social mobility through education, outcomes of 144–45; social security, lack of control over policies 149; Social Work (Scotland) Act (1968) 151–52; universal credit, development of 149; universal tenancy, rhetorical commitment to 143; university fees, effects on social mobility 144–45; user-directed social services, resistance to development of 153; World Health Organisation (WHO) 'Instrumental activities of daily living' scale 154–55
social security administration 135
Social Work (Scotland) Act (1968) 151–52
socialism: political polarisation on threat of 10; socialist planning, 'myth' of 11
socioeconomic inequality 44, 46, 55
soft budget constraint (SBC) 95, 96, 104
Solon the Wise of Athens 239
Spain: autonomy for regions in 237; constitutional arrangements in 231; Socialist Workers Party (PSOE) in 82
special advisers 130
Spencer, J.R. 200
Spruyt, H, 198
Squires, J. 164
Stafford, Alyson 133
stateless nations 182, 183
status and relationships within UK and internationally 4, 195–210; arguments in favour of independence, general tenor of 197; Assymetrical Juridical Quasi Federalism 209; *In Bed with an Elephant: A Journey through Scotland's Past and Present* (Kennedy, L.) 195; Canada, reference point for Scotland 203; Church of Scotland, status of 201; Commission on Local Democracy Report (2014) 204; comparisons with other states 202–3, 204–6; component jurisdictions of UK, distinct differences between 195; consitutional status 196; constituent jurisdictions of UK, distinctions between 201–2; constitutional and statutory position of local government, international comparators 205–6; Convention of Scottish Local Authorities 204; Council of Municipalities and Regions (CCRE) Report (2009) 204; country, description of Scotland as a 198, 199; Criminal Justice and Public Order Act (1994) 200, 201; distinct 'polities' within a state, realities of 199–202, 261; Draft Scottish Independence Bill (Scottish Government, 2014) 198–99; education in Scotland, distinctive nature of 201; English Votes for English Laws 196; exceptionalism of comparative democracies 206–9; geography of history 207–8; outcomes 206–7; unicameralism and security 208–9; extradition as power reserved to Westminster 199–200; further reading, sources for 209–10; future prospects 209; Global Wealth 203; institutional incoherence of UK political jurisdiction 197; legal system in Scotland: distinctiveness of 199; separate status of 200; Local Government, Planning and Land Act (1980) 201; Local Government (Scotland) Act (1978) 200; nation, description of Scotland as a 198, 199; National Health Service (Scotland) Act (1947) 196; polity, forms of 196, 199–202; popular media, discussions in 196; quadripartite relationship between devolved jurisdictions and UK Parliament 196; Scotland Act (1998) 199–200; *Scotland's Future: Your Guide to an Independent Scotland* (SNP, 2013) 197–98, 210n1; Scottish Parliament and UK Parliament, relationship between 196; Sewell Convention 200; Smith Commission 196, 199–200; social/geographical labelling 195; state of other nations 202–6; state of our nations 196–99; terminological confusion 195–96
Steel, David 51
Stewart, D. 14
Stiglitz, Joseph 134, 173
Strachan, Y. 165, 173
Strategic Board 127–28
Stratigaki, M. 164
study sources *see* further reading
Sturgeon, Nicola 53, 130, 134, 163, 168, 171, 172, 255, 256
subsidiarity, local government and 108, 109, 113, 119–20, 121, 261; decentralisation and, empowerment and 121; devolution and 108–10; 'service delivery' perspective and, tensions between 116, 117
substantive representation 163–64
Sun 246, 247, 254, 255–56
Sun on Sunday 250
Sunday Herald 245, 250, 255, 256
Sunday Mail 245, 247
Sunday Post 245
Sutherland, Sir Stewart 67
Swinney, John 68, 130
symbolic representation 163

Tanner, D. 10, 12
'tartan monster' problem 183
tax-and-spending 260
Taylor, Brian 43
territorial policy communities, Scottish policy style and 214–18
Thatcher, Margaret (and government of) 20n21, 27, 42, 49, 61, 63, 188, 243; 'Thatcherism,' Scottish reaction to 14–15
Thomas, George 12
Thomson, Ken 133
Thoughts on the Constitution (Amery, L.S.) 232
Thurmond, Strom 183
Tierney, Stephen 53
Times 246, 254
Tisdall, K. and Hill, M. 215
Tolmie, A. 168
Tomkins, A. 198
top-down UK policy process 215
Torrance, David 14, 28, 86, 130
Toye, R. 10
Treaty on European Union (Maastricht Treaty, 1992) 189
Tremblay, M. 172
Trinity Mirror Company 247
Trump, Donald 19n16
Turner, E. and Rowe, C. 80
Tuscany 186

UN Education and Cultural Organization (UNESCO) 180, 183–84
unicameral legislature 262; democracy, quality of 44, 46, 50, 55
unionism and nationalism, historical perspective 1–2, 6–21, 260–61, 262; asymmetric devolution 9, 18; Barnett formula 18; Britishness, shared history of 6; Community Charge ('Poll Tax'), reaction to 15; Conservative party in Scotland, decline of 14–16; perspectives on 15–16; Crowther-Kilbrandon Commission 12; Declaration of Perth (1968) 12; devolution: independence demands and 17–18; Unionists as party of 10–11; economic performance 16; education, Scottish interest in 14; English votes for English laws 17–18; federal structure: Crossman's argument for 12–13; problem of including small units within 9; franchise, extensions of 7, 10; 'Goschen formula' for funding 18; Great War 10; Highlands and Islands Development Board 12; historical past, SNP and Yes campaign eschewal of 6; Home Rule bills (1886, 1893, 1912) 18; ideological divide 11; ideologically-driven Conservative policies 14–15, 16; independent Labour candidates, threat to Liberalism from 8; inter-war period, Labour and Unionist domination of 10–11; Irish Home Rule 8; Liberal/SDP Alliance 14; Liberalism, dominant position of 7–9; matriarch of devolution, Thatcher as 15; monolithic Liberalism? 7–9; nationalism, unionist surveys of 12; NHS, Scottish interest in 14; 'no taxation without representation' argument 18; oil reserves, discovery of 13; Orange Protestantism 10; pledge of Scottish parliament, Blair's honouring of 17; political consequences, longer-term (of 1980s period) 16–17; political history 6; political landscape, change in (1974–82) 13; political traditions 6; post-war infrastructure, debates about reconstruction of 11; 'property-owning democracy,' notion of 14–15; redistribution of parliamentary seats 9; Reform Acts (1832) 7; regional policy expenditure 16; religious alignment of Scottish voters 15–16; rural to the urban, shift in representation from 9; Scotland Act (1998) 17; Scottish 'Claim of Right' 17; Scottish Constitutional Convention 17; Scottish distinctiveness, Unionist tradition of recognition of 12; Scottish Home Rule Association 8–9; Scottish National Party (SNP): organisation building 13; rise of 11–12; socialism, political polarisation on threat of 10; socialist planning, 'myth' of 11; 'Thatcherism,' Scottish reaction to 14–15; unionism, demise of inclusive form of 6–7; unionist duopoly? 9–18; Unionist Party: popularity of 6, 10; social conscience and 11; voting system for Holyrood, design of 17; West Lothian question 18; Whig domination (1832–1918) 7; Young Scots Society 9
Unionist Party: dominance of 25; popularity of 6, 10; social conscience and 11
United Kingdom: administrative styles, preservation of 124, 126–27; British policy style 213; equality landscape of 170–71; general elections in Scotland (since 1945) 25–30; quadripartite relationship between devolved jurisdictions and UK Parliament 196; Scotland's relationship with 259
universal credit, development of 149
universal tenancy, rhetorical commitment to 143
university fees, effects on social mobility 144–45
USA Today 247

valence voting 36–7
value added tax, comparisons between 2004 considerations and 2014 recommendations on 93

Index   281

van Biezen, I. et al. 76
Van Dorpe, K. and Horton, S. 138
Veenendaal, W. and Corbett, J. 46
voting behaviour 2–3, 24–40; Alternative Member System (AMS) 24; Britishness and 37–8; class as basis for 36; Conservative party in Scotland, decline of 26–7, 28; dealignment thesis 36; distinctiveness of Scotland, context of 36; electoral politics, fundamental changes in (1979–96) 27–8; explanation for 35–7; First-Past-The-Post (FPTP) electoral system 24–5, 27, 28, 30; further reading, sources for 40; general elections (1945–1970), seats won at 27; general elections (1974–2015), seats won at 27; importance of Scottish elections? 33–5; Labour party in Scotland: decline of 28–9, 39; domination in Scotland (1997–2015) 28–9; Mixed Members System (MMS) 24, 31; national identity (1999–2014) 37; New Labour, landslide victory for (1997) 28; Orange Protestantism 26; partisan identity as basis for 36; party system, fragmentation of 26–7; percentage of seats won at Scottish general elections (1945–2015) 30; plurality in elections 24–5; proportionality in elections 24–5; referendum (1979) 27; referendum (1997) 30–31; referendum effect 39–40; regional list result, 2011 Scottish Parliament election 26; Scotland Act (1998) 30; Scottish Assembly, proposals for 27; Scottish Election Study 38–9; Scottish National Party (SNP): electoral success 37–9; as governing party in Scotland 31–2; rise of 26–7, 32–3; Scottish Parliament: disappointment at achievements of 31; election results (1999–2011) 32; elections seen as distinct but with UK influences 35; elections to 30–33; variety of results 261; electoral system 32; first election to (1999) 31; multi-level voting effects 34–5; share of constituency vote in elections to (1999–2015) 33; share of regional vote in elections to (1999–2015) 34; split voting for 33; Scottish Parliament, first election to (1999) 31; Scottish Unionists, dominance of 25; Scottishness and 38; SDP-Liberal Alliance 28, 29; second order elections, effects on 34; share of vote won at UK general elections in Scotland (1945–2015) 28–9; Single Transferable Vote (STV) system 30; UK general elections in Scotland (since 1945) 25–30; valence voting 36–7; voter turnout, democracy and 54–55

Walby, S. 164
Wallonia 183
Walpole, Sir Robert 243
Watt, Nicholas 42, 53
Webb, P. et al. 76
Weber, Max 74
Weir, Lord William 60
Welfare Reform Act (UK, 2012) 135
Welsh Assembly Government 56, 99, 129, 162, 237
Wessels, Bernhard 45
West Lothian Question: constitutional reform 231; unionism and nationalism, historical perspective 18
Westminster system: democratic deficiencies in 54; divergence of Scotland from 259
Whatley, C. 6
Wheatley Commission (1969) 110–12, 113; assumptions underpinning recommendations 110; rationalistic design, frustrated localism and 111; recommendations of 111; revolutionary effect of 110–11; services and service delivery, emphasis on 112
Whig domination (1832–1918) 7
Whitelaw, William 235
Whiteley, P. and Seyed, P. 70
Whiteley, P. et al. 70
Wilcox, S. 142
Wilkinson, R. and Pickett, K. 203, 207
Williams, C. 164
Williams, M.H. 77
Wilson, Brian 251–52
Wilson, Harold (and governments of) 60, 232–34, 235, 236
Wings over Scotland 249
Witcher, S. 164
Wolfe, Billy 62
Women for Independence 54
Woodburn, Arthur 20n26
Woodhouse, D. 222
World Health Organisation (WHO) 'Instrumental activities of daily living' scale 154–55
Wright, A. 74
Wyn Jones, R. and Scully, R. 25, 26, 34

Young, L. 71, 72, 86
Young Scots Society 9
Younger, George 14, 63

Zahariadis, N. 220
Zapatero, José Luis Rodriguez 82